FIELDS OF WHEAT,
HILLS OF BLOOD

ANASTASIA N. KARAKASIDOU

FIELDS OF WHEAT, HILLS OF BLOOD

Passages to Nationhood
in Greek Macedonia,
1870–1990

THE UNIVERSITY OF CHICAGO PRESS
CHICAGO & LONDON

The University of Chicago Press, Chicago 60637
The University of Chicago Press, Ltd., London
© 1997 by The University of Chicago
All rights reserved. Published 1997
Printed in the United States of America
06 05 04 03 02 01 00 99 98   2 3 4 5

ISBN: 0-226-42493-6 (cloth)
ISBN: 0-226-42494-4 (paper)

Library of Congress Cataloging-in-Publication Data

Karakasidou, Anastasia N.
    Fields of wheat, hills of blood : passages to nationhood in Greek
Macedonia, 1870–1990 / Anastasia N. Karakasidou.
        p.   cm.
    Includes bibliographical references and index.
    ISBN 0-226-42493-6 (cloth : alk. paper). — ISBN 0-226-42494-4
(pbk. : alk. paper)
        1. Assiros Region (Greece)—History. 2. Ethnohistory—Greece—
Assiros Region. 3. Nationalism—Greece—Macedonia. I. Title.
DF901.A75K37   1997
949.5′607 — dc20   96-34475
                                                                 CIP

♾ The paper used in this publication meets the minimum requirements of the American
National Standard for Information Sciences—Permanence of Paper
for Printed Library Materials, ANSI Z39.48-1984.

for my father

CONTENTS

LIST OF MAPS

PREFACE

Macedonia is a word that has long evoked in the minds of many, Greeks and foreigners alike, visions of an ancient land, both mighty and splendorous. These images have been constructed through archaeological discoveries and historical legends surrounding such figures as Alexander the Great or his father, Philip II of Macedon. Enshrined in imaginations and popularized through glossy photographs in bound volumes on ancient art and archaeology, for many years Macedonia seemed to belong to a long past era of ancient history. Since the early 1990s, however, the name Macedonia has come to elicit sharply different images, particularly for those who follow developments in the Balkans. Late-twentieth-century Balkan nationalisms have given rise to competitive, even antagonistic, legitimation ideologies that make the Ancient Macedonia of coffee-table picture books the center of discord and controversy.

At the turn of the twentieth century, Greece and Bulgaria had been engaged in national struggle over the region of Macedonia. Today, at the threshold of the twenty-first century, the axis of competition has shifted, as the Former Yugoslav Republic of Macedonia (FYROM) has risen to independent statehood, encompassing a population of Slavs, Albanians, Muslim Turks, and *Roma* gypsies, among others. National activists and elites in contemporary Greece and the FYROM have become locked in a protracted contest to "prove" the supposed "national identity" of the Ancient Macedonias. Such debate has puzzled many foreign observers, particularly those who question how a population living two thousand years ago could possess a "national identity" (in the sense used by contemporary protagonists in this contest) long before anything remotely similar to the very modern concept of a "nation" was created. But such are the arguments through which the respective cultural warriors of the Greek and Macedonian national causes today sometimes attempt to affirm their political legitimacy over the region.

Quite often, the rhetoric of national competition between states (or, more properly, nation-state elites) harkens back to distant historical developments to legitimize present-day claims of—or demands for—sovereignty. The proud aura of Ancient Macedonia and its glorious heroes of ages past represent a mythological ancestral land and ancestors invoked by modern-day hegemonists—national ideologues and nationalist historians alike—in both Greece and the FYROM. Academic arguments and political rhetoric invent a national time, which is then used to legitimize a national space. Protagonists on each side of this dispute have constructed, in effect, a putative descent of their nation from glorious personages in ancient settings in order to provide their citizens with a national genealogy and an ideology of nationhood that links space, time, and notions (or metaphors) of kinship and descent. Yet they also attempt to delegitimize claims put forward by their antagonists, sometimes accusing each other of appropriating, stealing, or counterfeiting history.

Harnessed to serve the interests or purposes of the nation, itself an artificial and highly reified entity, history becomes a commodity. It is zealously possessed, but it must be circulated in order to increase and realize its value. It is this paradox between exclusion and inclusion that also lies at the heart of the concept of "nation" (Hobsbawm 1990). In the competitive discourses of nation-building in the southern Balkans, the word "Macedonia" has become not merely the name of a disputed region but also a symbol of national identity and its rightful historical glory.

The manner in which I originally conceived this study, before Macedonia had appeared in media headlines as a topic of political controversy, reveals that I too had been immersed in this national fiction making. Born and raised in Thessaloniki, the principal commercial center of Greece's northern province of Macedonia and the city in which my relatives still live, I had grown up amid conflicting images of cultural diversity and homogeneity. When I began to formulate a doctoral dissertation project in 1988, I was seeking to understand how the culturally diverse peoples inhabiting that region had come to feel themselves as part of a single national culture, that of Greece. The common popular perception, with which I too had been enculturated as I grew up, was that Greek Macedonia was inhabited by two groups: "locals" (*dopyi*) and "refugees" (*prosfighes*) from the 1922–23 Greco-Turkish War who had settled among them. Both groups were regarded as Greek. I wanted to explore how these people, at times seemingly so different, had come to regard each other as members of a single collective group, enabling them to interact and intermarry despite other appreciable differences.

It was, I admit, a topic of deep personal interest. I myself was the product of a mixed marriage between a "local" and a "refugee." My father had been a Turkish-speaking Christian Orthodox refugee from the Cappadocia highlands of Asia Minor. Orphaned in the war of 1922, he and his siblings had come to Greece with little more than the clothes on their backs and but a few words of Greek in their vocabularies. My mother, on the other hand, was the daughter of a Greek-speaking Thessaloniki merchant, a man from highland Halkidhiki who as a child had left his natal village and walked alone and barefoot to Salonika. There he eventually built a once successful import-export business (lost in the Great Depression) and married the daughter of one of the city's then prominent shoe merchants. Before her marriage and during the last years of the first decade in this century, my grandmother had been a teacher of Greek, posted to the village school of Laina in the Langadhas basin just north of the city.

Perhaps in my search for what made my parents, different as they were, both Greek, I was also looking subconsciously for the basis of my own Greek identity. Born and raised in Greece, I had gone to the United States on a college scholarship in 1975. Yet I found myself returning each summer to my family in Greece, in Macedonia, in Thessaloniki, my place of birth and sense of home. As a doctoral candidate in anthropology at Columbia University, I therefore welcomed an invitation by members of the Archaeology Department of the University of Thessaloniki in 1988 to participate in an ethnoarchaeological survey of the Langadhas basin. I arrived in the middle of May of that year, funded by a predissertation summer grant from the MacArthur Foundation, in the hopes of finding an appropriate site for my fieldwork. The colors of the Macedonian hills in late spring were still green, as the heat of summer had not yet begun to ripen the wheat crop in preparation for harvest. For several reasons, following an initial survey of the basin, I selected the township (*kinotita*) of Assiros as the focus of my study of interaction between "locals" and "refugees."

The character of my project made the adoption of a single village field site too restrictive for a study of social and economic exchange. As an administrative unit, the township was a source of local archives (township, school, and church) for its three component villages: Assiros, Examili, and Mavrorahi. The first two were located on the fertile basin plain and were characterized by a mixed economy of cereal (mainly wheat) agriculture and animal husbandry. Assiros, by far the wealthiest of the three settlements, was also the township seat. Examili was a smaller village situated on the semiperiphery of the township plain, at the foot of rising hills. Mavrorahi, by contrast, was a largely depopulated hamlet situated in the hills to the north, where husbandry was the principal source of livelihood for the five families that remained. Each settlement, moreover, offered what appeared to be different demographic and ethnic aspects. Assiros was inhabited predominantly by locals and refugees (and their descendants) from East Thrace (referred to as *Thrakiotes*), as well as a small group of settled Sarakatsan pastoralists. Examili, too, was populated by *Thrakiotes*. In addition, the families in Mavrorahi were Pontics (*Pontyi*), former refugees from the Pontos region of Asia Minor's Black Sea coast.

During that summer of 1988, I spent my first month in Mavrorahi before moving to Assiros village on the basin plain below. It proved to be a far more challenging experience than I had anticipated, for I soon realized that despite my native fluency in Greek there was nevertheless much that I was missing because of my inability to speak the Pontic dialect. Moreover, now as I reread my field notes from Mavrorahi, I realize that I had been also hampered, although unconsciously, by a frame of mind that led me to relate to the Pontics there as one Greek to another. There are many unstated assumptions in my diaries from that first month of fieldwork, as well as many loopholes and questions that I now beg to answer. Some of this may no doubt be attributable to lack of experience, but there is a consistent pattern in those notes to suggest that my own sense of Greek identity had, at the time, hampered a critical investigation of how local notions of identity had been constructed and transformed over time.

After a month in Mavrorahi, I spent the next ten weeks in Assiros village on the basin plain, engaging in informal interviews, examining the new township family registry (established in 1957), and collecting life histories from *dopyi* locals and *Thrakiotes* refugee families alike. I also recorded census data from the township secretary's office and participated in formal and informal community events. It was in Assiros that I began to appreciate the complex and puzzling relationship between locals and refugees.

These were ascriptive labels of identity that village residents themselves used, but they were also obfuscating categories that masked much diversity. "Refugees," for example, were not contemporary refugees but rather those villagers (and their descendants) who had come to Greece as refugees in the 1920s. Nor, I found, did the refugees constitute a single, uniform ethnic or cultural group, being divided by differences of language, custom, class, and other factors. Similarly, "locals" had presented themselves as the indigenous population of the area, yet were by no means a homogeneous group either. Assiros, I never stopped learning, was a *mazemata:* a collection of people and social groups from different places, many of whom had arrived and settled in the area since the second half of the nineteenth century. Elsewhere in Greek Macedonia, the term [*en*]-*dopyi* ('local') is used to refer to Slavic-speakers who had inhabited the region prior to its incorporation into Greece in 1913; in the Edessa and Florina prefectures, for example, the phrase *dopyos Makedhonas* ('local Macedonian') is used by many to signify a Slavic-speaker (and his descendants). In Assiros, by contrast, the term *dopyi* designated anyone who had been present in the area before the arrival of the refugees, regardless of natal language or other differences.

With these new insights, I returned to the township in April 1989 for a full year of field research, supported through grants from the MacArthur Foundation and the Wenner-Gren Foundation for Anthropological Research. This time, I shifted my focus to the establishment and early history of the Assiros village and its once thriving market. Over the next thirteen months, I devoted myself to an ethnographic history of the transformations involved in the construction of a common Greek national identity among both the various peoples or groups that made up the contemporary *dopyi* category in the local lexicon, as well as between them and the refugees from Turkey. This second session of fieldwork was joyfully interrupted by the birth of my son, Nikos, and I spent most of those days researching Greek historiography on the region and on the Macedonian issue in general at the library of the Institute for Balkan Studies in Thessaloniki.

When I returned to Assiros in April 1990, I began reading the local township archives, located in the basement of the township office building. Most of these documents consisted of loosely bundled papers that were unorganized, uncatalogued, and soiled with dirt, dust, and mice droppings. No one, I was told, had looked at them since they were moved into the basement, and the township office staff was preparing to burn them in order to free up storage space for other purposes. During this period, to borrow a phrase from Nicholas Dirks (1993:xiv), "I lived between history and anthropology" trying, as Comaroff and Comaroff (1992:5) put it, to expose "ethnographic island(s) to the crosscurrents of history." These archival documents, which contained a wealth of information far beyond the scope of this study, constituted an important source of primary data on local history that often helped to substantiate (or sometimes to refute or contradict) information derived from oral histories. As such, their diversity deserves special mention, having included: the minutes and decisions of the township council; various township registries (i.e., the Old [1918] and New [1957] Household Registries, the Male Registry [for conscription purposes], the Marriage Registry, the Baptismal Registry, and the Landholding Registry); and large bundles of official papers received from, or sent to, outside state agencies such as the General Directorate of Macedonia, the Tobacco Board, the Forestry Service, and other government offices. There were also local records pertaining to property transfers, land redistributions, and agricultural subsidies. In addition, the local church office maintained a small historical archive. The Assiros village school and school board likewise had extensive records pertaining to student enrollments as well as occupational and educational information on each student's father. With the exception of the church archives (to which the village priest permitted me only partial access), I was given free and unrestricted access to all these records. Information derived from these documents is marked by the general citation ATA (Assiros Township Archives).

My last session of fieldwork in Assiros took place in the summer of 1991. We had just come from China, where my husband had been conducting his own doctoral field research. Returning to Greece, I began to appreciate more fully the importance of open public narratives about local history. In China, interviews and conversations had often been sedate, frequently falling into whispers lest someone overhear what was being said to the foreign ethnographer; access to virtually all written records had been tightly restricted. In Assiros, on the other hand, discussions in the *kafenia* (coffeeshops) were usually lively. Interviews were constantly interrupted by onlookers or eavesdroppers, who engaged both the respondent at hand as well as each other in animated and often argumentative debate over what was being related to me. The Greek *kafenion* was a public forum in which the debatability of the past (*pace* Appadurai 1981) was enthusiastically pursued. Such oral accounts provided glossy threads of narrative with which I have woven the historical reconstruction of this study.

By my third field session in Assiros, it had become apparent that a much broader, more protracted *longue durée* of Greek nation-building had been developing in Macedonia since the mid-nineteenth century, if not earlier. It is this important process of historical transformation that I have chosen to research, document, and interpret in the chapters that follow. As I mentioned earlier, my efforts toward this end began well before the Macedonian controversy had returned to dominate headline news, political rhetoric, and popular consciousness in the southern Balkans. By the time I completed my doctoral dissertation in 1992, however, war and peacekeeping troops, civil unrest and ethnic cleansing, embargoes and sanctions had become contemporary icons of life in the region. In Greece, for example, the name Macedonia quickly became the focus of an emotive and sometimes volatile debate over history, national pride, and international politics. In many ways, the word Macedonia itself has become a metonym, albeit a highly contested one, for recurrent crises provoked by competitive nation-building campaigns in and among neighboring states in the region. There was, for a time, growing apprehension that violence or even armed confrontation might once erupt in and over Macedonia, the site of no less than six wars in this century alone.

I am consciously disinclined to define the geographic boundaries of the region of Macedonia (see map 1). Most authors writing on the area do offer such definitions, and many insist that all should. Yet in my research I have found that constructs of geographic, linguistic, or ethnological boundaries, not to mention political borders, belie the fluid and ever-changing patterns of exchange and interaction that characterized life in the region, at least until the latter part of the nineteenth century. During the late Ottoman era, or roughly from the mid-nineteenth century to the defeat of Ottoman forces in Macedonia during the First Balkan War of 1912, the village of Guvezna, as Assiros was then known, lay between the converging frontiers of mutually opposed nation-building campaigns in Greece and Bulgaria (and to a lesser degree in Serbia). Both before and after the region of Macedonia was partitioned between these three nation-states in 1913, national intelligentsia in those countries wrote their own histories about the Slavic-speakers in Macedonia, fiercely debating whose accounts were more factual, whose assessments of national identity were more accurate, and whose statistics were more scientific (e.g., Belic 1919). In this debate over who and what the Slavic-speakers of Macedonia were or are, the rhetoric of essentialism was and still is dominant. Each side has repeatedly accused the others of falsifying facts or deluding themselves, while their own accounts are heralded as authentic facts and indisputable truths (compare, for example, Tosheff 1932, Kolisevski 1959, and Martis 1984). Others are consistently portrayed as chauvinistic aggressors, while one's own nation is heralded as an enlightened liberator. Such national historiography is conducted and written much like colonial historiography, ultimately used to justify political rule (see Dirks 1993:xiv).

By 1992, such discourse had attained new public prominence in Greece. Yugoslavia had disintegrated, tensions were high in the region, and Greece appeared headed towards a confrontation with the newly independent FYROM. When I filed my dissertation in the spring of that year, I requested that it be placed under restricted circulation and not be released by University Microfilms for a period of two years. I had been motivated out of concern for the people of Assiros, fearing that during such a period of political high anxieties and virulent emotional patriotism my findings might be appropriated and used by some to advance their own agendas, with little or no regard for the confidentiality, sensitivities, and well-being of the Assiriotes. In my Afterword, I offer a brief synopsis of how guardians of the Greek cause in Macedonia have reacted to my work and an assessment of the implications of their actions for contemporary scholarship—and for historical anthropology in particular.

In the time that I have spent revising the dissertation for publication, a large volume of water has flowed under the proverbial bridge. My research interests have taken me westward, to work among Slavic-speakers in western Greek Macedonia; eastward, to Muslims in Greek Thrace; and southward, to those in Athens who influence national consciousness in Greece. My findings, interpretations, and opinions have not always found welcome among Greek circles, both in Greece and among diaspora communities abroad. Many have rebuked me for not supporting Greek national interests in the Macedonia controversy, but I have been motivated by concerns that extend beyond national partisanship.

The public attention directed at my work has not always been welcome or comfortable. Some Greek critics, emotionalized by a sense of patriotism, have denounced both me and my work, accusing me of everything from "stupidity" and "cannibalism" to being a "secret agent" of the FYROM. My work has been misrepresented and misquoted, in some cases even altered and then disseminated in an eerily Orwellian manner; my qualifications and integrity as a scholar have been questioned and criticized by nonacademics, including journalists, politicians, ecclesiastical leaders, and members of the lay public. As a native Greek writing critically on the Macedonian issue, I have felt at times like a woman who unwittingly violated taboos by peering behind the veils and revealing the "sacred flutes" of Greek national ideology.

The issue of native anthropology is, I believe, an important one in this context, although not because native scholars have some allegedly inherent privileged knowledge about their own culture. There are ample examples that render such contentions frivolous if not spurious. Ethnographic practice, it was explained to me in graduate school, was based upon a distancing from one's own native cultural assumptions and categories of thought, a process effected through immersion in an alien or foreign culture. Only then, I was cautioned, could one begin to engage in critical introspection. The native ethnographer, therefore, who is also an unconscious cultural practitioner, participating uncritically in the social phenomena he or she seeks to analyze, is headed for trouble. But so, too, I found, is the anthropologist who actively and critically comes to engage the basic assumptions of her native culture.

Perhaps it was a progressive sense of cultural homelessness, born of spending more than half my life in a foreign country and returning each summer to a Greece that seemed ever less familiar, that prompted my growing appreciation of comparative cross-cultural theory in anthropology. In any event, it was undoubtedly my training as an anthropologist that brought me to engage critically the basis of Greek national identity and to historicize modern nation-building in the country of my birth. I make no claims to privileged knowledge of Greek culture, be it based on innate genes, national ancestry, or the intimacy of childhood socialization and native enculturation. On the contrary, it is often difficult for native scholars to become conscious of, let alone to liberate themselves from, the assumptions of their own culture. It is the burden of culture that conditions one to look at the world in one way and not another.

Yet it is here, in the realm of culture, that the frontiers of late-twentieth-century nationalisms converge and where native anthropology assumes a new political dimension. Anthropological inquiry takes one into the forests of culture, where how one looks at the trees often determines how one interprets the woods. Notions of national identity are a strong part of popular culture in Greece, and the self-evident truths of an internalized national history can foster emotional reaction to perceived challenges. By critically revisiting some of the assumptions that have gone into the making of national ideology in Greece, I have been regarded by some as a prodigal native daughter gone astray. I have been asked often and repeatedly whether I still feel Greek, and how I can justify my particular scholarly activities at a time when the nation of the Hellenes and the state of Greece are besieged by foreign enemies seeking to dismember them.

During my research and the public reaction to it, however, I have enjoyed the good fortune of a small but supportive circle of friends and colleagues who have provided me with a source of inspiration, motivation, and emotional strength. In 1992, I was selected as the inaugural Hannah Seeger Davis Postdoctoral Fellow in Hellenic Studies at Princeton University, where I found excellent library resources and an environment in which to think and write. That year also brought the blessing of a second child, my daughter, Kalliopi. A subsequent Harry Frank Guggenheim Fellowship enabled me to spend an additional semester (fall 1993) at Princeton as a visiting scholar in Hellenic Studies and the Council of the Humanities, as well as the following academic year (1994–95) as a visiting scholar in the Department of Anthropology at Harvard University, whose research environment and library collections were of singular value. To the many individuals who have come forward, some forcefully, most quietly, to offer support and encouragement in the face of difficult times, I feel a profound sense of gratitude.

Before concluding these prefatory comments, I therefore wish to include a personal note to those who have traveled with me through the fields and hills of Macedonia, in reality, in memory, and in the world of allegory. Of these, foremost is my late father, Nikolaos Karakasidis, whose unwavering commitment to social equality and human decency remained steadfast throughout his life. Karakasidis was himself a Turkish-speaking *prosfighas* from Asia Minor whose life had been deeply affected by the Greek nation-building process. He had been raised in a Greek national orphanage in Western Greek Macedonia, following his compulsory evacuation to Greece in the wake of the Asia Minor War of 1922. There he had acquired a sense of belonging to the Greek national collectivity and had learned to memorize the Orthodox mass in Greek. And yet every evening Karakasidis would tune his shortwave radio to an Istanbul station and sing along with the slow Turkish songs, explaining to me their verses. He knew Turkish culture, and I have always thought of him as a Turkish-speaking Greek, although I was surprised to learn at an academic conference in Ankara in 1994 that, in Turkey, *Karamalidhes* such as my father were regarded as Christian Turks. In many ways it was *for* him that I began the search into the sacredness of the Greek nation, and it is to his memory that this work is dedicated.

My other fellow traveler in this odyssey has been my companion and husband, Gregory Ruf. Together we drove across the fields and hills of Macedonia, sat in wicker chairs in *kafenia*, drank with local villagers, and when evening came discussed life histories, characters, and the happenings of the day. One of my most challenging critics, often sending me back to my field notes with his incessant questions over ethnographic detail, he always tried to revitalize my sense of purpose when scholarly activities began to seem trivial as violence continued to ravage the Balkans and other areas of the world. This exploration was performed *by* him as much as by me.

My greatest intellectual debt lies with Joan Vincent. As my graduate advisor at Columbia, we forged a professional relationship as well as a friendship. It was her guidance that saw me through the research and analysis leading to the original version of this manuscript as a doctoral dissertation. The high standards of excellence she set were inspirational, and she has my unbounded admiration and gratitude. Michael Herzfeld of Harvard University's Department of Anthropology has my deepest appreciation for his steadfast friendship, unconditional support, and constructive criticism during some of the more bleak moments over the past few years. His intellectual energies also have been a constant source of inspiration, challenging me to rethink some of my arguments and reminding me of the importance of the comparative dimension of anthropology. Moreover, his support during a difficult period of personal attacks on both me and him was guided by well-reasoned ethical standards that were beyond reproach. I have come to regard Michael Herzfeld as one of my most valued friends and colleagues.

There were also those who permitted me to ask questions of them, to live among them, and to share my life and my family with them during my fieldwork. All remain "nameless" on the pages that follow, out of concern rather than callousness for I do not wish for them to bear any unpleasantness as a result of my work. The people of Assiros, Examili, and Mavrorahi helped me materialize my research goals. With few exceptions, they were willing and eager to talk, and to remember, reconstruct, and debate their pasts. They accepted me, sometimes as an outsider (*kseni kopella* or "stranger girl"), sometimes as an insider (*dhikia mas kopella* or "our girl"), but always as someone who took an interest in their lives and experiences. I have tried to protect my friends in the township by employing pseudonyms for those who were willing to share their knowledge and lives with me. I have opted to use the real names of these communities, as noted above, largely in the hope of redressing some of the injustices committed by an Athenian journalist who authored an unwarranted attack on them in 1993 (see Afterword).

My mother, Kalliopi Mavrou, never failed to remind me of a sense of purpose in my work and pushed me to see this study through to its conclusion. Her periodic kind and unpretentious presence "in the field" provided an important balance to the notion of the objective outside researcher and helped to personalize me to villagers in Assiros. When my days were filled with research and writing, she undertook household chores with an altruism that only a mother can offer and which over the years have made me very much "my mother's daughter." My sister, Maria Karakasidou, was a supportive pillar throughout my fieldwork, as well. Armed with good humor and common sense, she was a second participant observer while in the field, taking sensitive photographs and introducing me to social circles in the villages that might otherwise have been closed to me had she not been present. During the summer of 1995, which I spent intensely revising this manuscript for publication, both my mother, Maria and my sister Efterpi cared for my children with a love that made their absence, however intolerable for me, a bit less painful to Nikos and Kalliopi. My son, Nikos, was born in the field, in a sense. But, on the other hand, Nikos was witness to the writing of two dissertations, two books, and too many papers, which most regrettably took much of our time and energy. I hope the unconsciously registered memories of fieldwork, of our travels through the fields and hills of Macedonia, and of the experiences that followed, will help him one day to understand the purpose of my absences, both literal and figurative.

Andonis Liakos, professor of history at the University of Athens, read an earlier draft of this manuscript, a deeply appreciated courtesy he has extended to several of my papers as well. He discussed history with me, encouraging me to probe deeper in many fundamental questions and constantly raising my ethnographic focus to larger contexts. He displayed a trust in me that was emotionally moving as well as intellectually challenging. He is a valuable friend who continually generates new hypotheses and research questions; I could not have completed this study without him. Charles Stewart and Mark Mazower likewise offered valuable criticisms and suggestions that helped me to rethink and develop further some of the arguments advanced in this work. In addition, Loring Danforth, P. Nikiforos Diamandouros, and Ricki Von Beschoten also devoted their time to close readings of various drafts of this manuscript and offered extensive comments. In the course of my revisions, I have tried to take their constructive criticisms, substantive concerns, questions, suggestions, and alternative viewpoints into consideration. Any shortcomings the manuscript contains is certainly no fault of theirs, but rather rests with me alone.

My personal gratitude to several friends and colleagues also deserves note here: Adamantia Pollis provided me with determined moral support during the course of presenting portions of this and other works to Greek audiences that were sometimes less than amicable; Kostas Kotsakis and Stelios Andreou, of the Aristotelian University of Thessaloniki's Department of Archaeology, invited me to participate in their archaeological survey of the Langadhas Basin and discussed with me the longue durée of the region's settlement and development; Nora Skouteri-Didhaskalou, along with Andreou and Kotsakis, collected signatures of protest against the harassment I was receiving during the summer of 1994, and I am grateful for their support and courage; Sarah Wyatt and others at International PEN prompted greater responsiveness on the part of Greek authorities to the threats I was receiving that year.

Markos Meskos showed himself to be a steadfast friend of poetic compassion, sharing his extensive personal archives of press clippings and aiding me with the translation of many Slavic words and expressions; Kostas Kazazis, of the University of Chicago, offered similar assistance in translating Turkish and Slavic terms; Makis Seferiades shared many insights from his own research on Greek politics during the interwar period; John Chapple undertook the difficult task of compiling the index; Ken and Diana Wardle of Birmingham University, who had been excavating and analyzing a prehistoric settlement near Assiros since the mid-1970s, provided me with a social milieu of "outsiders" which acted as a safety valve for research tensions and frustrations, while Paul Halstead of Sheffield University, whose innovative ethnoarchaeological research in Assiros sometimes overlapped with my own concerns, freely discussed his material with me and pointed me in new directions; the librarians at the Institute for Balkan Studies in Thessaloniki, Efrosini Panayiotidou and Thomi Karakosta-Verrou, gave me free access to all their resources, and the staff of the Historical Archive of Macedonia offered gracious assistance during the course of my research there.

None of this work, of course, would ever have been possible without the financial support of institutions such as the Wenner-Gren Foundation for Anthropological Research and the MacArthur Foundation. As noted above, these organizations provided generous grants which enabled me to conduct the lengthy fieldwork and archival research upon which this study is based. I would also like to thank Dimitri Gondicas and the faculty of the Hellenic Studies program at Princeton University for their support and their spirited defense of principles of academic freedom. I hold a sense of special affection and gratitude towards Edmund Keeley, who never failed to remind me that intellectual integrity is worth fighting for, however lonely that road may be at times. Like Frost, I took the path less traveled.

To all of these people, and to the many more whom space prevents me from mentioning here, I extend my gratitude. They witnessed how this work developed and materialized. Their expectations initiated me, inspired me, and guided me. If, in any way, I have failed them, I ask for their forgiveness.

A. N. K.
Thessaloniki
June 1996

INTRODUCTION

For more than a millennium, the overland trade routes linking the empires and economies of Europe and Asia wove their way along river courses and over mountain passes, crossing the Balkan peninsula as they channeled an ever-changing flow of goods and people. A number of these major trade routes met at the port of Salonika (Thessaloniki), situated in a natural harbor on the northern edge of the Thermaikos Gulf of the Aegean Sea (see map 1). Its excellent physical setting made this urban area the principal bulk-breaking point for commerce throughout the northeastern Mediterranean, the southern Balkans, and Macedonia in particular. For several centuries this richly cosmopolitan city, populated by Jews, Greeks, Turks, Slavs, Armenians, Russians, Italians, Britons, French, Austrians, and many others, has been a key regional center of commerce and finance, politics and religion.[1] The deep red walls of its former Byzantine citadel and old city sprawl along the hillside and rise with a commanding view above the modern urban port, now Greece's second largest metropolitan area with a population of more than 700,000.

Running north from Thessaloniki, the old caravan trade route to the town of Serres and to Bulgaria and beyond passed through the Langadhas basin (see map 2).[2] Today, a modern four-lane national highway follows the course of these old trade routes, leading up to a pass in the pine-

Map 1. Geographic area of Macedonia and the Southern Balkans

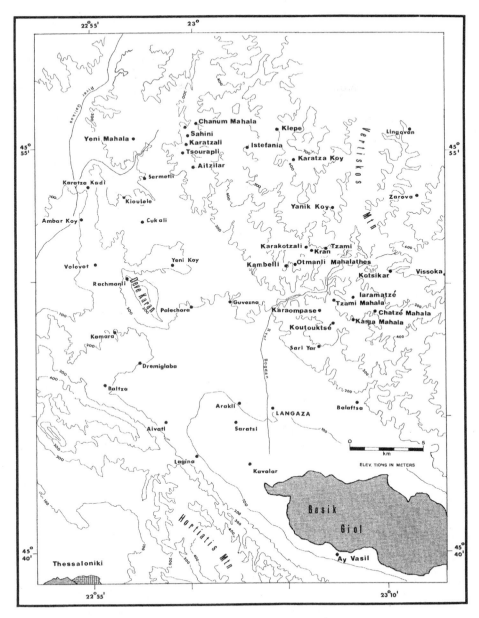

Map 2a. Langadhas Basin, late nineteenth century

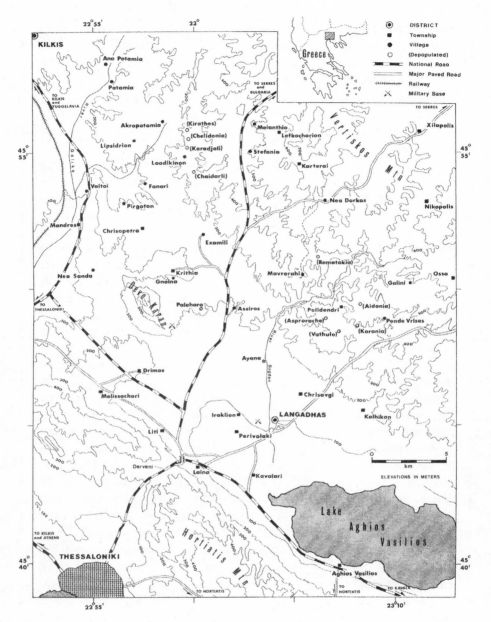

DISTRICT
Township
Village
(Depopulated)
National Road
Major Paved Road
Railway
Military Base

Map 2b. Langadhas Basin, present day

forested hills that ring the city to the north. The Derveni pass, the ruins
of its former toll station still visible at the edge of the basin on the northern side of the hill, was the last mountain barrier for Salonika-bound
caravans. As one crests the forested high hilltop, the wide expanse of the
Langadhas plain unfolds to the north.[3] In the spring all is green, with
grass and wheat stalks vying with each other in the various land parcels.
By midsummer, the land resembles a sea of golden brown as the wheat
crop ripens.

While the name Langadhas is derived from the former Turkish name
Langaza, meaning "woods," most of the basin forest-cover has long disappeared, leaving the area to swelter in a summer Macedonian sun. Despite recent industrial development, the air is cleaner in the basin, and as
the early morning mist clears visibility extends far across the basin floor
to Mount Vertiskos, rising fifteen kilometers to the north.[4] Prior to the
construction of the national highways to Thessaloniki, the district
(*eparhia*) seat of Langadhas was the hub of a complex web of small roads,
paths, and trails that crisscrossed the basin and ran up to the hills encir-
cling it. Located nineteen kilometers northeast of Thessaloniki, Langadhas is the administrative, financial, and formerly the commercial-market
center of the basin.[5]

A richly complex cultural tapestry characterizes the population of
most basin communities. The inhabitants are descendants of people with
historically diverse backgrounds and livelihoods, and whispers of these
assorted pasts are still audible. In addition to (now former) Slavic-
speakers, there were also settlers from southern, central, and island
Greece (who, along with Slavic-speakers are referred to as "locals" [*dopyi*]). There were also settled Sarakatsan and Koutsovlach (or Aroumani
Vlah) semipastoralists, and a mix of East Thracian (*Thrakiotes*), Pontic
(*Pontyi*) and Asia Minor (*Mikrasiates*) Greek refugees (*prosfighes*) who
had settled in the area after the 1922 war with Turkey (Chapter 5).[6] Over
half a century of migration and intermarriage have had their effects, and
most basin villages today are made up of a mixture of these groups (see
Table 2), no matter how culturally, socially, and spatially segregated
these groups had been in the recent past.

As one journeys across the basin floor, continuing up the two-lane
national road towards Serres, past the large military camp at the foot of
extinct volcano Deve Karan ("Camel's Hump," elevation 569 meters),
the road turns sharply westward, curving around a prehistoric *toumba*
archaeological site.[7] Here the lowlands of the basin plain begin a gentle
climb northwards towards the Vertiskos highlands and the town of Serres
on the next basin plain to the east. Lonely trees dot the wide, rolling fields

of wheat, suggesting a forest now gone. Just beyond this bend, twenty-some kilometers north of Thessaloniki, a small side road leads off to the east, towards a group of modern looking two-story houses. A government signpost and the omnipresent political graffiti of the conservative New Democracy political party announce that one has arrived at the village of Assiros.

ASSIROS TOWNSHIP AND ITS VILLAGES

The present-day township (*kinotita*) of Assiros is an administrative unit of plains and hills that encompasses the villages and lands of Assiros, Examili, and Mavrorahi, covering a total area of 67,500 *stremmata* (over 16,800 acres).[8] The village of Assiros is the administrative seat of township government and by far the wealthiest of the three settlements. Its oldest sections lie out of sight from the passing road, nestled in a gully at the conflux of two streams. Here too lies the *aghora* ("market"), the social, political, and economic center of Assiros and the focus of public life for a population of roughly 2,000 village residents (see table 3). So named because of the once bustling market it had hosted for neighboring villages and passing caravans, the *aghora* displays many symbols of the presence of the Greek state and the nation of the Hellenes. It is here that one finds civil and ecclesiastical administrative offices, a village green and playground, a small monument (*iroon*) dedicated to local war heroes, a large new Church dedicated to Saints Constantine and Eleni (under construction since 1990), as well as a number of stores, coffeeshops, *ouzeries,* small restaurants, and two kiosks (*periptera*) that offer newspapers, cigarettes, toiletries, ice cream, and a public phone (see map 3). In fact, many of the administrative actions of the local township government are discussed and sometimes even planned in the café-*ouzeries* of the *aghora.* Above the *aghora,* atop a small hill that forms the eastern side of the dell, sits the older Church of Profitis Ilias (The Prophet Elias). Its patron saint, it was said, had been a sailor who forsook the sea and climbed, with his small boat upon his back, atop a tall hill to live out his days. The church-owned wheat fields behind the church stretch in a northeasterly direction to the foothills of the Vertiskos mountain.

Today, the two small streams that carved this dell, the Tourkolakkos and Ambelolakkos, have dried to a mere trickle, largely as a result of over-irrigation and public works projects. But they were once strong enough to etch their signatures across the surrounding landscape, creating three small hills upon the sides and tops of which generations of village

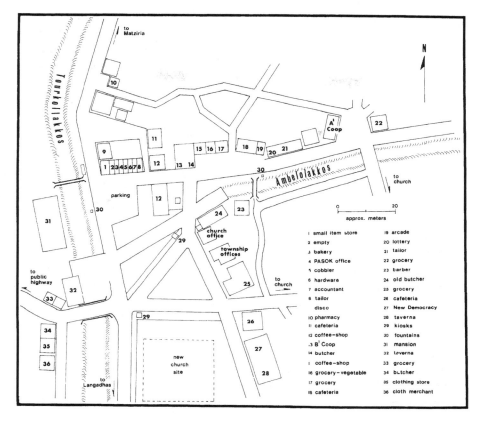

Map 3. The Assiros *aghora*

residents built their homes. Present-day Assiros consists of seven fairly discrete neighborhoods or *mahaladhes*:[9] the *Kato* (Lower), *Pano* (Upper), *Pera* (Over There), and School or Turkish *mahaladhes,* as well as neighborhoods known as *Neapolis* (New City), *Sarakatsaneika* (Where the Sarakatsan Live), and *Matziria* (Where the Refugees Live). The narrow, twisting paths and streets of most of these neighborhoods testify to their unplanned developmental sequence (see map 4). Over the years, family homes have slowly spread up and out of the low-lying dell and across the plain in a westerly direction toward the passing road. Houses closest to the *aghora* are mainly older one- or two-story stone structures, whitewashed with lime and sporting timbered balconies and tiled roofs. Most are surrounded by a retaining wall, enclosing animal pens and a small structure in the yard often used as sleeping quarters by the elderly. Homes in or near the *aghora* are packed closely together, and are linked by a

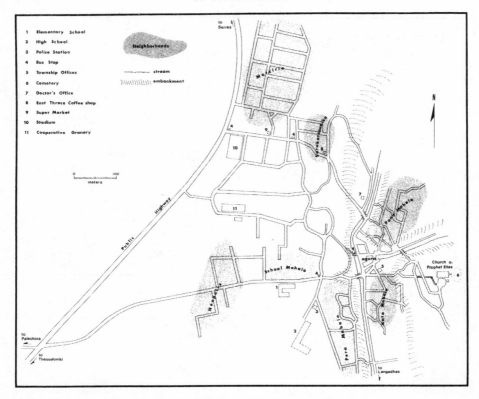

1 Elementary School
2 High School
3 Police Station
4 Bus Stop
5 Township Offices
6 Cemetery
7 Doctor's Office
8 East Thrace Coffee shop
9 Super Market
10 Stadium
11 Cooperative Granary

Map 4. *Mahaladhes* of the Assiros village

lacework of small back doors and tiny pathways that make it possible for neighbors (especially neighborhood women) to come and go through each other's homes without actually stepping out into the "public realm" of the main street (see also Friedl 1962). As one moves outward from the village *aghora,* up the embracing hillsides and across the plain, the houses are taller, larger, and more spread out, displaying more modern architectural styles. Many of these were built after the devastating earthquake which rocked Thessaloniki and central Macedonia in 1978.

Across the present-day national road, some 7.5 kilometers northwest of Assiros, the village of Examili sits at the base of rising foothills on the edge of the Langadhas plain (see map 5). Animal husbandry (primarily of cows but also some sheep and goats) and tobacco production are the chief occupations of Examili's permanent residents, although many also cultivate wheat.[10] According to the current township registry, Examili is populated by 312 *Thrakiotes* families: former East Thracian refugees and

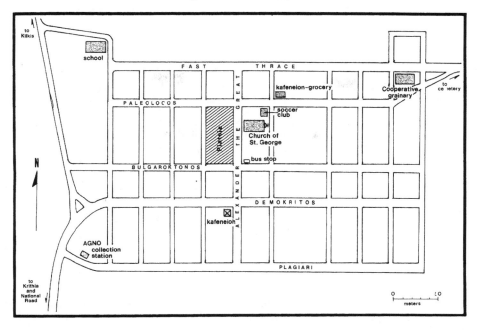

Map 5. The village of Examili

their descendants. The physical appearance of the village, like that of many rural settlements established by refugees in the 1920s, bears testimony to the presence of state planning and assistance in its construction. Streets and housing plots in Examili are laid out in grid-like fashion. Roads running east-west were named, during the military junta (1967–74), to remind inhabitants of their ancient past both in Greece and in Thrace: East Thrace, Playiari (a village in Thrace from which some Examili inhabitants came), Demokritos (the ancient Greek mathematician), and Paleologos and Voulgharoktonos (both Byzantine emperors). The only two paved thoroughfares in Examili are the east-west Demokritos Street and the north-south Street of Alexander the Great. At the center of the village lies a small public commons (also named after the Great Alexander) and the Church of St. George (Aghios Yeorghios).

The village of Mavrorahi lies at the edge of an escarpment, some 480 meters above sea level, on the southern knees of the Vertiskos mountain that forms the northern ecological boundary of the Langadhas basin. A single winding dirt road leads to the village from the old Thessaloniki-Serres highway, branching off just south of Dorkas or Dorkadha (formerly known as Yianik-Koy). Following a rising and falling ridge crest for four kilometers, the road passes through deep brown dry brush punctuated by small patches of wheat, rye, and tobacco. This is excellent pastoral land, but lack of water and poor soil make agriculture difficult. Formerly known as the Otmanli *mahala* of Tzami, once inhabited by Muslim herders, Mavrorahi was repopulated in 1922 by some thirty-five Pontic (*Pontyi*) Greek refugee families, most coming from the area of Trapezous on the Black Sea coast. Part of Assiros township since 1924, Mavrorahi now has ninety-two registered inhabitants, although only five families inhabited the settlement year-round during my field research. Around a small plaza at the center of the settlement are a now-abandoned school, a former Turkish mosque (*tzami*) that was converted to a church and then to a school for arriving refugees, a public water fountain, a heroes monument (*iroon*), and several stone houses built in the 1920s (see map 6). The settlement has only one *kafenion*, a small pale-yellow single-room house, the interior of which is lit with a single bare light bulb.[11] The village economy is now sustained by animal husbandry, a few almond orchards and tobacco plots, wage labor in the nearby Dorkas yoghurt factories, and the retirement pensions of the village's elderly citizens.[12] Although Mavrorahi used to be quite prosperous before the 1960s, raising more than 15,000 animals, its depressed economy now barely supports the few families who remain. The image of a now largely depopulated hamlet, teetering on the brink of oblivion, remains embodied in my memories of old Yannis, who has since passed away, sitting on the bench outside the *kafenion* in mid-afternoon, his head slumped in quiet slumber between a pair of crutches he fashioned from two tree branches.

At first glance, the ecological, economic, social, and even ethnic complexities of the basin area conveyed to me a sense of cohesiveness, a kind of unified culture that permeated these diverse communities and tied them together. But as my inquiry progressed, I began to realize that this was a relatively recent phenomenon, created through a protracted process of socioeconomic restratification and national homogenization. The contemporary ethnoscape of the area differs from its cultural tapestry of the late Ottoman era.

OTTOMAN GUVEZNA AND ITS CULTURAL DIVERSITY

Elderly inhabitants still recalled how the area had been once populated largely by Slavic-speaking Christian sharecroppers and herders, Greek-speaking merchants and traders, Turkish-speaking landowners, sharecroppers, and administrators, Ladino-speaking Jewish merchants and

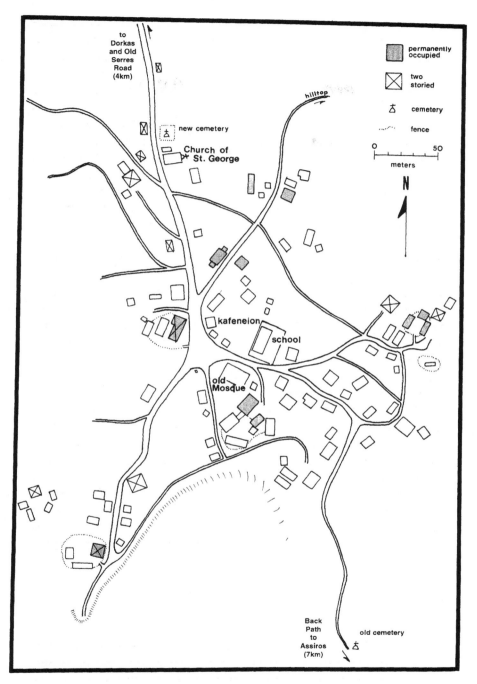

Map 6. The village of Mavrorahi

shopowners, Vlah-speaking pastoralists, as well as Armenians,[13] *Roma* (Gypsies),[14] and other groups. In the late nineteenth century, the two-story wall-enclosed homes of the clustered neighborhoods in Guvezna, as Assiros was then known, were inhabited mainly by grocer and merchant families. Also near the village *aghora* millers, tax-farmers, blacksmiths, saddle-makers, bakers, barbers, *khan* (inn) operators, shepherds, and share-croppers, both Muslim and Christian Orthodox had lived and worked. Divisions of labor and occupational specializations, based largely along cultural or ethnic lines, were crosscut by patterns of social, economic, and ritual exchange.

Nearly everyone in the Guvezna area spoke Turkish during the late Ottoman era. Yet by the mid-eighteenth-century Greek had become the language of the marketplace throughout the Balkans. As Stoianovich (1960:291) put it, "Balkan merchants, regardless of their ethnic origin, generally spoke Greek and assumed Greek names." It remains unclear whether the Christian merchants of Guvezna originally spoke Greek as their natal language. But evidence does suggest that most had been mid-nineteenth-century migrants from the area of Trikala (in Thessaly), who had settled permanently in the village and had established an economic niche for themselves by feeding and trading with the passing caravans.

The cultural field of late-Ottoman-era Guvezna and the neighboring settlements with which its inhabitants traded was both fluid and diverse, with shifting boundaries of identity, interest, and solidarity. The majority of the population in Guvezna and its immediate area had been sharecroppers, both Turkish-speaking Muslims and Slavic-speaking Christians, who worked the agro-pastoral *chiftlik* estates of Ottoman and Christian landlords (see chapter 1). In the nearby *chiftlik* of Gnoina (see map 2b), for example, there had lived Slavic-speaking sharecroppers and herders whose more upwardly aspirant families sent their children to the Greek school of Guvezna to become teachers, priests, grocers, or artisans. In the hills north of Guvezna, there had been the Otmanli *mahaladhes,* herding hamlets populated by relatively impoverished Muslims who traded with the Christian merchants of Guvezna.

Not far to the south was the town of Langaza (Langadhas), the administrative seat of the local *kaza,* where Ottoman local officials and tax collectors were centered. To the east were the mainly Slavic-speaking villages of the Vertiskos mountain, although some, such as Sohos, had a substantial Greek-speaking commercial elite (see Cowan 1990). Beyond the western rim of the basin had been the largely Slavic-speaking villages of the Avret Hisar *sanjak,* with its administrative seat of Kukush (Kilkis).

Many inhabitants of the settlements within this area were, to some extent, involved in economic exchange with Guvezna, some even marrying their daughters to men there (see chapter 2). Yet these patterns of exchange and interaction were traumatically disrupted at the turn of the twentieth century, when notions of national identity were imported into the region by agents and activists of the Bulgarian, Greek, and, to a lesser extent Serbian nation-states bordering Ottoman Macedonia (see chapter 3).

By no later than 1880, an Orthodox priest had been appointed to Guvezna. This priest, who also functioned as a teacher, had been under the jurisdiction of the Ecumenical Orthodox Patriarchate in Istanbul (Constantinople) and its Metropolite in Thessaloniki. He conducted his services and lessons, however, in Atticized classical Greek, a language of liturgical ritual that few of Guvezna's inhabitants could understand. Around the same time, or shortly thereafter, Greek teachers began to be appointed to the village by the Greek consulate in Thessaloniki. They soon replaced the village priest in educating the children of those families who could afford schooling. The Greek-speaking merchants of Guvezna, who lived in the *aghora* below the hilltop church, financially supported both the church and school, and oversaw the affairs of the Christian inhabitants of the community. These public concerns focused mainly on the collection of fees for the Patriarchate and taxes for Ottoman overlords, as well as on the enforcement of settlement security, since the countryside was infested with bandits and national propagandists (see Chapter 4).

Today, on the surface of everyday life and affairs, the contentious issues of national ideology that violently tore at the social fabric of Guvezna earlier this century seem distant and forgotten. Yet many of the economic subtexts of nation-building continue to find expression in contemporary legacies and historical consequences. Of even greater importance, however, is that many ideological issues of nationalism in Macedonia, which had their genesis in the late nineteenth century, continue to confront some Assiriotes even in the late twentieth (see Afterword). As national partisans in the Balkans now arm themselves to regain or defend their reputed ancestral lands, and as international diplomats sharpen their pencils to redraw borders and boundaries yet once again, public attention focuses on the past in Macedonia. Issues of distant origins, ancestral descent, and language and identity feature prominently in public commentary surrounding the past and history in Macedonia, just as they do in the basic assumptions, conceptual categories, and traditionalizations of national ideologies in Greece, Bulgaria, the FYROM, and other Balkan nation-states. Having made their passages to nationhood, Greeks, Bulgarians, Serbs, and Yugoslav Macedonians now look back on their pasts in different ways.

LOOKING-GLASS HISTORIES
Borders and Scholars

> The Slavs have light-colored hair and blood; they have blue eyes. The Greeks have dark hair, fair color, and sparkling eyes. The Slavs are broad faced, fat, and somehow unrefined. The Greeks are flexible, clever, and fun-loving. The same characteristics we admire in ancient [Greek] statues, nature reproduces in Greece everywhere. The intellectual qualities of the two races are also obviously different. The Greek is active, fast in perception, capable, eloquent in speech, qualified in many tasks, and impatient for innovation. The Slav is slow, and passive, and his interest is hardly triggered by anything which does not concern him immediately.
>
> Professor Cornelius Felton (cited in Tozis,
> *Makedonika* 1941–52,2:329)

It is often claimed that the rulers of ancient Macedonia built one of the greatest empires of antiquity, stretching at its height from the Balkans to the Indian subcontinent. Over the course of the next two millennia, however, various parts of Macedonia came under the dominion of a succession of imperial state systems. Roman rule was followed by domination by the Byzantine Empire, and Slavic migrations and settlement in the region during the sixth and seventh centuries significantly altered the ethnological composition of Macedonia. During the ninth century, many Slavs were converted to Christianity, principally through the missionary work of Cyril and Methodius, and their disciples.[15] As the Byzantine state shifted its resources to defend its eastern borders from encroaching Ottoman forces, parts of Macedonia in the fourteenth century came under the brief control of the Serbian Empire of Dusan, until the Ottomans overran and occupied the region from the fourteenth to twentieth centuries (Singleton 1976:38).

Quite often, when politicians and scholars in the southern Balkans speak or write about present-day Macedonia, the images they invoke have a certain distinctiveness. In Greece, for example, it is argued that Macedonia cannot exist as a separate nation because the Macedonian state of antiquity was an integral part of the "nation" (*ethnos*) of the ancient Hellenes.[16] The region's present-day inhabitants, it is asserted, are the direct descendants of the ancient Macedonians, and since those ancestors were Greek so too are their contemporary geographic descendants (see, e.g., Martis 1984). Some Greek scholars have gone to considerable lengths to argue that there has never been a non-Greek Macedonian ethnic or national group;[17] that no Slavic language can rightfully be called Macedonian; and that the word Macedonia properly refers to a region which legitimately belongs to Greece (Kyriakidis 1955; Vakalopoulos 1988a,b).[18]

Such schools of thought, moreover, frequently maintain that Greek language, culture, and civilization are pure and homogeneous. They imply that a Greek nation, apparently impervious to change, has survived since ancient times as a vestibule of high culture in the path to civilization, both for the world in general and for the Balkans in particular. It has been argued that Macedonia, as part of this Greek nation, was able to withstand centuries of Slavic migrations by Hellenizing the intruders, that is, by diffusing Greek High Culture while remaining unaffected by outside forces (Vakalopoulos 1970:2–3). Thus it is sometimes asserted that the inhabitants of Greece (including Macedonia) all spoke Greek, shared a common Christian Orthodox religious and cultural tradition, survived and rebelled against Ottoman occupation, and possessed a common cultural memory of what Kofos (1991:7) called the "glorious history of the ancestors." On the basis of such notions, many writers have argued that the population of Greece, including Macedonia, constituted a nation, that of the Hellenes, exhibiting a common Greek national consciousness through the centuries.[19]

Bulgarian scholars and officials, on the other hand, especially those at the turn of the century, frequently attested that all Slavic-speakers in Macedonia were "Bulgarians" (cf. Kiril 1969; Nikov 1929; Radeff 1918; Tosheff 1932).[20] While definitions of nationality proposed by Greek scholars draw heavily on religion and the influence the Ecumenical Orthodox Patriarchate had over the Christian population of Macedonia for hundreds of years (see chapter 3), Bulgarian writers have stressed language, the visible marker upon which Bulgarian national and ecclesiastical autonomy from the Ecumenical Patriarchate was based in 1870 (see Chapter 4). By contending that Slavic-speakers in Macedonia spoke Bulgarian, such arguments sought to legitimize attempts by the Bulgarian nation-state to extend sovereignty over them. For their part, Serbian authorities, both political and intellectual, insisted that Macedonia had been Serbian at the time of the Ottoman conquest and that its predominant language had been Serbian. They largely held Bulgarian national propaganda responsible for the Bulgarization of the Macedonian Slavic-speakers, who had turned to them in the hopes of liberating themselves from the Ottomans. I will not deal extensively with historical Serbian involvement in the Macedonian controversy because the activities of most Serbian national propagandists had been largely limited to the northern part of the region that was incorporated into Serbia in 1913 (i.e., the present-day FYROM as well as a small area south of the current Greek state borders).[21] Likewise, I will not address at length the contemporary activities of Macedonian national activists in the FYROM, as their efforts have had little direct influence on Greek nation-building in Assiros (but see Afterword).[22]

The debate between authorities of these three nation-states focused largely on demographic numbers and the supremacy of one group or category of individuals over others. Many of the census figures collected and published during the turn-of-the-century national conflicts in Macedonia are problematic, based largely on arbitrarily defined and usually national demographic categories. For example, Christoff (1919:31), using figures from a report on the causes and conduct of the Balkan Wars commissioned by the Carnegie Endowment for International Peace (1914), pointed to the confusion inherent in demographic debates that lack standard criteria for category definition or group membership (table 4). Greek advocates, basing their calculations mainly on Church affiliation and estimates of the degree to which Greek civilization had influenced urban centers in the region, claimed that Greeks were the dominant population of Macedonia, numbering 652,795. Bulgarian demographers, basing their figures on language, claimed that Bulgarians were predominant, numbering over one million. Serbians, on the other hand, defining national groups in terms of language dialect and customs, maintained that Serbs far outnumbered all other national groups in Macedonia, with over two million inhabitants in the region. For these reasons, I find such census data highly suspect, and consider much of them so compromised as to be of little use other than to illustrate how they were employed for political purposes as part of a numbers game by national powers in the region.

The controversy over Macedonia, however, took on new critical dimensions following the establishment of the Yugoslav Socialist Republic of Macedonia in 1944. Yugoslav Macedonians and their FYROM successors have been engaged in their own nation-building enterprise, constructing distinctive myths of collective origin and claims of descent from Alexander the Great. Some have maintained that Greeks had no historical presence in the region, and many have lobbied for formal international recognition of a Macedonian national group (Apostolski et al. 1969; Koliševski 1959).[23] These developments have raised anxieties in Greece, where much of the scholarly literature on the subject of Macedonia emanating from the FYROM has been dismissively labeled as "Skopian" propaganda.[24] Many Greeks now express fears of renewed Slavic territorial designs on their country embodied in talk of Greece's "minority problem" or of "unliberated brethren" living in Greek Macedonia.

Yet the arguments of national elites in the FYROM are often no less essentialist or primordial than Greek, Bulgarian, or Serbian counterclaims: that a Macedonian nation of Philip and Alexander did once exist in antiquity but that it was subsequently amalgamated with Slavic settlers migrating into the region during the sixth and seventh centuries. Since the Balkan Wars of 1912–13, they contend, the modern Macedonian nation has been divided between three larger nation-states: Yugoslavia has controlled "Vardar Macedonia," Bulgaria "Pirin Macedonia," and Greece "Aegean Macedonia" (Keramidziev 1951; see map 1).[25] Their accusations against those states who tried to block their passage to nationhood are indeed revealing. Kolisevski, the president of Yugoslav Macedonia in the 1950s, openly accused Bulgaria of "pharisaism," since it denied the separate nationality of the Macedonians and attempted to assimilate them. "Bulgarian leaders," he admonished, "have no respect for the lessons taught by history" (Koliševski 1959:54).

But these are looking-glass histories. They search backwards over the hills and valleys of historical events to trace the inexorable route of a given (or "chosen") population to the destiny of their national enlightenment and liberation. They transform history into national history, legitimizing the existence of a nation-state in the present-day by teleologically reconstructing its reputed past. Pedigrees of national descent are constructed, refined, and lengthened, and the ancestors of a "nation" become a vehicle for majority-group legitimation, a process rather typical of nation-building in general (Hobsbawm 1990). Yet perhaps we are looking through the wrong side of the metaphoric looking-glass. The insights such histories offer are often far removed from material realities, but they do illustrate how contemporary national identity may distort our visions of the past.

The Slavic-speakers of Macedonia had indeed their own vernacular language and dialects, kinship terminologies, and customs. Yet the denial or negation of this distinctiveness (which represented the ubiquitous "Other") and the promulgation of pan-Hellenism, or pan-Bulgarism and pan-Macedonianism for that matter, were, however, a fundamental component of nation-state building processes in the region. These developments were no mere "negotiation" of new identities among and between various social groups. In Greek, Bulgarian, and Macedonian national historiography alike, such transformations have been categorized as national "liberation." But as part II will show, the sharecroppers, shepherds, and laborers of Guvezna were arguably more oppressed in the early decades following the advent of Greek rule in 1913 than they had been under the Ottomans.

Much of the evidence that national historians have marshaled to support their respective claims rests on implicit assumptions of the preservation of a "national consciousness" through the centuries. Such arguments, however, are often theoretically, methodologically, and empirically flawed, sometimes deteriorating into polemics rather than critical scholarly studies. General scholarship of this kind does not regard identity (or even nationality) as a historical construct of its time. In this sense, many national scholars in the southern Balkans have failed to recognize the fundamental truism that reality is constructed, as are our cultural representations of Self and Other.

CONTESTING CULTURE, TRANSFORMING IDENTITY
Nation-Building as Cultural Revolution

The formation of modern nation-states, a process which started in Europe as early as the Middle Ages but received fresh and critical impetus from the French Revolution, entailed the transformation of diverse peoples inhabiting a given territory into the single people of a nation (see Weber 1976). The development of capitalism provided a new, unifying economic structure through which such transformations were effected (Smith 1987: 131–33). New state-level institutions of centralized administrative control, including a state monopoly on the legitimate use of force, accompanied the emergence of this new economic system and provided both the institutional channels of national enculturation and the necessary coercive means for the passage to nationhood. Nation-building, in much the same way that Corrigan and Sayer (1985) have characterized state formation, is a process of cultural revolution. Through it, education, religion, and institutions and symbols of state control shape the creation of a national identity, a new conceptual or intellectual framework for interpreting historical experience. Although the particular historical context in which different peoples have undergone their respective passages to nationhood vary, the passages have significant structural similarities across time and space.

❋ One theme that appears in much of the literature on national movements is the notion of an ethnic group on its way to national enlightenment, going through an initial stage of self-consciousness and then on to national liberation through political self-determination in the form of statehood (see Smith 1987). In such tadpole theories of the ethnic origins of nations, ethnic groups are often seen as a transitional stage in the formation of nations and nation-states. Many studies of this kind have drawn heavily on the nearly canonized approach of Barth (1969) to ethnic groups and boundary maintenance. Barth's notion of an ethnic group implies a social aggregate that demonstrates a consistent pattern of acting, conceiving, and portraying their collective membership in a group on the basis of diagnostic cultural criteria. While Barth had stressed the processes of boundary construction and maintenance in the formation, development, and definition of ethnic groups, many scholars who have used his theory assume the existence of ethnic groups and focus instead on how their identity has changed.

Such theoretical conceptualizations are hampered by the fact that these criteria often vary, and by the fact that members of an ethnic group, whether self-proclaimed or externally ascribed, also distinguish among themselves on the basis of material interests or idiomatic notions of identity other than ethnicity. In fact, terms such as ethnicity, ethnic identity, and ethnic group are often poorly conceptualized and ill-defined, providing little more than a convenient generic category into which stateless peoples or cultural minorities within a nation-state are lumped, usually on the basis of such diagnostic criteria as self-ascription, descent, language, religion, and customs. Many scholars thus engage in a mobius strip of reasoning, unable to distinguish between ethnicity and nationality or to determine precisely when an ethnic group becomes a nation.[26] Some have found themselves unable to clarify when particular ethnic groups took form, or have essentialized present-day characteristics of ethnic groups by projecting them on to the past or even by assuming their eternal, primordial qualities. In fact, ethnic groups are no less "imagined communities" (*pace* Anderson 1983) than are nations.

But group formation is a discrete phenomenon distinct from ethnicity or ethno-genesis per se. Weber (1968) and others have argued that ethnicity should be seen as an instrument or a tool used by rational human actors in their interpersonal relations. As such, it provides one of many possible symbolic media through which people may unite in the pursuit of their particular goals or interests. Glazer and Moynihan (1970) have recognized that ethnic groups are basically interest groups. The political dimensions of this theme were further developed by Abner Cohen, who described ethnic groups as people sharing common interests and who "coordinate their activities in advancing and defending these interests by means of communal type organization, manipulating in the process such cultural forms as kinship, myths of origin, and rites and ceremonies"

(1981:308). Ethnic changes do occur, but they are precipitated by "radical changes in the political-economic contexts in which people live" and therefore should not be explored independently of them (Keyes 1981:27). This connection between ethnicity, occupation, production, exchange, and stratification seems to be ethnicity's most prominent and salient aspect. As Joan Vincent put it, "the playing of ethnic differences has been important in maintaining the bottom layer of the stratification system" (Vincent 1974:378).

As far as ethno- or national genesis in nineteenth and early twentieth-century Macedonia is concerned, one must be careful not to put the wagon in front of the donkey, so to speak. Not only must changing contexts of time, space, and broader social relations be brought to bear on any discussion of such groups or nongroups, but so too must the course of group development be reconstructed. The key issue assumed in this study is not ethnicity but rather the central importance of material factors involved in the reproduction of life and the production of society, whether local or on a grander scale.[27] The particular set of historical relationships found in a specific field of interaction may vary, but the developmental process of social groups can necessarily be understood only in relation to other developing groups, not only those in the past and present, but also those still in the process of becoming. Identity is a fluid, historically rooted construct; boundaries created between groups and loyalties cultivated to groups frequently shift and change. Haarland's work among the Fur in the western Sudan (1969) offers an example of the shifting boundaries that may occur between occupational groups. He demonstrated how agriculturalists transformed themselves into nomads in an attempt to keep cattle for a cash economy, and in so doing slowly became reidentified as Baggara, a nomad group, for "a person who pursues a nomadic subsistence is categorized as Baggara" (Haarland 1969:70).

Conceptualizing Ethnicity in the Context of Nation-Building

Part of the conceptual difficulty with the notion of ethnicity lies in the fact that it is itself an abstraction created by nation-building processes. In much the way Fried (1975) argued that notions of "tribe" take form only through the processes of political and economic marginalization in the course of centralized state formation, so too are notions of "ethnic" minorities created in contradistinction to national majorities. Nationalism and national ideology "Otherizes" those who do not meet their definitional criteria of group membership; the formation of a self-conscious nation or national majority then minoritizes such Others; and the attainment of territorial nation-statehood effectively ethnicizes those minorities.

The earlier emergence of nation-states in Western Europe, as Verdery (1983:8) argued, "changed the rules of the game for all subsequent players, setting up imperatives that may have run counter to local developments in other societies." Nation-building processes in the Balkans had certain important distinctions from those in Western Europe. Much of the region's population had lived under foreign, non-Christian occupation for several centuries. Yet the Ottoman Balkans had been a highly multicultural area of the world, characterized by fluid exchange, both social and economic, between various peoples. With the advent of nation-states, however, the boundaries that people once crossed with relative ease were tightened, reified, or closed.

For these reasons, I prefer to discuss ethnicity in this work as a heuristic rather than "emic" category. In this manner I hope to avoid essentializing ethnic identity, an epistemological pitfall that often occurs in the context of nation-building. In this sense, I regard ethnicity as based upon observed or analytically derived patterns of interaction, traced through time, which illuminate certain aggregates of people. As such, ethnicity is conceptualized here on the basis of a Weberian-derived notion of ideal-type. Self-ascription is only one possible definitional criterion of ethnicity, and to rely on it as an analytical mode of reasoning is to risk essentializing certain cultural features, morals, values, and norms in order to justify such self-claims. The parameters in a material or social-relational definition of ethnicity include commonality of language, religion, occupational interaction or modes of livelihood, cultural institutions for property transmission, descent reckoning, patterns of affinal alliance, and shared "traditions" of a common past or collective history, be it reputed or demonstrated.

This leads to the complex issue of terminology. During the years I have spent researching and writing this study, I have considered a number of possible alternatives to describe the (former) Slavic-speaking inhabitants of the Guvezna area. Given the plethora of competing claims and politicized terms currently used in the late twentieth century to describe Slavic-speakers in late-nineteenth-century Macedonia, I believe that to adopt any one of these self-ascriptions or imposed categorizations is to risk reifying or even essentializing it over other alternatives. Those present-day inhabitants of Assiros who are descendants of Guvezna's Slavic-speakers conceive of and conduct themselves as nothing less than Greek citizens and full-fledged members of the nation of the Hellenes; they maintain strong convictions that Macedonia is Greek, and some believe that they themselves are the Greek descendants of Alexander the Great (see chapter 1). Yet they do not call themselves Macedonians. Some may have considered themselves as Macedonians in the past, and several referred to their former Slavic language as Macedonian (*Makedhonika*). But today, with the development of national ideology in the FYROM, the label "Macedonian" has come to convey a meaning markedly different from that in the nineteenth century. In fact, when Bulgarian propaganda intensified throughout Macedonia at the turn of the century, many inhabitants of Guvezna began to refer to the local Slavic vernacular as "Bulgarian" (*Voulgharika*). Chapter 3 explores this transformation in local terminology and labels of identity, and the role that ritual or liturgical language, the printed word, and the power of guns and swords played in shaping local consciousness of membership in a broader, grander, national collectivity.

Yet to refer uncritically to nineteenth-century Guveznans as "Greeks" or "Bulgarians" is to adopt national categories that were subsequently imposed on inhabitants of the area. Similarly, I have opted not to refer to them as "Macedonians" or "indigenous Macedonians" (*dopyi Makedhones;* a self-ascription employed by inhabitants of western Greek Macedonia today) because to do so either leads to ill-founded associations with the FYROM or invokes a primordial identity harkening back to the ancient Macedonians of Alexander's era. As such, it would ignore or dismiss the profound transformations in regional culture and local notions of identity that undoubtedly occurred over the centuries and millennia that followed, particularly after Slavic migrations into the region in the sixth and seventh centuries. Yet even the term "Macedonian Slavs" is untenable because it is overly inclusive: not all Slavic-speakers of Macedonia were Slavs.[28]

Likewise, the term "Slavophone Greeks" (a label commonly employed in contemporary Greece) is equally inappropriate, as not all Slavic-speakers in turn-of-the-century Guvezna were Hellenized, let alone Greek. Nor, in the case of nineteenth-century-Guvezna, does the term "Slavo-Macedonians" seem appropriate, as it too was a latter-day construct, coined by the Greek Communist Party (KKE) in the 1920s. Although in early works I have employed the term Slavo-Macedonian in reference to self-conscious notions of ethnic identity that developed among Slavic-speakers in western Greek Macedonia during the twentieth century (see Karakasidou 1993*b*, 1994*a*, 1995*a*), I find such nomenclature inappropriate for the Guvezna context. In Guvezna/Assiros, twentieth-century Greek nation-building led *not* to the creation of notions of a Slavo-Macedonian ethnic group but to the amalgamation of local identities under the encompassing rubric of Greek national identity. Present-day Assiriotes would be highly insulted if anyone were to label them as Slavo-Macedonians, and I too would object to such characterizations on analytical grounds.

In my quest for a relatively neutral analytical terminology, I have therefore decided on "Slavic-speakers," which although perhaps not perfect seems to be the lesser of all evils, so to speak. At least, I hope, it avoids projecting latter-day national categories or ethnic self-ascriptions onto the past. But I wish to underscore that I use the term Slavic-speakers to denote a population cohort rather than a self-conscious group, ethnic or otherwise. The Slavic-speakers of nineteenth-century Guvezna were a diverse collection of people, divided among themselves by different and sometimes conflicting interests, as I will show in the chapters that follow. In much the same vein, it is important to note that Guvezna was by no means a "typical" village in turn-of-the-century Macedonia. The degree to which people were involved in the activities of competing national causes varied considerably, not only across the physical breadth of Macedonia but also within the social space of particular settlements, such as Guvezna, and sometimes even within individual families.

By the 1900s, the Langadhas basin had become embroiled in the increasingly violent territorial and ethnico-religious disputes between two young, expansionist states vying for control over Macedonia: the Greek kingdom to the south and the Bulgarian principality to the northeast. Partisan warfare began in earnest at the turn of the twentieth century, when the fields and hills of Macedonia became stained with the blood of "heroes and assassins" (Christowe 1935). This was a period of intensive nation-building activity in the area. The Macedonian Struggle (1903–8), and the Balkan Wars (1912–13) that led to the partition of the region, were historical moments of crisis that tore apart the nexus of exchange that had structured social life in Guvezna and had given meaning to the lives of local inhabitants (chapter 4). The bodies of partisans and victims of these armed struggles were buried beneath the Macedonian soil, remembered today as ancestral martyrs of their respective nationalist causes.

In this process, heralded by some as national liberation and emancipation, patterns of local life and interaction, of identity and culture, were disrupted, destroyed, and created anew. Under the new regime of national ideology, local culture became a pawn of the illusory community of homogeneous nation-states. The contests and oppositions that arise under such pressures are not only over personal, cultural, or social identity, but over the means of producing and reproducing that identity.

National historians, folklorists, and other scholars have been concerned with "proving" the Greek, Bulgarian, or Macedonian heritage of the region's Slavic-speaking population, and thus demonstrating conclusively that the territory legitimately belongs to their respective nation-states. But history, it seems, has left us with no one Macedonia, no single history, no solely legitimate Macedonian people whose name and identity others now seek to usurp for themselves.

LOCAL ELITES AND NATIONAL AGENTS
Greek Nation-Building in Macedonia

The era of Ottoman rule in Macedonia came to an end with the First Balkan War of 1912, when an alliance of Bulgaria, Greece, and Serbia drove Ottoman forces from the region. The following year, in the Second Balkan War, Greece and Serbia joined together to push Bulgarian troops and agents from Macedonia. The Treaty of Bucharest (1913), brokered by the "great powers" of Europe, concluded these armed hostilities and formally partitioned the region between the neighboring young nation-states of Greece, Bulgaria, and Serbia.

Throughout the first half of the twentieth century, agents and authorities of each of these three states established and expanded institutions of national influence or control into their newly acquired territory. National elites and their local agents in each of these countries also pursued assimilationist policies towards the culturally or ethnically diverse new subjects who had come under their national political sovereignty. Chapter 6 examines this process in the Greek Macedonian township of Assiros. Not unlike the British colonial effort in India, these new institutions introduced "a new language and grammar of tradition" through which such agents of national ideology sought to project their own political orientation to the new citizens of their nation-states (Dirks 1993:xxiii). Some Slavic-speakers chose the road to national enculturation; others resisted it. But the words and deeds of local elites and national activists had a profound affect on reshaping the identity and consciousness of the peoples of Macedonia.

Historically, in the course of state formation or expansion, the political and economic elite who control the institutions of cultural hegemony adopt various means in order to integrate their subject populations and express their unity (Krader 1963:13). Both Barth (1969) and Gellner

(1983) have emphasized the role of local elites as agents of ethnic change. In southern Macedonia, such elites happened to have been Greek or a similar Hellenized population. As the Ottoman Empire disintegrated, these local elites, alongside the "imported" partisan warriors from the neighboring Greek nation-state to the south, took up the task of manipulating economic relations, political loyalties, religious sentiments, and collective identity throughout the region, transforming the population of a diverse ethnic tapestry into Greek nationals. Nationalism was the ideology that this productive and reproductive process wrought. It emphasized the collective destiny of the nation, and collapsed the personal experiences and memories of individuals with those of the new national group. As Faubion (1993:xiv) maintained, national action is a practice governed by norms which are "collectively ordained and collectively sanctioned."

Such is the hegemonic character of national ideology. It provides a common conceptual framework, a consciousness, a feeling or sentiment, which helps unite diverse peoples under one new political unit, expressed through the idiom of "nation" (Fallers 1974). National ideology appropriates cultural identity, wresting from family and the locale control over economy and iconic imagery. In Greek Macedonia, this process was accomplished through the agencies of bureaucratic administration and regulation, education, religion, the military and the police, as part II of this work will show. Social structure, organization, and identity in local communities were destroyed and transformed and replaced by new structures, organizations, images, and identities manufactured and propagated by new national ruling classes and their local agents.

Yet such classes and political units also had to be maintained and reproduced over time, and the ideology of nationalism was a prominent force in this reproduction process. Through nationalism, the state, which may be discussed in infinite detail as an administrative unit of the political economy, acquired a cultural hegemony over its "citizens." Materially and ideationally the nation-state became a unit of distinct culture which actively and passively guided the perceptions of its population. To understand how this transformative process takes place requires a close and critical examination of changes in the enculturation processes. Nationalism is a direct by-product of nation-building and state expansion. As Gellner argued, nationalism creates nations, and not vice-versa.

> Admittedly, nationalism uses the pre-existing, historically inherited proliferation of cultures or cultural wealth, though it uses them very selectively, and it most often transforms them radically. Dead languages can be revived,

traditions invented, quite fictitious pristine purities restored. (Gellner 1983: 55–56)

Purpose of national. But one must also note that, after the creation of a nation, nationalism comes to play a key part in the reproduction of that state of mind and in the preservation and defense of the territorial nation-state.

Chatterjee (1993:110) argued that, "Like other modern ideologies, [nationalism] allows for a central role of the state in the modernization of society and strongly defends the state's unity and solidarity." Yet one must be wary of addressing the relationship between nationalism and the state in teleological terms. Changes in state formation are not necessarily dependent upon developments in national ideology. Nationalism creates and transforms the nation, simultaneously. Today, the nation of the Hellenes is quite different from that of the 1910s, as it now includes a large number of diaspora communities that are actively involved in issues concerning the motherland. The nation, in a sense, is continuously undergoing transformation. Even the claims that national collectivities make for their history change, often being pushed further back in time with the publication of new archaeological findings. Innovations in state organization, on the other hand, are more administratively oriented, and tend to revolve around the notion of citizenship. In a sense, the nation of the Hellenes is a conceptual entity entirely distinct from the citizens of Greece. Hence, many Greeks today are forceful critics of the state and those who work for it, while at the same time they are equally impassioned defenders of the nation. Nationalism provides a sacred aura to the nation, its history, and its "heroes and assassins."

The timeless narratives of national ideologies offer a sense of durability or continuity across time, space, and social organization. But the multiplicity of voices and discourses embodied in family genealogies and local history in Guvezna/Assiros cuts across the coherently presented national culture of Greece. We live in a historical moment during which "the very concepts of homogeneous national culture . . . are in profound process of redefinition" (Bhabha 1994:5). In this study, I attempt to venture beyond the shadows of the Greek, Bulgarian, Serbian, and Macedonian nation-states and their bird's-eye views of ethnicity, nationality, and history. While critically engaging the hegemonic claims of national historiography and its patriotic discourse, I present a historical ethnographic reconstruction of the process of nation-building and state-formation in a community of southern (Greek) Macedonia over the past century. I will search backward to locate those moments of historical transformation that gave rise to the rhetoric of primordial, essential characteristics of one nation over another, such as those of Professor Felton above.

My purpose is not to present the voices of national historians, or for that matter those of the so-called subalterns who have quietly censored their own accounts of what happened in turn-of-the-century Macedonia (see Afterword); this study is more than a simple "ethnography of the past" or a "narrativized anthropology" (see Dirks, Ely, and Ortner 1994: 6). Rather, I endeavor to show how anthropology and history converge in the study of power. As Comaroff and Comaroff (1992:17) put it, "There is no great historiographic balance that may be restored . . . merely by replacing bourgeois chronicles with subaltern accounts. . . . For historiography, as for ethnography, it is the relations between fragments and fields that pose the greatest analytic challenge." This is the challenge that I undertake here.

In the chapters that follow, I argue that the national identity of the township's inhabitants has been a product of a process of homogenization and amalgamation that took place both *before* and *after* the incorporation of this region of Macedonia into the expanding Greek state in 1913. As state encroachment on local community autonomy increased, local relations of class, status, and occupation—the material bases of ethnicity—were recast through the state's efforts (in education, public works, mass communication, national symbols, and religion) to transform sectarian identity and create a common national culture of coexistence among the previously distinct local social groups. The relationships between economic development, state consolidation, and the construction of nation and nationality are presented throughout the text.

In the course of this narrative, I search backwards over the hills and valleys of historical events to trace the course of local history in a township on the Greek-Bulgarian frontier during the years leading up to and following its incorporation into the expanding Greek state in 1913. Some readers may find the terrain I cross to be difficult at times, while others will no doubt object to some of my conclusions. Yet only through laborious treks can one hope to leave bird's-eye views of ethnicity, nationality, and history and venture out from beneath the shadows of nation-states and nationalist historiographies. Let me, then, polish the metaphoric "looking glass" and turn my attention to a Balkan community on the southern fringe of Europe where empires once met and frontiers converged.

PART I

CONSTRUCTING VISIONS OF
THE HISTORICAL PAST

The Politics of Reading,
Writing, and Telling of History

1

BETWEEN ORAL MEMORY
AND WRITTEN HISTORY

Re-Membering the Past

> While a plain is coming to life, overcoming its dangerous waters,
> organizing its roads and canals, one or two hundred years may
> pass by. Similarly from the time when a mountain region begins to
> lose its population until the moment when the economy of the
> plains has absorbed as many waves of immigration as it can use,
> another one or two centuries may have passed. These are pro-
> cesses which span the centuries and can only be grasped if the
> chronological field of study is extended as far as possible.
>
> Fernand Braudel

I first went to Assiros in early July 1988, when the village's ripe golden
fields of wheat were being harvested and trucks heavily ladened with
grain, accompanied by rumbling combines, were a constant spectacle.
Late Sunday morning, on the second day of my fieldwork in the village,
my sister Maria and I sat at a *kafenion* in the *aghora* where many elderly
village men gathered each day for coffee, conversation, and perhaps a
game of cards or backgammon. As we drank our coffees, we were approached by one of the township's employees, a middle-aged man in
charge of the village water system who eventually became my friendly
"shadow" during my stay in Assiros. He asked us what we wanted, and
I briefly explained my interest in researching local history. He immediately took his leave of us, promising to return with an elderly man he
considered to be an authority on the history of the village. This was to
be my first interview in Assiros.

When the resident expert on local history arrived, he told me that
Assiros was a new village, but that it had ancient origins. "The name
[Assiros]," he maintained, "is derived from Assi, a nearby ancient city
that was flourishing during the time of Lysimachos, after Alexander the
Great." He went on to talk about the Ottoman era, which ended in 1912,
three years before his birth. In fact, when asked about the origins of Assiros, most villagers similarly responded with legends that harkened back,
like this one, to the ancient era of Alexander the Great. Their narratives

invoked a conceptual space in which myth, legend, and history blurred, almost indistinctly, a state of mind in which ancestral origins referred not to family but to membership in a larger collectivity: that of the nation of the Hellenes (*Ellines*). Such descent stories linked present-day space with that of antiquity, and local symbols with grand events, famous personages, and national icons in an often elliptical or cryptic manner. While the empirically minded may be tempted to dismiss such accounts as products of the imagination, these tales nevertheless suggest lines of inquiry and offer insight on the development of local expressions of national historical consciousness.

One great difficulty with national historiography, indeed its veritable Achilles' heel, has been a long-standing bias in favor of written data, even officially compiled data, at the expense of more popularly collected and disseminated oral histories. There is often an implicit assumption that merely equipping (or arming) a scribe or historian with pen and parchment somehow absolves such an individual of bias and discrimination in the compilation, recording, editing, analysis, and presentation of facts. But facts and fabrications often vie for legitimacy and hegemony in the historical records (Moore 1986), whether published in volumes that adorn the shelves of today's government archives and libraries of knowledge or passed verbally in coffee-shop discussions, schoolroom lectures, church sermons, or conversations on a doorstep or at a kitchen table. Such reasoning has become well accepted in anthropology but is only beginning to be appreciated in other academic disciplines.[1] This is particularly true in Balkan countries, where the writing of history has often been very much a highly value-ladened, even jural act (i.e., the "righting" of history). In such a context, written history is sometimes just as subjective or selective in its reconstruction of the past as the local memories and oral histories that national historians so often dismiss or disparage.

The legends that Assiros villagers presented to me sometimes offered conflicting versions of particular aspects of their ancestral origins, but all shared a consistent theme in their strong insistence on a Greek heritage and ancestry stretching as far back as the Great Alexander.[2] Consider one such account, related to me by the well-read daughter of a prominent village politician who insisted that she was the only person in Assiros to know its "real history" (*praghmatiki istoria*):

> After the reign of Alexander the Great, an Assyrian King dismounted
> from his horse at a spot southeast of the *toumba,* and established the village
> of Assi. [Nearby,] situated, between the two streams Tourkolakkos and
> Ambelolakkos, was another small community inhabited by people living

in huts. This settlement was called "Gvos," a Slavic name meaning "deep forest" or "pink grapes," referring to the color the village vineyards derived from the local soil. Southeast of Gvos, on the exact spot where Aghia Anna [St. Ann] now stands, was a settlement the Turks called "Kioutsouk Stanbul" or "Small City" because it was like a miniature Istanbul. This town had been destroyed after the Turks occupied Macedonia. Its inhabitants had been killed off either by cholera or by the plague. Someone severed his finger in an accident, but instead of throwing it away, he put it in a place where chickens hatched their eggs. From there, bacteria spread throughout the town, decimating its population. The nearby settlement of Palehora was flourishing then, a big community comprising an array of huts, and Gnoina had a large population then as well. The Turks from Thessaloniki built their summer houses at Gvos, and renamed it Guvezna. There were plenty of water buffalos wallowing in the abundant supply of water from Lake Aghios Vasilios, which at that time reached as far north as the Vertiskos foothills.

This account opens with a prominent point of reference in the local landscape, the prehistoric *toumba* mount that rises just southwest of the present-day settlement of Assiros and which is visible from a considerable distance. While British archaeologists have excavated this Bronze and Iron Age *toumba* extensively,[3] most elderly Assiriotes still believe that the mount, like many others dotting the countryside of northern Greece, was not a prehistoric settlement but rather a garrison post constructed by Alexander the Great, the epic ancestor. This they unanimously claimed to have learned from their former schoolteacher, the son of a Greek-speaking migrant settler from Thessaly. This woman even went so far as to sketch for me a diagram of the *toumba's* internal layout, including tunnels, ovens, and burning wood, explaining that this mount was part of an elaborate communication system devised by Alexander to relay messages to and from other fortifications in the area.

It is significant that villagers associate the *toumba*, the most prominent local landmark dating from antiquity, with Alexander the Great. Many, in fact, explained to the British archaeologists at great length that their interpretations of Alexander were all wrong. Alexander, the great Macedonian emperor, has become an impassioned present-day national symbol of the Greekness of Macedonia, both past and present. In Assiros, the most extreme assertion of descent from Alexander was embodied in a locally infamous account that the community had been founded by settlers from "Porno," said to be a village near Serres so named because the Great Alexander frequented brothels there (*porni*, Greek: "prostitute").

Origin myths regarding Assiros also shared a certain timelessness. In them, dates are often confused or linear chronology becomes irrelevant as local interpretations and recountings of history hinge on symbols and events rather than on points in time. The above accounts of both resident experts each began, for example, with Alexander the Great and then jumped to the Ottoman occupation of Macedonia, leaving a chronological gap of some 1,500 years. In such legends, time looms like a huge ungovernable dimension, and figures such as the Great Alexander belong to both the near and distant pasts. Constructions of descent from Alexander were based either on alleged events of his time, or on more personal claims such as those of bastard ancestry. But they all rooted local origins in the age of antiquity and to Alexander, the glorious Macedonian conqueror who now features so prominently in Greek national ideology.

Present-day Assiriotes stress the pure and ancient Hellenic origins of their village. Consider how, during my first session of fieldwork in Assiros, a leading township official took the initiative to show me a letter from the township archives that reputedly linked contemporary Assiros and its inhabitants to the ancient Hellenes. This invocation of literary authority, dated 20 September 1956, was written by an Athenian schoolteacher and listed a series of names resembling that of Assiros (such as "Assa," "Assira," "Assiritis," and "Assoros") which the author claimed to have encountered in ancient Greek writings.[4] If the orthography of a name may be used to explore its etymology, the suggestion of a link between the name Assiros and the ancient town of Assi, allegedly established by one of Alexander the Great's officers, becomes stronger. As the first resident expert on village history I encountered pointed out, in the Greek spelling of Assiros the middle vowel is *ita* (*H*), the same as the final vowel in Assi, rather than *ipsilon* (*Y*) as in the Greek spelling of Assyria. Yet the name "Assiros" was officially given to the village in 1927, replacing the Turkish name "Guvezna," which apparently had replaced the even earlier Slavic name, "Gvos."[5] The name "Assiros" had been adopted at the suggestion of an outsider, a Greek schoolteacher who had been posted to Guvezna at the turn of the century. The teacher was said to have been very knowledgeable about the ancient history of the area, and his suggestion had been accepted without question or dissent. Yet despite the place-name changes, elderly villagers frequently interchanged the names they used in reference to various settlements in the area. Many elderly Assiriotes often used the former Ottoman or Slavic names of surrounding villages, especially if they were reconstructing a story about local history.

Local origins legends such as those recounted above also linked settlement and habitation in the area to symbols of both Greek antiquity and the Byzantine era. Consider, for example, "Aghia Anna" or "Ayana," which is mentioned in almost all such tales. In Assiros, both names were used alternatively in reference to an abandoned settlement site southeast of the village (see map 2b). The site was located atop a high promontory overlooking the river Boidana, a Hellenized form of the river's former Slavic name, "Bogdan," meaning "Sent by God." Archaeologists maintain that the site had been inhabited as early as the Neolithic Age.[6] It is possible that the settlement of antiquity (i.e., "Assi") referred to in the ancient Greek sources cited above was a precursor of Aghia Anna/Ayana; some Assiriotes claimed to have found coins at Aghia Anna emblazoned with the head of Aris (the ancient Greek god of war) and with a lion on the reverse, bearing a small inscription referring to the Hellenistic King Lysimachos (306-281 B.C.E.). On the other hand, Aghia Anna may have been the Christianized name of an entirely different settlement.[7] Some Assiriotes also claimed that Aghia Anna is mentioned in the archives of Mount Athos, suggesting that it may once have been a monastery estate during Byzantine or early Ottoman times.[8] The Christianized name of Aghia Anna links the settlement site's ancient past with the still distant though less remote Byzantine era, while reference to Mount Athos, the holy center of Orthodox Christianity, adds a further element of glory to these popular associations.

By all local accounts, Aghia Anna had been an important town. Its sophisticated layout, Assiriotes claimed, resembled Istanbul and was therefore referred to by former inhabitants of the area as "Kioutsouk Stanbul" ("Small City"; as opposed to "Istanbul," "The City").[9] As villagers in Assiros described it, Aghia Anna covered an area of thirty to fifty *stremmata* and controlled a large hinterland of small scattered hamlets reaching northwestward to the present-day village of Peristeri (see map 2b). It had been surrounded by fortifications and was said to have contained distinct neighborhoods, broad streets, tall buildings, a cemetery or tomb network, watermills, and vineyards, as well as a sophisticated water system consisting of an aqueduct and clay pipes which brought water in from a nearby spring. Many local legends attest that Ayana had been rich in gold, panned from the sands of the river, and goldsmith shops were said to have been located within the fortified settlement itself.[10] Destroyed either by the Ottomans, an earthquake, or an epidemic, its inhabitants were said to have dispersed to surrounding villages, including the small nearby community of "Gvos."

Local beliefs surrounding Ayana, with its reputed origins in the time of Alexander the Great, establish a present continuity between the near and distant pasts. Ancient Greek settlements in Macedonia bearing names similar to that of Assiros and recorded by ancient scholars, as well as rumors of ancient golden coins with Greek inscriptions found at the site, contribute to this local mythology of Hellenic ancestry, as do local interpretations of the nearby prehistoric *toumba*. But the legends offer few clues about the Christians inhabiting the settlements of Gvos, Palehora, or Gnoina. The name "Gvos" had been used in several local accounts of Assiros origins, and it bears a resemblance to that of "Grozdovo," a name the Serbian traveler Gopcević attributed to Guvezna/Assiros in 1889 (Lefort 1986:152). Yet few in the village offered detailed accounts of Gvos (i.e., of their own settlement), preferring instead to speak of the nearby *toumba* (and its associations with Alexander the Great) or nearby Ayana/Aghia Anna (and its archaeological links to Byzantium).

At the same time, however, local origin accounts often contained particular elements that suggested diversity, or more specifically the purity of some and the difference of others. Consider, for example, another account concerning the establishment of the village, this one offered by another elderly man who was also recognized by his friends at the coffeeshops as an authority on local history:

> Around the time that the Great Alexander was returning from war at Troy, an Assyrian King established himself at a site just south of Assiros called Aghia Anna, or Ayana, and the village [of Assiros] is named after this Assyrian. This village was very different from those surrounding it. Although King Darius of Persia once passed through the area, he did not come to Assiros but instead went to Gnoina, which explains why the Gnoinans spoke differently from us, addressing people as "dare," whereas we use the term "re." Another Persian King, King Xerxes, once passed through Drimos, and that is why villagers there wear blue skirts [*foustanelles*], which they say were characteristic of the ancient Persians.

An important quality to such legends is the antihistoricity embedded in the use of time. Such tales create a conceptual space of national time, in which the period of Alexander the Great is collapsed with that of the prehistoric Trojan War. This antihistoricity and nonlinear use of time were recurrent in all the origin accounts I solicited, and represent the "deep structures" of these ancestry myths. They link the particular to the general, and the locale to the nation of the Hellenes.

While emphasizing ancient royal ancestry and a link to the Christian "Aghia Anna," local origin-accounts also voiced claims of difference through which Assiriotes attempted to distinguish themselves and their past from those of other villages in the area, such as Drimos, Gnoina, and Palehora. In the tale above, for example, differences of language and dress were said to mark the inhabitants of present-day Drimos as different from those in Assiros. Yet some Assiriotes claimed that the people of Drimos were the real descendants of Alexander the Great (rather than the Persian King Xerxes) because they wore blue *foustanelles* with a blue shirt that reached down to their knees. Other Assiros residents, however, particularly some elderly villagers, labeled the inhabitants of Drimos as *Harvatadhes,* maintaining that they had actually come from a place in Serbia called Harvat. Still others contended that the people of Drimos had come from the Black Forest (*Melas Drimos*) in Germany.[11] Despite the linguistic markers said to distinguish the inhabitants of Assiros and Drimos, the spoken vernacular now used in both villages is quite similar. Referred to as *dopya* ("local") language, it is basically Greek with loan words from Turkish and Slavic. Many elderly Assiriotes were conscious of their pluralistic vernacular. Most had received only rudimentary schooling and still spoke with what they themselves called a "heavy" (*varia*) accent. The younger generation, on the other hand, had received far more extensive schooling; they spoke a more "proper" form of Greek and had only limited knowledge of the local "heavy" dialect. In contrast, the inhabitants of nearby Liti (formerly Aivati) were unanimously regarded by Assiriotes as descendants of a "Bulgarian race" (*ratsa*), because they formerly spoke Slavic (and by the accounts of some Assiriotes still do).

It is noteworthy that the inhabitants of present-day Gnoina and their ancestors were also distinguished in the above legend by language markers. The Gnoinans were identified in most accounts of local history as Slavic-speakers, a claim that appeared to be supported by the surnames of those who were said to have inhabited the settlement during the late Ottoman era. Many of the stories told in Assiros marked the Gnoinans as somehow anomalous "Others." Yet local township records on places of origin, as well as local oral accounts pertaining to the Ottoman era, maintained that the inhabitants of Guvezna had extensive relations of exchange (both marital and economic) with those in Gnoina during the late nineteenth century, and had participated with them in many of the same religious ceremonies. Nevertheless, in contemporary Assiros there are many stories told about "Gnoina" which underscore perceptions of qualitative difference, often marked by language, religion, or unnatural phenomena.

In these tales, present-day place names were used to describe alleged events of the past. Superficially, this may seem to be an unconscious projection of familiar contemporary names back in time. But like legends of the origins of Assiros addressed above, these tales of "Gnoina" also employed the antihistoricity of national time, collapsing distant origins with recent pasts in constructed traditions of Otherness. In such a manner, these tales indirectly serve to highlight the Greekness of the Assiriotes. In fact, the entire area to the immediate west of Assiros, including the abandoned settlement of Palehora and the present settlement of Gnoina, was often referred to in general by Assiriotes as "Gnoina."[12] Their stories about Gnoina thus referred both to the nearby settlement of the present day as well as to the abandoned community of the nineteenth century. As such, these tales of "Gnoina" mark important cognitive boundaries between the contemporary Greekness of Assiros and the foreign quality of the area's Slavic past. By commenting on the alien and even eerie past of the "Gnoinans," Assiriotes distance themselves from *that* past, and in so doing illuminate some of the conceptual oppositions upon which contemporary notions of Greek identity are based.

CONSTRUCTING OTHERNESS
Vampires, Bulgarians, and the Ghosts of "Gnoina"

Oral accounts in Assiros claimed that the original inhabitants of present-day Gnoina were descendants of the ancient Persian king, Darius, and that they were brought to "Gnoina" by Alexander the Great to cultivate the land there. Some Assiros villagers maintained that the "Gnoina" area had ancient Greek roots, too. Some told of a *toumba* or hill called "Kastraki" ("Castle"; apparently a reference to a Byzantine site adjacent to present-day Gnoina), atop of which Queen Antigone (a character in ancient Greek dramas) had lived in her own castle amidst riches and splendor. It was said that the "Gnoinans" had been Christians who spoke a "heavy" language, some claiming it had been close to "Persian." Others, however, insisted that it had been "Bulgarian," because a "Gnoina" woman married into Guvezna was able to speak with Bulgarian troops during the German occupation of Assiros in World War II (see chapter 7). She was said to have welcomed them and told them that they were all of the same "race" (*ratsa*).

For their part, present-day residents of Gnoina denied they were Bulgarian, claiming that the Bulgarians had worn white headbands (*sarikia*), while they did not. They were probably referring to Bulgarian propagandists and partisans who had been active in the area at the turn of the century (see chapters 3 and 4). During the Macedonian Struggle, Bulgarian partisans were said to have helped the people of "Gnoina," protecting them from the depredations of Greek partisans by evacuating the elderly to Aivati (Liti), then a reportedly pro-Bulgarian stronghold in the basin.[13]

Assiriotes also enjoy relating tales of strange supernatural occurrences in "Gnoina." One story, for example, concerned the funeral preparations for a recently deceased man. It was said that when his arms and legs were untied, he suddenly sat up, causing terrified onlookers to flee in every direction. He called to two of the fleeing men by name: "Traiko! Petko! Don't run away!" The man reportedly lived for another ten years. The names by which he was said to have addressed his friends or relatives (i.e. "Traiko" and "Petko") shed considerable light on the ethno-national question at hand, for they are Slavic names.

Similarly, another Assiros story concerning "Gnoina" claimed that the soil above the graves there would continue to rise up and that the dead who were buried there did not rest in peace. This probably implied that "the Gnoinans" did not have a proper Orthodox Christian burial, one administered by an Orthodox patriarchate priest. In fact, many Assiriotes claimed that there had been no priest in "Gnoina," and that vampires haunted the settlement. Other stories told of an invisible woman, named "Lengo," who used to urinate from the roof of a house in "Gnoina." A Muslim *hodja* (*imam*) came, read something out of his book, brought the invisible woman down from the roof, and killed her. Although he was said to be the only one who could see her, all the spectators to the incident saw her blood.

Tales of such supernatural phenomena as ghosts, vampires, and exorcisms attribute to "Gnoina" an eerie, godless aura in the minds of present-day Assiriotes, and suggest the strong formative influence of religious ideology in local conceptions of social relations and identity. Most Assiriotes look upon "Gnoina" as a strangely alien place. In fact, when my friends in Assiros learned that I was interviewing people in Gnoina, many tried to dissuade me from going there, some joking that the place was "full of vampires" (*ghemato vrikolakes*).[14] Language differences were clearly a marker of "Otherness," and present-day Assiriotes built upon this theme of Otherness in a plurality of ways that differentiated and distanced themselves, and their history, from the Slavic-speaking "Gnoinans."

Yet prior to the ecclesiastical schisms and national competition at the turn of the century, Guveznans and Gnoinans, despite whatever differences they may have perceived among themselves, participated in a common ritual community under Orthodox Christianity. In fact, the Guvezna priest had performed many weddings and baptisms in Gnoina, and such rituals in both communities were described as having been similar to those in Guvezna. Yet Gnoina apparently acquired its own church and priest later in the nineteenth century (see chapter 3). A man in present-day Gnoina maintained that the "Gnoina" community had a priest, referred to as *Betis*. Such a priest may have been sent by the Bulgarian Exarchate, which might help to explain why present-day Assiriotes regard the former inhabitants of "Gnoina" as not proper Christians. The Patriarchate and its loyalists regarded the Exarchate and its supporters as "schismatics" (see chapter 4).

Some local area residents maintained that the Gnoinans had been obliged to form their own ritual community after facing growing discrimination from the priests in Guvezna. One present-day Gnoina resident told me a story of a woman (in "Gnoina") who had gone to Guvezna to seek a forty-day blessing (*sarandismos*) for her newborn child. The priest there allegedly demanded a payment of two *tenekedhes* (large tin cans or drums) of wheat, which sent the woman's husband into a rage. (It was explained that the usual payment in return for a *sarandismos*, as well as for a monthly blessing [*aghiasmos*] to bring "light" to a house, was a gift of firewood collected from the surrounding hills.) The woman, it was said, eventually went to a village in the Kukush area (which had many Bulgarian Exarchate churches) to get her blessing.

Despite such manifest ambivalence in the present day, ethnographic evidence such as family genealogical reconstructions and local oral histories all indicate that "the Gnoinans" had maintained strong marital and ritual kinship ties with Guvezna, as well as with Arakli and Langaza, both largely Slavic-speaking settlements. For their part the men of Guvezna, as I will show below, tended to marry brides from Ambar-Koy (Mandres), Balaftsa (Kolhikon), Langaza (Langadhas), and Zarova (Nikopolis), all of which were largely Slavic-speaking settlements.[15] This is not to suggest that the inhabitants of Guvezna had a preference for marrying Slavic-speaking (much less "Bulgarian") women. Their marriage patterns, as common throughout the world, often followed their economic activities, as the following chapters will show.

OF ANCESTORS AND KINGS

Still further mystery, however, seems to surround the Assyrian king who appears in many local origin accounts. He was said by some to have come to the area in the days of Alexander the Great, or by others to have arrived sometime after Alexander's death, or even in 1828, as a retired Greek policeman assured me one hot summer afternoon as we talked in an Assiros *kafenion*. He claimed to have read this in a book (note again the invocation of literary authority) loaned to him by a fellow police officer. The book supposedly described the former ethnological makeup of the region, alluding to a population of non-Greek origin; the few Assiriotes who made claims of descent from non-Greek ancestors also referred to this book. It was said to have disappeared from Assiros under mysterious circumstances. Some contended that it had been confiscated by security officials during the Metaxas dictatorship in the 1930s, which may explain how and why policemen posted to Assiros claimed to be familiar with it.

A similar version of the settlement's origins portrayed this Assyrian king as a liberator who saved the inhabitants of Aghia Anna from "Turkish" (i.e., Ottoman) persecution by bringing them to Gvos:

> An Assyrian king came to the area after the time of Alexander the Great. Then Aghia Anna had fallen under Turkish rule and the inhabitants were said to have been suffering immensely. The Turks appropriated all the produce of the Aghia Anna lands, which had been converted to a *chiftlik*. As there were no police in the community, the Turks were free to harass the Greeks, raping women and abducting children to make Muslims and Turks out of them. One day, the Assyrian king, who had by then established himself in nearby Gvos called on the inhabitants of Aghia Anna, who told him their misery. He listened compassionately, and told them to trust him and to not be afraid. Urging them to leave their possessions, he brought them to Gvos, which means "low spot" in Slavic. The people followed him, resettled there [here] and led a quiet life, never to be bothered by the Turks again.

This account bears many of the hallmarks noted earlier, namely, the anti-historicity of nonlinear time. But it ascribes a new element of persecution and tragedy by attributing the eventual demise and abandonment to the depredations of Turks, the perennial enemies of the Hellenes since the fall of Byzantium.

Yet, a number of elderly Assiriotes, born in the 1910s and 1920s, claimed that it had been their ancestors who two or three generations earlier had migrated over the mountains from Trikala (Thessaly) and established themselves in the village of Guvezna, where Muslims had been tilling the land of nearby agro-pastoral *chiftlik* estates (see below).[16] Assuming such claims to be fairly accurate, one may tentatively date the arrival and settlement of these Greek-speaking village ancestors between 1835 and 1880.[17] And yet other Assiros families claimed that their ancestors had originated elsewhere, from places as distant as Montenegro or as near as Langadhas. Assiros, as I noted in my Preface, was described as a *mazemata:* a mixed community of Greek- and Slavic-speaking Christians who had arrived in Gvos/Guvezna/Assiros at different times.

These contemporary oral accounts of the past may or may not accurately present history, and ultimately in many cases we may never know. But they are themselves part of the historical record as it develops in the present. Their motifs mark boundaries that exclude "Others" from the national pedigree to which these narratives lay claim. Told in school, homes, and *kafenia,* the accounts of Assiros's origins construct a proud heritage of ancient descent and links to glory or even royalty. Historical reconstructions of broad diachronic processes therefore present the ethnographer, much like a mystery detective, with a difficult task. They require a laborious search and "excavation" of a wide variety of disjointed, often cumbersome, confusing, or perplexing pieces of data and arcane clues. Until the final puzzle begins to take shape, these appear more like the fragments of a shattered artifact. They must be painstakingly extracted from a bed of rest and patiently considered again and again in alternative relations to other similar (or dissimilar) pieces until a general hypothesis may be formed to link them together.

But while legends relating to the establishment of Assiros may be perfectly correct and legitimate to their narrators, they are in essence myths of origin. They make use of key symbols, events, and personages to convey their own hidden meanings, but especially to emphasize certain key aspects of their descent stories which distinguish the Assiriotes and their ancestors from "Others," not only Muslims and "Turks" but also Christian inhabitants of other nearby settlements. By pursuing these threads through stories and memories of the less distant past, one may hope to reconstruct a feasible hypothesis concerning local history and labels of identity in Guvezna since the late nineteenth century. Some of the elements in these descent stories, moreover, intersect with information recorded elsewhere. Such written records, to which I now turn, offer some indication of the context, form, and extent of local historical transformations. But since not all of the historical record is preserved in print, and what is "preserved" is sometimes as selective as malleable memories are, both oral and written sources must be addressed critically. After reviewing available written sources on local history, I will return to the issue of personal memories to seek an appreciation of the content and meaning of local historical change for those who experienced it.

Landownership, Settlement Status, and Tax Privileges in Guvezna
The Written Record

Ottoman forces swept across the southern Balkans in the second half of the fourteenth century, with the regions of Macedonia and Thrace coming under Ottoman rule between 1361 and 1384. The Byzantine cosmopolitan commercial port and Orthodox religious center of Salonika (Thessaloniki) fell to the Ottomans a half century later, in 1430. Constantinople, the seat of the Byzantine Empire, surrendered in 1453 following a protracted siege (Stavrianos 1959:45–46). The Ottoman Empire, which ruled over Macedonia for roughly five hundred years, divided its population into religious-based *millets* and its territories into provinces (*vilayets*), prefectures (*sanjaks*), districts (*kazas*), and municipalities (*nahiyes;* see Gibb and Bowen 1950:137–44). The Christian population of Guvezna, for example, belonged to the Christian Orthodox *Rum millet,* and the settlement itself was situated in the *kaza* of Langaza, in the *sanjak* of Salonika, and the *vilayet* of Salonika.

A large volume of goods and people moved across Ottoman Macedonia, following transcontinental caravan routes and growing regional commercial trade. By the nineteenth century, if not earlier, rural Macedonia had become intimately tied to the growing capitalist economy of the European nation-states, effecting a devolution of power to regional and local landholders and estate managers. The opening of new markets encouraged migration, both within Macedonia and across its borders with neighboring states, such as the independent kingdom of Greece, established in 1829. During the late Ottoman era, the tax status of particular settlements in rural Macedonia strongly influenced migratory patterns, occupational livelihoods, and prospects for social mobility among local residents. While land in the empire was, in principle, ultimately the property of the sultan, rights of access, use, management, and eventually even de jure ownership were granted or transferred to local officials and later to Christian subjects of the empire and even to foreign owners.

Many scholars have characterized the economic system of the Ottoman Empire as a particular form of feudalism.[18] The sultan delegated use-rights to land and administrative oversight in a number of ways. Following the Ottoman conquest, most lands in the Balkan peninsula had been classified as *timars,* large noninheritable estates that were cultivated by Christian and Muslim sharecroppers and managed by cavalry officers known as *sipahi* (Gibb and Bowen 1950:237).[19] Fifteenth-century Ottoman tax records pertaining to the area, for example, mentioned a *timar* called "Gaina," inhabited by Muslims and situated in the northwestern Langadhas basin (Dimitriadis 1980). Described as having only eight houses, Gaina most likely referred to the now abandoned settlement site, just west of present-day Assiros, popularly referred to by area residents today as "Palehora" ("Old Village"). There was no indication of any Christian inhabitants on this *timar,* but the same Ottoman records also mentioned a nearby Muslim garrison post named "Cedid," manned by eleven Yuruk soldiers, a short distance to the west. Cedid apparently had been an earlier name of the small settlement, now called "Gnoina."

Another principal form of property holdings in Ottoman lands, granted by sultans to influential palace servants, were *wakf* properties (Inalcik 1985:107). These charitable trusts endowed for a pious cause were held mainly by such institutions as churches, mosques, schools, or hospitals (Gibb and Bowen 1950:165). *Wakf* trusts enjoyed certain privileges over *timar* estates, mainly lower tax rates and convertibility to private ownership.[20] They constituted a major proportion of landed property in Macedonia, and were the predominant form of landholding among Christian churches and monasteries throughout the Ottoman Balkans. Ghazi Evren *bey* (*bey,* Turkish: "landlord," "governor"), the Ottoman military leader whose forces conquered most of Macedonia in the fourteenth century,[21] had been granted vast tracts of land in Macedonia by Sultan Vayiazit I in recognition of his achievements. Much of this property had been designated as *wakf,* and was thus inheritable by his descendants and transferrable by his own authority.

Inhabitants of Ghazi Evren's *wakf* estates fared better than those living on *timars,* as the tax burden for the estates was lighter and was paid to a specially designated *wakf* collector (Dimitriadis 1980:407–8). Sixteenth-century Ottoman tax records indicate that Ghazi Evren possessed several *wakf* estates in the Langadhas basin, including the settlements of "Guveyna" and "Guveyna-Yeni" (Dimitriadis 1980). "Guveyna," it appears, was a new name for Gaina, the (former) *timar* settlement mentioned above. Guveyna-yeni (*yeni,* Turkish: "new"), on the other hand, apparently was a new settlement situated nearby, or at least a newly classified *wakf* trust.[22] Although much of Ghazi Evren's *wakf* estates remained intact until the Ottomans were driven from Macedonia in 1912, those around the settlements of Guveyna and Guveyna-Yeni apparently underwent significant changes in trusteeship or ownership as well as in names (see table 5). In these sixteenth-century Ottoman tax records, Guveyna and Guveyna-Yeni were recorded not only as *wakf* but also as *chiftliks,* both populated by Christians (Dimitriadis 1980:410), suggesting changes not only in ownership and management but in the composition of the agricultural labor force as well.

In fact, patterns of landholding and estate management throughout the Ottoman Empire began to undergo critical transformation in the late sixteenth century with the development of a commercial market in land, based in large part on the introduction of the *chiftlik* estate system.[23] Unlike *timars*, these large inheritable *chiftlik* properties could be leased or transferred to private stewards and effective owners, who became a new class of landholders known as the *chiftlik-sahibi* (Braudel 1966:594; McGowan 1981:56–79; Stavrianos 1959:138–142).[24] Many urban Muslims (and Christians, particularly in the last decades of Ottoman rule) who possessed the requisite funds found the purchase of *chiftlik* lands attractive and profitable. Cultivation rights under the *timar* system came to be replaced by tax revenues collected in cash or kind from *chiftlik* sharecroppers, whose landlord extracted from them the bulk of their harvest. Gradually, many *timar* and *wakf* lands throughout Macedonia were converted into or acquired the status of *chiftlik* holdings, and additional laborers were sought as resident cultivators.

By the late eighteenth century, Ottoman tax lists indicated two *chiftliks* in the area of present-day Assiros, both named "Guveyna" and both with similar taxes, but one now inhabited solely by Christians and the other by Muslims. Apparently, for reasons still unclear, the Christian sharecroppers of one settlement (former Guveyna-Yeni) were relocated, perhaps even concentrated in the other *chiftlik*, while Muslim sharecroppers were brought in to repopulate the former "New Guveyna" as resident cultivators. Both *chiftliks* were registered in these documents as charcoal-producing communities (*komurkesan*), and as such enjoyed special tax privileges. Although they were required to provide Ottoman authorities with a stipulated amount of firewood and charcoal every year, to be used in mining industries, such communities were exempted from grazing taxes (*celeb tahriri*) and tended to attract population from surrounding areas (Dimitriadis 1980:414). The Yuruk garrison post of Cedid mentioned in fifteenth-century tax rolls, on the other hand, was listed in eighteenth-century records as "Yeni-Koy," a *hanekesan* (Greek: *sinikismos*, "community"), which paid taxes according to its number of *hane* or households. Yeni-Koy reportedly provided the Ottoman army with niter for gunpowder, and continued to receive exemptions from the regularly issued supplemental taxes issued by the Ottoman Porte (Dimitriadis 1980:427).

These details, however incomplete, suggest that the introduction of the *chiftlik* economy was accompanied by, or even generated, a considerable degree of physical mobility among the inhabitants of Ottoman Macedonia. In fact, the *chiftlik* system inaugurated major changes not only in landownership and taxation but also in commercialized agro-pastoral production. Many such estates were devoted mainly to wheat, cotton, or tobacco cultivation for export to foreign markets in European countries, such as Austria, England, and France (McGrew 1985:30; Pamuk 1987:9).[25]

In fact, the late nineteenth century had witnessed the opening of new cultivated areas in Macedonia and a sharp rise in both wheat and cotton production. Cotton cultivation, in particular, increased dramatically during the 1860s, when U.S. cotton exports, devastated by the American Civil War, fell short of the demand in European markets (Gounaris 1989: 142).[26] Macedonian cotton, especially that produced in the Serres Valley, was exported along caravan routes through Sofia or Bosnia to Italy, Germany, and France (Zdraveva 1981:178), or was transported to the port of Salonika and then shipped out by sea. Notwithstanding the dismal descriptions of many contemporary observers (see below), turn-of-the-century Macedonia was no stagnant backwater of feudal Ottoman society. Rather, it was intimately tied to the developing capitalist world economy centered in northwestern Europe, where market conditions influenced the production and shipment of grain, tobacco, and cotton crops.[27]

Owners and managers of *chiftlik* estates controlled access to information on market conditions and made decisions regarding what crops would be cultivated. Since the eighteenth century, the pastoral sector of the *chiftlik* system had been boosted by the growing profitability of wool for export markets (Vucinich 1965:118). As Vergopoulos (1975:137) put it, "Wherever the *chiftlik* developed, the herding group (*tselingato*) followed closely." The mutually supportive character of agriculture and husbandry was bolstered by the increasing commercialization of agro-pastoral production. In addition, during winter months many *chiftlik* owners rented their lands to transhumant pastoralists and stockbreeders as seasonal encampments (Karavidas 1931:36).

Commercialization and market-oriented production under the *chiftlik* system were no doubt linked to the slow decline in centralized Ottoman administrative control. By 1900, *chiftliks* had become the most common form of landholding in both Macedonia and Thrace; a total of 552 such estates existed in Macedonia alone, over 90 percent of which were located along major trade routes on the plains and in the valleys (Perry 1988:25; McGrew 1985:30–31). In fact, at the time of its incorporation into the expanding Greek nation-state in 1913, some 41 to 52 percent of all cultivated lands in Macedonia were *chiftlik* properties (Vergopoulos 1975:135).

The new commercial *chiftlik* estates were taxed more heavily than other forms of property, and levies were increasingly imposed in cash rather than in kind. Or, rather, sharecroppers would pay their fees in kind to local tax-farmers, who then sold such products to merchants for cash, a portion of which they remitted to authorities of the Ottoman Porte (for Muslim farmers) or to the Orthodox Patriarchate (for Christians). Rural cultivators, Muslim and Christian alike, shouldered the heaviest burdens under this regime of surplus extraction and, depending on the specific arrangements made with the landowner, were arguably worse off than under the *timar* system. Poverty drove many either to migrate illegally to the cities (where taxation could be evaded) or to take to banditry (Vucinich 1965:49–52). *Chiftlik* owners, in turn, became increasingly dependent upon migrant laborers from hill and mountain areas, as more and more Ottoman subjects (*rayah*) left their farms rather than endure what many regarded as unattractive or disadvantageous cultivation arrangements (McGrew 1985:35).

By the mid-nineteenth century these transformations in the regional and global political economy led to important changes in local settlements. An Ottoman tax document from 1861–62 reveals several changes in both the names and classificatory status of the Langadhas basin settlements mentioned above (Dimitriadis 1980). It lists a Christian-populated *chiftlik* called "Guneyna," still registered as a charcoal-producing *wakf* of Ghazi Evren and consisting now of twenty-four houses.[28] Yeni-Koy, once a *hanekesan* community in the eighteenth century, was now recorded as a Christian *chiftlik* of seven houses.[29] Most notable, however, is the appearance of a new settlement named "Guvezna," referring to a "village" (*horio*) with a mixed population of eleven Muslim and eighty-four Christian households. Apparently sometime prior to the mid-nineteenth century, a new group of Christians had come or were brought to the former Muslim *chiftlik* of Guveyna-Yeni, transforming it substantially enough to have it reclassified as a village. By the 1860s, the settlement had also lost its status as a charcoal-producing community.

This change in status was not the result of the proliferation of private landowning among local cultivators, for such communities were known as *kefalohoria* ("head" or "free" villages).[30] Rather, a particular flow of people into the local field of action appears to have effected this new classification. A few decades earlier, in 1831, the French traveler E. M. Cousinery described Guvezna as having a mosque, two fountains, freshwater springs, many taverns or inns, and winter quarters for caravans, but had made no mention of a Christian Orthodox church (Lefort 1986: 152).[31] This suggests not only that at least by the third decade of the nineteenth century Guvezna had become a stopover for overland commercial trade, but also that a Christian population, if present at all, was small and of little prominence.

Yet by the mid-nineteenth century, economy and society in Guvezna began to undergo yet another series of fundamental changes. As noted earlier, genealogical reconstructions of family histories for present-day Assiros villagers who claimed their ancestors had come from Trikala, date the arrival of these Greek-speaking migrant settlers to the mid-to-late nineteenth century, or the 1830s–1880s in particular. Most of these newcomers established themselves, as their family occupational histories revealed, as merchants and artisans. These Christians soon came to dominate the flow of goods in and out of the settlement and by the end of the nineteenth century had built a church and brought in a teacher of Greek to educate their children. But what brought these men to Guvezna? Here, again, local oral histories provide an important supplement to the written historical record, for Ottoman tax records make no mention whatsoever of trade caravans passing through Guvezna or of an important market that developed there.

CARAVAN STOP AND GROCERY SHOPS
Memory, History, and the Makings of a Market Town

Sources limpides et lieu d'hivernage des caravans

Cousinery (1831)

By the mid-nineteenth century, the town of Serres had become a major commercial center whose surrounding plains produced cotton and tobacco for export to European and Asian markets. Vakalopoulos (1987) argued that the Crimean War (1853–56) had closed Russian ports on the Black Sea, making Salonika the principal bulking point for regional export products in the third quarter of the nineteenth century (or roughly 1845–75). Many of the agricultural exports from Serres were transported to Salonika, often by camel caravan, before being shipped further abroad. At the same time, the American Civil War had heightened concerns of British manufacturers over maintaining adequate supplies of bulk cotton for their booming textile industries in Manchester, Birmingham, and elsewhere, and the British began to import new American cotton seeds to Macedonia.[32] Although foreign construction of railways through Macedonia in the 1860s precipitated the gradual decline of the caravan trade, not all merchants could move their commodities by rail. As long as Serres remained a regional center for trade and bulking, villages along its caravan routes generally prospered.

Guvezna was one such community, which by the late nineteenth century had developed its own bustling market, held every Monday, the day before the Langadhas animal market.[33] Caravans regularly took three days and two nights to travel the route between Salonika and Serres, from where many continued on to other important market towns to the east, such as Drama and Nigrita, or to the north to Bulgaria and beyond. Situated at the foot of a mountainous section of this road, Guvezna became an important layover stop for caravans delayed by poor weather during the winter season (Lefort 1986:152). In fact, it was one of two main overnight stops for Salonika-Serres caravans, as the route was said to have passed close to the village *aghora*.[34] Local memories and the memories of memories maintained that by the turn of the twentieth century the village had two *khans* (inns), where merchants and wagoners found safe shelter for both camels and cargo and where drivers could receive food, drink, and a bed for the night.

Guvezna's thriving market and agro-pastoral *chiftlik* commercial economy attracted growing numbers of new settlers, both from other communities within Macedonia as well as from Greek-speaking communities to the north and south. The relatively shielded location of Guvezna, situated in a forested dell, provided some security from marauding bandits of the nineteenth century and from the national partisans of the early twentieth-century Macedonian Struggle who preyed on the inhabitants of the basin (see chapter 4). The repeated theme in local origin-accounts of patronage and protection offered to local Christian inhabitants is supported by evidence that urban Muslims indeed took rural cultivators under their protection and resettled them on newly colonized *chiftlik* lands.

> [W]hile *chiftlik* peasants were poor, they were at least comparatively safe. Christian peasants not living on *chiftliks* were often beset and terrorized by hostile Muslims . . . perpetrating wanton murder, raping and extortion (Perry 1988:25).

In much the same way, a landowning patron was credited in local origin-legends with having brought the former inhabitants of Aghia Anna (or others) to Guvezna (or "Gvos"), offering them protection from harassment and persecution.[35] Perhaps this owner had been from the eastern provinces of the Ottoman Empire (i.e., an "Assyrian"), or perhaps the Christians of Aghia Anna had been compelled (by banditry or other

forces) to abandon their settlement and move under the protection af-
forded by a powerful Turkish *bey*. Such scenarios had been common in
Ottoman Macedonia, and such dependents were required to pay the *bey*
an annual fee called *kism* (Greek: *kesimi*), similar to a tribute (McGrew
1985:39). On the other hand, it is also possible that Aghia Anna was
destroyed by epidemic and that the survivors were absorbed by the nearby
chiftlik as sharecroppers. Vucinich (1965:49) maintained that villages
ravaged by epidemics were, in fact, sometimes turned into private possessions where rural cultivators were offered protection.

With the decline of Italian maritime commerce in the eastern Mediterranean and the growing importance of many overland Balkan trade
routes during the eighteenth century (Tsoukalas 1977:47), *chiftliks* in Ottoman Macedonia became intensely involved in export-oriented agro-
pastoral production. Many such estates had been situated either alongside
major caravan routes or in depopulated areas undergoing recolonization.
The repopulation of the countryside, the Ottoman Porte had hoped,
would increase productivity and tax revenues while also reducing the endemic rural banditry in Macedonia.[36]

Moreover, Guvezna's then abundant water supply also made for an
added attraction. Guvezna eventually became famous for its excellent
vines, pleasant climate, and an unusual absence of the notorious mosquitoes that infested the plains of Macedonia.[37] Attracted to the site, a number of Ottoman Turks apparently moved in and built summer homes
there, reportedly renaming it "Guvezna" (Turkish: "Deep Red Earth,"
from *guvez*, "dark red" or "violet" + the suffix *-na*, signifying "place").
During the mid-nineteenth century, a number of unmarried young Greek
(or Greek-speaking) men, mainly from the area of Trikala in Thessaly,
came to the Langadhas basin and established themselves in Guvezna as
merchants, millers, wagoners, and tax collectors.

I leave the issue of the cultural or ethnic identity of these migrant
settlers open, for while their descendants claimed that they had been
Greek, other evidence suggests that they may have been Hellenized Vlahs
who spoke Greek. A number of scholars have written on Vlah acquisition
of Greek identity through mercantile occupations and formal education
in the late nineteenth and early twentieth century (e.g. Balamaci 1991;
Vouri 1992). As one descendant of these settlers told me:

> Our grandfather's father came from Trikala. There are Vlahs there. All of
> them there from the mountains were Vlahs. The Trikaliotes have strange
> words, they speak differently. From Trikala, they say they are all Vlahs.
> Our grandfather spoke no Macedonian [*Makedhonika*]. He only spoke

Turkish. He had a mill in Balaftsa [Kolhikon]. They spoke Macedonian there.

While this account suggests that his ancestors were Hellenized Vlahs rather than native Greeks per se, I am reluctant to project such origins on all Greek-speaking mercantile settlers who arrived in Guvezna during the mid-nineteenth century, as this man was the only one in Assiros to explicitly make such a claim. Descendants of other Greek-speaking merchant settlers depicted their ancestors as Greeks.

These settlers, along with the recently absorbed inhabitants from Aghia Anna (or elsewhere), with transhumant pastoralists who wintered in the area, and with sharecroppers, laborers, and shepherds from other nearby *chiftliks* such as Palehora and Gnoina, gradually came to form the nucleus of the nineteenth-century Orthodox Christian population of Guvezna. As the village and its market flourished, more settlers followed. Later, the terror of the turn-of-the-century national conflicts between Greece and Bulgaria brought even more Christians, both Greek-speakers and Slavic-speakers, to the village (see chapter 4).[38]

Some of the newcomers were sharecroppers and others found employment in the shops of the merchants and artisans or as laborers for local landowners and herd-owners, Christian and Muslim alike. In a collection of traveler accounts from Macedonia, Lefort (1986:152) described the settlement of "Gkioubezna" as having ninety-five houses in 1862, 992 inhabitants in 1913, and 1,906 inhabitants in 1920, indicating that its population had more than doubled during the second half of the nineteenth century, and had doubled yet again in the first few years following its incorporation into Greece in 1913.[39]

Being registered as a "village" (*horio*) in late-nineteenth-century Macedonia had certain implications for social and economic organization. Taxes, for example, were collected from the village as a unit, rather than from individual households or families (McGowan 1981:138–39). Locally, notable property holders, in either agro-pastoralism or in commerce, often took an active interest in seeing that the community's tax obligations were met. Tax burdens were distributed among village residents on a family rather than on an individual-head basis, a practice that fostered the development of large, extended domestic units. All families, large and small, rich and poor alike, were required to pay a share. Wealthier families would often offer loans to those who could not meet their payments, since defaulting on taxes could bring reprisals against the entire community (Vergopoulos 1975:58).[40] Those with village resident status who disapproved of arrangements in their settlement had the alternative of moving to another village or to a city (Dimitriadis 1980:435). Yet many village poor became indebted to better-off families, and sometimes ended up working off debts as servants or semi-indentured laborers.

As they grew in wealth and influence, these mostly Greek-speaking Christian notables came to play, as a group, an increasingly influential role in overseeing the affairs of the village. In addition to overseeing local tax collection, they came to exercise a degree of authority over the civil, judicial, and religious affairs of other Christian villagers. They also mediated relations between Guvezna Christians and both Ottoman authorities and the Ecumenical Orthodox Patriarchate, which had jurisdiction over members of the Orthodox Christian *Rum millet.* As later chapters will show, this Greek-speaking commercial elite came to exercise strong influence over new local conceptions of identity, both before and after violent national competition erupted over Macedonia.

Private interests and public roles contributed to the growing power, authority, and group identity of this nascent local Christian elite, who were referred to in Guvezna as *tsorbadjidhes.*[41] These Christian local notables fared relatively well under the Ottomans, at least compared with Muslim and Christian sharecroppers of *chiftlik* estates. Most were Greek-speakers, either by birth or by virtue of their roles as property managers, merchants, stockbreeders, local administrators, tax collectors, moneylenders, and leading participants in local church and school affairs. In mediating relations between local Christian inhabitants and both Ottoman and Patriarchate authorities, the *tsorbadjidhes* of Guvezna were not unlike the local Christian notables of "free villages," who

> managed the transfer of agricultural surpluses from the Christian cultivators to Turkish landowners and officials, and in so doing won for themselves local power and modest wealth. [Moreover] under the lax property laws . . . they could often convert their tax-farming profits into landed property. (McGrew 1985:37)

In Guvezna, however, the Christian *tsorbadjidhes* did not acquire sizeable tracts of agricultural and grazing land until the first decade or so of the twentieth century (see chapter 6). Rather, their earlier property holdings were concentrated in the *aghora,* while agro-pastoral lands in the area continued to be held mainly by Muslim *chiftlik* estate owners.

By local oral accounts, most *chiftlik* sharecroppers and laborers in late-nineteenth-century Guvezna, however, lived and labored under circumstances markedly poorer than those of the new Greek-speaking Christian merchant settlers. Despite its rising local prominence, in 1854 Guvezna was depicted by a French visitor, A. Boué, as a "miserable hamlet" located between two streams (Lefort 1986:152). In fact, accounts written by early-twentieth-century contemporaries visiting the Langadhas basin mainly depicted a poor and struggling population. For example, G. F. Abbot (1903), a British folklorist who passed through the region while enroute to Istanbul on the eve of the Macedonian Struggle (1903–8), observed that bandits roamed the basin countryside, commerce was terribly underdeveloped, and the area's inhabitants were sharply divided by both language and "race" (see chapter 3). Kontoyiannis (1911:241–54), a teacher in Thessaloniki who took students on a tour of the basin during the years between the bloody Macedonian Struggle and the First Balkan War (1912), had been struck by what he perceived as the desolate lack of progress or civilization in the basin, and had regarded the local agrarian population as melancholic, beset with sad folk songs, and suspicious towards outsiders. Such accounts may suggest that conditions in the basin had deteriorated in the late nineteenth century, a time of growing national competition between Greece and Bulgaria over the region of Macedonia. But the observations of such literate outsiders were also framed by notions of "progress" and "civilization" they held in their own minds. Like landscape painters, their depictions emanated from a vantage point outside (and "above") life in the basin.

2

EXCHANGING IDENTITIES

The Makings of the Guvezna Market Community

> [U]ntil the beginning of the nineteenth century, the Slavs, Greeks
> and Vlahs still constituted one Christian community, united in the
> Rum millet. A peasant felt himself first of all as a member of a
> family, a village community and maybe a small culturally distin-
> guishable unit, and, secondly Rum.
>
> Hans Vermeulen

Oral accounts of living conditions and land tenure in Guvezna and
its environs during the late nineteenth and early twentieth centuries
provide an ethnographic texture to documentary evidence of transformations in the political economy, as discussed in chapter 1. Their often rich
detail provides insight on how perceptions of identity and difference were
framed by local residents themselves, as well as on how such notions were
sometimes reshaped or redefined over time.[1] As such, they provided an
important complement to archival sources written by "outsiders." For
example, oral accounts from contemporary Assiros supported evidence
from available Ottoman archives that agriculture and landowning were
predominantly in the hands of Muslims.[2] But they also revealed the importance of the Guvezna market—and the Christian merchants who
dominated it—in shaping the flow of economic, social, and even cultural
exchange, a key issue that receives no direct mention in Ottoman sources.

By the close of the nineteenth century, occupational specialization in
Guvezna had become well pronounced (see table 6). One's relative position in the local division of labor was an important facet to constructs
of identity in Guvezna during the late Ottoman era. Issues such as vernacular language and religious affiliation, often cited as key aspects of Greek
or Bulgarian national identity, became politicized markers only with the
onset of the national competition over the region of Macedonia (see chapters 3 and 4). Yet by that time, divisions of labor had established the
foundations of a local status hierarchy in the market village, from which
a new pattern of social stratification emerged following the turn-of-the-
century Macedonian Struggle and advent of Greek rule in 1912. The
growing influence of prominent Christian merchants and grocers facili-

tated their economic diversification into other profitable commercial activities, notably tax farming and livestock breeding. The wealth generated
through such enterprises made these families well positioned to extend
their political influence even further, when new offices and powers of
township government were established in the 1910s (see part 2).

LANDOWNERS, SHARECROPPERS, AND "THE CHRISTIANS OF GUVEZNA"

The largest landowner in Ottoman Guvezna was said to have been the
Toptop or Tortop *bey,* also known as Tsei *effendi* (*effendi,* Turkish:
"master") or Soucri Tortop, who possessed 5,000 *stremmata* (1,250
acres) of land. Some described the Toptop *bey* as an Ottoman minister
for the *vilayet* of Salonika, while others depicted him as a customs officer
in Thessaloniki. Apparently an absentee landlord who often visited Guvezna on his holidays, the Toptop *bey* possessed a large mansion (*konaki*)
above the Tourkolakkos ("Turkish Creek"), the stream on the western
side of the village *aghora.* This hilltop neighborhood was where most of
the village's Muslim inhabitants lived and where the mosque was located
(see map 4).[3]

A second large landowner in the village had been an army officer
named Shei *effendi,* or Seremet *bey,* who owned large tracts of land northeast of Guvezna stretching from the village of Lingovan (present-day Xiloupolis) in the northern hills to the Arakli *chiftlik* to the south (see map
2b). Shei *effendi* was said to have often arbitrated disputes between Christian and Muslim villagers in Guvezna.[4] He too had his own *konaki,* and
operated an inn (*khan*) patronized mainly by Muslims from surrounding
mountain hamlets, especially those from the Otmanli *mahaladhes.* He
also possessed his own threshing floors as well as a barn in which he
stored hay. Shei *effendi* employed an estate steward for his *chiftlik,* a man
named Kerim *effendi,* who was well respected and treated as a landlord
himself. Kerim had married Shei's sister, and for thirty years managed
Shei's properties.

Oral histories also maintained that while most of the land in turn-
of-the-century Guvezna had been managed by these Ottoman Turks, by
1912 both Muslims and Christians in the village owned private plots of
land.[5] This shift in landholdings, particularly ownership by Christians,
may have been precipitated by the new Turkish constitution of 1908,
which institutionalized private landownership in the Ottoman Empire
(see chapter 4). Some local accounts maintained that until 1908 the Chris-

tian population of Guvezna could not possess land unless it was granted
to them by Ottoman authorities. For example, Guvezna Christians were
said to have been allotted some 1,600 *stremmata* for their vineyards.

Similarly, after its establishment in the second half of the nineteenth
century, the local Orthodox Christian church had been granted *wakf*
charitable trusts in Guvezna, both outlying agricultural fields as well as
plots within the village proper.[6] After the advent of Greek rule in 1913,
these *wakf* properties came under the joint ownership of the local township (*kinotita*), church, and school, which managed them as a tripartite
trust corporation until the Greek government ordered its dissolution in
1930 (see chapter 6). It was said that once land became transferable in
1908, a number of Christian families who had already amassed considerable wealth through mercantile or pastoral enterprises were able to take
advantage of this legal reform. Other villagers, however, claimed that by
1910 the Turks had become suspicious that they would soon be forced
to leave the area, and began selling their land to local Christians rather
than wait for its appropriation.[7]

Regardless of how they acquired land, a number of Guvezna Christians rose to local notable status through their new landholdings. Consider the following paraphrased account of one such man, Nikolaos Tamtakos, who came to possess such extensive lands that villagers came to
address him as *bey,* an honorific title usually reserved for Ottoman landowners and administrators:

Nikolaos Tamtakos (born 1882) was the son of a settler from some-
where in southern Greece who had arrived in Guvezna around 1870. His
original surname was Stavrakis. His mother had been a Slavic-speaker from
Aivati (Liti). Tamtakos had once served as an officer in the Ottoman army,
stationed both in Asia Minor and in Serbia. He spoke fluent Turkish. Tamtakos was president of the Guvezna Christian community, both under the
Ottomans as well as after 1913. Well-off financially, he was considered a
true patriot because he was said to have used his good relations with the
Turks to save many Greeks from suffering and death. Using his political
position, Tamtakos was able to allot himself 600 *stremmata* of land. He
planted half with wheat, while the other half he left fallow during the winter
and planted with summer crops such as corn, sesame, and watermelons.
The 300 *stremmata* of wheat fields gave him some six tons of grain every
year, a pretty fair yield considering that no fertilizer was used. He also had
his own threshing floors (*alonia*), located across from the schoolhouse on
the spot where the police station now stands. He either kept the grain at
home or sold it to merchants after enough had been ground at the water

mills by the river to cover his family's domestic needs, both human and animal. He had four to six horses to plough his fields, which were worked by his children and six servants, "*Koinari* Turks,"[8] whom he provided with food in return for their services. Tamtakos did not raise livestock, but bought cheese and milk from local animal breeders, or exchanged his chickens and eggs (he was raising some fifty chickens) for dairy products.

Tamtakos and his family lived in a big house, famous for its spacious balconies and storage cellars. There he received guests, mainly prominent "outsider" men who were passing through the area or Guvezna notables who dropped by for a visit. He would order the women of his household to spread a rug over the floor while his guests sat on low stools or cushions, drinking *ouzo* from his own vineyards and eating bread and raisins. Tamtakos had married a "Bulgarian" woman from the village of Ambar-Koy (present-day Mandres) who bore him three children before she died. His second wife was also a "Bulgarian," from Langadhas, who was a good housewife.

Tamtakos was the founder of a large patriline which is still present in Assiros (see Genealogy A), and all his daughters married locally, i.e., within the village. Some of his descendants asserted to me that the father of Tamtakos had come originally from Mani, a Greek royalist stronghold in the southernmost Peleponnese. They explained that they had heard that the name "Tamtakos" was a common one in that part of Greece. Although the mother of Tamtakos and both his wives had been Slavic-speakers, many villagers insisted that he himself spoke Greek and Turkish but not "Bulgarian."

While the accounts of Tamtakos' ancestry may be factual or fictitious, it is notable that his reputed Greek ancestry was given strong emphasis. Generally speaking, most male villagers often emphasized the Greekness of their male ancestors, but few made any attempt to conceal Slavic-speaking or "Bulgarian" women who had married into their family patriline. As I will argue in chapter 4, such patriarchical assumptions or patrilineal biases peripheralized female ancestors in local constructs of identity. They also misunderstood the reality of how language (and culture) is learned and transmitted.[9]

While the tale of Tamtakos illustrates how Christian notables rose to landowner status at the turn of the century, the majority of resident Christians in the area lived as sharecroppers on local *chiftlik* estates, or as seasonal laborers or shepherds paid in cash or kind. Local sharecropping arrangements between landowners and cultivators were tempered by particularistic ties between patrons and clients that could cut across religious distinctions or other lines of difference. Most Christian and Muslim sharecroppers on area *chiftliks* were referred to as *yarandjidhes* (Greek: *misaridhes,* "half and half"). They were provided with seed, a pair of oxen, and housing by *chiftlik* owners, who in return retained half the harvest after taxes. The following composite life history provides a glimpse of the variation in conditions faced by rural cultivators during the late nineteenth century. I recount it here in some detail, as it concerns a family that came to feature prominently in local history and to whom I will return repeatedly in chapters that follow.

Nikolaos Asteriou, originally a native of Montenegro (Greek: Mavrovouni), fled Serbian authorities in 1869 at the age of eighteen and made his way down to the Kukush (Kilkis) area of Macedonia, settling in a village just beyond the hills that ring the Langadhas basin to the west. That village, at the time, had been inhabited mainly by Slavic-speakers, and Asteriou found work there as an agricultural laborer for a local *bey.* One day, the visiting *bey* of the *chiftlik* of "Gnoina" (i.e., Guneyna, or present-day Palehora) saw Asteriou in the fields and, recognizing him as a dedicated worker, invited him to resettle on his own *chiftlik.* Asteriou had been around twenty years old when he moved to Guneyna (i.e., circa 1871). As an employee of the local *bey,* he enjoyed good standing with his patron, who soon found for him a Slavic-speaking wife from Langadhas. Together, he and she established what eventually became one of the largest and most prestigious families in contemporary Assiros (see Genealogy B).

Working as a laborer on the Guneyna *chiftlik,* Asteriou's status rose as the *bey* provided him with animals, fodder, seeds, machinery, and land, for which he paid with produce. From every eight *koutlous* (approximately one kilogram) of wheat, the *bey* took six for his own use, leaving Asteriou with the remaining two. He was soon promoted again, this time to *yarandji,* a half-and-half sharecropper. Productivity increased and both Asteriou and the *bey* were pleased. Four years later, the *bey* promoted him yet again, this time to *altedji.* Their sharecropping arrangement reverted to a 6:2 division of the harvest, but now Asteriou retained the bulk of it. As a *yarandji* and *altedji,* Nikolaos Asteriou gradually saved enough wealth to begin purchasing land and house plots in nearby Guvezna village, acquiring some 200 *stremmata* (roughly fifty acres).

Such arrangements between landowners and laborers were particularly "advantageous to the agricultural laborer, a mountaineer, who desired only periodic work as a plains cultivator to supplement a meager living from a small farm or flocks in the mountains" (McGrew 1985:33). Asteriou apparently stayed on at Guneyna because of the very favorable

treatment he received from his landlord. As an immigrant from Montenegro, he also met the criterion of "foreign status" that Vergopoulos
(1975:95) noted was required for those who sought to settle and work
on a *chiftlik*. The fact that his patron also found Asteriou a Slavic-speaking bride from Langaza was probably an added incentive, as it tied him
to a larger network of new affinal relatives in the area. Asteriou, however,
invested his profits in Guvezna, rather than in Guneyna, because the former had (by then) the privileged classification of village (*horio;* as opposed to *chiftlik*) and therefore possessed an open market in land.

Sharecropping arrangements at the Yeni-Koy *chiftlik* (present-day
Gnoina) were said to have been less favorable than those offered to resident cultivators in Guvezna or Guneyna. Farmers in Yeni-Koy, however,
had cultivated wheat as well as corn, and had maintained large animal
herds on nearby Deve Karan mountain, but rates of agricultural surplus
extraction at this *chiftlik* were reportedly quite severe. Sharecroppers at
Yeni-Koy not only were obliged, like cultivators elsewhere, to surrender
one-tenth of their harvests for the 10 percent *dhekati* tax (see below), but
the local *bey* reportedly retained as much as 80 percent of the remaining
harvest, leaving cultivators with little subsistence grain. As compensation,
inhabitants of Yeni-Koy had been granted the status of *kehayiadhes* (livestock owners) by the local *bey*, and were permitted private ownership of
animals. Both these livestock and husbandry by-products were exempt
from taxes.

All these *chiftlik* estates in the area included grazing lands in the
nearby hills, where both Muslim and Christian herders raised sheep for
export wool. Ottoman landlords apparently owned these grazing lands
and extracted rent from herdowners who needed access to pastures. For
example, half-and-half *misaridhes* sharecroppers in Guneyna (Palehora),
including Asteriou in later years, rented some 4,000 to 5,000 *stremmata*
of grazing land from their local *bey*, on which they raised both sheep and
cows.[10] Oral histories of the Velikas family (see Genealogy C), widely
regarded in Assiros as one of the oldest resident families of the village,
maintained that a substantial portion of their income had been derived
from pastoral activities. The family was said to have settled in Guvezna
at an early date, bringing their herds from Apostolari (the present-day
name of a village in the Kilkis prefecture) and renting land from one of
the Guvezna *beys*. Over the years they acquired large parcels of their own
land in Guvezna and since 1913 have been one of the most prominent
families in the village.

Inhabitants of Guneyna (Palehora), such as Asteriou, enjoyed special
tax exemptions on their husbandry activities owing to the *chiftlik*'s

charcoal-producing status since at least the late eighteenth century. More-over, although details remain sketchy, sometime in the nineteenth century Guneyna reportedly became a "foreign-owned" *chiftlik* and its inhabi-tants acquired the protected status of "foreign citizenship," which later exempted them from military conscription as well.[11] Such privileges en-abled many Guneyna families to accumulate large savings in gold pieces, and many were said to have built up large, "extended" domestic units. One such localized descent group had been the Stoinos family (a name with Slavic roots), who had maintained a joint family of some fifty-five to sixty individuals on a single budget and common property holdings.[12] Consisting of five brothers, their spouses, their children, and five agnatic (i.e., patrilineally related) cousins, the Stoinos family all lived, worked, and ate together as a single unit under the managerial direction of the eldest brother.[13] Ottoman authorities rarely involved themselves in local affairs in Guneyna, technically a foreign settlement. During the turn-of-the-century Macedonian Struggle, its Slavic-speaking inhabitants fre-quently fell prey to the harassment of Greek "Macedonian Fighters" (*Makedhonomahi*). The Stoinos family, for example, eventually used its gold pieces to purchase the lands of Shei *effendi* when they abandoned Guneyna and moved to Guvezna in 1905, fleeing persecution by armed partisans (see chapter 4).

Husbandry, therefore, had been a key part of the agro-pastoral econ-omy of many *chiftlik* estates. As one elderly villager in present-day Assiros put it, "Those who had the money or the surplus produce could rent space from the Turks in their grazing lands. That way they could slowly build a flock and make a profit." One of the wealthiest men in Guvezna at the turn of the century had been a Christian named Yeorgios Halepis (see Genealogy D), who according to local oral accounts owned 3,000 sheep and goats. Halepis was a widely feared man, who was alleged to have employed violence, even murder, against his rivals and enemies. As one Assiros villager put it,

> Old Halepis was a brave man (*pallikari*). He had been a crop-watcher. He was in charge. He carried his pistol and no one dared to do anything. He had 2,000 sheep, 1,000 goats, and herds of cows. He was illiterate, but he was smart. He had gold pieces hidden in sacks.

Halepis was said to have hired Muslims to tend his flocks but also to have housed the shepherds in a hut where he would beat them if they asked for their pay. It was alleged that he not only refused to pay them but also refused to let them leave. Many upwardly mobile Christians sought to expand into highly profitable stockbreeding enterprises, as did

Halepis. The cash and capital they derived from these pastoral activities could be reinvested in the expansion of other family commercial enterprises and in additional purchases of land. This contributed to the rising status of such merchant-landowner-stockbreeding Christian families as *tsorbadjidhes* local notables, and eventually to their consolidation into a local elite class (see chapter 6). Vergopoulos (1975:146) argued that under the Ottomans, Christian notables often constituted a bourgeois stratum of local society as powerful as Turkish landowners. In Guvezna, most of these Christian notable families got their start in Guvezna as migrant settlers who predominantly established themselves as merchants, grocers, and artisans in this first overnight stop for trade caravans from Salonika to Serres.

"PEOPLE OF THE *AGHORA*"

Among the first young unmarried Greek-speaking men said to have come to the Guvezna area from Thessaly were Dimitris, Sapountzis, and Sigaras, followed sometime later by Gaitetzis, Mantsos, Kondos, and Stavrakis. To some extent, the claims of their descendants to Greek ancestry in Thessaly involved a measure of creative ancestral editorializing. The constructed character of such descent accounts is suggested, at least, in assertions that because particular surnames were allegedly common in certain areas of Greece to the south, the ancestors of such families came originally from those areas. In fact, several of the surnames by which these families are now known were adopted subsequent to their settlement in Guvezna.

The migration of these men into Macedonia had been motivated, most likely, by either political or economic factors. Some of their descendants claimed that these ancestors had escaped from Ottoman authorities in Thessaly. Thessaly did not become part of Greece until 1881; if they had fled that region from Ottoman agents and officials, they would have done so before then, as indeed many of their descendants asserted or implied. Whatever the elusive (and perhaps irrelevant) "origins" of these men, it is possible that they or their relatives had been engaged in pro-Greek national activities in Ottoman Thessaly. In fact, one villager in Assiros, related to one of these men from Thessaly, asserted that they had come to Guvezna for propaganda purposes (*yia propaghandha*), to Hellenize the inhabitants in this part of Macedonia.

On the other hand, it is also possible that the strong *chiftlik* system in Thessaly, where large estates of concentrated landholdings continued to dominate the regional economy even after incorporation into Greece, had prompted these young adventurers to migrate north across the Macedonian frontier in search of land or new livelihoods. As one of their descendants in present-day Assiros put it,

> The village here was pure Turkish, and people from elsewhere came and found jobs as merchants, tinkers, cobblers, and the like. They came over here from Trikala, armed like *kapetanarei* [captains or partisans]. They got in here among the Turks and they made a village. That is how they got to own most of the housing plots in the village. The Dimitris family was down by the river. Tamtakos was up on top, at the Pera *mahala*. Gaitetzis was over at the Pano *mahala*. Kondos was down here in the *aghora*. None of them have legal deeds for their properties.[14]

These initial migrant settlers married Slavic-speaking women from surrounding villages or (in a few cases) from Guvezna itself. Their descendants claimed that when their forefathers had arrived, there were no women in the village to marry; that, they explained, is why they took Slavic-speaking brides from elsewhere. Perhaps all village women at the time had been Muslims, or perhaps there were not enough Christian women in Guvezna for all of these settler men to marry. On the other hand, it may also have been that local Christian families in Guvezna preferred to marry their daughters exogamously to other villages in the area.[15]

Having first established themselves through businesses and the services they provided to passing caravans as merchants, grocers, or artisans, these Greek-speakers expanded their activities to cater to the needs of surrounding settlements that looked towards Guvezna as their market town.[16] For example, they traded extensively with those from the Muslim hamlets in the hills to the north and northeast of Guvezna. These Otmanli *mahaladhes* (situated in the area of present-day Mavrorahi) were described as a number of small, impoverished herding hamlets, whose residents had been engaged in sheep and goat husbandry.[17] The Muslims inhabiting Otmanli constantly had family members conscripted into the Turkish army and were forced to pay heavy taxes. Poverty-stricken herders possessing no land of their own, they were allotted only enough land to sustain small gardens. "Twenty Turks ate from the same plate," Assiros villagers claimed today, "eating fig leaves to assuage their constant hunger and gathering up leftover bread discarded by the Greeks."

These Muslims came down to Guvezna to sell butter, eggs, and wool, and to buy staple goods from shops there. They either bartered for their supplies or paid for them with cash they received from Guvezna cheese-makers who traveled daily to the mountain hamlets to obtain fresh milk. As one Assiros villager maintained, these Muslims

> were getting exploited by those who had the grocery stores. The store own-
> ers sold the produce in Thessaloniki and brought groceries back to Gu-
> vezna. They exploited a vast area reaching down to Strimoniko [a village
> on the Strimon River, along the route to Serres].

Many Assiriotes claimed that by trading with the Muslims of Otmanli, for example, the baker and saddle-maker Artousis (see Genealogy E) ac-quired some thirty-three *okadhes* (or 1,312 ounces) of gold.[18] Born in 1873 in the Slavic-speaking village of Aivati (Liti), Artousis had been adopted by a childless Guvezna couple whose surname suggested his adoptive father was an Orthodox priest. After the death of Artousis, his widow was said to have collected the gold pieces from his bakery and saddle-making businesses and given them to her two sons as venture capi-tal. The Artousis brothers jointly opened a store that sold groceries, fab-ric, yarn, and other general merchandise. Profits from the family's mer-cantile enterprises were reinvested by the two brothers, who in the 1910s expanded their joint property holdings through the purchase of the Aralki *chiftlik* south of Guvezna.[19]

By the turn of the twentieth century, therefore, many of these Gu-vezna merchant families had become the wealthiest Christians in the vil-lage. Consider the family of Yeorgios Kondos (born 1876), whose grand-father, Andonios, was said to have come to Guvezna from Trikala sometime around 1850. Reportedly classified as a "foreign citizen," Kondos had been entitled to certain tax exemptions under the Ottomans and gradually had accumulated considerable wealth. Through wages earned as a miner with a British company in Halkidhiki, Yeorgios Kondos became rich and built a large house in the village *aghora*.[20] His garden was so famous throughout the area that he hired two local men to guard it from thieves. Originally, he would come to Guvezna from Halkidhiki only on holidays, but later he married a woman from Palehora and settled permanently in Guvezna. A good portion of the *aghora* is still owned by his descendants. Kondos married his only son to a Slavic-speaking woman from Ambar-Koy, from whence many Guvezna Christians took wives in the late nineteenth century. His daughters, however, married into prominent Christian families in Guvezna itself. In 1895, the eldest wed Mantsos, a wealthy merchant and tax farmer, while the younger married Pashos, stepson of the village Greek teacher, Garoufalidis.[21] Kondos divided his property equally between his only son and his two daughters, giving the latter sizeable landed dowries consisting of properties in or near the *aghora*. Such dowries were markedly absent from the marital exchanges practiced by Slavic-speakers in the area.

With time, the Guvezna *aghora* came to have a number of grocery stores patronized by traveling caravans, inhabitants of neighboring settlements of the surrounding plains and hills, and Guvezna inhabitants as well. The largest store, it was said, had been owned by a Jewish man called Sakito. In the early 1900s, armed partisans of the Greek cause began to harass and terrorize Jewish merchants in the area, demanding money and goods from them. Sakito was eventually obliged to leave the village, and his business was taken over by his former Guvezna employees, Vranas and Maritsis. Vranas later opened a cheese-making shop next to his grocery store (as well as a small *kafenion* and an inn), and eventually became one of Assiros's most powerful political figures in the 1920s and 1930s (see Genealogy F). Maritsis also opened his own grocery at the other end of the village *aghora*.

Stylianos Maritsis (b. 1868) was said to have come alone to Guvezna around 1880, although no one could recall from where. His first wife had been from the Galianos family (see Genealogy H), prominent Guvezna notables of Arvanitis descent who claimed to have migrated to the area from Attica. After he took over the Jewish grocery, Maritsis began to acquire gold pieces. Next to his grocery store he built storage rooms, which he kept full of corn, barley, and rye. He operated his diversified business together with his son, Yeorghios, and traded extensively with the Muslims inhabiting the surrounding hills. Maritsis would load the produce of those Muslim herders onto wagons and take it down to Salonika, where he sold it to a Jewish merchant.

These shops, of course, also catered to local Guveznans. Most villagers, as present-day Assiriotes claimed, bought their supplies on credit, and were thus constantly in debt to the Guvezna merchants, who kept detailed accounts of all transactions. Debts were usually settled at harvest time, when villagers would pay merchants and creditors in grain. Many Assiriotes alleged that grocers sometimes took advantage of a villager's inability to read or write by overcharging or by falsifying records. Such transactions continued up until the 1960s. After that point, as I will show in part II, outside wage-labor opportunities brought a welcome source of cash flow into the homes of many laborers, who no longer sought local credit.

The Guvezna grocers employed some twenty transporters or wagoners (known alternatively in Assiros as *kiradjidhes, aghoyiates,* or *karaghoghis*)[22] from the ranks of local men to ferry goods for them in and out of the village. Each grocery shop owner, for example, employed one or two wagoners to haul periodic purchases of goods from Jewish merchants in Salonika to Guvezna. Some wagoners made the trip from Salonika to Serres twice a week. For some, it brought wealth through diligence. Among such wagoners was a Thessaly settler named Tanaras, who also doubled as a saddle-maker (*samaras*). He was a prominent Christian leader in Guvezna during the last quarter of the nineteenth century. Also a *dhekati* renter, Tanaras eventually acquired so much wealth that he owned ninety pair of oxen and 700 *stremmata* of land. But he eventually defaulted on his *dhekati* payments, went bankrupt, and committed suicide.[23]

Another profitable occupation in which Greek-speakers of Guvezna were involved was that of milling or processing harvested grains. Guvezna had several families involved in the operation of mills in the region which were leased out by the Ottomans. The Dontas, Sapountzis, and Dimitris families had all been involved in milling since at least the turn of the century.[24] A branch of the Dimitris family (see Genealogy I) was among the first to operate mills in the basin area. Arriving in Guvezna from Trikala sometime around the 1850s, Konstantinos Dimitris had married a Guvezna woman who bore him two sons, Athanasios and Fotios. When the former came of age, he entered a public auction in Balaftsa (Kolhikon), a village of Slavic-speakers, and won the right to rent the water mills there from the Ottomans. The family resided in Guvezna, but ran this operation in Balaftsa until 1940, milling flour for local villagers and selling any surplus on the market. Their position vested them with both economic power and political influence. Using the capital generated by their milling operations, the Dimitris family was able to acquire land in both Balaftsa and Guvezna. However, the family lacked legal titles to these properties and eventually lost most of them during the land redistribution programs of the late 1920s (see chapter 6).

The Dontas family, also said to be descendant from a Trikala settler, operated a water mill near the river Bogdan until 1941, and withheld 10 to 15 percent of the flour. Although their enterprise was large enough to employ one full-time worker, they had no storage facilities at the mill. Their proximity to Langadhas allowed them simply to load sacks of flour on horseback, ford the river, and carry the flour down to Langadhas for the Tuesday market. The marriages of the Dontas brothers reflected the value this water-milling family placed on relations with surrounding communities. One brother married downstream, to Balaftsa, another upstream to Zarova, and the third to a woman from Guvezna. All three brothers were millers.

Marriage exchange and affinal alliances of this sort were not unusual.

Indeed, the examples of Dimitris and Dontas are illustrative of the larger network of exchange maintained by the merchant-landowning families who were rapidly rising to prominence in Guvezna at the turn of the century. The Dimitris family, for example, gradually accumulated wealth and their daughters subsequently married into several other prestigious and wealthy Guvezna families during the 1930s, when marriage patterns among Guveznans turned overwhelmingly village endogamous. Dimitris' prominent new affines included Velikas, a stockbreeder; Vranas, a grocer and politician; Aivadjis, a grocer; Asteriou, a teacher, stockbreeder, and politician (see chapter 4); and Voukas, a crop-watcher who later became a large landowner.

These examples illustrate the flourishing commercial economic activity and the degree of fluid mobility that characterized life in Guvezna at the turn of the century. Businesses were opened and others were closed. Land transactions were numerous and popular, for aside from commercial ventures land represented one of the few means through which upwardly mobile Christians could invest their accumulated wealth. The Greek-speakers who settled in Guvezna opened groceries and prospered.

Thus in Guvezna there gradually developed a group of Christian notables whose collective label of identity, *tsorbadjidhes,* became synonymous with wealth and power in the local lexicon. Many of these families, it was widely said, were much better off than the vast majority of area inhabitants, Muslims and Christians alike. Their wealth was created through mercantile enterprise, landholding, or stock-breeding, or a combination of these activities. Although they displayed their wealth modestly, with discreet expressions of affluence, they were far more open and conspicuous in their display of power and influence. The *tsorbadjidhes* of Guvezna exercised an influence not unlike the committees of prominent Christian notables (*dhimoyerondia*) elsewhere in both Macedonia and southern Greece, including in the nearby villages of Baltza and Drimos.[25] They were empowered with the responsibilities of managing the affairs of local Christian inhabitants. Powerful and respected, they arbitrated and adjudicated disputes, assessed fines and collected taxes, managed the village Orthodox church and school (both established in the 1870s), and oversaw the auction of various privileged positions in the village, i.e., *dhekati* tax collectors, crop-watchers, renters of various village- or township-owned *wakf* properties.

For example, local collection rights to the *dhekati* agricultural tax (or 10 percent tithe) required of all rural cultivators, were usually auctioned to prominent Christians. Villagers in Assiros maintained that the local *dhekatistis* (*dhekati* collector) first collected the tax in kind, then

sold the produce to millers, wholesalers, or other merchants, both in Guvezna as well as in Thessaloniki. The *dhekatistis* then remitted a portion
of the cash he received to Ottoman authorities, whose representative
would ride into the village on horseback carrying the Ottoman flag. The
dhekati collector retained a portion of the revenues he collected, usually
in the form of gold pieces.[26]

The *tsorbadjidhes* were also responsible for calculating and assessing
the amount of taxes each family or taxable household unit owed, and it
auctioned the right to collect those taxes.[27] Many local notables themselves participated in these auctions. Those who won such contracts were
required to secure the signatures of two guarantors (*enghiites*), "people
of the *aghora*" (*anthropi tis aghoras*) who ran businesses and possessed
considerable money and prestige. Such procedures of issuing and collecting various taxes remained in effect until the 1940s (see chapter 6). Just
as Vergopoulos (1975:344) noted for the case of Thessaly, a "substantial
number of those Greeks who were 'tax renters' . . . under the Ottomans
[eventually] became *chiftlik* owners" after Macedonia's incorporation
into the Greek state.

Clearly, a process of group formation was already underway among
Christian local notables in Guvezna at the close of the nineteenth century.
By the 1920s, following incorporation into the Greek state and the subsequent decline of the Guvezna market, these merchant-millers-landowners
had adopted endogamous patterns of social closure that confined most
property circulation within a relatively small cohort of increasingly elite
families.

MOBILIZING RESOURCES IN A RITUAL COMMUNITY
Women, Marriage, and the Structuring of Exchange

As noted earlier, the Greek-speaking migrants who settled in Guvezna
during the mid- and late-nineteenth century married extensively with
Slavic-speaking women from nearby communities.[28] This had been facilitated by the fact that as Orthodox Christians both belonged to the same
ritual community, the *Rum millet,* under the Ecumenical Patriarchate and
its local priests. By marrying in this way, they apparently followed existing patterns of marital exchange-practices by Christian sharecroppers
whom they found *in situ* at the time of their arrival. Women's labor,
recall, had been a key aspect in local family economies. As the Greek-
speaking merchant settlers in Guvezna gradually diversified the family
economies into stock-breeding and later agriculture on their newly ac-

quired lands, more pronounced divisions of labor developed within their families. The Christian men who established themselves in the commercial niche attended to their shops or transport activities, while their wives and daughters worked in the fields. Moreover, the property that moved with women between families, whether in the form of bridewealth or dowry, was a critical matter in betrothal arrangements. Through the affinal ties created by marriage, families could explore new channels of resources or cultivate new clientele for their businesses.

Many of the families most intensively involved in agro-pastoral production had been large, extended domestic units in which women's labor was a key component, both in the house and in the fields.[29] These extended families were characterized by what anthropologists term joint organizational form (i.e., two or more married siblings, with or without parents and/or children, sharing a common domestic budget and economy, usually managed by one or both parents or a coalition of married siblings).[30] Such domestic arrangements entailed a sizeable labor force, in which women played important roles.

Evidence of family organizational form, however, does not necessarily imply static structural types associated with particular ethnic groups, a pattern frequently suggested in ethnographic literature on the Balkans.[31] The mere presence of joint families does not mean that such families were Slavic ones. It suggests, rather, that conditions of production in the region fostered particular patterns in family developmental cycles (Goody 1958). Extended family economies were especially encouraged among large agro-pastoral families whose livelihood and well-being were linked to their own labor force, and where particular taxation policies were conducive to the development of larger family units.[32]

In such contexts, the importance placed on women's labor was marked symbolically in different ways. It had been common practice for the family of a groom to present a series of betrothal payments (bridewealth) to the family of a bride.[33] In Assiros, negotiations (or "bargaining," *pazarema*) over bridewealth was initiated by the groom's family, who approached the bride's and declared, "We hear you have a heifer [*dhamala*] for sale."[34] Such animal metaphors symbolized a woman who had reached her prime productive and reproductive age. Yet even after betrothal, some engagements were broken off after the two families failed to agree on a date for the wedding. Families of the grooms sought earlier marriages in the spring, so that they could take advantage of an additional laborer during the agricultural peak season in summer. For the same reasons, families of the brides preferred a wedding in the autumn or even winter.

Daughters of most Slavic-speaking families received a trousseau (Greek: *rouha*) when they married, but not a dowry (see also Cowan 1990). Yet, when Ioannis Pashos, son of a Slavic-speaker from Palehora, married the daughter of Kondos, a Greek-speaking settler from Trikala, he received property in the Guvezna *aghora* and his father-in-law's tobacco business as dowry (*prika*). The mercantile way of life, with its undertones of bourgeois culture, introduced new forms of property transmission in local society, many of them expressed through a Greek idiom, the lingua franca of the Balkan commercial world. For some of the wealthy large extended joint families in Palehora that were made up of sharecroppers and herdowners, the prospects of an affinal tie or alliance to a merchant family in Guvezna was a matter to be considered, discussed, or even traditionalized. The dominance of those mercantile families in local society and economy was underscored by many of the ritual practices surrounding the institution of marriage. When the Slavic-speaking bride of one of the Dontas brothers arrived in Guvezna on horseback from Balaftsa, her groom commanded her to dismount, kneel, and bow in front of his family's milling enterprise. Through such symbolic displays of submission or subservience, the Greek-speaking commercial notables of Guvezna cultivated an image of themselves as powerful local families.

The Christians of Guvezna were a diverse population cohort marked by differences in language, livelihood, property assets, and places of origin. The market was a social space open to all, but some dominated a greater share of the exchange there. These "people of the *aghora*" dominated this central forum of exchange in local life. Imaginings of Alexander and the Byzantines notwithstanding, the Greeks of Guvezna emerged with the new commercial market in the late nineteenth century. Consciously or subconsciously, these local elites expressed a sense of common, shared identity through their mutual patterns of ritual exchange. While everyone exchanged in the mundane field of the commercial market, patterns of ritual exchange involving more intimate aspects of life (such as marriage) had a far greater selectivity. The *tsorbadjidhes* married in a particular manner, and transferred property amongst each other over generations through practices of inheritance and betrothal and marriage payments. Patterns of marital exchange and alliance developed between certain Christian families, linking some in, and excluding others from, a generalized circulation of property within the community through time.

It was only after the introduction of national propaganda into the local scene that language differences between Greek-speakers and Slavic-speakers came to mark new and highly significant social and political boundaries. Prior to this, the multilingual character of the Guvezna marketplace had made it an important center for exchange in the basin. Marriage and affinal alliances with local Slavic-speaking families had provided Greek-speaking migrant settlers (from Thessaly) not only with access to local property but also with a wider network of patronage that supported their commercial enterprises. Affinal connections with surrounding villages in the area, such as Ambar-Koy, Balaftsa, Langadhas, and Zarova, helped these new settlers establish, extend, and diversify their networks of exchange. Later, with the advent of national competition over the region, the Greek-oriented Guvezna market and its mercantile elite took an active role in the growing political struggle, either as agents and advocates of the Greek cause or as patrons and protectors of Slavic-speaking affines.

LANGUAGE, LABELS, AND IDENTITY
Interest Groups and Ethnic Empowerment

But during the turn-of-the-century national struggles some of the Slavic-speaking women from Ambar-Koy and elsewhere who had married into Greek-speaking families in Guvezna found themselves forbidden by their husbands or in-laws to speak their native languages in their new households. It is important to note that, prior to the turn of the century, language differences did not represent a significant social or political boundary between the populations of Macedonia. Greek-speaking men who had settled in Guvezna apparently had little or no difficulties in marrying Slavic-speaking women. Some, perhaps, could speak Slavic even before they arrived in Guvezna; others undoubtedly learned enough of it after they arrived to get by in their commercial livelihoods and in their interaction with affines.

It was only later, during the period of the Macedonian Struggle when such men began to forbid their wives to speak "Bulgarian," that language became a source of tension and conflict, eventually becoming a veritable national barrier that divided and polarized the countryside. As a descendant of an old Palehora family put it,

My uncle married a woman from Vissoka [present-day Ossa]. She was a Bulgarian-speaker [*Voulgharofoni*]. She spoke Macedonian [*Makedhonika*]. Bulgarian is a different language. She spoke Greek as well. And my mother, my father, and my mother-in-law all spoke Macedonian. It was the custom [*ethimo*] here. We were used to it. We call the aunt [*thia*] "tsino" and the water [*nero*] "voda."

Note that here the labels "Macedonian" and "Bulgarian" were used interchangeably in reference to Slavic-speakers, a confusion attributable largely to the imposition of national labels on local patterns of speech and language, a theme to which I will return in chapter 3. Yet the above statement also points to differences in kinship terminology among local inhabitants (see table 7). Families in Guneyna (Palehora) and Yeni-Koy (Gnoina), for example, distinguished between father's sister (*tsino*) and mother's sister (*teto*), distinctions that are not prevalent in Greek kinship terminology.[35] By the turn of the century, however, such language differences took on the significance of national diacritics, as they came to be employed as markers of group identity.

Yet the importance of such distinctions within the symbolic media of language and kinship terminology was shaped and understood by the relative position of Greek-speaking and Slavic-speaking families in the local division of labor. As the Greek-speaking Christian notables of Guvezna prospered and diversified their economic activities, they assumed patronage roles for poorer families of Slavic-speaking sharecroppers, agricultural laborers, and shepherds. This entailed not only a growing web of employment relations but also baptismal sponsorship and ritual kinship relations based on a Greek idiom. New dominant idioms of identity were in the making. Guvezna was not only being transformed from a *chiftlik* to a village but to a village dominated by a Greek-speaking Christian mercantile elite. Meanwhile, a national identity was in the process of forming, of being created, among villagers of different cultural or ethnic backgrounds.

The merchant settlers who arrived from Thessaly or elsewhere and established themselves in Guvezna (and subsequently their families) defined themselves as Greek, claimed to have come from Greek areas to the south, spoke Greek, and held the Orthodox faith of the Ecumenical Patriarchate. As a whole, they made their living off the passing trade, and practiced tactics of closure and alliance necessary to maintain themselves, to protect their property, and to advance their interests. Along with upwardly mobile and wealthier families from among the local Slavic-speaking population with whom they married, these families came to act as a fairly coherent group. They possessed enough solidarity or consciousness to see themselves as sharing certain interests not held in common with other local inhabitants. Later, as post-1913 Greek state expansion further transformed material conditions of life in the area, these *tsorbadjidhes* notables came to form an elite local class whose interests were oriented more strongly towards the Greek state and its developing nation (see part II).

A by-product of this process was the construction of a similar national (i.e., Greek) identity among the economically less prominent Slavic-
speaking population of the settlement, whose labor products and sur-
pluses the Greek-oriented *tsorbadjidhes* needed. These Slavic-speaking
families were, on the whole, not very wealthy, and perhaps they did not
always share the same set of interests as their new neighbors. The label
"Bulgar," as Vermeulen (1984:234) pointed out, was often applied to
poor, Slavic-speaking, Orthodox Christian peasants, shepherds, or laborers of lower social status to whom were ascribed a "peasant" culture.
The *bakal* (Turkish: "grocer"), on the other hand, was generally known
as a Greek, regardless of what language he spoke (Vermeulen 1984:232).
Undoubtedly, local Slavic-speaking laborers held contradictory views of
their new Greek-speaking neighbors and creditors. They too shared a
sense of local identity about who they were and who among their neighbors were "different," "outsiders," or "Others." But it was only when
competitive national propaganda agents became active among the population that those perceptions of difference came to be expressed and reified through the new conceptual categories of national identity.

The *communitas* shared by local Slavic-speakers had been rooted in
their common rituals, the rhythms of the agricultural cycle, their networks of barter and exchange, and their subordination to tax collectors
and merchant creditors. Some had married into the families of these newcomers, or had joined their households as domestic servants. Others had
apprenticed themselves to the Greek-speaking grocers, millers, merchants, and artisans to learn a trade, a craft or a vocation. Through such
exchanges, many local Slavic-speakers had been drawn into more generalized, higher-order economic trade and social intercourse, and more
readily acquired a Greek-oriented national identity. Among those who
had not yet acquired a national identity, the process of Hellenization encountered relatively little resistance. But for those who had formed some
sense of affiliation with a distinctively non-Greek group—in other words,
those who had acquired a non-Greek national identity such as Bulgarian
or Macedonian—Hellenization required a reorientation, a reeducation,
so to speak, about who one was. A new language of national traditions
came into being.

But even among the ranks of these local Christian notables there were
a few voices of dissent raised in response to the increasingly dominant
ideology that maintained everyone in the village was of Greek origin and
descent. Consider the example of a prominent merchant in Guvezna during the first half of the twentieth century: Ioannis Pashos, son-in-law of
the merchant Kondos. Pashos had been born in 1880, apparently in Pa-

lehora where his family had been herdowners. His father had married the daughter of a Greek-speaking settler from Trikala. Pashos' father, however, had died young, and his widowed mother remarried to an "outsider," Garoufalidis, the prominent Greek teacher of turn-of-the-century Guvezna who was himself a divorcé. It was in the context of this Greek-oriented household that Pashos was enculturated. After he married the daughter of Kondos, Pashos took over the latter's lucrative tobacco-processing business. Together with a Jewish partner they employed local girls from the village, having them work from three o'clock in the morning to process tobacco for little pay. Pashos' prominent position in the economic field of Guvezna led him to become active in local politics, and he eventually became a resourceful and respected village leader. His tobacco business failed, however, during the Depression of 1929 and his Jewish partner committed suicide. Pashos himself was imprisoned for a time, apparently because of his debts. After his release, he diversified his business dealings and opened a grocery store and a coffeeshop in Guvezna.

The important role that Pashos came to play in local politics, however, was derived from his educated background. Stepson of the turn-of-the-century village Greek teacher, Pashos was himself trained as a Greek teacher and received postings to several different villages in Macedonia during the early-twentieth-century national struggle. He reportedly resigned his position and left teaching because he had been unwilling to work as a classroom teacher by day and then join Greek partisan "Macedonian Fighters" at night to terrorize local Slavic-speakers. Yet when the Bulgarian army came to Guvezna during the First Balkan War of 1912, Pashos fled to Salonika, telling local villagers that "real Bulgarians had come to the village, not Macedonians." His actions and words suggest that he supported neither the Greek nor the Bulgarian cause in the national struggle over Macedonia. Later, during the 1920s and 1930s, Pashos joined the pro-royalist Populist Party in Greek politics. Although nominally he came to represent Greek conservatism during the interwar period, decorating his home with portraits of the Greek king and heroes of the 1821 Greek War of Independence, he was prosecuted by authorities for his pro-Macedonian positions in the late 1930s (see chapter 6).

For those Slavic-speakers who had resisted both Greek and Bulgarian national labels, family or descent group had been the principal focus of their sense of collective identity. Some had conceptualized their identity as "Macedonians" (*Makedhones*), but had used the term as a marker of their sense of common regional or cultural identity. In this sense, it was used in a manner fundamentally different from its meaning (and historicity) in the FYROM, and yet still distinct from the manner in which it is often used in Greece to signify Hellenic racial continuity from the ancient Macedonians. A man from the village of Xiloupolis, raised by his Slavic-speaking grandmother, asserted that he spoke only "Macedonian" (*Makedhonika*) until he began Greek primary school. He claimed that his mother had been obliged to go to night school in the 1930s for Greek language lessons while she was pregnant with him. "The Macedonian language is lost," he told me. "It has vanished. What a pity." Other voices, sometimes public, often private, were more militant. One of the few elderly Assiriotes to speak directly about the Macedonian issue maintained that a certain village leader "used to say in the 1930s that the Macedonian nation [*Makedhoniko ethnos*] is lost." "Don't listen to what the politicians say," he told me. "They are themselves from Macedonian villages. What do you think the Langadhas area was?"

Dominating an occupational niche at the conflux of local and regional interaction and exchange, however, the *tsorbadjidhes* came to be the community leaders, the landowners, store operators, employers, ritual patrons, tax collectors, and usurers. The complex of social and ideational relationships that made up what might analytically be termed their "ethnicity" facilitated not only their coalescence as an interest "group," but also their eventual empowerment as a dominant ruling class in local society following incorporation into the expanding Greek nation-state in 1913. They not only objectively shared certain interests as a collective group but also came subjectively to recognize how those interests were linked and actively organized in the production and reproduction of life and livelihood in this local setting. The *tsorbadjidhes* were, in a sense, "a force in the formation and consolidation of nationhood and the territorial state" (Sahlins 1989:8).

COMMON CULTURE THROUGH THE MARKETPLACE

The primordial sentiments that today bind the Assiriotes *as* Assiriotes, as descendants of ancient Hellenes, were not the product of an "unbroken narrative" of the nation (cf. Geertz 1973:341). Rather, this collective self-hood was a constructed tradition that grew out of practical necessity and common interests, mediated by the growing power and authority of a nascent local elite and by political incorporation within the expanding Greek state. It was not so much a matter of choice or primordial attachment as it was a result of historical contingency. Before the onset of violent national competition over Macedonia, notions of "blood and kin ties, language, customs, religion and the land" were the "referents of their identity" (Blu 1980:228–30) that bound local inhabitants together through the Guvezna marketing system in a common quest for subsistence. The marketplace or *aghora* was a key institution in facilitating the interaction among the local populations. It is no coincidence that the coffee shops and *khans* of the village were located in the marketplace. This was the central forum of interethnic, intersettlement, and interfamily exchange. Through the relationships they developed within the formal "public" realm of the market, these Slavic-speaking and Greek-speaking families began to intermarry and establish more diffuse and generalized networks of ties between each other.

This was the symbolic paradox of the market: it was the very mundane aspects of exchange that made the local marketplace so central— and sacred—to local community. As a forum of cross-boundary transaction, the *aghora* brought together people of different backgrounds, occupations, livelihoods, religions, languages, and cultural values. Specialized divisions of labor in the regional commercial economy had strengthened the importance of the market as a key forum for such exchange. In some cases these transactions were temporary, immediate, or of short duration: the limited, often circumstantially dictated, exchanges of immediate or direct reciprocity. But other contacts and relationships were more protracted, being maintained and reproduced in either similar or new forms: the extended long-term relationships of generalized reciprocity embodied in patterns of ritualized exchange, such as marriage. The sacredness of the market lay in its collectively acknowledged necessity of existence, its central importance to the lives and economies of families who used it. This sacredness was paradoxically based on its "profanity" as a public, mixed or "impure" forum of intercourse and exchange (see Durkheim 1965). And this sacredness protected the market's profanity. Greek may have been the language of those who controlled market exchange, but those who used that market were certainly not all Greek-speakers, let alone possessed a sense of Greek identity.

The Christians of Guvezna had been a diverse population cohort marked by differences in language, livelihood, property assets, betrothal practices, and places of origin. By the mid-to-late-nineteenth century, a resting stop near a *chiftlik* along the Salonika-Serres caravan route had been transformed into a thriving commercial market village, complete with local banks and foreign-insured businesses. In a manner of speaking, the origins of modern day Assiros lay in the Guvezna *mazemata* and its common culture of the marketplace. Even marriage patterns followed the contours of the local marketing systems. Greek had been the language of the *aghora,* and many of those who dominated economic exchange in the marketplace aspired to a Greek idiom of expression in their ritual and educational activities. The *aghora* of Guvezna provided a higher-ordered organizational structure for exchange in the area, akin to what Sahlins (1989:7) called a "boundary zone": a space through which people moved in and out. Those who dominated that space, the "people of the *aghora,*" acquired a prominent notability in local society.

Whether or not the commercial market created an ethnic-based division of labor in Guvezna, it certainly fostered the maintenance, reproduction and restructuring of such a regime over time.[36] This is not to suggest that until the turn of the twentieth century social life in Guvezna had maintained essentially the same form and patterns of interaction for centuries; clearly, evidence presented in these first two chapters indicates just the contrary. Yet when local market conditions and the broader regional forces structuring the flow of exchange there were altered by the advent of national competition over Macedonia, many relationships between families of different backgrounds began to unwind. An intense period of crisis set in as new labels of identity were introduced into currency in their local marketplace, with violent repercussions.

The boundaries imposed upon the inhabitants of Macedonia during the turn-of-the-century national contest radically upset the dynamics of exchange, interaction, and coexistence that had developed in the countryside during the late Ottoman era. The ritual community shared by local Christians was torn asunder with the schism between the Ecumenical Patriarchate and the Bulgarian Exarchate in 1870. In Guvezna, the descent-group banners that families had once carried and displayed in their wedding rituals were replaced by the flag of the Patriarchate, and later with the Greek flag (see chapter 7). The creation of national ecclesiastical domains (of Greek and Bulgarian Orthodoxy) in the late nineteenth century was reified in the movement of those respective nation-states into Macedonia in the early twentieth century. In the first decade of this century, Guvezna lay between the converging frontiers of the Greek and Bulgarian national movements in Macedonia, and it witnessed the violence of that armed struggle repeatedly through the years that followed.

3

CONVERGING FRONTIERS OF GREEK
AND BULGARIAN NATIONALISM

Religious Propaganda, Educational Competition,
and National Enlightenment in Macedonia,
1870–1903

But, save for a few scattered heaps of stones among the cornfields,
to-day no memories remain of the mighty Macedonians, no record
is left of the Great Alexander. . . . The plough of the Balkan
peasant traces its furrow over Pelias. . . . The past appeals
but little to him whose lot it is to struggle with the heavy cares
of the present.

Richard Von Mach, *The Bulgarian Exarchate*

The twentieth century dawned across the low hills of southern Macedonia with the rumblings of shot and cannon, and with the clashing
of knives and swords. The cries and laments of war came closer by the
day, and growing numbers of Bulgarian and Greek national partisans
entered the region as teachers, priests, fighters, or agents provocateur.
These developments heralded the impending clash of the converging frontiers of two modern state-expansion and nation-building campaigns.
While the contest had major ramifications for the nation-states involved,
the impact of the conflict on the inhabitants of the region was far more
profound and tumultuous than many abstract discussions of nation-
building would lead one to understand.

Modern nation formation in the Balkans was intimately linked to
broader diplomatic developments and shifting "balance of power" alliances in Europe and Asia. As the Ottoman Empire declined and disintegrated, national liberation movements took root in Christian areas of the
Ottoman Balkans. Through a variety of channels, including commerce,
education, and Protestant missionary work, the revolutionary spirit of
the European Enlightenment diffused to regional intellectual and political
elites, who often used it to construct an ideological framework for popular mobilization and armed insurrection. These enlightenment ideologies,
however, as this chapter will demonstrate, were essentialist in their char-

acter and rhetoric. They stressed the innate and primordial characteristics of one's own national group while "Orientializing" those of others. The rhetorical debate in this contest focused on the progressive capacities of each national group, creating new ideological hierarchies of identity in which some national groups were deemed more worthy of European support and empowerment than others. In their discourse, these Enlightenment writers created the ideological bases for emancipation and liberation from the Ottomans. But they also fostered new partisan constructs of identity, solidarity, and difference that encouraged separation and stigmatization.[1] The Kingdom of Greece was the first nation-state of the southern Balkans to gain independence from the Ottomans, in 1829,[2] while the Treaty of Adrianople guaranteed the autonomy of Serbia the same year. The autonomous principality of Bulgaria was created in 1878.

The early stages of the Macedonian conflict, i.e., those decades immediately preceding the armed confrontations of the turn of the century, were characterized largely by a propaganda war between Greece and Bulgaria (as well as between Greece and Serbia) for the "hearts and minds" of the Slavic-speakers of Macedonia.[3] The broad and general outlines of this struggle can be seen in the literature, nationalist writings, and diplomatic communiqués of that era. It has been documented extensively, though rarely completely, by national historians on all "sides."

HEGEMONIC NATIONAL CENSORSHIP
Propaganda War, 1870–1903

The roots of national ideological and political conflict between Bulgaria and Greece over the population and region of Macedonia may be traced to the establishment of the autonomous Bulgarian Orthodox Church, known as the Exarchate, in 1870.[4] Two years later, on 23 March 1872, the first Bulgarian Exarch, Antim, proclaimed the independence of the new church, and Orthodox Christians who followed the Exarchate were subsequently declared "schismatic" by the Ecumenical Patriarchate (Tosheff 1932:36). The establishment of the autonomous Bulgarian Orthodox Exarchate in 1870, however, had provided nascent Bulgarian national elites with a strong organizational foundation from which to construct their own nation and their political state.

For over four hundred years following the conquest of Byzantium, the Ottoman administrative system had organized populations and defined "nations" through the *millet* system, which classified inhabitants on the basis of religion. *Millets* were administrative rather than territorial jurisdictions, and the Christian and Muslim "nations" of the Ottoman Empire, divided under this system, were administered according to different regulations, offices, and procedures. While Muslims belonged to the Muslim *millet,* all Orthodox Christians belonged to the Orthodox *Rum millet,* and were subject to the direct and indirect control, supervision, and administration of the Ecumenical Orthodox Patriarchate in Istanbul, which enjoyed a privileged and powerful position in the Ottoman Empire.

The Orthodox *Rum millet* included a diverse Christian population dispersed across vast territories of the Ottoman Empire. As Vucinich (1965:59) pointed out, "a *millet* did not embrace a unified territory, or a homogeneous ethnic group, or peoples enjoying the same political and judicial status." Instead, as Kitromilidis (1989:152) argued, "Balkan Orthodoxy was composed of an ethnically diverse assortment of collectivities differentiated primarily by their languages." Nevertheless, the centrality of religion and religious authority provided the basis of both Greek scholarly definitions of nationality or ethnicity in Macedonia. Indeed, R. Just (1989) has suggested that the *Rum millet* was an institutional precursor to the Greek concept of *ethnos* (nation).

The Patriarchate, through its strong influence with the Ottoman Porte, had been able to have both the Bulgarian and Serbian Orthodox Churches eliminated in 1765 and 1767 respectively (Friedman 1986: 289). Since at least 1840, Bulgarian religious personnel, and intelligentsia, as well as American missionaries had been campaigning for the use of Bulgarian native language(s) in churches, or had sought appointment of Bulgarian priests and bishops to predominately Slavic-speaking communities. The Ecumenical Patriarchate had resisted, fearing such moves would compromise its "ecclesiastical and economic interests" (Augustinos 1977:19). As the Bulgarian Orthodox Church movement gained headway, the battle between the two Churches became a clearly political, or ethno-national, conflict. Brailsford, a British journalist who personally observed the turn-of-the-century national struggle in Macedonia, wrote of the backward conditions of oppression under which Bulgarians had been living during Ottoman rule and under the ecclesiastical *cum* secular authority of the Patriarchate. As he noted, "A Greek can never bring himself to regard the Bulgarians as a race with the same right and title as his own. They are simply excommunicated schismatics" (Brailsford 1906:196).

When Bulgarian ecclesiastical and secular elites managed to secede from the Patriarchate in 1870, they laid the foundations for their passage to nationhood. Bulgarian secular administrative and national autonomy

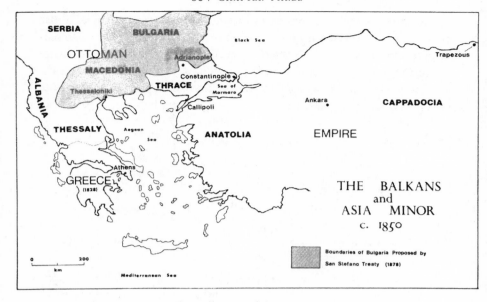

Map 7. The Balkans and Asia Minor, c.1850

from the Ottomans was subsequently acquired in 1878 when the Treaty of San Stefano (signed 3 March 1878), following the Russo-Turkish War (1876–78), defined the territorial boundaries of the new autonomous principality of Bulgaria. Its borders, established by Russian and Ottoman negotiators, encompassed as much as three-fifths of the Balkans (Christoff 1919:13–14), embracing an area of 164,000 square kilometers and a population of some 4,580,000 inhabitants (Angelopoulos 1973: 12). The southern expanse of this "Greater Bulgaria," as it was called by some critics, extended to the Lake of Besik-Giol (Aghios Vasilios) in the Langadhas basin (Natsas 1953:184), and included the market town of Guvezna (see map 7).

A few months later, however, diplomatic maneuvers by the Greek kingdom and growing apprehension among leading European powers of Russian expansion into Ottoman Europe prompted a renegotiation of Bulgaria's borders. Until then, the positions of most European "Great Powers" regarding Macedonia had been ambivalent, influenced mainly by balance-of-power configurations at particular historical moments.[5] The Treaty of Berlin, signed 13 July 1878, reduced the territory of the autonomous Bulgarian principality significantly and returned Macedonia to the jurisdiction of the Ottoman Empire. Soon afterwards, national competition for control over Macedonia began in earnest.

At first, Greek and Bulgarian organizations competed to establish churches and schools, until full-scale fighting erupted between armed partisan groups. Permit me to present an account from a Patriarchist Orthodox priest from Nevrokopi, near the town of Drama in present-day eastern Greek Macedonia, who had witnessed propagandizing efforts by both Greek and Bulgarian agents:

> Before 1862, the Bulgarians and the Greeks of the town made up one Orthodox community. But the [Bulgarian] gangs came, and working in secret drew the town notables to their side. The Greeks did not allow the teaching of Bulgarian in schools, and the Bulgarian children had to leave. Then the Bulgarians requested that the left chanter in church be permitted to chant in Bulgarian. After all this, the Greeks "woke up" [*ksipnisan*] and a *tsorbadjis* [Greek landed notable] took charge. The Church tried to bring peace, and gave the eastern part of the school house to the Bulgarians. The Turks were janus-faced, collecting taxes from both groups. But the Grand Vezir sent an order to count Greek and Bulgarian inhabitants of the town, and the group which was found in the majority would be granted the undisputed use of the town's cathedral dedicated to the Virgin Mary. The archbishop, a wealthy landed man who used to lend out gold pieces, entered the dispute, siding with the Greek cause. After that, violence began to mar the dispute, people were assaulted and both the school and church were burnt down. (From Theodoritos 1941–52)

In fact, the author of this account was himself assaulted and forced to flee the community.

Several inferences may be drawn from this account. Evidently a sizeable population of "Bulgarian-speakers" lived in this town, among at least some of whom Bulgarian nationalist propaganda and agitation had found fertile ground. Moreover, it suggests that the local landed notables were themselves divided along linguistic or national lines; whichever side they took, and whatever the nature and extent of their participation, they made a critical difference. The involvement of the archbishop appears particularly decisive in this instance, principally because of the financial resources he commanded. Caught between two emerging nation-states struggling for control over them, the Slavic-speaking population of the area lacked either a national consciousness of their own or sufficient resources to consolidate themselves independently of both Greek and Bulgarian dominance.[6] As one contemporary observer put it, "Macedonia is racked by political intrigue without, and within by turbulent, ambitious, mischief-making factions, which are neither of the people, nor voice their legitimate aspirations. It is the saddest part of Macedonia's unhappy lot

that its worst enemies are those whose professions of friendship are loud-
est" (*The Population of Macedonia* 1905:3). The new labels of identity
that national activists sought to impose upon the region's Christian population ruptured the ritual and economic community that the latter had
once shared, creating deep social schisms that eventually erupted in violence and bloodshed at the turn of the century.

COLLECTIVITIES, SOLIDARITIES, AND FAITH

Vincent (1993:128) has noted, in terms reminiscent of Fried's discussion
of the "notion of tribe," that ethnicity is a cultural construction born
within empires, either political (e.g., those of the Ottomans, Hapsburgs,
or the Soviets) and economic (such as that of modern global capitalism).
Considering the ways in which political empires are frequently built upon
economic empires, one might also consider a third form of imperial domination and hegemony: that of religious empires, such as the Patriarchate
or the Exarchate. In addition to its administrative and educational roles
under the Ottomans, the Ecumenical Patriarchate also had a monopoly
on officiating at and performing all significant rituals of passage for Christians in Macedonia until its dominance was challenged by the Exarchate
and nascent Bulgarian national elites. The role of the Orthodox Church,
both in molding social relations through marriages and baptism, as well
as in expressing these relations through sermons and teachings, has been
considerable, as too has been its influence on the content of education
and popular ideology.

One common issue to emerge from the diverse literature on nation-
state building has been the connection between religion and nationalism.
For example, the Russian Orthodox Church was considered to have been
instrumental in the development of unity between tribes, ties which later
became the foundations for the creation of the Russian nation-state
(Baron 1947:166).[7] In Romania, too, the role of institutionalized religion
in the 1690s was critical to the formation of Romanian ethnic (and subsequently national) consciousness (Verdery 1983:348). There, the newly
created Uniate Church, with its privileged clergy, provided the necessary
organizational support or conditions for the development of a common
national identity (ibid., p. 118).

Greece was no exception, for "the Byzantine identification of religion
and politics . . . [has] coloured and shaped the direction of an emergent
Greek nation" (Smith 1986:115). As a centralizing institution, the Orthodox Church offered a mechanism of homogenization and assimilation.

In due time, Greek Orthodoxy was reborn as a national consciousness which sought to absorb "geographically isolated and culturally incompatible" groups (Tsoukalas 1977:32). The Orthodox Patriarchate, which in terms of language was more Greek than Ecumenical, imposed and enforced its religious hegemony through sometimes harsh measures, including the burning of Bulgarian liturgical texts (Baron 1947:185–89).[8] Anderson (1983:28), writing of how "imagined communities" of nations emerged out of religious communities, noted that other fundamental changes were necessary to complete such processes. Print capitalism, for example, was instrumental in laying the foundations for national consciousness. The written word helped to build the image of a timeless antiquity stretching down to the modern day. The leaders of the nationalist movements that swept Europe in the eighteenth, nineteenth, and twentieth centuries relied heavily on "national language" as a metaphoric banner around which to rally supporters.

American missionaries working in Bulgaria in the 1850s created the first standardized Bulgarian script, choosing to base the national language on the dialect of Thrace and eastern Macedonia rather than on that spoken in the regions of northern Bulgaria. Until the work of such American missionaries, memories of an ecclesiastical past in Bulgaria had been preserved in large part only by Slavonic monks. The American Board of Missionaries, with their network of locally posted missionaries, intentionally or not assisted nascent Bulgarian national elites to forge a different picture of the past.

Dr. Elias Riggs, for example, crossed "European Turkey" in the late 1840s and in 1847 compiled a Bulgarian grammar primer. According to Tsanoff (1919:ix), it had been the American missionaries who had discovered (or, we might say, helped to invent) the Bulgarian nation. They published some of the first books in Bulgarian, and in 1864 began putting out the first monthly magazine in the region written in Bulgarian. *Morning Star* (*Zornitsa*), as it was called, later became a weekly, was distributed widely throughout the countryside and was read aloud in coffee shops in towns and villages. In fact, *zornitsa* eventually became a generic term for newspaper in Bulgaria.[9] Apart from the work of Bulgarian clergy, intellectuals, and political elites for the national awakening of the Bulgarian peoples, it had been the provisioning of the written word that provided the impetus for unification under the banner of Bulgarian national ideology. As Prince Ferdinand of Montenegro once remarked, "had there been no American missionaries, there would have been no Bulgaria" (cited in Haskell 1919:3). Not only did they translate the Bible into Bulgarian, but their linguistic work also enabled them to preach to local inhabitants in their own language, an approach that diverged radically from that of the Patriarchate.

Through the centuries, the Ecumenical Orthodox Patriarchate often operated as a pseudo-state within the Ottoman Empire, spanning the collectivity of the Orthodox *Rum millet*. The excellent relations between the Patriarchate and the Porte were evidenced in the wide and sweeping powers the sultans had granted the Patriarchate to collect taxes, mediate disputes, hear lawsuits, and even imprison criminals among the Christian population.[10] Brailsford (1906) noted the power of the Orthodox Church during his travels through Macedonia at the turn of the century, calling it a "national organization" with its own aristocracy, the bishops.[11] It had its own hierarchy of officials empowered by the sultan himself to collect taxes, to run large *wakf* landholdings, to manage education, and to arbitrate disputes. At the apex of this hierarchy was the patriarch himself, who maintained many of the outward appearances of a Byzantine emperor and came to be regarded as an *effendi*, a king, or an ethnarch (i.e., leader of an *ethnos*) rather than merely the spiritual head of a religious group (Papaioannou 1991:15–30).[12] In many ways the Patriarchate, controlling the Orthodox Christian *Rum millet*, represented the only "national" institution to affect the lives and thought of Ottoman Christians of any ethnic background. As Stavrianos put it, "It is an irony of history that the patriarch of Constantinople enjoyed greater ecclesiastical and secular jurisdiction under the Ottoman Sultans than under the Byzantine emperors" (Stavrianos 1959:103).[13]

In August of 1872, roughly five months after the first Bulgarian Exarch had proclaimed the independence of the new Bulgarian national church, the patriarchs of Ecumenical Orthodoxy convened a major synod and condemned the "racism" (*filetismos;*[14] Kitromilidis 1989:181) of which they had accused the Bulgarians of practicing by accepting into their church only members of their race. In their opinions, the Bulgarian Church was not ecumenical, but rather used religion to promote the idea of the racial community of the Bulgarians. Similar arguments might also be advanced regarding the secession from the Patriarchate of the Greek, Serbian, and Romanian Churches, which became autocephalus in 1833, 1879, and 1865, respectively (see Frazee 1983). But those three national churches emerged within independent nation-states: they were territorially defined national political units that sought to impose a common religion upon their populations. The Bulgarian Church at the time of its secession from the Patriarchate lacked the institutional and financial support of a nation-state government and was much more vulnerable. Except for the case of Serbia, the quest of these national churches for administrative and financial independence from the Patriarchate was greeted with resistance. The Greek Church and the Patriarchate, for example, did not properly restore their relationship until some twenty years later, in 1850.

It was the same kind of national separatism that troubled the Patriarchate with the establishment of the Bulgarian Exarchate. The Patriarchate had opposed ethnic, racial, or national separatism in Macedonia and Bulgaria, just as it had opposed the Greek War of Independence in 1821. In Bulgaria, the declaration of an independent church preceded the creation of an independent Bulgarian state, but was nevertheless a key moment in the Bulgarian passage to nationhood. The chauvinistic character of the church was evidenced in its appeals to the Slavic-speakers of Macedonia, who were labeled in Exarchate rhetoric and proselytizing as "Bulgarians." They, the religious institutions, immediately tried to appeal to the primordial sentiments and cultural features, so as to lead these ethnically diverse peoples in a passage to nationhood. With the establishment of the autonomous principality of Bulgaria a few years later in 1878, modern nationalism became the name of the game and soon open warfare between the contending new nation-states in the region became a vehicle of "national liberation."

Under the Patriarchate, Orthodox mass had been conducted in Byzantine or Church Greek, an atticized construct. Greek was also the language taught in churches and other schools throughout the Macedonian countryside, as well as in cities, towns, and marketplaces where the literates and the prospective literates mainly lived. The Patriarchate had been ideologically opposed to the nationalization of churches, because it detracted from the ecumenical character of Christian Orthodoxy (Kitromilidis 1989:181); but it provided the organizational framework for the creation of new national identities. Its clergy in Macedonia became the targets and then the agents of the creation, reproduction, and subsequent legitimation of such national identity.

Most priests in rural Macedonia came from the ranks of local villagers themselves. Brailsford (1906:62) found them to be generally uneducated (at least by British standards), leading the life of a "peasant," mumbling incomprehensible words in a "dead" language (i.e., atticized Greek) during their rituals, and acting as petty officials empowered by the Church hierarchy to be leaders of local villages and Christian notables. Even Dragoumis (1992:49) claimed that priests were distinguishable from the local peasantry only by their cloaks and hats. Similarly, Papastathis (1987) claimed that most priests had been illiterate, or semiliterate, with relatively little knowledge acquired through scholarly study. However, the rural priests of Ottoman Macedonia exercised a spiritual or ideological hegemony through their monopoly on iconic imagery and rituals that cultivated a *communitas* reinforced by religious faith. Liturgical language and script were powerful vehicles for the creation, preservation, and transmission of collective faith, memory, and myth.

With the establishment of the Exarchate, Bulgarians began to take control over secular and ecclesiastical institutions in Slavic-speaking communities in Macedonia (Perry 1988:27). Official recognition from the Ottoman Porte gave Bulgarian elites a degree of legitimacy in their separatist struggle for regional autonomy.[15] Augustinos (1977) claimed that following the formal establishment of the Exarchate, Bulgarians were permitted to expand their interests outside the "nation" of Bulgaria, for the sultan had decreed that any village could join the Exarchate provided that two-thirds of its inhabitants voted for such a move. This stipulation was included in Article X of the sultan's *Firman* (dated 11 March 1870) establishing the independent Bulgarian Exarchate (Augustinos 1977:20, Stavrianos 1959:519; Von Mach 1907:13–15).[16] This decree also laid the foundations for the turn-of-the-century political, economic, and ideological contest over Macedonia between Greece and Bulgaria. The spiritual power necessary for the "liberation" of the Macedonian countryside came from nationally-oriented religion.

The Patriarchate, however, opposed the attempts of the Exarchists to establish their supremacy. Together with Greek literary associations and other nationally-oriented organizations, the Patriarchate built churches and schools and began to mobilize the population of Macedonia through the rhetoric of common membership in the nation of the Hellenes. Through religion, an equation between Orthodoxy and national Greek sentiment and orientation was constructed. Greek national identity, as its ideologues have maintained, was preserved by the Church through religion and identification with the high Church clergy. But to argue that all of Macedonia, its history, and its heritage belongs only to one national group would be, as Brailsford (1906:195) put it, "much as though the 'Roman' Catholic Church should claim the greater part of Europe as the inheritance of Italy."

Yet Bulgarian activists also built schools and churches, and likewise attempted to mobilize the population. Their rhetoric, however, focused on common oppression, or what they called the "double yoke" of Ottoman and Patriarchate overlordship. With religious autonomy, Bulgaria was on its way to national liberation. Russia's victory in the Russo-Turkish War of 1877–78 obliged the Ottoman Porte to grant the region of Bulgaria status as an autonomous principality. As one turn-of-the-century British author (writing under the pseudonym "Diplomatist") put it in his book, *Nationalism and War in the Near East,* "The Christian churches of Macedonia are of ethnological rather than ethical importance. . . . [They] have contributed nothing as evangelizing influences to the maintenance there of peace and good-will; while, as educated influences, they have contributed only to the growth of nationality (chauvinism), and have failed to exercise any influence on the new spiritual life of the Balkan Peninsula" (cited in Haskell 1919:2).

Consider that prior to the attempts of the Orthodox Church to educate its parishioners, the inhabitants of Macedonia quite probably knew very little about the ancestors of the nation of the Hellenes, such as the Greek heroes of antiquity or even Alexander the Great. Even if one assumes that those inhabitants, regardless of their ethnic identity, knew about the heroes of Ancient Greece and even felt or expressed an affiliation to them as ancestors, one is nonetheless left with the question of how such knowledge or sentiment was constructed and transmitted over time. The songs and tales of traveling storytellers, who came from the north as well as from the south, may have been one important medium of transmission. But undoubtedly the greatest storytellers of all were the local priests (and, later, schoolteachers), who blessed the Patriarch every time they celebrated mass and regarded him as the heir of the Byzantines. Thus these priests, whose eulogies drew on tales of the glory, bravery, stoicism, and above all Christian devotion of Byzantine heroes of the past helped to foster a form of consciousness among the Christian population of Macedonia.

Consciously or not, the activities of scholars, educators, and politicians have been an integral part of this competitive nationalist legacy. Nation-building in Greek Macedonia has been a long and complex process in which the expanding Greek state penetrated local communities of the region and radically transformed economic, political, religious, social, and cultural relationships of the late Ottoman era. Greek national historiography has generally failed to address the critical issue of how Greek national or ethnic consciousness originally emerged and how it has been transmitted and reproduced across time.[17] Some have assumed, for example, that Greek national consciousness existed as an ideology among nationless Greek-speaking and Slavic-speaking peoples scattered throughout Macedonia and elsewhere.[18] Greek scholars have staked such claims on suppositions of a link between the twentieth-century population of Macedonia, the Byzantines, the ancient Hellenes, and Alexander the Great.

But one might also consider, in the spirit of critical debate, the claims of many contemporary ethnological demographers that the majority of the inhabitants of late-nineteenth-century Macedonia were neither Greek nor Greek-speaking,[19] but rather became Hellenized. No doubt the efforts of the Ecumenical Patriarchate featured prominently in this process, for across the centuries it had enjoyed a monopoly over ritual and educational practices as well as over iconic imagery throughout Macedonia. But to this nexus of powers that formed and shaped identities must be added the institutions and arrangements of commerce and marriage, such as those outlined in chapter 2. In addition to the Orthodox Church, the efforts of local Greek-speaking mercantile elites had been central in this process of Hellenization, as too had been practices of social and cultural reproduction embedded in marriage and child-rearing.

In early-nineteenth-century Macedonia, in addition to religious monopoly under the Orthodox Patriarchate, Greeks generally enjoyed commercial dominance. Moreover, where commercial towns developed, the early establishment of schools under the auspices of the Patriarchate soon followed. By and large it was education and the development of a local "literate" class in the Greek-speaking market towns of Macedonia, such as Guvezna, that fostered a historical prejudice against "illiterate" Slavic-speaking agricultural communities in the region.[20] These literate Greek centers controlled political, jural, and ecclesiastic hierarchies, and monopolized the manufacture and interpretation of iconic and symbolic imagery. Greek language, Brailsford noted, was the commercial and polite language of the Balkans (1906:86), and "the Greeks are well known through their commercial colonies and their romantic history, while the Bulgarians are a purely local race which has no roots beyond the east" (ibid., p. 106).

Strong differences existed between Greek market towns in Macedonia and their surrounding hinterlands, particularly in the realms of language, mode of subsistence, and social organization. The stories and tales related about "Gnoina" (in chapter 1) are very indicative of these marked differences. The rural populations over which the petty and elite clergymen ruled were by no means a cohesive, let alone universally Hellenized, group from any standpoint. The institutions of church and school were efficacious vehicles in the creation of a new national Greek identity among local Slavic-speakers, as were socioeconomic stratification and local relations of patronage and dependency.

Politically expedient but ahistorical and rather polemical claims that the inhabitants of Macedonia are, were, and always have been Greek— or Bulgarian or Macedonian—as some contemporary national partisans assert, grossly underappreciate the complex processes by which ethnic and national consciousness is created, transmitted, and reproduced across time and space. Arguments such as those of Bulgarian elites that "Macedonia is populated by a mass of stern, enlightened Bulgarians, with a deep national consciousness" (Tosheff 1932:4), or that the Bulgarian Exarchist propaganda was responsible for the Bulgarization of a Greek or Serbian population (Cvijić 1907), lead to an essentialism, evoking the preservation of a national psyche throughout the centuries. They also contribute to ideologies of nationalist racism and to campaigns of ethnic cleansing that continue to haunt the Balkans even today. Nationalism, as Chatterjee (1993:4) put it, is a "dark, elemental, unpredictable force of primordial nature threatening the orderly calm of civilized life."

IRREDENTISM, BYZANTINE HELLENISM, AND THE EXPANSIONIST GREEK STATE

I am one of the last Greeks who regard [Macedonia] with the Byzantine memory and with the hope that it could become Greek.

Ion Dragoumis, *Martyrs' and Heroes' Blood*

Greek involvement in the contest over Macedonia and the dispatch of partisan forces there was both a reaction to Bulgarian activities in the region as well as part of the "Great Idea" (*Meghali Idhea*), an irredentist ideology that regarded Macedonia (along with Asia Minor, Crete, Eastern Rumelia, and Thrace) as yet unreclaimed territories of the ancient Hellenes. Many turn-of-the-century Greek irredentists had been inspired by images of the glorious Byzantine Empire (which they argued had been a Greek empire), and had hoped one day to liberate Constantinople (Istanbul) from infidel Turks. By that time, irredentists were striving to gain a dominant position of political influence in the small, independent Greek kingdom to the south.

In the construction of the ideology of the Greek nation, a continuity with the past has been overstressed. Herzfeld, in his inspirational book, *Ours Once More* (1982a), addressed this process by which cultural continuity across time was constructed by Greek scholars in order to defend notions of national identity. Greek folklore, he noted, has been at the service of the new Greek state's mechanisms of legitimation since the turn of the century.

In order to justify the creation of the state (*kratos*) in the terms of ideological philhellenism, it was necessary to show that *ethnos* (the nation) and *laos* (the people, *Volk*) were one and the same thing, with the sole difference being that the *laos* did not include the educated elite. (Herzfeld 1982a:13)

Elite intelligentsia, at the head of the newly established state political economy of Greece, needed to construct a cultural and national identity to shore up the economic foundations of their new kingdom.

The work of Konstantinos Paparrigopoulos (1983), widely regarded in Greece as the father of modern Greek historiography, was instrumental in this effort, emphasizing the role of Byzantine Orthodoxy in the alleged continuity of Hellenism from ancient to modern times. Fueled by irredentism, and guided by a "defense of Hellenism," ideologues and armed partisans in Greece were well positioned to carry their campaign into Macedonia. The young Greek kingdom, however, did not always have the means to satisfy demands of such agents of nationalism for funds and arms. Following a failed attempt to incorporate Crete into the Greek kingdom in 1897, the Macedonian frontier to the north was presented by some in Greece as a potential catharsis for the isolation, defeatism, and melancholy that seemed to pervade the country.

The Paparrigopoulos paradigm of Byzantine Hellenism strongly influenced Ion Dragoumis (1878–1920), for example, a prominent figure in early-twentieth-century Greek national efforts in Macedonia who is regarded as a historical symbol of the Greek nation.[21] Son of a bourgeois mercantile Athenian family with roots in western Macedonia, Dragoumis was twenty-four years old when he obtained a post as secretary at the Greek consulate in Monastiri (Bitola) from December 1902 through June 1904 (Souliotis-Nikolaidis 1993:15).[22] Dragoumis' sister, Natalia, had married Pavlos Melas, who later became a heroic national martyr in the Macedonian conflict.[23] Some Greek historians have maintained that Dragoumis' philosophical nature and refined psyche made him a visionary prophet of the Greek cause in Macedonia (A. Vakalopoulos 1987:15), or that his ideological and intellectual strength was derived from his readings of Herbert Spencer, Maurice Barres, and (especially) Friedrich Nietzsche (Koliopoulos 1987). But it had been Paparrigopoulos' notions of the continuity of Hellenism from ancient to modern times through the vehicle of Byzantium that most influenced Dragoumis' perspectives on Macedonia.

In May 1992, the Nea Thesis publishing house in Athens ran a 2,000-copy reprinting of Dragoumis' *Martyrs' and Heroes' Blood* (*Martiron ke Iroon Ema*), an account of a young Athenian man, "Alexis," who upon graduation from the University of Athens law school at the turn of the twentieth century went to Monastiri/Bitola to find work close to his uncle. The story, a blend of romantic vividness, intellectual argument, and political proselytizing contains a certain degree of literary ambiguity, leaving a reader a bit dubious as to where the lines of fact and fiction cross. Despite the numerous questions that might be asked regarding the protagonist, "Alexis," his character, and his opinions, the account is an excellent example of the impassioned rhetoric surrounding Hellenism and Macedonia.

The paramount themes Dragoumis sought to develop in *Martyrs' and Heroes' Blood* were the prospects for the rejuvenation of Hellenism and the call to arms and personal involvement for the Greek cause in Macedonia. There is indeed an important philosophical quality to the work. Throughout the story, the young Alexis is reflecting on the worth of the individual and one's place in society, on the conflicts between good and evil and between the nation (Hellenism) and the state (the Greek government), and on the salvation of the individual through one's dedication to personal sacrifice in the name of national emancipation. Dragoumis argued that fighting for Macedonia could help Greeks overcome their "mediocrity" *(metriotita)* that had become pervasive following their defeat in Crete in 1897. "You should know," he mused through Alexis, "that if we run to save Macedonia, Macedonia will save us. She will save us from the dirt in which we are rolling, from mediocrity, and death. If we run to save Macedonia, we will save ourselves" (Dragoumis 1992: 10-11). To this end, Dragoumis styled his brother-in-law, Melas, as the quintessential hero to be admired and emulated. In his introduction, Dragoumis maintained that, until the early and unfortunate death of Melas in 1904, the latter had single-handedly led the cause of Hellenism in Macedonia, offering people belief once again that Greece could and would survive, despite the events of 1897. He urged the "Children of Greece" *(Ellinopoula)* never to forget the death of this "brave young man" *(pallikari)*.

Throughout much of the text, Dragoumis wrote in broad, general categories of "Greek" and "Bulgarian." Yet occasionally, particularly when articulating a detailed ethnographic point, he also spoke of "Macedonians of Macedonia" and the "Vlahs of Hellenism." The context of national struggle in Macedonia at the time of Dragoumis' writing shaped a broad rhetorical framework of Greek-Bulgarian opposition in his political discourse. The equally important context of local conditions, as he himself had observed and experienced them, revealed another level of group labels and ideological characteristics masked by the principal Greek-Bulgarian dichotomy, such as the Macedonians of Macedonia (who opposed both Greek and Bulgarian activities) and the Vlahs of Hellenism (who rejected Romanian propaganda and considered themselves members of the Hellenic national collectivity). The depiction is significant, for it addresses the active role Hellenized Vlahs played in establishing the hegemony of the notion (and the policing) of a modern Greek state in Macedonia.[24] As for the "Macedonians," Dragoumis maintained that their language is closer to a mix of Greek and Slavic than to Bulgarian.

Yet the theme of Hellenic continuity in the region via Byzantium is a motif that appears repeatedly in the work.[25] Dragoumis depicted the national competition of his day between the emerging nation-states of Greece and Bulgaria as an ancient conflict, routed in the Byzantine past:

> The king of Bulgaria, Samuil, after he fought twenty years to overthrow the [Byzantine] empire and take over rule, grew fatigued, finding before him [Byzantine emperor Vasilios II] the Satanic Bulgarian killer (*satanikos Voulgharoktonos*), and in the end he died defeated. Bulgarians tried a few times to raise their heads, but fell asleep very tired and since then have never confronted the Greeks with arms. (Dragoumis 1992:138)

Note that Dragoumis advocated a particular brand of humanism shaped by national ideology. He denounced Emperor Vasilios' blinding of captured Bulgarian troops as "inhuman" but went on to argue that it would have been better simply to have killed them. "Even today," he wrote, "with 15,000 less Bulgarians we would be better off" (Dragoumis 1992: 138).

Elsewhere in the book Dragoumis wrote of a conversation between Alexis and a visitor, aged sixty-four, who for fifteen years had run an artisan shop in the town of Melnik (in present-day Bulgaria). His visitor admitted that he was illiterate, but insisted that he considered himself "a Byzantine." For Dragoumis, the national conflict of his day between Greece and Bulgaria represented a resumption of the Byzantine struggle against the barbarian Slavs. He argued that generations of barbarians from the north had tried to challenge the Greek *ghenos* (descent group), but that now a new Vasilios would arise to seek out Bulgarian barbarians in the "mountains, in the caves, in villages, and in forests, and they will kick them out or kill them" (Dragoumis 1992:139).

The superscription of centuries-past conflicts between Hellenic Byzantines and neighboring barbarian Slavs onto contemporary national competition between Greeks and Bulgarians in Macedonia owes much to the influence of Paparrigopoulos's work. Paparrigoupoulos himself had criticized the Ecumenical Patriarchate for not being more actively engaged in Hellenizing the population of Macedonia. Yet the *Phanariotes* Greek elite under the Ottomans did contribute, perhaps inadvertently, to the Hellenization or Greek nationalization of the Christian population of the Ottoman Empire by fostering a sense of belonging under the Ecumenical Orthodox Church, which they virtually controlled.[26] This was accomplished primarily through educational and cultural programs, as well as through literary associations established to shape public opinion, to support Greek education, and to lobby government officials.

Associations for the spread of the ideology of Hellenism in Macedonia were established in both Athens and Istanbul, the respective decision-making centers of the new Greek state and the Patriarchate with its *Phanariotes* elite.[27] Often described as "literary associations," in contradistinction to their more militant counterparts that were dispatching (sometimes armed) national partisans along with teachers and propaganda materials to Macedonia, these organizations provided coordinated channels for communication and action on the Macedonian issue. Two in particular, the Hellenic Literary Association in Istanbul and the Association for the Propagation of Greek Letters in Athens (headed by Paparrigopoulos), both established in 1874, were instrumental to the cause of Hellenism in Macedonia. As president of the Association for the Propagation of Greek Letters, Paparrigopoulos wrote to the Greek foreign minister in 1888 urging the ministry to provide scholarships for the training of priests, teachers, and other local agents in Macedonia, especially the area north of Thessaloniki (Belia 1987:31).

The impact of such literary associations, at both the national and local levels, was profound. In the early 1870s,

> literary associations were formed or reactivated in many towns, and primary schools, boarding houses for girls and nursery schools were established in villages. Most funds were contributed locally, but assistants and teachers, textbooks and even grants were forthcoming from the Association for the Propagation of Greek Letters. These efforts soon brought results: by 1876 the advance of Bulgarian propaganda had been arrested. (Kofos 1975:35)

As many as 176 educational and philanthropic associations and brotherhoods were established in the decade 1870–80 alone (Papadopoulos 1987:27). In 1892, a Greek teacher working in Langadhas established a literary association known as *Philoproodhos* ("Friends of Progress"), which drew members not only from the town itself but also from nearby villages. The association was reportedly disbanded by Ottoman authorities in 1904 because of alleged propaganda activities by its members, who quite likely were armed partisans as well (see chapter 4). The association's name is enlightening, as the ideology it preached of common descent and national purity was regarded by its founder as a "progressive" development in the turn-of-the-century Langadhas basin.

Such efforts by Hellenic activists and Patriarchate loyalists, whether guided by financial interests, irredentist visions, or religious zeal, were instrumental in transforming some of the Christian inhabitants of Macedonia into a militant Greek group, prepared to struggle actively for their existence and expansion.[28] The unifying ideological themes in this process were "common blood" and "common faith," but equally important were the organizational and financial resources that nationalist forces in the Greek kingdom and the *Phanariotes* were able to offer such a movement. While growing national autonomy in Bulgaria during the 1870s contributed to the establishment of similar and competing efforts, Slavic-speaking agriculturalists of Macedonia by contrast generally lacked the organizational guidance and material support of a political, economic, and intellectual elite of their own. Their commercial and educated elites tended to associate themselves with either Greek or Bulgarian interests. Moreover, within the hierarchy of identities under which Slavic-speakers of late-nineteenth-century Macedonia lived, being an Orthodox Christian was generally far more significant or meaningful than being a Slavic-speaker or a Macedonian per se.

The ideological institutions of church and school, as well as the economic institution of the marketplace, were the principal forums through which competitive Greek and Bulgarian national interests struggled for cultural and political hegemony in Macedonia. Changes in marriage patterns, kinship and gender relations, and the organization of domestic life in rural communities of Macedonia provided more subtle psychological and cognitive means of educating and enculturating family members. Greek national identity was not a "natural development" or the extension of a "high culture" over the region of Macedonia, although it is now frequently portrayed as so. The ideology of Hellenism imposed a homogeneity on the Macedonian region and its inhabitants. By reviving a vision of Byzantine or ancient Greek culture, and projecting it on the region's population through the medium of an increasingly Greek version of Orthodox Christianity, agents of Greek national ideology fostered the creation of a Greek national consciousness among the region's Slavic-speaking population.

Nationalism, the sustenance of standardized, homogeneous, central high culture, as Gellner (1983:55) argued, is crafted in situations where such "well-defined educationally sanctioned and unified cultures constitute very nearly the only . . . *natural* repositories of political legitimacy" (emphasis added). Local sensitivities and sensibilities, the conceptions of identity and perceptions of difference shaped through local exchange and interaction, became irrelevant or at worst anomalous to this "great arch" of nation-building. It is not coincidental that the Assiriotes claimed descent from the inhabitants of Byzantine Aghia Anna rather than from the vampires of "Gnoina," Montenegro, or other places of origin. School and church offered a venue for the popular transmission of a standardized ideological framework (Hellenism) across a broad area. Religion and education boosted rural literacy rates and opened new channels of social and economic mobility, channels that would promote ties between rural communities in Macedonia and the new Christian nation-states to the north and south. In Guvezna, school and church together played a major role in the promotion of Hellenism and Greek national interests.

CULTIVATING NATIONAL CONSCIOUSNESS
Greek Schooling and Education in Rural Macedonia

The school, as always in our history, became the workshop where national consciousness was strengthened, and the nursery where faith in the nation's ideals was deeply cultivated. . . . Without this infrastructure, one wonders, how useful would have been the support generally of the Greek state and especially the dispatch of partisan bands [somata] in Macedonia from free Greece.

Stefanos Papadopoulos, "Education in Macedonia"

[handwritten annotation: proselytism in school]

Schools throughout modern Greece have long been regarded or even revered as bastions of the idea of the nation and the freedoms for which it stands. The Guvezna primary school was perhaps the single most important locus for the proselytization of Greek language, as well as for the creation and reproduction of a Greek national identity and national culture among the village's diverse population. The historic role of the school in local nation-building efforts was noted by the township president in a letter to the Committee of Townships and Municipalities of the Ministry of the Interior (dated 29 September 1956): "[I]n the center of the village's *aghora,* there stands today the old schoolhouse which was built by the Christian Community during the years of slavery, and in this lighthouse the Greek language and local morals and traditions [*ithi ke ethima tou topou*] survived" (ATA 1956). The portrayal of the school as a "lighthouse" (*faros*) is a motif that appears in other accounts as well, depicting education as a vehicle of enlightenment and liberation, especially for the young generation.

Despite their political differences, the Greek state and the Patriarchate collaborated extensively in educating Patriarchate loyalists (i.e. non-Exarchists) in Macedonia, regardless of whether their natal language had been Greek, Slavic, Vlah, or Arvanitika. In 1871, the Greek foreign minister inaugurated Greek educational propaganda efforts in Macedonia, issuing a communiqué to Greek consuls in the region on 4 January 1871 which urged them to establish schools for boys and girls in large communities (Belia 1987:29). Funds for teacher training as well as for the construction and maintenance of schools came from various literary and philanthropic associations in Athens and Constantinople such as those mentioned above, and from the Greek government.

Literary associations and diplomatic consulates also provided schools with free books of patriotic content, such as Dimitsas' (1879) history of Macedonia from ancient times to the Ottoman conquest, written in *Katharevousa* (atticized classical Greek). Another book distributed to Greek schools in Macedonia was *The Prophecies of Alexander,* written by Athanasios Souliotis-Nikolaidis, a Greek agent of the Macedonian Struggle who posed as a merchant in Thessaloniki and established a partisan secret society known as the *Orghanosi Thessaloniki.* Also written in *Kathareousa,* it described prophecies Alexander the Great had reputedly made from his deathbed concerning subsequent developments in Macedonia and the liberation of the region that would eventually come with the help of the Greeks (Souliotis-Nikolaidis 1993). These prophecies shared a close symbolism with the Apocalypse of St. John, and yet ended with Alexander's own prediction that Macedonia would become part of Greece. Similar sagas of Alexander the Great were even printed in Slavic with Greek characters (Kofos 1991:7). The associations and consulates also provided literary poems and stories with patriotic content, particularly from writers with ties to Macedonia. Poems were even adapted to martial music for schools, such as the marching song, still sung in Greece, "They Will Never Take Her [i.e. Macedonia]" (*Dhen Tha Tin Paroune Pote).* Written by Kostis Stamatopoulos, a Thessaloniki poet from a large and famous mercantile family, and set to music by a composer from Corfu, this song was sung in Greek schools throughout Macedonia (Plastiras 1987). Newspapers in Greek language also began to appear, the first being *Hermes (Ermis),* published on 13 May 1875 in Thessaloniki. The rapid proliferation of these new popular media vehicles played a critical role in the development of national ideology and consciousness in Macedonia, where the written word was portrayed to the largely illiterate rural population as the vestibule to sacred and ancient knowledge.

Despite the activities of these national institutions in educational work, most local school financing remained dependent upon local communities themselves (Papadopoulos 1987:26). Between 1878 and 1905, the number of Greek schools in market centers and large towns in Macedonia had risen by 81 percent (Belia 1987:33).[29] Through education, the spiritual power of resistance was cultivated in those who attended school and learned to read. Moreover, the school system provided an organizational infrastructure not only for national propaganda but also for the subsequent introduction of armed partisans into Macedonia (see chapter 4).

But these numerical gains were not always accompanied by an enthusiastic response from local inhabitants, and Greek educational propaganda efforts in Macedonia were not considered a major success. One of the chief obstacles in the campaign had been the lack of competent teachers to fulfill the mission of "teacher-apostles" that Ion Dragoumis had urged in his writings (Belia 1987:37). Books and materials, moreover, were written in classical atticized Greek (*Katharevousa*), rather than the spoken vernacular (*dhimotiki*) used by Greek-speakers in Macedonia.[30] But teachers dispatched to the region often gathered information for the Greek national cause by organizing local "centers of national activity" (Belia 1987:40). Cast in roles of educators and historical illuminators, teachers played a key role in shaping new notions of collective identity based on constructed traditions.

ENLIGHTENING EDUCATION

Popular legends in Greece often speak of how the Christian population, living enslaved under the Turks, were forbidden to practice their religion or to educate their children in Greek language and history. Local "traditions" in contemporary Assiros, as elsewhere in Greece, tell of covert midnight school lessons conducted by priests in a secret school (*krifo skolio*) hidden in the basement of the church, where pupils learned the Greek alphabet by the dim light of an oil lamp or even simply by the light of the moon.[31] The widespread character of such tales, alternative versions of which were also circulated in Bulgaria, suggests their importance in the national "traditions" constructed in both countries.

Consider how Tosheff, a member of the Bulgarian Academy of Sciences and a former minister plenipotentiary, described Bulgarian educational efforts in Macedonia prior to the establishment of the Exarchate in 1870:

> Generally speaking, the thirst for enlightenment and education by the Bulgarians of Macedonia from early times is most striking. Upon their own initiative they took care of their cultural needs. . . . [T]he Bulgarians taught

their children in the so-called [secret] "cell schools" which gradually were
replaced by regular elementary and other schools. (Tosheff 1932:68)

In fact, there is considerable myth-making in such national traditions.
Christian education had not been forbidden under the Ottomans. But
sparse resources often led to lessons being conducted in makeshift classrooms or even in commercial storage space, as was the case in Guvezna,
where conditions were often cramped and lighting was dim.

What Ottoman authorities did object to, however, was the promulgation of national propaganda and the encouragement of agitation, which
became a regular feature in both Greek and Bulgarian schools in Macedonia after the 1870s. It was these activities that constituted the "secret"
element in such national myths, and which led to the arrest and imprisonment of Stylianos Asteriou, the son of Nikolaos, and which eventually
prompted both Asteriou as well as Ioannis Pashos to quit the teaching
profession (see chapter 4).

Students in late nineteenth and early twentieth century Macedonia
did not attend school six to eight hours a day, as many children today
do. Many of them carried more important responsibilities of family labor
as well, whether in agriculture, husbandry, commerce, or even such domestic chores as the collection of firewood. In all likelihood, pupils attended school before or after their daily chores had been completed.
Whether they studied by day or night, they undoubtedly used candles or
oil lamps, for many buildings in Macedonia (churches included) had low
rooms with small windows. Pupils studied under the paternal eyes of local
priests, who added the Light of God to the dim glow of wax candles and
oil lamps. And what did the Light bring? What did such pupils study?
They learned to read, to write, and to do basic arithmetic. In effect, they
were learning the two languages of commerce: Greek letters and mathe-
matics. Regardless of their backgrounds, through schooling pupils were
transformed not only into Greeks but also into merchants, teachers,
priests, artisans, scribes, and the like. The cultivation of national consciousness and interest-group identity went hand in hand.

Few students of the Guvezna primary school in the early twentieth
century ever graduated, and in 1911 only three were earning excellent
(*arista*) grades (Assiros School Archives [ASA]). Yet the importance of
Greek education was not measurable in terms of grade scores, graduation
rolls, or placement in institutions of higher education. It lay, rather, in
the transmission of basic Greek lessons, especially language, math, religion, and history, to local children.[32] From the ranks of those educated
at the turn of the century came the politicians, administrators, and record

keepers of the new local township bureaucracy that was established following the advent of formal Greek rule: Pashos, Artousis, and Asteriou being among the most prominent examples (see part II). The post-1912 educational curriculum in Greek Macedonia and its obligatory attendance requirements, along with national holidays and celebrations, played a very important role in the construction of national sentiment and in the reinforcement of subtle ideological and psychological bonds of hierarchy and authority.[33]

Religion and language studies were crucial to the formation of a concept of "nation" in the minds of students, which then became legitimized or reified into the "natural order" of the cosmos. An elderly Pontic refugee in Mavrorahi, who had been sent to school as an adult under the mandatory educational policies for non–Greek-speakers during the Metaxas dictatorship of the 1930s (see chapter 7), recounted a memorable lesson in which his teacher explained that if the queen bee dies, the other bees cannot survive without her. That, the teacher told the class, was also the nature of life in the Greek motherland (*mitera patridha*). And thus the authority of the Greek king was legitimized.

But the hegemony of Greek national ideology in Macedonia was not achieved through educational efforts and religious proselytizing alone. The first decade of the twentieth century witnessed the eruption of violent armed conflict between opposing national partisans over the region. As terror gripped the lives of many families and blood was spilled across the hills of Macedonia, the new national labels and categories of identity promoted by secular and religious partisans came to take strongly emotive connotations in the minds of local inhabitants.

CALL TO ARMS, 1900–1908

Bulgarian propaganda in Macedonia enjoyed far greater success than its Greek counterpart, owing largely to the central use Bulgarian activists made of the language issue. By the turn of the century, national and ecclesiastical elites in Sofia had formulated clear ideas regarding the future of Macedonia, once freed of Ottoman overlordship. Many argued that Macedonian Slavs were Bulgarians, or a subgroup thereof. Once the region could be liberated from the Ottomans, Macedonia would become part of Bulgaria. National activists in Bulgaria did indeed promote the notion of an autonomous Macedonia, although they maintained that "Macedonia for the Macedonians" (a phrase reputedly coined by the British politician Gladstone [Chakaloff and Shoomkoff 1904:5]) represented *only* an intermediate phase of the region's progressive incorporation into Bulgaria.

But language had been a key factor in drawing support for the Bulgarian cause from Slavic-speakers in Macedonia. This was particularly true of liturgical language, since it meant that finally rural inhabitants could hear mass and other rituals conducted in a language they could understand. As one elderly man in Assiros told me, "The ceremonies in the Bulgarian churches were the same [as those in Greek churches]. They only differed in the language used." The standardized national Bulgarian language used in Exarchate churches was much closer, apparently, to the spoken Slavic vernacular in Guvezna than was the atticized construct used by the Patriarchate priests. This opened new opportunities for Slavic-speakers in Macedonia to seek education or new livelihoods in Bulgaria, and many who were thus exposed to Bulgarian national ideology actively fought for its cause back home in Macedonia.

The influence of Bulgarian national ideology on Slavic-speakers in turn-of-the-century Macedonia was profound but by no means universal. Other Slavic-speakers were drawn to Hellenism, while some even advocated an independent Macedonia. In 1893, the Internal Macedonian Revolutionary Organization (IMRO) was established secretly in Thessaloniki, dedicated to inciting a general rebellion among Slavic-speakers in Macedonia against the Ottomans and to the eventual creation of an autonomous Macedonian state (Stavrianos 1959).[34] IMRO activities brought many rural Slavic-speakers into contact with the organization, especially through the activities of schoolteachers and Exarchate clergy who (like their Greek counterparts) also often operated as political agents. It is unclear to what extent the rural population of Macedonia supported the aspirations of Bulgarian nationalists within the IMRO, but the movement was apparently riven by political and ideological factionalism from its inception.[35] In particular, members shared significantly different views regarding Macedonia, Macedonians, and their relationship to Bulgaria.

In 1895, the Supreme Committee, or what alternatively became known as the External Macedonian Revolutionary Organization (EMRO) was established in Sofia. Referred to by some as the "Supremists," these pro-Bulgarian activists had split with the IMRO to proclaim that their ultimate goal was the annexation of Macedonia to Bulgaria. EMRO opposed both the formation of Macedonian national consciousness and IMRO designs to create an independent Macedonian state (Stavrianos 1959:520; Trajanovski 1981:198). National elites in Sofia provided financial resources, ideological support, and arms to partisans, creating a formidable military force. Nevertheless, they continued to be opposed by the less well financed IMRO, whose leaders (the so-called "Centralists") called upon the peoples of Macedonia to rise up for political and economic transformations and to fight for a Macedonia that was either autonomous or independent (Kofos 1987:299). IMRO, however, lacked the necessary resources to operate its campaign effectively. The dispatch of Bulgarian Exarchist propagandists and EMRO partisans to Macedonia created a great deal of confusion among many local Slavic-speaking Christians, as there were two separate pro-Slavic national partisan forces operating in the region with very different agendas. In contrast, despite their other differences, both the Greek state and the Patriarchate were united in their views about the future of Macedonia and the status of its statehood.

With the formation of the pro-Slavic Macedonian political movements, armed partisan groups (*comitadjidhes,* or "committees") began to operate in the Macedonian countryside.[36] Local Slavic-speaking men were recruited into these groups, and many joined out of political conviction or belief. Sometimes, *comitadjidhes* formed alliances with armed bandits who roamed the countryside, stealing from the rural population indiscriminately. The bandits who joined with the Bulgarian partisans began to concentrate their terror and looting on Patriarchists (see Smith 1908), while those who allied themselves with Greek "Macedonian Fighters" (*Makedhonomahyi*) similarly attacked Slavic-speakers. In the Langadhas basin, there had been a notorious *Makedhonomahos* known as "Kapetan Thanasis" who so terrorized an extended family in Palehora that they were eventually obliged to abandon their lands and seek refuge in Guvezna in 1905.

While established historiographical convention in Greece generally dates the onset of the "Macedonian Struggle" (*Makedhonikos Aghon*) to the murder of famed Macedonian fighter Pavlos Melas in 1904,[37] the Ilinden uprising of autumn 1903 represented the first non-Greek nationally-oriented armed insurrection in Macedonia against Ottoman rule.[38] On July 20 (August 2, by the new calendar), IMRO led an uprising near the mountain town of Krusovo in the present-day FYROM.[39] Rebels cut telegraph lines, destroyed bridges, blockaded roads, burned houses and crops on eleven Ottoman estates, and attacked Ottoman garrisons.[40] Leaders of the rebellion demanded autonomy for Macedonia from the Ottoman Porte, but the uprising was eventually suppressed and most of its IMRO leaders were tracked down and killed.[41]

The Ilinden Rebellion of 1903 represented a moment of revolutionary consciousness in the minds of many Slavic-speakers in Macedonia.[42]

self-control

Greek historians and textbooks, however, have downplayed the historical significance of the incident, depicting it as only a local agitation. Yet Dragoumis (1992:82), who had been employed at the Greek consulate of Monastiri (Bitola) at the time of the uprising, reported that pro-Bulgarian agents and activists had prepared for the rebellion for quite some time, selling arms to the local population and even planning tactical details. They had garnered support among Slavic-speaking sharecroppers working on Ottoman *chiftliks* by promising a redistribution of land. Moreover, Vakalopoulos (1988a:219) noted that while the uprising may have been a distressing event to many Greeks, it also generated new efforts on the part of pro-Greek Macedonian organizations that were forming in Athens at the time. In fact, a new wave of armed Greek partisans were dispatched to Macedonia following the incident, and the bloody Macedonian Struggle between Greece and Bulgaria began in earnest.

As in many nationalist movements, commercial economic interests were a key subtext to the conflict over Macedonia, at both regional and local levels. Macedonia had been an economic frontier, and its rich grain lands and critical trade routes made it a focus of both business and government interest. While trade may have followed the flag in the case of British colonial interest in India (cf. Bailey 1957), in Macedonia flags followed trade. By the early twentieth century a large number of influential citizens in the independent Greek kingdom to the south, as well as international friends or "philhellenes" (*filellines*) had recognized the necessity of armed struggle to secure for Greece as much of Macedonia, its produce, and its trade as possible.

For example, one Greek writer in Bern, Switzerland, urged all Greeks wanting to save Macedonia to support the armed struggle (Kepetzis 1908: 33). Another scholar of great influence over politicians, ideologues, and partisans had been Neokles Kazazis, professor of the philosophy of law at the University of Athens. Son of a mercantile family, Kazazis in 1892 established a national patriotic association called "Hellenism" (*O Ellinismos*) for the "investigation and cure of Hellenism's rights" (Anagnostopoulos-Paleologos 1987:264). The association organized demonstrations, sent students to fight in the 1897 war in Crete, and sponsored partisans in Epiros. It also conducted an important campaign to "enlighten" the perceptions of both nonliberated Hellenes as well as Europeans on the Macedonian controversy. Kazazis's activities had been very successful in France, and his association began publishing a (French-language) journal, *Ellinismos,* in 1898, which proved a major factor in mobilizing French philhellenes for Greece.[43]

Similarly, a "Macedonian Committee" (*Makedhoniko Komitato*) was established in Athens, on 22 May 1904, with the full support of the Greek government (Gounaris 1989:183).[44] Its founders were "urban middle class businessmen, officers and professionals of nationalism" (Sowards 1989:75). Its president, Dimitrios Kalapothakis, had been an energetic man from Mani (a strong royalist region of the southernmost Peloponnese) and editor of the patriotic newspaper *Embros* published in Athens (Vayiakakos 1987).

During the crucial period from 1904 to 1906, the Macedonian Committee had been directly responsible for the organization and oversight of Greek partisan groups in western Macedonia, near the area of Bitola. It dispatched military officers and/or secret agents to the Macedonian countryside to work as teachers, agronomists, clerks, consulate staff, and the like (Vakalopoulos 1987:15). The Macedonian Committee, however, was often at odds with the partisan and propaganda activities of the Greek consul general of Thessaloniki, Lambros Koromilas, who controlled agents and operatives in central Macedonia (Gounaris 1987:113). While the consulate was generally more cautious and conservative in its covert activities for fear of hostile diplomatic reactions from the Great Powers in Europe, the committee was unrestrained by such issues or by the regulatory oversight of state bureaucracy and thus tended to work with a more active, impassioned agenda.

Rising tensions and growing conflicts prompted both Greek and Bulgarian national activists to organize, train, supply, and dispatch groups of armed partisans to Macedonia to protect the interests of their respective "nationals."[45] Austro-Hungarian documents maintained that the first state-sponsored "Macedonian Fighters" from (southern) Greece to come to Macedonia arrived in the *vilayet* of Thessaloniki in 1904, but that even they had failed to incite the local "Grecicized Slavs," as these documents referred to them. The earlier Greek partisans who had been active in the region as early as 1878 or 1896 had not been as well organized or funded as these later irregular forces, and had often operated as little more than bandits. By contrast, these new 1904 "Macedonian Fighters" had been organized in groups known as "bodies" (*somata*).[46] Each *soma* was referred to as a "school" (*sholio* or *skolio*) and its members were salaried "students" (*mathites*).[47] The leader of each *soma* was paid seven *lire* per month, while rank-and-file members earned 2.2 *lire* (Papathanasi-Mousiopoulou 1982–83:462). Elderly residents of the Langadhas basin recalled that the countryside had been infested with banditry, suggesting that raids by Greek and Bulgarian partisans, selective or indiscriminate, placed considerable hardship on rural inhabitants of Macedonia (see also K. Vakalopoulos 1983). Local villagers reportedly switched their allegiances between Greek and Bulgarian sides, depending on circumstances. Some who burned their candles at both ends, so to speak, later suffered recriminations. Others, such as Halepis, a large stockbreeder in Guvezna who supported both the Greeks and the Bulgarians, were more successful, not only surviving the war years but even profiting from them. Yet in general, the numbers of casualties during the Macedonian Struggle were high, and as in the case of most civil conflicts many of its victims were noncombatants.[48]

By spring 1907, the Great Powers of Europe had begun to complain about Greek activities in Macedonia (Gounaris 1987:113). Too much blood was being spilled, and the violence seemed to be escalating. Levels of terror, destruction, and death had become so severe that by 1908 "Macedonia had become a battleground among the Balkan nations over the dead bodies of those whom they allegedly wished to liberate" (Fisher-Galati 1972/1973:467). That year, conflicts in Macedonia and the Ottoman Balkans in general took on a significant new dimension with the Young Turk uprising and the promulgation of the New Ottoman Constitution on 11 July 1908. The Young Turks, led mainly by an educated officer corps exposed to Western ideas, initiated a number of reforms in Ottoman administration and political economy, including the revision of property laws so as to grant non-Muslims the right to own and inherit private property. These developments were welcomed by both Greek and Bulgarian national elites, as they presented an opportunity to consolidate and expand commercial interests in Macedonia. By then, the Macedonian struggle between Greece and Bulgaria was subsiding towards a tenuous and inconclusive suspension of hostilities. Yet the continuing decline of central Ottoman control over the Macedonian hinterland, coupled with growing national rivalries in commerce, administration, taxation, education, and religious affairs, bred further impetus for violent confrontation at both regional and local levels.

When Greece joined Serbia and Bulgaria in alliance against the ailing Ottoman Empire in what became the First Balkan War of 1912, the activities of each national group's partisans were officially suspended. But evidence gathered throughout central Greek Macedonia suggests that partisan actions, covert or overt, continued, and that many powerful local residents used the opportunity of the Turkish defeat to seize landed properties (see chapter 6). In Macedonia, a reign of terror fell not on the heads of a national aristocracy as it had in France in 1778, nor on urban laborers as in Germany in 1848. Rather, its victims were primarily rural cultivators, priests, teachers, and petty merchants of the "blood-soaked mountains and plains" of the Macedonian countryside (Haskell 1918a:4).

The first decades of the twentieth century were, therefore, an intense period of nation-building in Macedonia. Revolutions were made and broken. Large tracts of territory were "enclosed" within the new borders of nascent nation-states, just as large plots of land were also "enclosed" in local communities following the liberalization of property laws in 1908 and the "liberation" of Macedonia from Ottoman rule in 1912. Orchestrated by elite members of nations still in the process of forming and defining themselves, these conflicts in Macedonia might more aptly be termed wars of national creation rather than the more teleological wars of "national liberation." They revolutionized not only power structures in many local communities but also the ways in which people conceived of themselves and others. Greek and Bulgarian church officials and educators, sometimes the same individuals, preached and taught about identity, history, faith, solidarity, and loyalty. Education was a principal means by which new national identities were legitimized and accepted. Nation-building in Macedonia was structured by an ideology of purity, whose force and impact are best illustrated through local historical ethnography.

The violence and terror of the Macedonian struggle (1903–8) and the Balkan Wars (1912–13), as I will show in the following chapter, tore apart the regional social fabric as many communities—Slavic-speaking and Greek-speaking alike—were prayed upon by bands of armed national partisans, both Greek and Bulgarian. The growing crisis precipitated a great deal of physical and social mobility. Rural inhabitants of Macedonia who remained faithful to the Ecumenical Patriarchate and associated themselves with Greek interests were intimidated, assaulted, or forced from their homes and land by armed groups of Bulgarian *comitadjidhes*. On the other hand, those who for whatever reasons sought to distance themselves from Greek concerns and joined the Bulgarian Exarchist Church were subject to similar actions by Greek partisans or "Macedonian Fighters." Some of these Exarchist families left for Bulgaria, either voluntarily or marching with the Bulgarian army; others were killed or had their homes, businesses, and means of livelihood destroyed. Many Slavic-speakers, like Asteriou, the *chiftlik* sharecropper from Montenegro, attempted to Hellenize themselves, adopting the mantle of Greek nationality and largely denying (publicly at least) aspects of their cultural background that might be deemed anomalous to such new nationally oriented identities. As the tide of conflict washed across the wheat fields of the Langadhas basin, economic and social closure in the area came to be expressed through a new idiom: national identity. For many, national enlightenment and national liberation represented the threshold leading from barbarism to civilization.

In this process, previously existing locally and occupationally defined identities shared by Christian families participating in the Guvezna marketing community were negated and their legitimacy was denied. The imposition of new national categories meant that Slavic-speakers were now *either* Greeks *or* Bulgarians. In Guvezna, being a "Macedonian" was simply not an option. The essentializing and fanatic rhetoric of that period divided the rural population of Macedonia into those who sided with the so-called "schismatic" Bulgarian Exarchate and those who supported the Patriarchate and the Greek national cause. Slavic-speakers who sided with the Greeks came to be called *Grecomans* by the Exarchists, while in Greece and among Patriarchists in Macedonia they were referred to as "Bulgarophone Greeks" (Christoff 1919:34). Although there had been opposition by Slavic-speakers to the proselytizing efforts of both Greek and Bulgarian national agents, such dissent failed to culminate in a successful independence movement, at least in Guvezna.[49]

In the course of their interaction with me, villagers in contemporary Assiros frequently took pains to ascribe both to themselves and to others in their past or present social field, certain labels and alleged or stipulated lines of national descent. But neither field notes nor recollections have revealed any instances in which villagers used either the term *ethnotita* (ethnicity) or *ethnikotita* (nationality).[50] Rather, in discussing the actions of groups or various categories of people, local residents used proper (though equally unspecific) nouns that referred to national groups, such as *Ellines* (Greeks), *Servyi* (Serbs), *Tourkyi* (Turks), and *Voulgharyi* (Bulgarians). Some, however, especially those whose families came from Gnoina/Palehora, used the term *Makedhones* (Macedonians) in reference to the Slavic-speaking population of the area prior to 1913, as indicated in previous chapters. But those who did so insisted unequivocally that such people had a sort of commonality which marked them as somehow different from others. When pressed to clarify such distinctions, Assiriotes overwhelmingly insisted that local Slavic-speakers had spoken a language similar to yet distinct from Bulgarian. Yet nonetheless, most still referred to them and to Slavic-speakers in general as "Bulgarians" (*Voulgharyi*) or "Bulgarian-speakers" (*Voulgharophonyi*), two broad and politicized labels that date to the ideological and military conflict between Greece and Bulgaria over Macedonia at the turn of the century.

As that conflict intensified, rural inhabitants of the Langadhas basin began to seek security and protection in larger, more well defended settlements such as Guvezna. Most new settlers who sought refuge in the village during those years were not Greek-speakers from the south, but rather Slavic-speakers from nearby villages, most of whom had established affinal ties to Greek-speaking Guveznans before the national struggles gripped the area. This prompted more well-established, Greek-speaking families of local Christian notables to close ranks, turning increasingly endogamous in their marriage strategies as they sought to consolidate their resource bases. It was these dominant Christian families, most with commercial, educational, religious, and other ties to Greek interests, that came to play the most critical roles in mediating the changes of twentieth-century Guvezna. In this process, Slavic-speaking Christians were re-born, so to speak, into new social roles and identities. The conflicts that fueled such developments were couched in a new conceptual framework of nationalism that was revolutionary in that it transformed the ways in which people thought about themselves and others. Once Greek national interest and identity had achieved a degree of hegemony over the region, alternative identities based on linguistic or cultural difference became antinational and anti-Greek, vaguely threatening and potentially subversive.

4

THE MACEDONIAN STRUGGLE IN GUVEZNA

Violence, Terror, and the Scepter of National Liberation,
1903–1908

> The position of the Macedonian Fighters [*Makedhonomahyi*] who
> with their blood haunted the land of Alexander the Great, stands
> next to [that of] the 1821 fighters. If [the 1821 fighters] resur-
> rected the Greek state, [the Macedonian Fighters] renewed [it]
> with their heroism and supplemented [it with] their deeds.
>
> A. Vakalopoulos, "The Macedonian Struggle"

By local accounts, a number of Guvezna men were directly involved
in the armed struggle over Macedonia. As one Assiriotis explained
to me, speaking of the fathers and grandfathers who had lived during the
turn-of-the-century national conflict, "The old men in the village were
illiterate, but they were smart and they loved each other. They were looking for liberation." These Christians had actively supported those who
sought to drive out the Ottomans, hoping that success would bring new
opportunities to expand their own economic interests and influence in
the Guvezna market community. Nearly all these local activists, which
included both "locals" born in the area as well as "outsiders" who had
arrived only recently, had been Greek-speaking merchants, teachers, or
priests.

Religion has been an important force in modern national liberation
movements throughout the world, and it certainly played a central role
in the turn-of-the-century national competition over Ottoman Macedonia. As illustrated in chapter 3, popular conceptions of identity had a
strong religious element, shaped in large part by the administrative institutions of the *millet* system. Guvezna's first priest-teacher, papa-Angelos,
had been an influential leader in this Greek cause, despite having been
an "outsider," because he was literate and had received formal schooling
and training. During the era of the Macedonian struggle (1903–8), religion and education provided an institutional context for the promulgation of enlightenment ideologies of national identity and liberation. They
also offered an organizational structure for the activities of armed and
unarmed partisans of the Greek and Bulgarian national causes.

In Guvezna, popular identification of the village as a Christian (i.e.,

Greek Orthodox) community focused on the construction of the Church of the Prophet Elias, erected on a highly visible hilltop perch above the settlement, apparently in the 1880s.[1] Local accounts explaining the church's prominent location told of how construction had begun at a site down in the dell near the two streams, close to an "old little chapel" (*palio eklisaki*) dedicated to St. George (*Aghios Yeorghios*), a popular saint among pastoralists in Macedonia. Yet each morning, it was said, villagers awoke to find that the icon of the Prophet Elias had "walked up the hill" during the night. After repeated incidents of this sort, Christian villagers proclaimed the phenomenon a miracle—a message by the prophet or even by God himself that the new church should be built atop the hill, on a spot slightly higher than that occupied by the Turkish mosque on the opposite hilltop.

Such tales voice a popular theme in contemporary Greek national ideology, namely the age-old competition between Greeks and Turks. But the principal political and religious tensions of the 1880s were not those between Christianity and Islam (or Greece and Turkey, for that matter) but rather those arising from the competition between the Ecumenical Patriarchate and the Bulgarian Exarchate. Local tales surrounding the "miraculous" icon of the Prophet Elias further stressed this national religious dichotomy. The icon, it was said, had been brought to Guvezna by a Palehora family, apparently after a Bulgarian Exarchate priest had been dispatched to Palehora sometime after 1870. By contrast in Guvezna, asserted one elderly Assiros man, "they were all Christian Orthodox [i.e., Patriarchate loyalists]. . . . There were no heretics." In other words, in the context of the contemporaneous contest between Hellenism and Bulgarian nationalism in Macedonia, the siting of the new Guvezna church had another significance. It was established through a joint effort of Greek-oriented *tsorbadjidhes* in Guvezna and pro-Patriarchate Slavic-speaking families from Palehora, and became a visually prominent structure on the local landscape that marked the settlement, obscured from sight in the dell below. "Bulgarians," in the words of one villager, would not dare "set foot in the village" (*na valoun podhari*).

Cooperation and mutual support between the Church and Greek-oriented merchants, whether conscious or not, was manifest in a number of examples. Cowan (1990) described such phenomena in the market town of Sohos, situated in the hills east of Guvezna:

> In 1770, for example, the wealthy thread merchant Hadzihariskos (who, as the prefix to his name announces, had demonstrated his piety by making a pilgrimage to Jerusalem)[2] master-minded and financed the secret con-

struction of the town's main church. To ensure that it was not subsequently pulled down, he made a number of generous gifts to well-placed Ottoman officials. This act was undoubtedly an assertion not only of his religious devotion and patriotism, which Sohoians today invariably stress, but of his own wealth and influence. (Cowan 1990:40)

In Guvezna, ecclesiastical authority came to play a significant role in village political life, or in the exchange of personnel between clerics and merchants (as well as teachers and merchants). Local priests were either "outsiders" sent to the area (such as papa-Angelos, mentioned above), or had come from the ranks of local notable families (such as Papailiou; see below). Yet all shared a common dedication to the creation and promotion of an anti-Bulgarian feeling of national belonging and, ultimately, a sense of Greek national heritage. When the armed struggle began, these spiritual leaders also took to carrying guns at night to protect the village from Bulgarian outsiders.

Local accounts, for example, maintained that during the first decade of the twentieth century Guvezna had a priest by the name of papa-Souliotis, said to have come to the village from the Peloponnese in southern Greece.[3] It was he who had reportedly organized the local *somata* (armed groups of pro-Greek fighters) and the more irregular partisan groups (*Tsetes*).[4] Papa-Souliotis had also been involved in lucrative tobacco production in Guvezna. As such, he commanded significant amounts of personal and family wealth and was not a "poor" priest whose daily subsistence was dependent upon the donations and contributions of parishioners, as was often the case after 1913. Papa-Souliotis hired local villagers, particularly women, to work his land. He was not only alleged to have used a considerable portion of his cash income to finance the Greek *somata,* but was also said to have employed his laborers to run messages between various units involved in the Macedonian Struggle.

Another Guvezna priest intimately involved in the Macedonian conflict had been papa-Yiannis Papailiou, brother of a landowning police officer. When he died in 1939, a township council meeting eulogized Papailiou, enshrining him in township records as a "brave man" who did many good things for the township and who had participated in the Macedonian Struggle. In respect for and in recognition of his contributions, the township voted to cover the expenses of his funeral, which was held in great grandeur and attended by a number of priests and excellent chanters from Langadhas (ATA 1939).

Yet as noted earlier, the relationship between religion and education at the turn of the century had been intimate and pervasive. Local schools often operated directly or indirectly under religious guidance, and the Church provided a well-developed organizational network through which the national struggle for Macedonia was conducted. All appointments of professional teachers to Greek schools in Macedonia had been made by the Greek consulate of Thessaloniki, often if not regularly in conjunction with the Metropolite of Thessaloniki, which appointed local priests.

PREACHERS AND TEACHERS
Constructing Traditions of Enlightenment in Guvezna

The Assiros school archives help to illuminate the important role that schooling played in forging a Greek national consciousness among the residents of Guvezna. One document in particular, an account of the school's establishment and its relationship both with the Church and with the ideology of Hellenism, suggests that church, school, and local merchant capital were key elements in the Greek national cause in Macedonia.[5] According to this text, the first schoolroom in Guvezna was established in 1835, in the vestibule of the "old little church" of St. George that once sat in the dell. There, the account maintained, Greek letters "saw black days that were lit only by the burning oil of sacred lamps and the illuminating words of the priest."

Guvezna's first teacher had been the village priest, papa-Angelos, originally an "outsider" from nearby Baltza (Melissohori) who had resettled in Guvezna and established a prominent family group that came to own a number of properties in the village *aghora*. For unexplained reasons, after 1860, lessons reportedly were no longer conducted in the church but rather in "dark rooms of low houses," suggesting that classrooms were convened in private homes or storage rooms. Around 1900, on the eve of the Macedonian struggle, the township funded the construction of the first separate schoolhouse. The Greek army was said to have occupied the building from 1912 to 1915, and classes were moved to a storage room provided by Vouninoudis, a village shoemaker, and the house of Tsountas, a village grocer, so that "young Greek children [*Ellinopoula*] could learn the Greek language [*Ellinika grammata*]." During the years 1916–17 the church vestibule once again became the locus of instruction, until a new school building was erected in the village square in 1918 with funds from the local Christian community.

The formal establishment of the Guvezna school is one example of the near-frenzied competition between Greek and Bulgarian activists attempting to set up schools and churches throughout Macedonia at the turn of the century. Bulgarian efforts were particularly noteworthy. Whereas in 1886–87 there had been 353 Bulgarian schools with 516 teachers and 18,315 pupils in the region, by 1912 there were 1,196 Bulgarian schools, with 2,096 teachers and 70,000 students (Tosheff 1932: 67).[6] Yet pro-Bulgarian activists, educators, and propagandists never acquired a significant influence in Guvezna. As the account of the school's origins suggested, the support and assistance of prominent local Christian notables, especially village commercial and mercantile elites, were critical to the propagation of Greek letters in local society. Without the active involvement of such individuals, situated at key interstitial positions, the famous national societies—such as the Association for the Propagation of the Greek Letters—would have had only limited influence on the local level. It had been primarily Greek-speaking and Greek-oriented local notables, such as the artisans, grocers, and merchants of Guvezna, who supported Greek schools locally, sent their children to them, and created the first generation of an educated village elite.

In fact, a representative of the Greek Ministry of Education, dispatched to Macedonia in 1905 to ascertain the degree to which Greek education had spread throughout the region, had been particularly impressed by the support given by local notables in "Giouvezna" (Guvezna) to Greek schooling and religion.

> This village lies on both sides of a stream which passes through Langadhas to the south and ends in the Aghios Vasilios lake. It is made up of approximately 150 Greek families and Greek speakers. Cohabitating with them are 40–50 Turkish families. In the east end of the village on a hilltop is a small church, visible from far away. There exists a school in which nine male teachers and one female are teaching, while the township guards their well-being. And the inhabitants of this village were distinguished always for their dedication to the [Greek] *ghenos* and the Church (Chatzikiriakou 1962:12).[7]

The financial backing of Guvezna Christian notables and the close association of church, school, and township administration had been critical during the early years of this effort. In 1914, the District Director (*Eparch*) of Langadhas reported to the Prefect (*Nomarch*) of Thessaloniki that the Guvezna school had no funds of its own, that the schoolhouse belonged to the township, and that the school was run with money from church property.[8] In 1929, wealthy local tobacco merchants and the Greek state (*kratos*) jointly financed the construction of a new two-story school building, which was used until the 1978 earthquake left it structurally unsound and a new facility was constructed.

To better understand the relationship between the local Greek notable establishment of Guvezna and these institutions of nation-building, consider one specific example. In 1967, the village school sent a list of its most prominent teachers, past and present, to the Greek Ministry of Education at the latter's request.[9] Among those names on the list was that of Yeorgios Garoufalidis, son of Triandafillos, who had been a schoolteacher in the village until his retirement in 1924. A non-native of Guvezna, Garoufalidis had been born in 1857 in the important market and religious center of Serres. There he attended the Ottoman Gymnasium and received additional educational training at the Maroulios School, an educational academy which trained many teachers of Greek. Before coming to Guvezna, Garoufalidis had been appointed by the Greek consulate in Thessaloniki (which, as noted earlier, collaborated with the Metropolite of Thessaloniki in appointing all Greek teachers in Macedonia) to serve as a teacher in several locations in the European part of the Ottoman Empire, including schools in the cities of Constantinople, Thessaloniki, and Monastiri (Bitola). His contributions to the spread of the Greek language and civilization in Guvezna, as well as those of his son, Alexandros,[10] were indeed considerable and worthy of recognition.

Yet far from being an "urban intellectual," Garoufalidis had accumulated experience in rural educational activities, particularly when he served as a schoolteacher in several villages in the "Bulgarian"-influenced Yiannitsa area to the west of Thessaloniki, a site of major armed conflict during the Macedonian Struggle. As one local villager put it, Yeorgios was "the teacher, the chanter in church, the man who drew up notary public deeds, a social worker, a doctor, an ecologist, and a bookbinder who was responsible for school and out-of-school activities. He taught the children [proper] behavior and music." The songs that Yeorgios Garoufalidis used to teach his students were about the heroic acts of Greek patriots. Playing his violin, Garoufalidis would follow the students as they sang, evoking powerful images and lessons for young children in turn-of-the-century Guvezna. Here is a sample that is still remembered in Assiros today:

> Mitrousis Kapetanios
> brave man from Serres
> Was fighting with stamina
> from the bell tower

With four brave men
　　with body and stones.
Seriously wounded
　　by Greek traitors
Who helped the Turks
　　to encircle them
"Mitrousi, give up!"
　　with his loud voice
"I am not afraid of the Turk
　　because I am a Christian
I fight with Him
　　I will stay alive."

By all accounts, Garoufalidis had been a competent and influential
teacher, much admired by many local villagers.[11] He was said to have
owned an excellent personal library, of which present-day Assiriotes
spoke with great admiration and respect. A photograph of him, dressed
as a proud "Macedonian Fighter" (*Makedhonomahos*) with his weapons,
still adorns the house of his granddaughter.

Three other Guvezna teachers had also been active supporters of the
Greek cause in Macedonia. These men were born in Guvezna during the
1880s, and were appointed to teaching posts in various villages. The first,
Dimitrios Sapountzis, was one of two sons of the miller and stockbreeder
Nikolaos (himself the son of a priest), who apparently settled in Guvezna
before the birth of his children (see Genealogy J). Sapountzis taught in
Kato Seli (Veroia district, western Macedonia), Tsernovo (the same area),
and Profitis (Langadhas district) before being appointed to Guvezna in
1900, where he remained until his retirement in 1948. Sapountzis also
maintained and updated village (and subsequently township) records,
and later taught the township-sponsored Agricultural Sunday School in
the 1930s.[12] He was remembered as a temperamental man who was not
averse to using corporal punishment on his school children, but he was
also renowned for his knowledge of national and local history.[13] Another
Guvezna man who became a teacher was Fotios Koroupis, son of a Guvezna priest. Koroupis received appointments in Galliko, Chalastra (both
in the then Slavic-speaking Axios/Vardar valley region), and Guvezna.
The third local teacher, Stylianos Asteriou, was the son of the upwardly
aspirant settler from Montenegro whose life history and career as overseer of the Guneyna (Palehora) *chiftlik* was recounted in chapter 2.

An account of the life of teacher Stylianos illuminates not only how
after his retirement from teaching Stylianos and his own sons built them-

selves into a large landowning and stock-breeding family (Genealogy B), but also how powerful local families with links to Greek interests came to play a major role in the ethnic and national transformation of Macedonia.

Stylianos Asteriou (b. 1885) was the third and youngest son of Guneyna *chiftlik* overseer Nikolaos, of Montenegro.[14] His father had decided to send him to Greek school in Guvezna, and during the 1890s Stylianos walked to school from the family's home in Guneyna/Palehora.[15] He performed well in his studies under the teacher, Garoufalidis, and prompted by the urgings of the village church chanter, Nikolaos decided to send his youngest son to train as a teacher at the Educational Academy [*Dhidhaskalion*] in Thessaloniki, which was operated by the Orthodox Metropolite, the Greek consulate, and prominent Greek notable families of Salonika. [In the view of local villagers this was an extraordinary accomplishment, testifying both to Stylianos' talents as well as to the financial resources of the family.]

Living and working conditions in rural Macedonia were, however, often difficult for teachers during the first decade of the twentieth century. Assigned to posts by the Greek consulate in Thessaloniki, many were expected to teach by day and to join Greek partisans fighting for the Macedonian cause at night. Stylianos' first appointment was to the Greek-speaking village of Horouda, in the hills of Vertiskos, where he taught for six years until the "revolution" of 1903.[16] Later, he was reassigned to the "Bulgarian" village of Petrovo [present-day Petra, Kilkis District], whose inhabitants were described as "Bulgarian-speaking Greeks." A Greek priest accompanied Stylianos to Petrovo, although [or perhaps because] the village already had a Bulgarian priest. Stylianos and the Greek priest obtained an old storage room and divided it, using one part as a school and the other as a church.

The school did well under Stylianos, but a villager named "Christos" kept warning him to be careful. When the school year ended, Stylianos locked up his classroom and returned to Guvezna. The following week a Turkish gendarme [*soubashi*] came on horseback from Langadhas and asked the Guvezna village president where he could find Stylianos. Villagers warned the young teacher and helped him to hide near the village church, on a plot of land rented by his father, who had by then moved the family from Palehora to Guvezna. The village president tricked the Turk by presenting another man as Stylianos, but the gendarme returned the following week and threatened Nikolaos and his wife with exile if they did not surrender their son. Stylianos gave himself up, and was taken by the gendarme to Langadhas, tied to a wagon. There he was detained in the basement of the Langadhas director's offices, before being moved to Youmenissa west of the Axios (Vardar) River valley [where Stylianos was handed over to Bulgarian authorities]. There he was held for a long time awaiting trial, and was eventually sentenced to be hanged four times [*tetrakis*].[17]

Meanwhile, a Guvezna man from a large mercantile family, Apostola-koudhis, was working for a British company digging for gold in the Gal-likos River of the Kukush (Kilkis) area, west of Deve Karan mountain. He and Yeorgios Halepis, head of the largest stock-breeding family of Gu-vezna, went to Youmenissa to seek the assistance of a Bulgarian army major who was a first cousin of the mother of Stylianos' fiancée. Stylianos' future mother-in-law was a "Bulgarian" from Ambar-Koy (Mandres) who had married a Guvezna man and bore him a son, only to be widowed shortly thereafter. She remarried, with another Guveznan, who forbade her to speak "her language." She bore him two daughters; Pashalina (who mar-ried a mill owner in 1923) and Yerakina, who eventually married Stylianos Asteriou. After the marriage, Stylianos likewise did not permit his mother-in-law to speak "Bulgarian" in his household either, and he himself spoke mostly Turkish to her. "Martso,"[18] he used to tell her, "You can speak all the Turkish you want. But not that language."

The two Guvezna men, Apostolakoudhis and Halepis, rode for eight hours on horseback to Youmenissa. The Bulgarian major agreed to help his cousin's betrothed son-in-law. He went to the jail, found Stylianos, and beat him. But this was really only a show for the jailers, doping them into thinking the major had a personal hatred for Stylianos. The ploy worked, and the major was later able to get Stylianos released from prison, appar-ently under his own charge. Upon his return to Guvezna, Stylianos was again assigned work as a schoolteacher in Petrovo. This time he refused, declaring, "I will take a pan and sell *halvah* outside the Greek consulate in Thessaloniki, but I will never again become a teacher in Petrovo."

This account is particularly illustrative of the many-layered relation-ships of culture and power in turn-of-the-century Macedonia. It was the chanter of the Orthodox church who had suggested to the upwardly mo-bile and Hellenizing *chiftlik* overseer from Montenegro that his youngest son become a Greek teacher. As one Assiros villager, a grandson of a priest, put it,

The teachers were locals [*dopyi*]. They were primary school graduates and then they attended the *Dhidhaskalion* for just six months. Priests graduated [from their training] very fast as well. They turned them [both teachers and priests] into responsible nationalists [*ipefthinous ethnikistes*]. The money was coming from below [*Apo Kato*] [i.e., from the Greek state authorities to the south].

This and other details suggest that Orthodox churches and Greek schools shared the same space (sometimes physically as well as symbolically) for the propagation of Greek "High Culture" and national consciousness. While marriages between "Bulgarian"-speaking women and Greek settlers or Hellenizing Greek-speaking settlers were quite common, the account of Stylianos Asteriou reveals the degree of power and censorship that Greek (or Greek-aspirant) men could exercise within the domain of their family, some forbidding their Slavic-speaking wives or in-laws to use their native language even at home. It also suggests the intimate ties that existed between many Guvezna merchant families, as well as how through their positions they became mediators of exchange across ethnic, religious, or national boundaries.

Moreover, it is also apparent through such accounts that teachers were closely involved with partisan activities in the national contest for Macedonia, as many sources have described,[19] and that their propaganda work was regarded as illegal and grounds for imprisonment by Ottoman authorities. As one Assiros villager recalled, "the teachers, the priests, and the Greeks [all] carried weapons in their belts." Some, however, resisted Hellenization and declined to dedicate themselves to the Greek cause. Pashos, for example, the stepson of Garoufalidis, was also trained as a teacher but reportedly resigned his post in the early 1900s allegedly because he had been reluctant to take up arms and fight for the Greek cause. As one villager put it, "He did not want to be a teacher during the day and a Macedonian Fighter by night, terrorizing Macedonians." After leaving teaching, Pashos became an influential (conservative) political figure and a highly successful tobacco merchant in Guvezna.

Some families of teachers, priests, and merchants shared affinal ties as well, suggesting the degree of intimacy, or at least mutual support and cooperation, among these local Christian notables. For example, one of the two sons of Artousis, the big grocer, married the daughter of the priest papa-Andonis at the turn of the century. The teacher Koroupis had been the son of a priest, while the son of Sapountzis (another teacher) later became the village priest, a post he held until retirement in the early 1980s. These teachers and priests made up a village intelligentsia, conveying to the local population a sense of common membership in a broader, larger collectivity through their sacred knowledge, both religious and secular. They were agents of authority, and together with other local notables, especially the families of the *aghora*, exercised a profound influence over the lives of village residents.

MERCHANTS AND PARTISANS
Secular Agents Negotiating the Passage to Nationhood

Commercially prominent families in Guvezna also took an active role in the period of national partisan conflict in the early twentieth century. Some were local agents of a network of influence cultivated by the Greek consulate in Thessaloniki.[20] Recall the local merchant, Apostolakoudhis, who had been instrumental in saving the life of Stylianos Asteriou when the latter was imprisoned by Bulgarian authorities in Youmenissa. Apostolokoudhis came from a wealthy mercantile family which conducted most of its business in the Kukush (Kilkis) area, a heavily Slavic-speaking district northwest of Guvezna. Their founding ancestor was said to have come to Guvezna from Halkidhiki, one of the few areas of Macedonia that Bulgarian activists did not claim as "Bulgarian-speaking." One member of the Apostolakoudhis family was ascribed the title of "Macedonian Fighter." He had been in charge of a local *soma,* and was said to have terrorized families and looted homes in the area. As a young man, it was alleged, this Apostolakoudhis had murdered the Tortop *bey,* stopping his carriage near the ancient *toumba* and shooting him.[21] This young Apostolakoudhis was eventually murdered himself, "cut into pieces" in Drimos by rivals while looting the house of a Turkish landlord.

Another prominent villager actively involved with partisans in the Macedonian Struggle had been the wealthy merchant-industrialist, Salamas. Owner of a salami and sausage factory in Salonika,[22] he and his brother also ran a cheese-making shop in Guvezna. Salamas reportedly had been a gun-runner for Greek partisans. It was said that he used to receive arms from the Metropolite in Salonika and would transport them north to local distributors, such as the Guvezna *tsorbadjis* landowner and stockbreeder Stavrakis, who would then deliver them to Greek partisans in the countryside. Most likely Salamas worked as a local agent of the Thessaloniki Organization (*Orghanosi Thessaloniki*), a Greek partisan group that operated secretly out of Salonika (see Souliotis-Nikolaidis 1993).

Yeorghios Halepis, the feared pistol-toting *tsorbadjis* stockbreeder mentioned in chapter 2, also played an active role in the Macedonian Struggle. According to one of his descendants, however, Halepis had assisted both Greek and Bulgarian partisans, devising special signals to use with each side. When partisans of either faction came to Guvezna, Halepis reportedly hosted them at his home. As his wife cooked food for the soldiers, Halepis would secretly signal to their opponents and to local Turkish authorities that these partisans were present in the village.

The "Macedonian fighters" from "Old Greece" who had come north to participate in the Greek struggle for Macedonia often relied on local inhabitants for food and supplies, either through purchases and sympathetic donations or looting and confiscation. By the above accounts, at least four notable Guvezna merchants or stockbreeders, two priests, and five village teachers had been actively involved in the Macedonian struggle. Their combined efforts proved both critically important and largely successful. While present-day Assiriotes claimed that Bulgarian propaganda efforts achieved strong successes in some villages of the Langadhas basin, such as Aivatovo (Liti), Balaftsa (Kolhikon), and Vissoka (Ossa; see map 2a), Bulgarian agents and activists were never able to establish a foothold in Guvezna. As many present-day Assiriotes proudly proclaimed, "The Bulgarian element [stihio] never entered Assiros." They were all Greeks and spoke only Greek, or so villagers maintained in the 1990s.

Most Guvezna villagers, however, had remained largely bystanders in the armed struggle. While many commercial or educated families had identified strongly with Greek interests at the turn of the century, the majority of local Christians had felt little sense of affinity with any national collective, be it Greek, Bulgarian, or Macedonian.

> On those occasions when the Slavs of Macedonia did adopt a nationality before World War I, it was usually because they were won over by the consciousness-raising propaganda efforts of either the Bulgarians, Greeks or Serbs. Cases of families divided are extant in which, because one brother was educated in a Bulgarian school, another in a Greek school, and a third in a Serbian school, each adopted a different nationality. (Perry 1988:23)

School lessons on the ancient Hellenic roots of Guvezna/Assiros had left a deep impression on local memories, largely because such ideas were both radically new and emotionally appealing. As I have argued in chapter 2, identity had been principally a product of what one did for a living, one's social standing, and whom one married.

The new labels of identity introduced during these campaigns of "enlightenment" and "liberation" were heavily ladened with political and religious meaning. Those who supported Bulgarian activities were stigmatized by excommunication as schismatic heretics, and later harassed by Greek partisans. Those who attempted to stay clear of the political struggle sometimes fared no better, as their ambivalence had often been regarded as a symbol of secret leanings or hidden inclinations. This was particularly true of Slavic-speakers, who straddled the boundaries of these emerging national frontiers. To such people, Greekness or non-Greekness became issues of daily life only after partisans entered their communities and began to harass, threaten, loot, or kill. A good number of present-day Assiriotes, especially elderly residents who had moved to Guvezna from Palehora, recalled that the "Macedonian Fighters" were "like thieves" who would steal food and belongings from their homes. In response, many adopted the most expedient solution to such problems: they fled their exposed native villages for settlements that offered more protection and security.

The wealthy fled with their gold pieces and other forms of movable property, and often found it easier to reestablish themselves in new communities. For example, several Greek-oriented Christian families from nearby Slavic-speaking Aivati (Liti), where Bulgarian agents had been very active, moved to Guvezna in search of protection. As one Assiros man claimed,

> They did well here. They were people of the commercial world [*anthropyi tou emporiou*]. They did not want to go with the Bulgarians. One of them, Aivadjis, stayed [here]. He married Halepis' daughter. The others left and returned to Aivati when the Greeks came [*irthe to Elliniko*].

Despite the fact that Aivadjis had been a Slavic-speaker, as the son-in-law of the feared Halepis he nevertheless became well connected with the Guvezna elite. He rented shop space from the merchant Kondos and opened a grocery store next to that owned by Vranas. Poorer Slavic-speaking families from other nearby settlements such as Palehora and Gnoina, as well as from several villages in the Kukush area, also sought refuge in Guvezna during this period, fleeing their communities with their few possessions and taking whatever jobs they could find as laborers for *tsorbadjidhes* patrons. The case of Guneyna/Palehora and the fate of its Slavic-speaking residents is illustrative of such developments.

PALEHORA
Partisan Terrorism and Settlement Abandonment

As Bulgarian and Greek armed partisans moved throughout the Macedonian countryside at the turn of the century, they often harassed local inhabitants and targeted wealthy supporters of their opponents with terror and sometimes even murder. It was in response to such terrorism on the part of Greek partisans, for example, that the population of Palehora began fleeing the *chiftlik* in 1905.[23] Villagers in Assiros recounted that Greek partisans from the south often came to Palehora, demanded gold pieces from the families there, and frequently beat them regardless of whether they cooperated or not.

Consider the fate of the family of Yeorghios Stoinos, the largest joint domestic group living at the Palehora *chiftlik*. They had worked the land there as sharecroppers, and under their special Ottoman tax privileges had raised large herds of livestock, hiring shepherds from Slavic-speaking communities such as Yianik-Koy (Dorkas). But at the turn of the century, both the Stoinos family and their hired shepherd laborers came under harassment by bandit and Macedonian Fighter "Kapetan Thanasis" and his men, who accused them of being "Bulgarians" and terrorized them until they were driven out of the settlement.[24] The first branch of the family to flee Palehora originally sought refuge in the village of Balaftsa (Kolhikon), which had been populated by Slavic-speakers at the time. Soon, however, they moved again, to Guvezna, reportedly in search of a "better climate" (*kalitero klima*). Their resettlement in Guvezna had been facilitated by the fact that it had been the natal village of Yeorghios Stoinos' mother. Other branches of the family from Palehora followed, and they changed their surname to a more Hellenized form, recorded in the 1918 township registry as "Palepolitis" ("Person from the Old Town"). Even after moving to Guvezna, this Palepolitis family maintained a single domestic economy, consisting of five brothers, with their wives and children, all under the leadership of Yeorghios, the eldest brother and patriarch.[25]

Even so, Yeorghios Palepolitis and his family continued to be harassed by Kapetan Thanasis after they moved to Guvezna. They had purchased houses and some 250 *stremmata* in Guvezna from Shei *Effendi*, who was an absentee Muslim landowner, and attempted to continue their profitable agro-pastoral activities. To accommodate the family's large flocks and herds, Palepolitis had rented additional grazing land near the village of Yianik-Koy (Dorkas), from where his shepherds had come. But the predations of Kapetan Thanasis continued, and eventually Yeorghios was betrayed and kidnaped, held by the notorious Thanasis for a large ransom of gold pieces.[26] After being freed, Palepolitis sold all his landholdings in Guvezna and moved to Langadhas, from where his wife had come. There he finally found protection with his father-in-law, a very prominent Christian notable of great influence.

In the decades immediately following its abandonment by the

Stoinos-Palepolitis family, Palehora came to be inhabited sporadically by other families fleeing partisan terror, either Greek or Bulgarian. Its last inhabitants, a Sarakatsan family, remained there until as late as 1949. After that, the old village of Guneyna, its houses, streets, and graves, disappeared under fields of wheat.

Establishing a Greek Macedonia
Localizing National History

The early years of the twentieth century witnessed extensive population movements in the Macedonian countryside, as many Slavic-speakers and Greek-speakers alike fled the violence and terror inflicted upon them by bandits and armed partisans. Events of the bloody Macedonian Struggle (1903–8) and the Balkan Wars (1912–13), which led to the partition of the region of Macedonia and the incorporation of its southern half into the expanding Greek nation-state, subsequently became part of a proud national heritage in Greece. By the late twentieth century, many communities of Greek Macedonia have come to lay their own claims to a part of this glorious tradition. Stories are told of local contributions to the cause of national liberation, or of the role that rural communities have played in major events of this era of armed struggle; marble busts have been erected throughout villages of Greek Macedonia commemorating "Macedonian Fighters," national martyrs, and other heroes of the Greek cause through names inscribed in stone; and verses are sung of the exploits of Greek partisans in driving the Bulgarian presence from the region and in bringing emancipation to the oppressed Hellenism of Macedonia. Since assuming sovereignty over the southern half of the region of Macedonia, the Greek government has actively encouraged these developments, as part II of this work will show.[27]

Consider an account of Guvezna's role in both the First (1912) and Second (1913) Balkan Wars, related to me by an elderly Assiros man who claimed to have learned it from his former schoolteacher, Sapountzis. The tale recounts the "liberation" of the village from the Ottomans, not only linking Guvezna Christians to the Greek national collectivity but also purporting to explain how they came to be members of that collectivity. It also contains narrative elements suggestive of the double pasts of the Assiriotes, of relationships more complex than contemporary claims of Hellenic hegemony would lead one to believe.

In October 1912, during the First Balkan War which allied Greece, Serbia, and Bulgaria against Turkey, Bulgarian forces swept down on the plain of Langadhas from their positions in the occupied village of Yianik-Koy, present-day Dorkas. They reached a point on the northern outskirts of Guvezna where the Palepolitis family had constructed their houses. The Greek soldiers [Evzonakia],[28] however, were also scattered around the plains, and they continually reassured the Guvezna villagers that everything was under control and there was no cause for alarm.

The Bulgarian army established camp in the area up behind the village church, and the Bulgarian prince leading the force stayed in the house of a local Guvezna man [who was not from the ranks of prominent villagers]. Some Assiriotes had no problems communicating with the Bulgarian troops. On the afternoon of October 25 [1912], there came a Greek messenger with a few lightly armed evzones.[29] The next day the Bulgarian army marched down to Thessaloniki. The Turkish Pasha, at the urging of the Great Powers [principally the British], had already officially surrendered the city to the Greek army, which in fact was still encamped several kilometers away on the far bank of the Gallikos River. Today, the village's local national holiday is St. Dimitrios Day [October 26, also observed in Thessaloniki], because the village was liberated from the Turks the day before.

The Greek and Bulgarian armies began to engage in open battle against each other in the Second Balkan War of 1913, which pitted Greece and Serbia against Bulgaria. In their victorious campaign, the Greek forces also passed through Guvezna on their way to battle in the highlands to the north. The Greek-Bulgarian War began in Guvezna on 13 July 1913. On the preceding day, four Bulgarians were arrested outside the village and executed. The Greek liberating army also camped here. The great hero of the Balkan Wars, Velissarios, is said to have pitched tents for his men under the great plane [platani] tree in the village aghora. Officers were quartered in the home of a village grocer, Tsountas, whose house served not only as a field hospital for wounded soldiers, but also as the kitchen in which Greek troops maintained their cooking and dining facilities.[30] [The older villagers recall] the Greek troops ate a lot of lentils and chick peas.

The Greek forces were not allowed to move north of the 32nd kilometer [marker] of the national road, just beyond which the Bulgarians held two small hills, below the village of Karterai. The Greek King Constantine and his staff came as far as the 24th kilometer [marker], from where he dispatched a detachment to take the Lingovan [Xiloupolis] bridge and the bridge of Strimon. The Greek assault attacked the flanks of the Bulgarian forces. The Bulgarians had a big cannon which was firing continuously, but the Bulgarian soldiers were tied down and could not move. The Greeks took over those two small hills.

Eventually, the Greek forces pushed the Bulgarians back north and moved their forward command to Berova [present-day Vertiskos], awaiting orders from King Constantine. The next Bulgarian resistance they encountered was in Lahanas. The hero Velissarios collected his men behind the Guvezna church. He then attacked the Bulgarians around the Lahanas area. Although he did not have enough supplies, he won the battle. He himself died on a spot called Kresna, where his tomb still exists. The Bulgarians fled and they did not even have the time to destroy the Lahanas bridge. The Turks helped the Greeks and showed them all the paths. At 1:00 in the afternoon of 21 July 1913, Lahanas was captured by the Greeks.

On the second front, the Greeks were fighting the Bulgarians in Kilkis. King Constantine went up the Deve Karan mountain and watched the battle.[31] Kilkis fell to the Greeks on 21 July 1913, the same day as Lahanas. Guvezna lost four villagers in the fighting, and an additional six remained on the rolls of the missing.

This account claimed that the famous July 1913 Battle of Lahanas, a critical engagement of the Second Balkan War in which Greek forces allied with Serbia drove Bulgarian troops (and many Slavic-speaking civilians) from large parts of Macedonia, actually began in Guvezna. Yet it also revealed that both the Bulgarian and Greek armies had been active in the area, and that both were regarded as "liberators" by their supporters. Even the Greek king made an appearance on the local scene in this narrative. The commanding officer of the Bulgarian forces was quartered in the home of a local resident (perhaps a Bulgarian sympathizer?), while the staff of the Greek army stayed with Tsountas, the *tsorbadjis* grocer who had also lent space in his home for the village's Greek school. The story also maintained that at least "some" Guvezna villagers could speak "Bulgarian," and did so with the Bulgarian troops.[32] These soldiers remained in the village for about a week, other Assiriotes claimed, accompanied by fleas that infested many local residents.

Such accounts illustrate how memory, local knowledge, and historical authority may construct oral traditions that present proud and heroic images of a community's place in national history. They are personalized historical narratives that evoke emotional aspects of identity which are then linked to ideological constructs of the nation. In this manner, the role of "the local people" and the village itself take an active voice in national liberation, articulated through the Greek victory in the Balkan Wars. The Second Balkan War, they proudly maintained, actually began in Guvezna and the great heroes of the day had made an appearance there. Today, the heroes monument (*iroon*) in the Assiros village *aghora* commemorates those villagers who gave their lives in these and other wars of the national cause and the victory of Hellenism.

Yet at the same time, such localizations of national history may also censor other voices that ring anomalously in homologizing constructs of national heritage. Consider the fate of women who married into Guvezna from nearby Slavic-speaking communities, such as Ambar-Koy, Balaftsa, Palehora, or Zarova. Some, especially those marrying Greek-oriented Guvezna men, were actively forbidden by their husbands to speak Slavic at home or to teach it to their children. Others faced similar pressures after the enactment of Greek government-mandated official prohibitions against the speaking of any "foreign" or non-Greek languages in the 1930s (see chapter 6). By the 1990s, many Assiriotes had come to deny the past existence of Slavic-speakers in their village, despite the considerable evidence to the contrary, both written and oral, presented above. In fact, a great deal of self-censorship is often exercised by Assiriotes in conversation with outsiders, consciously or not.

CENSORING HISTORY
The Fate of Ambar-Koy Affines

Of course, the Assiriotes are by no means unique in the fact that they present only a part of themselves, their families, or their histories in the course of their social interaction. Such behavior, be it conscious or unconscious, lies at the heart of symbolic communication and has been a central aspect of social theories based on dialectical reasoning, from Goffman and Simmel to Freud, Marx, and Gramsci. What is significant in this particular context, however, is the highly politicized *national* element in this self-censorship. Greek hegemony in Macedonia has been ideological as well as political and economic. And the ideological content of notions of the Hellenic nation, which far from being ecumenical has shown itself to be rather intolerant of cultural or ethnic pluralism, has led many inhabitants of Greek Macedonia to deny or hide those aspects of their own personal or family pasts that may be perceived and regarded as anomalous or detrimental to the Greek nation (*ethnos*) in Macedonia.[33]

The assertion in the above narrative that "some villagers had no problems communicating with the Bulgarian troops" seems remarkably ironic when one considers that it was made by a man who in nearly every other context insisted that no one in Guvezna spoke Bulgarian. There are several feasible explanations that may be entertained to account for such apparently contradictory statements,[34] although the most plausible one concerns the manner in which speakers conceived of and used the term "Bulgarian" in such contexts. They were most likely referring to the national orientation of the local population, implying that regardless of their diverse pasts or vernacular languages they uniformly supported the Greek cause. As another Assiros man claimed, in describing how the day after Greek forces arrived in Guvezna villagers took the Greek flag up to the church, "The population here was pure Greek. We had no Bulgarians." But other evidence gathered from the area suggests that universalizing claims regarding the language, ethnicity, or even national orientation of all villagers, past or present, warrant careful scrutiny. Such claims may themselves be the product of the nation-building process in (Greek) Macedonia.

Contradictory testimonies and "hidden transcripts of resistance" highlight the importance of extended local ethnographic fieldwork and the solicitation of narrative accounts of the past. Such research methodology may reveal details that question broad or universalizing claims or disclaimers which may be given in response to direct, sound-bite-style questions from interviewers practicing hit-and-run methodologies. Consider the life histories of "Paskhalina," an elderly Assiros woman who on three separate occasions told me the story of her childhood during the Balkan Wars. Paskhalina and I often talked about her memories of youth and of farming techniques, but we especially discussed the Balkan Wars, for she had been born in 1906 in the village of Ambar-Koy in the Kukush (Kilkis) area. I first interviewed Paskhalina at her home, in the presence of her relatives, during my first session of fieldwork in Assiros in 1988. She spoke with me at some length, offering a detailed personal account of the misfortunes of her family. The following account represents a composite of that story, because the topics she covered were not necessarily discussed in the sequence presented below. I recount her narratives here at some length because their rather rich ethnographic detail may be of interest and use to other scholars engaged in comparative research.

THE FIRST LIFE-HISTORY OF PASKHALINA, "THE BULGARIAN"

In Ambar-Koy, Paskhalina's father had been a sharecropper who worked the land of the Turkish owner and received half of the crop. She also remembered that they had buffalo there whose skins they used to scrape with razors. When they later moved to Guvezna they had buffalo and sheep as well, but by that time they had become very poor. Paskhalina's father used to come to Guvezna very often to buy groceries and other provisions. He had good credit with the Guvezna grocers. The people in Guvezna, Paskhalina claimed, understood "Bulgarian." They were very friendly when they used to go to Ambar-Koy to buy the village's cereal crop or to marry their women. After the Balkan Wars Paskhalina's family moved to Guvezna.

Pashkalina remembered the day the battle took place [she was referring to the Battle of Kilkis on 21 July 1913 which found the Greeks victorious over the Bulgarians]. It was a day like all others when disaster struck, she said. Her mother prepared bread dough in the morning and covered it to allow it to rise. That's when the cannons started firing. Her brother and her sister had gone out to harvest the wheat fields, while she and her parents had stayed at home. The Bulgarian army picked up her brother and sister, separated during the battle, and took them to Bulgaria when the army retreated. Paskhalina and her parents fled. While the cannons were still firing above their house, she and her parents packed some belongings, loaded their animals, and left for Serbia. There they had a difficult time. The people did not want them, and soon they returned to this area. They had only a donkey, Paskhalina remembered, and they looked like beggars. When they returned, they found their village in ashes.

Her mother's relatives were in Guvezna. She had a sister called Dono [a Slavic name] who married a man in Guvezna. Her mother's brother was also in Guvezna. He had learned how to be a shoemaker in Thessaloniki and opened a store in Guvezna. He too married a woman from Guvezna. Her father also had some acquaintances here because he used to visit the Guvezna shops when he purchased the family's supplies. In addition, his sister had married a Guvezna man called Apostolakoudhis. They were well-accepted in Guvezna, rented a house, and the villagers supported them.

Paskhalina's two siblings remained in Bulgaria. After many years one of their neighbors in Assiros told them that his brother received a letter from Paskhalina's brother in Bulgaria. That's how Paskhalina was reunited with her siblings. In 1957 her sister visited Assiros and after that they kept exchanging letters. Paskhalina wrote in Greek, but her sister could only answer in Bulgarian [i.e., she knew no Greek]. The sister, however, knew a man in Bulgaria who was originally from Kastoria [in western Greek Macedonia, near the Albanian border], and he translated those letters into Bulgarian for her. Her sister had married a man from the area around Kilkis. Paskhalina's brother married a Bulgarian woman and had many children. Paskhalina met them all when she visited Sofia in 1960 and again in 1970. She said that she could not understand the language of her Bulgarian relatives. She claimed that they spoke something equivalent to the *katharevousa* form of Greek.[35] She was happy to see her brother again at that time, because he later died. Paskhalina cried when she remembered her mother, Stoino [a Slavic name], who used to work at the harvest and take a break in isolation from the others in order to cry for her lost children.

Paskhalina went to school in Guvezna and there she learned Greek. Her first day in school was St. Dimitrios' Day, the 26th of October, when the spring grazing cycle came to an end.[36] She remembered asking what *kalimera* ("good morning") meant. While she was in school she was very afraid because the other children used to threaten her, saying that they would slaughter her and her people. The teacher also called her by the nickname of *Voulgharoudha* or "little Bulgarian girl." Paskhalina remembered that for many years everyone called her "Paskhalina the little Bulgarian girl." She said that throughout most of her time in school, the other girls refused to play with her.

In Guvezna, her family was very poor. They rented a house close to the church from a woman who was also "a Bulgarian." Her father was a *dhoulos* or slave in the fields of the wealthy Voukinas, Halepis, and Apostolakoudhis households. He used oxen to plough their fields. He also took the village's calves out to graze. Paskhalina's family received some land after the 1929 land distribution (see chapter 6).

Paskhalina remembered that she worked hard as a young girl in a tobacco workshop. She also took care of a small boy. She preferred to work there because she received free food. Her mother worked in the harvest, but her family was always in debt. They used to buy their groceries on credit. After the wheat harvest, they would start hoeing the vines, and after the vines they would collect the fava beans. Their work never ended. Paskhalina married a Guvezna man in 1925 when she was nineteen years old. He was relatively poor, but his family had good connections with the local *tsorbadjidhes*. Her cousin from her mother's brother's family initiated the matchmaking (*proksenio*).

Later, in the 1960s, there was an incident which upset Paskhalina so much that she finally took the case to court in Langadhas. One of her female neighbors was from Palehora and she called Paskhalina "Voulgharoudha" ("the Bulgarian"), one day. This occurred despite the fact that Paskhalina had told the woman in the past not to call her "a Bulgarian." Along with her to the court she brought two witnesses. Paskhalina appeared in front of the district attorney in Langadhas and told him that she was not Bulgarian. She showed him her Greek identification card and she also told him that if she were Bulgarian her son would not have been able to join the Greek Air Force [the most prestigious body of the Greek armed forces where those with the right political connections can send their children.] She insisted that she did not want the people to call her "Bulgarian." The district attorney recommended to the woman from Palehora that she not do it again. Paskhalina was always proud to recount this story.

The second time I called upon Pashkalina she was ill in bed after suffering a fall, and her relatives thought she was dying. I brought her a small gift of biscuits, which she quietly hid beneath her pillow. We spoke only briefly. To the astonishment of everyone, Paskhalina recovered, and when I visited her again, in the garden of her house, there were several other people present, including members of her immediate family. During that interview we returned again to the events of her childhood, and her account was basically the same as that she had presented during our first meeting. I also asked her about kinship terms in "her language" (see table 7).

I last spoke with Paskhalina on a fourth occasion during the summer of 1991, when I called on her alone at home. I had reviewed my notes on our previous interviews, and hoped to clarify several points, particularly details relating to the dispersal and flight of her natal family. Stories of the Bulgarian army abducting children to Bulgaria are often heard in Greece, and I wanted to explore any traditionalizing in her account and perhaps to flush out any hidden transcripts. When I arrived, she bade me to sit across her bed, after she again hid under her pillow the new biscuits I brought. She preferred not to go out into the courtyard, she said, when the weather was hot. She was visibly distressed about something, and spoke to me quite frankly of her ailing health. She was then in her early eighties, and lived with her youngest son and his family. During our conversation, I raised the questions that her previous accounts had provoked in my mind. In response, she recounted her story for me once again, only this time with significant alterations in certain details. I asked Paskhalina why her previous accounts had differed from this third version. She replied that all these years she had been afraid to tell the truth, for fear of recriminations.

THE OTHER LIFE HISTORY OF PASKHALINA, "THE BULGARIAN"

Paskhalina remembered her date of birth because it was written in a registry, which was kept by the Bulgarians since Ambar-Koy had been under their influence. Paskhalina spoke "Bulgarian" when she was growing up in Ambar-Koy. But the "Bulgarian" she spoke, she claimed, is not the same as the Bulgarian spoken by her relatives who now live in Bulgaria. Paskhalina told me that she met a man in Veroia and they spoke the same language. They communicated without any problem. Paskhalina also communicated well with the people from Liti.

The village [of Ambar-Koy] had a Bulgarian church and a Bulgarian school. It was the Greek army that burnt her village and not the Bulgarians [as she had claimed in her earlier versions]. Her whole family had fled to "a Bulgarian village inside Serbia [*ena Voulghariko horio mesa stin Servia*]," where they were begging for bread. Her oldest brother and sister stayed there, as they did not want to return to Greece. The rest of the family were ashamed to tell the truth of this story, and began to weave a tale that those children had gone out to work the harvest while the rest of the family had remained in the village. This is how they were able to account for their family's separation: they claimed her brother and sister were abducted by the Bulgarian army. Later Paskhalina learned of a miller in Ambar-Koy who was from the village of Volvot (Nea Sanda), also in the Kilkis District, and who was an officer in the Greek Army. He confessed that he was responsible for burning the village, but said he was just obeying orders. Finding nothing of their home left, Paskhalina's family moved to Guvezna in search for a new home.

It was mainly her brother who did not want to return to Greece. As he and his sister were old enough to live on their own, they stayed in Serbia. In the village where they stayed, they worked as shepherds of the village herd (*agheli*). Then Paskhalina's sister walked all the way to Sofia, Bulgaria, and started working in the tobacco sorting plants there. Two of her father's brothers also stayed in Serbia. Most of the people of old Ambar-Koy are now in "Serbia," Paskhalina claimed, though some are in Bulgaria. She insisted there were no "Greeks" in Ambar-Koy.

Guvezna was called "Gostovo" in "her language." Paskhalina's father's last name in Ambar-Koy was Galtsanoff, but he later adopted a Greek surname. When Paskhalina's family returned to the area of Guvezna, they stayed in Palehora for a while, where another family from Ambar-Koy had also settled. Her family later came to Guvezna, but lived in fear because the policeman came often and told them to leave. Despite their hard work, Paskhalina's family had many problems in Guvezna because they were considered "Bulgarians." The police were always trying to kick them out. Her father's old business friends from the past now did not want them. They were really scared. At one point, they had to hide her father so he would not go to prison. The Guvezna villagers used to yell at them to go away.

They wanted to pitch a tent in the courtyard of the church but the villagers did not allow them. Paskhalina's father died of pneumonia in 1922.

Paskhalina's revised account is significant in several regards. It illustrated that Slavic-speaking inhabitants of Ambar-Koy had lived in relative peace, if not harmony, with Guveznans, even maintaining relationships of exchange with them prior to the national struggles of the twentieth century. The local economy was apparently well diversified. Like the villagers of Yianik-Koy (Dorkas) and Zarova (Nikopolis), the Slavic-speakers of Ambar-Koy had fled to Bulgaria or Serbia when violence and harassment in the Langadhas area escalated to intolerable levels. Although some remained in those countries, others such as Paskhalina returned to Greece, usually with assistance or support from kin, often matrilateral relatives and affines. But her last account to me also suggested that despite their conscious decision to return to Greece and to become Greek citizens, families like hers were treated by some as non-Greeks: scorned, ridiculed, harassed, and rejected. As late as the 1960s, some of her neighbors were still calling her "the Bulgarian" (*Voulgharoudha*), but by then Paskhalina was prepared to challenge them.

I felt honored that Paskhalina had developed enough trust in me to confide what she finally claimed to be the secret truth about her family. Her confidence was even more important from an ethnographic standpoint, as she had been one of only three Slavic-speaking women still alive in Assiros when I began my fieldwork there. During my first research session, one of those women, also from Ambar-Koy, had died before I was able to meet and interview her. The third I had been actively discouraged from interviewing and, on the one occasion when I did manage to schedule an appointment with her, it was canceled at the last minute with an apology that the *yiayia* was not feeling well. Nevertheless, I did learn a small part of those women's stories from other oral accounts that confirmed other testimonies I had heard regarding the years of the Macedonian Struggle: generally speaking, few local families were firm, loyal supporters of any national cause at the turn of the century. Most tended to go along with the interests of those who were most powerful or dominant at the moment, while trying to maintain a low profile. Some families, in fact, were even divided in the national orientation, support, or allegiance of their members. The Sanousis family, for example, had been sharecroppers on a Muslim *chiftlik* in the village of Sermetli (Fanari) of the Kukush district. Roughly half the family became supporters of the Bulgarian Exarchate, while the rest remained faithful to the Patriarchate. The latter were "drafted" by the Greek partisans, and moved first to Arakli (a

Slavic-speaking village close to Langadhas) and later to Guvezna. While pro-Exarchist members of the family eventually left for Bulgaria, the descendants of those who remained in Assiros discussed in detail the fact that they had relatives living in Bulgaria. For most of the interwar period and even after World War II, this Assiros family worked as "servants" (*douhlyi*) for the township elite and provided shepherds for the village's common herd (*agheli*; see chapter 6).

The terror of the Macedonian Struggle and the Balkan Wars had torn at the social fabric of the Guvezna market community, politicizing markers of identity and creating new divisions among the local population. The diplomatic settlements that marked the conclusion of those hostilities did not, however, resolve the larger "Macedonian Question." The years that followed witnessed voluntary and involuntary migration across the new state borders that came to divide the region. But the creation of a Greek Macedonia was a longer, more protracted process that continued well into the second half of the twentieth century (see part II).

AFTERMATH

The Treaty of Bucharest, signed on 10 August 1913, marked the end of the Second Balkan War. Under its terms, the region of Macedonia was partitioned between the kingdoms of Greece, Bulgaria, and Serbia. Greece received roughly half (51 percent) of the region, Serbia obtained just over one-third (34 percent), and Bulgaria a little less than 15 percent (Vakalopoulos 1988a:235). Yet administrative partition did not solve the "Macedonian Problem." Hostile incidents persisted throughout the region, both during the First World War and in the years following. As Tsanoff, a Bulgarian contemporary, put it: "No matter what boundary line might be drawn between Greece and Bulgaria . . . some Greeks will still be left in Bulgaria and some Bulgarians would be left in Greece" (Tsanoff 1919:xi).

Following World War I,[37] international diplomats had hoped that the Minority Treaty (10 September 1919) and the Treaty of Neuilly (27 November 1919) would settle lingering problems of the unresolved Macedonian issue, particularly through conventions governing a voluntary exchange of populations between Greece and Bulgaria. A significant portion of the Slavic-speaking population of central Greek Macedonia departed for Bulgaria at that time, declaring they "felt Bulgarian" (Sarandis 1987:35).[38] After the Treaty of Neuilly, some 46,000 Greeks left Bulgaria to resettle in Greek Macedonia, while 92,000 Slavic-speakers from Macedonia moved to Bulgaria (Pearson 1983:104). By 1920, there had been an influx of no less than 126,000 new immigrants with Greek national consciousness to Greek Macedonia (Kyriakidis 1941–52).[39]

Despite the exchange of populations, fighting continued sporadically in border areas until 1924. The Politis-Kalfoff Protocol (signed by Greece and Bulgaria on 24 March 1924) was to provide for the protection of the Greek minority in Bulgaria and the Bulgarian minority in Greece, but after the intervention of Serbia the protocol was never enforced.[40] Later the same year, the League of Nations pronounced its position that there was no Slavic-speaking minority population left in northern Greece. The basis upon which such conclusions were drawn remains unclear, but its repercussions were great. It signaled an end to the Great Powers' mediation of ethnic and national conflict in Macedonia, and permitted Greece as well as Bulgaria and Serbia to proceed with national assimilation and amalgamation programs.[41]

Having achieved sovereignty over the southern half of Macedonia, the Greek state undertook to transform regional and local administrative structures in order to integrate the region into the national economy and polity of Greece. New regulatory agencies and offices were established in rural communities, presenting local elites with new resources and structures of authority through which they could pursue their own economic and political interests while acting as local agents of the new state. Such developments were a key aspect of the protracted effort by Greek authorities to Hellenize their new frontier. They empowered certain families and individuals (with their own vested interests and agendas) to administer a series of state-sponsored initiatives, in such areas as economy and government, education and religion, policing and security, and ritual and culture. Their effect, if not intent, had been to create or raise the level of national consciousness and identity among the population of Greek Macedonia. Similar measures were adopted in Bulgaria and Serbia.

ETHNICITY IN THE (RE)MAKING
Constructing Nationality in Greek Macedonia

The cultural hegemony which Greek, Bulgarian, and Macedonian scholars have exercised in their respective nation-states regarding the Macedonian question has led to rather far-reaching (and sometimes far-fetched) assertions that Macedonia and its Ottoman era population have always been an integral part of the Greek, Bulgarian, or Macedonian nations that (or so their respective propagandists claim) have spanned the millennium.

Such arguments, as I have suggested in this part I, are not only theoretically, methodologically, and empirically flawed, but also tend to deteriorate into polemics rather than sustained critical scholarly studies.[42] They do not regard ethnicity (or even nationality for that matter) as a historical construct of specific time, place, and material context. But one must recognize ethnicity as an analytical concept, even in its popular usages. As such, it must be defined historically—not synchronically—and must be examined across the dimensions of time, space, and social organization.

In her influential work on Romania, Verdery (1983, 1991) has argued that ethnic identity, in general, is a "historically contingent social and cultural product" that emerges out of preexisting patterns of social interaction (Verdery 1983:14). She maintained, for example, that Saxon ethnicity emerged in the 1600s through the involvement of certain individuals in mercantile capitalism as both local manufacturers and short-distance traders (Verdery 1983:347).[43] Ethnicity is a fluid concept, however, subject to change as new economic conditions and political solidarities emerge. Any subsequent formation of a nationalist movement, *pace* Verdery, is dependent upon the degree of solidarity embodied in such collective identities, as well as on particular historical conditions of the moment. Yet in its polysemy, ethnicity may be a rather ambiguous or arbitrary identity that may mean different things to different people in different contexts and at different times. In Transylvania, group identities were national rather than ethnic because they emerged in the context of the social contradictions generated by nation-formation in the eighteenth and nineteenth centuries (Verdery 1983:16). When Transylvania became socialist, ethno-national antagonisms were suppressed as membership in different ethnic groups was collapsed into class membership.

In Guvezna, what scholars might term ethnicity was an ambiguous, fluid mental construct that was based on perceived patterns of relations rooted in material conditions of life. These subjective notions later came to act as a catalyst in the formation of what one might distinguish as a national identity. The process was not necessarily conscious, for, as Marx (1977) once noted, people make their own history but not always as they please. As I noted earlier, the Assiriotes did not use terms such as "ethnicity" (*ethnotita*) and "nationality" (*ethnikotita*) in describing, expressing, or otherwise characterizing local notions of identity. Rather, it is often scholarly or literary discourse—and the popular uses made of it—that creates such categories. When the distinctions between the two concepts are not held clear, their muddled use can lead to protracted political consequences, an issue to which I will return in my Afterword.

Patterns of social interaction that contributed to material and spiritual life provided the structural context within which new nation-state-oriented institutions and agents endeavored to create a national identity among inhabitants of the area. This "national enlightenment" gave people a new definition, a new identity, and a common culture of collectivity, community, and commonality that included the political and ideational categories of Greek nation-state universalism—and primordial essentialism. This was not always a conscious process, but it was guided by both positive and negative material incentives.

With the territorial partition of Macedonia, Slavic-speakers of the region were transformed from a people without a nation to a transnational ethnic group. The existence or legitimacy of their cultural background has been challenged and denied by national and local elites in Greece, Bulgaria, and Serbia. In Guvezna, the common culture of the marketplace came to be replaced by a common national culture of coexistence forged through institutions such as the military, administrative bureaucracy, school, and church. Ethnicity or ethnic identity, whether self-ascribed or externally imposed, is very much a product of broader, historical social contexts; it is inextricably linked to nation-states, nationalism, and national identity (see Fried 1975). It is thus epistemologically questionable, in both theoretical and methodological terms, to approach ethnic-group formation (or dissolution) outside the context of local and regional conditions of life within which people produce their livelihood and reproduce themselves. The symbolic media through which identity, assumed or ascribed, is created, expressed, transformed, transmitted, and reproduced are themselves the products of historical processes and specific circumstances.

The evidence presented in part I suggests that during the late nineteenth century Guvezna had become a pro-Greek stronghold in the Langadhas basin, despite the cultural or "ethnic" diversity of its inhabitants. Bulgarian nationalist propaganda and Exarchist proselytizing made little or no advances into the community, despite the heavy activities of their agents in the area. The few Bulgarian sympathizers in Guvezna were obliged to move out and resettle in pro-Exarchist villages in the basin, while other families, Patriarchate loyalists or those with a Greek national orientation, sought refuge in communities such as Guvezna. The local Christian notables of the village—the merchants, priests, and teachers in particular—were very particular about whom they allowed to stay in Guvezna. As one Assiriotis said, "Many bad people came to Guvezna, but they were forced to leave."

Religious affiliation and national orientation became a sort of litmus test applied to local residents. The turn-of-the-century national struggles

136 / CHAPTER FOUR

in Macedonia for "enlightenment" and "liberation" politicized religious ascriptions with a new national-oriented content. Identity as a member of the Orthodox Christian *Rum millet* of the Muslim Ottoman Empire had lost much of its significance, as categories such as Patriarchist and Exarchist, *Ellines* and *Voulgharyi,* Greek and Bulgarian came to be the principal poles around which local constructs of identity were redefined. It is, I believe, both theoretically and empirically unsound to speak of the inhabitants of Macedonia at the turn of the century as ethnic groups on their way to a natural development into national groups (cf. Smith 1987). They may have ended up as members of national groups, but the assumptions embedded in such naturalistic perspectives tend to essentialize latter-day categories of ethnic or national identity and to project them backward in time. The Christian population of Macedonia in the late nineteenth century had conceived of themselves and their neighbors in many different ways, as much in terms of occupational livelihood, economic status, and marital ties as by language, ritual, or religion. People undoubtedly thought about their social, economic, or political interests; wealthy or powerful local Christian notables (*tsorbadjidhes*) arguably had attained a conscious recognition of themselves as a local interest group. But these distinctions, and their markers of difference, focused not on ethnicity but on socioeconomic status and a family's material conditions of life. Boundaries were permeable and political loyalties often shifted.

The development of national identity was no natural stage in social evolution but rather a product of human agency, of both conscious design and unconscious reaction. Bulgarian agents, it was said in Assiros, used to bribe villagers with "cans filled with gold coins" in order to entice them away from the Patriarchate. In their propaganda, they promised liberation from the "double yoke" of Ottoman and Patriarchate oppression and taxation. Macedonian autonomists had also had an active presence in the area, although they generally lacked the institutionally organized financial, propaganda, and military resources of the Greek Patriarchists and Bulgarian Exarchists. But Greek mercantile interests, education, national propaganda, and armed partisan activities eventually proved dominant in this national struggle.

In the years following 1913, the inhabitants of Greek Macedonia underwent a homogenization of their nascent national consciousnesses, a process strongly conditioned by a dramatic restructuring of rural class relations at the local level. In 1914, Paskhalina "the Bulgarian" entered the Guvezna school as a monolingual Slavic speaker. Although during most of her school years the other female students refused to play with her, Paskhalina maintained that she had enjoyed school. It was a forum of conversion and transformation. Having entered school as a "Bulgarian," Paskhalina graduated as a Greek. Yet stigmas continued to follow her throughout the twentieth century. Indeed, as part II will show, many of the tensions and cleavages that ripped asunder cultural cohabitation in late-nineteenth-century Macedonia found new expressions of difference and solidarity with the advent of Greek rule.

GALLERY

Old Ottoman house in Mavrorahi. Photo by Maria Karakasidou.

Visiting in the Mavrorahi *Kafenion*, June 1988. Photos by Maria Karakasidou.

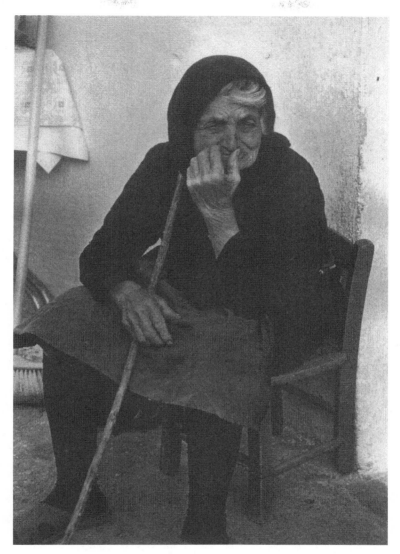

An elderly Pontic refugee in Mavrorahi. Photo by Maria Karakasidou.

Old Yiannis in Mavrorahi, June 1988. Photo by Maria Karakasidou.

Prefabricated house for refugees in Examili

At the AGNO milk-
weighing station in
Examili

An old mansion in Assiros,
ca. 1920

Two local Assiriotisses

An old man from Palehora

Local Assiros elderly

After family division, even the yard of the family house was divided.

Procession in the wheat fields, St. George's day, 1989. Photo by Maria Karakasidou.

Preparing the *Kourbani* food on
Prophet Elias day, 1989

Dancing with the flag at an Assiros
wedding procession. Photo by
Maria Karakasidou.

PART II

CLASS REFORMATION AND NATIONAL HOMOGENIZATION

*Processes of Consolidation
and Change Following the
Advent of Greek Rule*

5

CROSSING THE MOVING FRONTIER

Group Formation and Social Closure in the Era of Refugee Settlement, 1922–1940

If Greece exists today as a homogeneous *ethnos,* she owes this
to [the Asia Minor Catastrophe]. If the hundreds of thousands
of refugees had not come to Greece, Greek Macedonia would
not exist today. The refugees created the national
homogeneity of our country.

Augustinos Kandiotis, *Metropolite of Florina*

By the end of the Balkan Wars in 1913, the Greek state had secured
sovereignty over a large part of the region of Macedonia, including
the Langadhas basin and the market village of Guvezna. International
politics and diplomacy played a central role in reconstituting the cultural
and ethnic makeup of the region and in consolidating Greek sovereignty
over it. The treaties that ended the Balkan Wars redrew international
borders in the region and most of its pro-Bulgarian Slavic-speakers began
to move north to Bulgaria, a trend heightened after the defeat of Bulgaria
in World War I. Bulgaria, defeated by Greece and Serbia in the Second
Balkan War, had been allied with Germany in World War I. Finding itself
on the losing side of that devastating war, and accused of atrocities during
its occupation of parts of Macedonia and Thrace,[1] Bulgaria not only lost
Thrace (and its access to the Aegean coast) in the postwar settlement, but
also saw its claims to Macedonia come to an end.[2]

The Treaty of Neuilly (November 1919) at the conclusion of World
War I solidified Greece's presence in that part of Macedonia it had acquired after the Balkan Wars. The decision of Greek Liberal Party Prime
Minister Eleftherios Venizelos to align the country with the allies, in opposition to the king and pro-royalist political forces that had sought to
ally Greece with Germany, had brought the country these new territorial
gains.[3] Yet Clogg (1979:112) has argued that as early as 1915, Venizelos
has been "prepared to cede newly won territory in Macedonia to the
Bulgarians, if necessary" in order to acquire parts of Asia Minor, particu-

larly its Aegean coast and important commercial centers such as Smyrna (Izmir).

The years following a convention for the voluntary exchange of nationals between Greece and Bulgaria in November 1919 were marked by out-migration, displacement, and deportation of Slavic-speakers from Greece (Jelavich 1983:136; Ladas 1932).[4] Despite this substantial exodus, which incidentally did not occur in Guvezna, a heterogeneous population of Slavic-speakers, Greeks, Turks, Vlahs, Sarakatsan pastoralists, *Roma* gypsies and others remained *in situ* in what was now Greek Macedonia. Yet the Treaty of Lausanne (July 1923) following the Asia Minor War of 1921–1923, and the subsequent bilateral exchange of nationals between Greece and Turkey, became a critical development in the reconstitution of the region's ethnic tapestry. These military adventures and diplomatic maneuverings resulted in a profound restructuring of social relations in Macedonia. Nation-state borders were again redrawn, large numbers of people were forcibly uprooted from their homes, and new notions of identity and sentiments of commonality and difference were created in the process.

Liberal political leaders in post–World War I Greece, riding the crest of rising national sentiment, had rallied public support by championing the banner of the irredentist *Megali Idea,* a visionary quest that sought to restore to the Hellenes the glory that had been theirs in Byzantium. I will not address the factors leading up to the Asia Minor War here. Rather, I focus on the resettlement process which brought over a million Christian Orthodox refugees to the newly expanded Greek state, almost half of whom were settled in urban centers and rural areas of Greek Macedonia, including Guvezna. By exploring the saga of the refugees, the violence of their forced uprooting and "repatriation" (*epanapatrismos*) to Greece, as well as the resistance many encountered in communities where they eventually settled, such as Guvezna, I seek to highlight how their entry on the local scene and their struggle for interest representation became critical aspects in the emergence of a national culture of coexistence in Greek Macedonia. As I will show, refugee settlement had a profound impact on group amalgamation and national homogenization in Guvezna.

On the eve of refugee settlement in 1920, the rural Greek township (*kinotita*) of Guvezna had comprised the Guvezna village and the settlements of Palehora and Yeni-Koy (present-day Gnoina), and had been inhabited by 1,358 residents. With the arrival of refugee settlers after 1922, the administrative domain of the township underwent several significant changes. Between 1922 and 1928, the township population had more than doubled to 2,775 (see table 3). Two new villages, Examili and Krithia, both populated by recent Greek refugees from east Thrace (referred to as *Thrakiotes* or "Thracians"), were created in the western portion of Guvezna township. Meanwhile, refugees from the Pontos region of the Asia Minor Black Sea coast (known as *Pontyi* or Pontic Greeks) had settled in the hilltop hamlet of Mavrorahi (formerly the Otmanli *mahala* of Tzami), which by the late 1920s had lost its status as an autonomous settlement as its prized grazing lands were brought under the administrative control of Guvezna township.[5] By 1927, the settlement of Palehora had been permanently abandoned and most of its former inhabitants had moved over to Guvezna (ATA 1927). A dramatic development came in 1930 when the newly established refugee village of Krithia, along with nearby Gnoina (formerly Yeni-Koy), withdrew from the township following a protracted and bitter struggle with the Guvezna *tsorbadjidhes* elite, leaving the township with its present administrative configuration of the villages of Guvezna, Examili, and Mavrorahi.

The refugee settlement, which also included the sedentarization of Sarakatsan pastoralists in various townships of Greek Macedonia, had major ramifications on local life and economy, particularly in the realms of occupational specialization, divisions of labor, patterns of land tenure, and social stratification. It was also during the 1920s that Guvezna was renamed as "Assiros," after the suggestion of the well-respected teacher, Garoufalidis. The name Assiros replaced that of Guvezna in official township documents beginning in July 1927, but many local inhabitants continued to use the old name of the settlement for some years thereafter.

By 1922, many Ottoman or Turkish Muslims were still *in situ* in Greek Macedonia. But their conditions of life had changed dramatically from those of the turn of the century. The crisis facing landowning Muslims there had been growing, and many sought to sell their property holdings rather than risk their ultimate abandonment or expropriation. As this part II will show, from 1913 through the refugee settlement of 1922 and until the large-scale land redistribution in 1929, the powerful and influential Christian *tsorbadjidhes* families that had come to dominate Guvezna in the late Ottoman period progressively enlarged their resource base, purchasing or simply enclosing Muslim properties as their own.

Formal incorporation into Greece in 1913 also brought new institutions of local government to rural communities in Greek Macedonia. In Guvezna, the Christian notables who had sided with Greek partisans during the Macedonian Struggle quickly maneuvered themselves into these new local-level administrative positions within the bureaucratic structure of the Greek nation-state. The influence many had long exercised over local community affairs took new dimensions with the addition of formal regulatory powers backed by the coercive sanctions of the Greek state. Members of those notable families acquired official status as township administrators, becoming grass-root agents of the state (see chapter 6). Acting in such capacities, they pursued their own interests while mediating those of their constituencies and the state bureaucratic apparatus alike. As employment patrons and administrative authorities, affines and ritual kin, the Guvezna *tsorbadjidhes* enjoyed diffuse influence over other local families. This enabled them to enhance their own economic power and social standing in the community while also helping to effect the cultivation of a common national consciousness among these new citizens of Greece (see chapter 7). In part II of this work, I follow the process by which these families gradually transformed themselves into a dominant ruling class, despite their political or other differences. Although the institutions of school and church were important vehicles in the creation of a common Greek national ideology among the diverse groups inhabiting the area, the local *tsorbadjidhes* played a key role as local administrative agents in that process.

IRREDENTISM, CATASTROPHE, AND REPATRIATION
The Fruits of Nationalism

In 1921, the young Greek nation-state was drawn into its fourth armed conflict of the twentieth century: a war against Turkey for possession of Constantinople (Istanbul) and major commercial centers such as Smyrna (Izmir) on the Aegean coast of Asia Minor with large Greek-speaking populations. By that time, the Ottoman Empire had collapsed and the new nation-state of Turkey was taking form under the leadership of Kemal Ataturk. This secular nation-building movement not only included reforms in language, dress, and other cultural aspects, but also rendered Islamic faith as a secondary concern in state administration. These and other developments led to a confrontation between clashing nationalisms. On the one hand had been Greek nationalist forces harboring visions of new borders and a larger, greater nation-state; on the other, had been those in Turkey engaged in their own efforts to construct an imagined community of the Turkish nation.

The intervention of certain major European powers, particularly the British, contributed to both the commencement and conclusion of hostilities between Greece and Turkey.[6] Following initial victories by Greek forces in Asia Minor, their campaign soon floundered into a crushing defeat. Its irredentist vision in shambles, the Greek government returned to the negotiating table. Under League of Nations sponsorship, a conference convened at Lausanne, Switzerland, in 1923, attended by Greek Prime Minister Venizelos. The resulting Treaty of Lausanne (July 1923) yet again redrew the borders between Greece and Turkey, dividing the region of Thrace into eastern (Turkish) and western (Greek) areas,[7] and set forth the terms under which Greece and Turkey agreed to repatriate their respective "nationals."[8] Treaty negotiators had used religious, rather than ethno-national, criteria to determine who should stay and who should be relocated.

The massive population exchange that followed involved the influx of roughly 1.5 million Orthodox Christian refugees from Turkey to Greece and the exodus of almost 350,000 Muslims from Macedonia and Thrace to Turkey (Hirschon 1989:8).[9] The procedure was executed quickly, with minimal planning, and no substantial regulatory supervision. As a result, it took place under harsh or even appalling conditions in many areas. Hundreds of thousands of refugees were brought by boat to the ports of Thessaloniki and Piraeus, presenting Greek authorities with an immediately pressing problem of immense proportions. Those refugees who had been fortunate enough to bring wealth with them to Greece had relatively fewer difficulties settling in urban centers and re-establishing businesses or commercial enterprises. But most of these "repatriates" had lost their possessions, their savings, and in many cases even their family members. Homeless, jobless, and hungry, their plight presented a threat to the political stability of the Greek state, which already had been weakened by the draining burden of war and by factionalism between the Liberal and the pro-royalist Populist political parties (see below).

Searching for locations in which to settle this mass of humanity, the Greek government looked north to the newly incorporated lands of Macedonia, which still had a relatively low population density and an abundance of lands that once had been owned by the now departing Muslims. Mavrogordatos (1983b:185–86) maintained that, by 1930, 90 percent of the 578,844 refugees settled in rural Greece were concentrated in the regions of Macedonia and western Thrace. Thus Macedonia, Greece's newly acquired second "breadbasket" (after Thessaly), became the depository for East Thracian (*Thrakiotes*), Pontic (*Pontyi*), and Asia Minor (*Mikrasiates*) refugees. A large proportion of these refugees had been farmers and their resettlement prompted the enactment of land reform, long debated at the national level, throughout Greek Macedonia (see chapter 6).

The settlement of refugees, whose Greek identity had been tempered by the fire of war and (often) involuntary eviction from their natal homes, and the land reform campaigns that followed, added an important new dimension to Greek nation-building efforts in Macedonia. It contributed to redefinitions in perceptions of identity and to new social categories such as "local" or "indigenous" ([en]dopyi), as discussed below. During the interwar years, the Langadhas basin of central Greek Macedonia became a social field through which a highly fluid refugee population passed in search of an appropriate or accommodating place to settle. Although they had come from diverse origins, the refugees of the 1920s generally possessed an identification with the national collectivity of the Hellenes strengthened through their traumatic experiences of stigmatization, victimization, and expulsion from Turkey. Yet they were often unwelcomed and treated with contempt by those among whom they sought to settle in rural communities of Greek Macedonia, such as Guvezna.

REDEFINING IDENTITY THROUGH NATIONALISM

The story of the refugees has become a national epic in Greek culture and history. The ordeals endured, the desperation faced, and the strength demonstrated in the face of circumstances beyond their control was by no means unique to these refugees. Yet their saga has remained obscure to most Europeans, a forgotten or often ignored event in a corner of the southern Balkans. Still, it was there that nations and nationalisms explored some of the dialectical extremes on which their principles are based. While there is overwhelming concern among Euro-American politicians and diplomats over what nationalism has brought to Eastern Europe in recent years, many seem unaware of the fact that nation-building processes are a *longue durée* in which tragic and heroic acts become epic sagas, and "Others" are often depicted in unflattering stereotypes or as vicious enemies who have oppressed and hindered the liberation of a nation.

Even in the 1990s, the subject of this forced exodus of Christians from Turkey continues to raise strong emotions among Greeks, both refugees and nonrefugees alike. Consider, for example, the Pontics who had settled in the Otmanli *mahaladhes* (later renamed Mavrorahi) of Guvezna/Assiros township and who had endured a less than glorious "repatriation" to their new national homeland. In their accounts to me of those experiences, Pontics in Mavrorahi constructed heroic tales of their own odysseys and recounted with tears the harsh circumstances involved in repatriation, when they passed through fire and death at the hands of "barbaric" Turks who had killed their siblings, raped their women, and looted their belongings. The experience proved difficult for many to comprehend, accustomed as they had been to peaceful coexistence with Muslims in the Black Sea area.

Having left their homes in the mountains of Pontos, these refugees had gone down to the city of Trapezous (Trebizond; see map 7), a regional port on the southern coast of the Black Sea that had been designated as their collection point. There they were crowded by authorities into the French Lyceum building, while details pertaining to their repatriation were settled by diplomats. Detained in cramped conditions with abysmal sanitation facilities, many fell sick, and those who died were quickly buried in mass graves.[10] Those who survived the detention were eventually summoned to board ships waiting in the harbor to ferry them to Greece.

Disembarking in Thessaloniki, these Pontic refugees recalled having been shocked to see Greek gendarmes (most of whom had come from "Old Greece") beating up departing Turks. Once again, they were temporarily quartered in large rooms in a high school where again many fell ill, this time with typhus and meningitis. And once again, those who died were buried in mass graves. Some of the survivors jointly employed men to survey the countryside for suitable places to settle. One such scout returned to Thessaloniki to report to his group that a site had been located on a shrub-covered hillside at the northern rim of the Langadhas plain, not far from a village called Guvezna.[11]

Many *dopyi* resented the settlement of refugees in their communities, or initially regarded the refugees as somehow less Greek than themselves. Others considered them as total "Others" who had come to take away the lands they now claimed as theirs. Yet now the refugee saga is commonly used in Greece, by refugees and nonrefugees alike, as part of a national epic, as a forceful tool with which to decry the persecution of Greeks in general. They, too, now tell stories of refugee families having their homes looted of gold or of being robbed, beaten, raped, or killed as they boarded the vessels that would carry them to Greece. But the significance of the refugee settlement for the nation-building process in Greek Macedonia remains largely unappreciated. The Greek government reasserted its claims over the territory by encouraging and concentrating refugee settlement there. Through the Refugee Settlement Commission (RSC), the government provided each refugee family with a cow, a horse, an old Turkish house or a newly built home, timber with which to undertake construction and repair, and a temporary plot of land to cultivate.

It later implemented a land redistribution program to provide the refugees and other poor families of the region with enough land on which to subsist (see chapter 6). The only claim that refugee settlers had to the region was that they (too) regarded themselves as Greeks and, as part of the imagined community of the Hellenes, were entitled to a portion of the hereditary estate of the national clan, so to speak. Although some refugees did not speak Greek at the time of their arrival, their settlement in Macedonia, where the language issue recently had been of great political significance, added an important new dimension to local constructs of identity.[12] Moreover, many had brought with them to their new homeland oral traditions, crafts, dresses, songs, ceremonies, and symbols that differed from those of other inhabitants of multiethnic Greek Macedonia. Yet these refugees had been defined as Greeks by the national government as well as by international treaties, mainly on the basis of their religion. The overwhelming majority of refugees embraced this identity, but it was challenged or questioned by many inhabitants of northern Greece among whom they settled. Their integration within the culture and polity of the Greek nation-state became an integral part of the broader process of national enculturation among the population of Greek Macedonia.

The East Thracian, Pontic, and Asia Minor refugees had been Orthodox Christian families in another part of the Ottoman Empire, inhabiting the area around Constantinople, the northern and eastern shores of the Aegean Sea, the southern shores of the Black Sea, and the bulky highland plateau of Asia Minor. Some (such as the East Thracians) spoke Greek, while others (e.g., the Pontics) spoke a dialect thereof. Still others, such as the *Karamalidhes*, spoke Turkish but wrote it using a Greek script. Before their repatriation, some families had been grain merchants in their homelands, as my own Turkish-speaking ancestors had been, helping to feed the Black Sea and Constantinople grain trades with crops produced by Muslim and Christian agriculturalists alike. Others had been tobacco cultivators whose lives and livelihoods were oriented towards a different market. Still others had been herders, fishermen, artisans, mattress makers, and the like.

These families had lived a Christian "tradition" in Turkey, following the teachings and preachings of the Ecumenical Orthodox Patriarchate. In a manner of speaking, one of the few things that all these refugees shared was their common Christian Orthodox religion. Although they are often referred to as a single group, "refugees" (*prosfighes*), they came from various backgrounds with perceived significant cultural, ethnic, or regional distinctions, the remnants of which were still discernible in the early 1990s. During my fieldwork, I encountered a steady stream of jokes and stereotypes, many in poor taste, of the sort that are often directed towards other "races" (*ratses*), "nationals," or "ethnics." In Assiros, for example, local villagers ridiculed the ability of Pontic refugees in Mavrorahi to grow tobacco, claiming that when the Pontics saw tobacco for the first time they thought it was inverted lettuce. Even in the 1990s, tensions were still often expressed through the idiom of ethnic stereotyping, with Assiriotes calling the Pontic Greeks "stupid" shepherds who cannot speak Greek, while the Pontics claimed "true" Greek descent and labeled the Assiriotes as "Bulgarians" (see also Drettas 1985).[13]

It would, however, be equally mistaken to depict the refugees as a "pure" race of people descendant from ancient Greeks who had colonized the Aegean coast in antiquity or as pure-blood descendants of the Byzantines. Such claims are advanced not only by many refugees themselves but also some Greek scholars. Yet how likely was it that this so-called "race," whose alleged members often distinguished so many differences among themselves, had been kept "pure" through six hundred years or so of Ottoman rule? The fact is that terms such as "refugee," "Pontic," "Greek," "Christian," and "ancient" are all nation-like categories, inventive labels that subsume and obliterate a plethora of individual differences that constitute local culture and identity, which itself grows out of the production and reproduction of life. The source of such stereotypes, be they positive or negative, lay not in the realm of ethnicity per se, but rather in economic relations. The grazing lands of Otmanli, for example, were critical to power relations and social stratification in the township. After Pontic refugees occupied those coveted hills, the rhetoric of ethnic identity became a channel through which tensions and conflicts of material interest were expressed.

Refugees often referred to their place of origin as their "country" (*patridha*). It is not uncommon to hear such (former) refugees in Greece say, "In the *patridha*, we did such and such." In their *patridha*, the Christian inhabitants of Turkey had been a very diverse category of people who had constructed boundaries among themselves based on differences and regional distinctions in language, customs, and religious practices.[14] Hirschon (1989:5) has argued that such social boundaries were sometimes drawn even within particular locales despite apparent similarities among the population. Yet upon their arrival in Greece, many of these families shared a sense of commonality as *prosfighes* (refugees), resulting from the notion of displacement from their *patridha*, as well as a sense of solidarity born of the shared *pathos* and violence of their forced evacuation. Resettled in a hostile environment in the Yerania neighborhood in Athens, for example, refugees from Asia Minor grew increasingly vocal about their Greekness in order to legitimize their relocation (Hirschon 1990).

The collective refugee experience of repatriation to Greece was a dramatic rite of passage into the embrace of the young Greek state's national ideology. In an ironic twist of fate, these refugees were both the victims of nationalism as well as the unwitting agents of its legitimation. As Clogg (1979) put it,

> Although the exchange of populations necessarily occasioned a great deal of human misery. . . . it did ensure that Greece itself became an ethnically homogeneous society. . . . The result was that Greece was transformed into a country virtually without minority problems, by Balkan standards at least. (Clogg 1979:121).

Later, in the land redistribution campaigns that followed refugee settlement, the terms of their incorporation into Greece were negotiated and defined through local action, some of which was reminiscent of the violence that ravaged the region during the Macedonian Struggle and the Balkan Wars. While differences continued to exist, their idioms of expression were transformed by the new social conditions.

The refugees are still enshrined in much Greek historiography as exemplary victims of the persecution suffered by the Greek nation at the hands of its eternal enemy, the Turks. As Christians, they had sought refuge from the violence that had been done to them under the banners of Turkish nationalism and self-determination. The fact that many had not sought the wars that disrupted their lives, devastated their livelihoods, and killed their family members has often been ignored. Despite the chaos and violence, some had been reluctant to leave Turkey. Not all Greek communities in Turkey perished in flames as did Smyrna, the warships of the great nations of Europe sitting idly in the harbor as flame, sword, and shot ravaged the mass of humanity gathered on the waterfront. Some, such as the Pontics, had even sought to create their own nation-state (see Psomiades 1968). Yet reluctant or not, the refugees eventually boarded boats which "re"patriated them back "home" where they were "re"settled in an unfamiliar country amid an existing population that often feared or resented them.

Yet the term *patridha* was used by refugees in reference to the former homes in Asia Minor or East Thrace, and not to Greece, per se. In this sense, *patridha* may convey two very different symbolic connotations. It may refer to a physical homeland, from which people were obliged to emigrate. On the other hand, it may also embody the notion of a national collectivity and refer to a national homeland. The term "repatriation," therefore, merits the quotation marks that enclose it. For those whose sense of *patridha* had been focused on the lands and homes (outside of Greece) in which they had been born and raised, "depatriation" might in some cases have been a more appropriate characterization of their experiences. Yet the adoption or imposition of a national-based category of identity (one no doubt held by many but certainly not all refugees) defined the politically orchestrated and treaty-mandated population exchange as one of "repatriation" to a national homeland.

One of the greatest tragedies of nationalism is its tendency to censor history. The sufferings of one people are sometimes elevated to the status of a tragic epic of persecution which is then used to justify or to legitimize national struggle. Victims of nationalism become its martyrs, and their trials and tribulations are appropriated as poignant examples of national persecution. The victims of competing nationalisms (including so-called nation-less peoples who refuse to join an emerging national group) are often caricatured as villains or simply pass into oblivion, erased from historical memory as their alternative identities come to be regarded as anachronistic.

The horror of repatriation notwithstanding, Greek refugees were not the only victims of the Asia Minor Catastrophe. The hegemony of modern-day nationalism in Greece frequently precludes discussion of the similar plight of Muslim refugees who fled Greece (there are many similar epics of repatriation circulated in Turkey). Common perceptions of wealthy Turks oppressing poor, suffering Greeks during the Ottoman era are themselves little more than fictive stereotypes with political undertones. As indicated in part I, most of the Muslims of Ottoman Macedonia had been poor herders and sharecroppers rather than wealthy landowners or merchants. Indeed, many Muslim refugees were obliged to walk (some of them several hundred kilometers) to the Turkish border in 1922–23.[15] Many violent acts were committed by the Greek army and civilian population alike against Muslims evacuating the Langadhas area as well. Stories of such atrocities, including beatings, robberies, and even indiscriminate killings, were told by Assiros residents, both refugees and locals alike, who had witnessed the Muslim evacuation. Some European accounts of the Muslim exodus expressed similar horror.[16] Atrocities had not been limited to regular combatants in Macedonia; nor were the targets of such acts always men. While some Muslim women were regarded (or remembered) in Assiros as friends of the "Christians," others had been victims of crimes or cruel treatment. After the liberation of the region from Ottoman rule, for example, Muslim women in Guvezna were said to have been gathered together in the *aghora* and publicly ridiculed as they were forced to dance naked at gunpoint.

CATEGORIES, LABELS, AND GROUPS
Transforming Identity amid Cleavage and Tension

It was during the period of refugee settlement that the term *dopyi* or *endopyi* (*en*, "in" + *topos*, "place"; or "those in place"; local; indigenous) came into use throughout Greek Macedonia. It was, and still is, a term used to mark those who lived in the area prior to the arrival of the refugees. While in western Greek Macedonia it refers solely to Slavic-speakers (or *dopyi Makedhones*, as they call themselves) whose largely Slavic dialect is commonly called (*en*)*dopia*, in the Langadhas basin (*en*)-*dopyi* came to refer to all inhabitants of the region, including Greek-speakers, who had been *in situ* prior to the arrival of the refugees. In both cases, the term came to represent an invented tradition in the Hobs-bawmian sense, constructed in opposition to more recently arrived population cohorts. Adopted as a self-definition by the pre-refugee inhabitants of Guvezna/Assiros, it referred more to what they *were not*, rather than to what they actually *were*. It was a term that masked internal cleavages and differences among the "local" population, while implying a set of rights and claims to the territory vis-à-vis refugee newcomers. The term *endopyi* was itself a symbol of social and economic closure, an exclusive definition of nonrefugee group status which, most importantly, bridged cultural differences among Guvezna residents prior to refugee settlement.

Refugee settlement policy was formulated under the auspices of the League of Nations and administered through the Refugee Settlement Commission (*Epitropi Apokatastaseos Prosfighon*), established in 1924.[17] The trial settlement option permitted under Refugee Settlement Commission guidelines provided for much movement and relocation among the refugee population during the first few years following repatriation. Under the guidelines, newly arriving refugees were entitled to establish themselves in three different communities on a trial basis before they were required to make a decision on where to settle permanently. If they found no existing community appropriate, they could establish a new settlement themselves. Animosity between the pre-refugee population and the newcomers had been prevalent throughout Greek Macedonia, where conflicts over land became common in the 1920s (Mavrogordatos 1983a:76). With few exceptions, refugees settling in Guvezna/

Assiros township encountered a great deal of resentment and hostility to their presence from local inhabitants.

Indeed, the difficulties that confronted those who chose to settle permanently in the township were formidable. Economically marginalized and politically isolated, many refugee families had to endure social boycotting by the locals, who at best ignored their presence or at worst employed verbal abuse and physical harassment in an effort either to drive them away or to confine them to positions of economic and political dependency within local society. The land reforms and redistribution campaigns proposed by the government for the region of Greek Macedonia were perceived by many local landowners as a threat to their designs or claims on former Muslim or Turkish properties. Yet the politics of refugee self-determination, and the violence of confrontation and resistance, played a critical role in the restructuring of local community organization and the development of new identities, solidarities, and sentiments of difference. In Guvezna/Assiros township, the experiences of East Thracian and Pontic refugees in Krithia, Examili, and Mavrorahi offer very different perspectives on the dynamics of local-refugee politics during the interwar period. In Guvezna, there had developed a Greek-literate and Greek-oriented *dopyi tsorbadjidhes* elite by the time the refugees arrived. In many communities elsewhere in Greek Macedonia, *dopyi* "locals" largely came to be politically subjugated by incoming refugees who quickly assumed administration of many townships.[18]

In 1922, a sizeable cohort of refugee families from various places in East Thrace and Asia Minor came through Guvezna village in search of a suitable site on which to settle. Their arrival was not welcomed by the Guveznans, who directed their hostility particularly against the Asia Minor group, composed of some twenty families. The township president at the time had been Velikas, a large-scale stockbreeder and landowner, who soon instigated the departure of the Mikrasiates families by providing them with food for a week and ordering them to leave.[19] Some Assiros villagers claimed they had allowed the East Thracian refugees to stay because of their lighter skin color.

Coming from two different towns in East Thrace, these refugee settlers had arrived either individually or with members of their immediate family. Constituting more of a diverse social aggregate than a coherent "group," few shared a sense of common descent or common identity other than the fact that they were Thrakiotes refugees. Perhaps this lack of solidarity fostered perceptions among Guvezna's leaders that the refugees posed little threat to their political dominance. Those who stayed in Guvezna were assigned abandoned homes in the *Matziria* section of the village,[20] physically segregated from the village proper and its central *aghora* (see map 4).[21] In addition to their physical isolation, the refugees were also socially marginalized in village life and faced a great deal of resistance to their presence.[22]

Although refugees received relief assistance from the Refugee Settlement Commission, few local villagers assisted in providing food or shelter or in demonstrating compassion for their plight. East Thracian refugees in Assiros, for example, recounted a tale of a rich local miller, who responded to a refugee's plea for some food by asking for the refugee's daughter in return. The miller was said to have been punished by God when both his children died the next day. His avarice and lust for the helpless girl were described as acts intolerable to their common Christian Orthodox God. Hungry and poor, Thrakiotes refugees settling in Guvezna/Assiros township began working as harvest laborers for local landowners, or as shepherds for large herdowners, thus providing the local class of notables with valuable labor at critical times.

A separate contingent of East Thracian refugees also arrived in the Guvezna area in 1922 from a town called Krithia on the Kallipolis (Gallipoli) Peninsula of the Dardanelles in East Thrace.[23] Searching for a suitable place in which to settle, they initially selected the former *chiftlik* of Palehora. Yet *dopyi* villagers in nearby Drimos had coveted the Palehora lands and had hoped to acquire them after the Muslims departed. It was alleged that inhabitants of Drimos cut off the water supply to Palehora from a point upstream, provoking a crisis that obliged the refugees to abandon the former *chiftlik* and to relocate yet again. They finally settled in a nearby area, just north of Gnoina, the former *wakf chiftlik* of Yeni-Koy. There, homes were built for them with corrugated tin roofs, and they named their new community "Krithia," after their former town in East Thrace.

As the Gnoina *chiftlik* had been part of Guvezna township, the new village of Krithia built upon its lands was likewise designated as part of the township (ATA decree D. 12.28.1926). Prior to receiving land in the late 1920s redistribution, the refugees of Krithia had few resources. Most lived by cutting firewood and shrub (*pournaria*) from nearby Deve Karan mountain, which they sold in Drimos or Langadhas. Nevertheless, local authorities in Guvezna/Assiros almost immediately sought to subordinate the new settlement as an important local tax and revenue base for the township. Tax rolls from 1927 indicate that even prior to the land-redistribution campaign refugee farmers in Krithia already paid nearly one-fifth (19.1 percent) of the total agricultural tax in the township, a burden second only to that of Guvezna/Assiros itself (ATA 1927).[24]

Tax politics and other conflicts with residents of Guvezna/Assiros led to growing hostilities between inhabitants of the two villages. There were reports of Krithia herds and herders being chased off grazing lands, of families being forced off cultivated fields, of fistfights, and even shootings. Following a protracted struggle, also marred by violent incidents over land conflicts, Krithia in 1930 seceded from Assiros township and became an independent *kinotita* that included the small settlement of nearby Gnoina (ATA decree D 2.5.1930).[25] Slavic-speaking *dopyi* in Gnoina, who unlike the Guveznans had no Greek-literate elite, came to be dominated by the refugee newcomers. During the formal schism of 1930, the Krithiotes had demanded the eastern border of their township follow the public highway near Guvezna/Assiros. The Assiriotes, on the other hand, had long coveted the lands of the former Palehora *chiftlik* to the west of the road. Although Krithia eventually did win its independence from Guvezna/Assiros, the latter retained control over most of the disputed land and hostility between the two settlements continued.[26]

Yet still another group of Thrakiotes arrived in the Guvezna/Assiros area during the resettlement era and established a second new village in the township: Examili, named after a village in East Thrace from which some of these refugees had come.[27] During the first few years after establishing their new village, the settlers of Examili had governed themselves. Yet having come from different places of origin and different social backgrounds (like the Thrakiotes who settled in Guvezna), and not all having arrived on the local scene at the same moment, the East Thracian refugee families of Examili lacked the cohesion and solidarity of the Thrakiotes in Krithia. They were divided amongst themselves by perceptions of difference from the time of their settlement together. The political leaders of Guvezna/Assiros exploited these divisions, or so the inhabitants of Examili maintained, playing rival alliances or factions of refugees against each other.[28] In this manner, they were able to incorporate Examili within the township and to retain jurisdiction over village lands without much difficulty. This being despite the fact that one faction of Examili residents had sought to incorporate their village with Krithia after the latter had seceded from the township.[29]

In 1924 the RSC undertook to construct houses and roads for refugee families in Krithia and Examili, as elsewhere in Greek Macedonia where refugees did not occupy former Turkish homes. These new villages were designed and built on a grid-like pattern, and consisted of identical houses made from prefabricated brick and wood panels manufactured by a German company.[30] These two new settlements were situated near the western frontier of Guvezna township and were quickly integrated in the extensive commercial economy of the Langadhas basin, as subsequent conflicts over grazing lands during the 1920s and 1930s suggest (see chapter 6). Few Examili villagers, it was said, missed the Tuesday Langadhas market. The road leading to the town, many of them maintained, was jammed all day long with an endless chain of people, carts, and donkeys.

Between 1922 and 1925, some thirty-five families of Pontic refugees came to settle in the main Otmanli *mahala* of Tzami, which (in those years) had an ample water supply. Although Otmanli had at one point become a self-governing community, its autonomous status was abolished in 1925 by a government directive (ATA, 1925, Directive #D 14-4-1925). Pontic refugees in Mavrorahi (formerly Tzami) claimed that they had originally wanted to settle in a sixth *mahala,* Outs Agats, situated closer to the Guvezna plain. There the land had been more fertile and better suited for agriculture. Moreover, they had hoped that from there they could send their children to school in Guvezna. The township council blocked the plan, however, as it controlled the grazing lands of the Outs Agats area, which were prized by the village's large stockbreeders.[31]

Tzami/Mavrorahi and the other Otmanli *mahaladhes* had been situated much closer, in both physical proximity and ecological affinity, to the village of Dorkas (Karterai township) than to Guvezna/Assiros. Dorkas and Karterai had been resettled by refugees, mainly East Thracians, after their former Slavic-speaking inhabitants had been evacuated.[32] Over the years the Pontics of Mavrorahi have attempted to secede from Assiros township and join up with Karterai, but the local *tsorbadjidhes* elite in Assiros has refused to relinquish the prized grazing lands of former Otmanli.[33] Animal husbandry in Mavrorahi has brought considerable revenue to Assiros township. The animal head tax, as well as purchase and sales taxes, gave the township sizeable income (see chapter 6).

In addition to the Pontyi, Thrakiotes, and Mikrasiates, another group of outsiders also settled in Guvezna/Assiros during the interwar era: Sarakatsan pastoralists who, not unlike Vlahs,[34] had formerly roamed the Balkans in search of pastures for their herds.[35] In 1920, a Sarakatsan transhumant shepherd and his family arrived in the Guvezna area and occupied former Muslim houses in the small Otmanli *mahala* of Kalivia (or Vlahika),[36] located between Guvezna and Tzami/Mavrorahi. Situated in the low foothills approximately an hour's walk from either village, this hamlet came to occupy a middle position, both literally (in terms of space) and symbolically (in terms of social exchange and intercourse) between the different cultural or ethnic groups inhabiting Guvezna and Mavrorahi. The Sarakatsan used the Otmanli grazing lands as winter pastures for their herds, leading to a protracted conflict with large-scale stockbreeders in Guvezna/Assiros (see below). As transhumants, the Sarakatsan passed their winter months in concentrated residency among lineal and collateral agnates in Kalivia.[37] During the summer season, however, they migrated with their herds to the hills and mountains to the west, often in a large company of a dozen or so families.[38]

Since their settlement in Guvezna/Assiros, these Sarakatsan have been strongly endogamous and have not intermarried with the local Assiriotes. In a manner of speaking, they were nationally inclusive, sharing the same national sentiments as most Guveznans, but culturally exclusive. Sarakatsan in Assiros told me that they had been very pleased and proud when they became full Greek citizens in 1934, in accordance with a decision (#8037/11.12.1934) of the General Directorate of Macedonia, and were listed in the township conscription registry (*mitroo arrenon*). At that point, their *kehayias* took the surname of Politis ("Citizen"). No one questioned the Greekness of the Sarakatsan, and many of them in Assiros recounted the contributions various Sarakatsan had made to the Greek cause in the Macedonian Struggle.[39]

By 1928, refugee settlement in Guvezna/Assiros township had been more or less completed and the population had stabilized around four principal categories: (1) Endopyi locals in Guvezna/Assiros, who had been present in the village prior to the arrival of the refugees; (2) Pontyi refugees who had settled in Mavrorahi; (3) Thrakiotes refugees in Guvezna/Assiros, Examili, and Krithia; and (4) Sarakatsan pastoralists who had settled in the Otmanli *mahaladhes* and in Examili.[40] Members of the last three categories were, as shown above, unwelcome to the "locals," and frequently faced hostility, animosity, and threats. Each refugee group brought with it a distinct set of language, customs, rituals, and beliefs. Yet tossed into a hostile and unwelcoming environment, all claimed to be essentially Greek, despite what their regional or ethnic differences might have been or still are.

NASCENT GROUP FORMATION AND SOCIAL CLOSURE

There is no way I will accept the Caucasian,[41] the dirty, in my house. As far as I am concerned he can drop dead in the middle of the street. May they all be burnt in fire. Venizelos brought shit to Macedonia. They were all starving in Turkey.

a "local" Assiriotis

Threatened by the new arrivals, whom they saw as one potentially cohesive group, the local population of Assiros and the *tsorbadjidhes* in particular moved towards selective social closure. They turned associations and marriage exchange patterns inward, away from the refugees and other outsiders. While marital patterns in Assiros had already begun to move precipitously towards endogamy before the arrival of the refugees, the settlement process further heightened this tendency. The *tsorbadjidhes* created and maintained alliances within the village, adopting marital patterns characterized by strong class endogamy and ritual kinship ties across class lines.[42] "Local" poor sought marriage and baptism sponsors from the "local" elites, while refugees cultivated similar ritual kinship relations largely with other refugees in neighboring villages.

Local Assiros women frequently told me that they did not want to marry refugee men, and many of those who did claimed that they had acquiesced only because their families had been "poor," or because their preferred fiancés had broken off an original engagement and no other local man was willing to marry them. Endopyi parents, it was said, preferred to give their daughters to a gypsy rather than to a refugee. Local men were also said to have preferred not to marry refugee girls. Mavrorahi and Examili, on the other hand, were markedly village exogamous but strongly "group" endogamous. Thrakiotes in Examili married Thrakiotes in Krithia and other East Thracian refugee villages; Pontyi in Mavrorahi married other Pontyi. Having found themselves relatively isolated in a hostile environment, many sought to expand their social ties outward beyond the township and with people of the same cultural background.

Notwithstanding the preponderance of local endogamy, the character of community closure in Guvezna/Assiros during the interwar period was in many ways quite selective. The local elite adopted several different measures to ensure that no new groups would mount a serious challenge to their control over local affairs. To begin with, they actively discouraged many refugee families from settling in Guvezna/Assiros. Failing that, they often attempted to marginalize the role of small groups of newcomers in social life and political affairs of the township. Take, for example, the underrepresentation of refugees on the township council. While a few refugees appeared on the council's rosters during the interwar years, they were minority representatives who lacked significant power.

In other instances where newcomers occupied coveted lands or other strategic resources, the local elite attempted to dislodge them. The heavy taxation and licensing policies with which the township council harassed the settled Sarakatsan were but one example of such tactics. In some cases, locals extended limited or selective affinal and ritual kin ties to refugees, often in an attempt to win their political support. Control or influence over such patron-client intravillage alliances facilitated the consolidation of a dominant position on the part of Assiros locals.

Intervillage relations within the township were characterized in the past by sharper lines of division. Even as late as the 1990s, the Pontics of Mavrorahi and the Assiros villagers did not participate in each other's village patron saint day festival (*panighiri*). Although the East Thracians of Examili did come to Assiros for that village's celebration, the Assiriotes did not reciprocate. Among the older generations, the animosity directed at the refugee settlers by the local Assiriotes has had a protracted character that continued even in the 1990s, both within the village of Assiros itself as well as between Assiros and the refugee communities of Examili, Mavrorahi, and Krithia. In the past, when young refugee men in the village of Assiros wanted to go down to the coffee shops in the village *aghora* or to take a promenade (*volta*), they had to go in groups for fear the local men might physically assault them. Locals used to say, "The *matziria* is coming," and would then refuse to socialize with the refugees, insulting and ridiculing them instead. The refugees, for their part, had ridicule of their own with which they retaliated. Nevertheless, the lines of schism and division have apparently blurred with time, and many young people today do participate in intervillage social exchanges, crossing the lines their parents once drew so fiercely. It is now they who are on the cutting edge of modernity and definitions of identity (see chapter 7).

By the 1990s, social markers of group differences in the village were superficial in character. Processes of cultural amalgamation and national integration have been enormously successful in Assiros, though they were achieved through a protracted, diffuse, and sometimes violent campaign of both inducement and intimidation. Even children were drawn into such conflicts. Refugee children in *Matziria* often dared not leave their own neighborhood, as local children would throw rocks at them and chase them away. Parents of victimized refugee children went to the homes of the local bullies to complain, and they themselves became involved in the fighting. "It was something like the dispute between the North and the South," a refugee Assiriotis told me, referring to a popular mini-series on the American Civil War that aired on Greek television around the time of my fieldwork.

Yet both the village church and school were key institutions of cultural homogenization, although the educational environment of the local school was far from neutral or equal for all participants. Discrimination haunted refugee children in the classroom, as well. Several teachers confessed that, although the East Thracian children were, on the whole, smarter or better students than local children, pupils who came from the largest, wealthiest families of Assiros always received the high grades. Thus it was the children of the Assiros *tsorbadjidhes* who on holidays were given the honor of carrying the Greek national flag (*simeoforos*), or the privilege of standing next to it in the parade formation (*parastatis*). Similarly, it was always the children of wealthy local families who were asked to recite poems or perform theatrical displays of Greek heroism during national holiday celebrations. Today in Assiros, this form of discrimination has also disappeared. The local Greek Orthodox Church in Assiros played a critical role as a vehicle of cultural and social assimilation as well, as national church has been a central institutional mechanism of homogenization. A former Assiros priest (who served from the early 1950s to the late 1980s) displayed considerable discrimination toward the refugees, and made few personal or direct efforts to integrate them with "local" villagers. Indeed, the former priest even refused to allow one East Thracian refugee to become a chanter (*psaltis*) in the village church. Now, however, the village priest is of Pontic refugee descent and—despite initial resistance from "local" villagers—has created a "flock" of devoted followers from among local and refugee families alike. His success was epitomized in the fund-raising campaign he orchestrated in the early 1990s to cover the costs of building a new church of much larger proportions in the center of the *aghora*.

At the same time, public discourse in households, coffee shops, marketplaces, and judicial courts accompanied and narrated the emergence and consolidation of two newly defined social groups: locals and refugees. Even today, Assiriotes say negatively.

"Only the race of Alexander the Great is worthwhile. The rest are worthless and dirty people."

"Pontic Greeks and the rest are of dishonorable race."

"The Pontic Greeks destroyed Greece."

"Why do they blame us for not providing them with a sleeping place? Who wants to sleep in a strange place anyway? Why don't they want to go to their homes?"

On the other hand, most prominent among the positive remarks I heard about the refugees were the following statements:

"The Pontics were poor but they had good mattresses."

"If the refugees hadn't come we would still have been 'sleeping.' They brought money with them."

These comments apparently are not unique to the Assiros context.[43]

The settlement process thus not only fostered the creation of two new categories of people, "refugees" and "locals," but also juxtaposed them as mutually opposed social groups. Before the refugees' arrival, ethnicity and social stratification in the township was such that one could not speak of a single, unified, cohesive or even coherent Assiros population. Nor was the refugee population homogeneous. Following refugee resettlement, however, each of the refugee populations was transformed into a meaningful, distinct social group. The ever-changing population of Assiros once again underwent radical change, as the refugees came to occupy intermediate positions outside the village of Assiros (as a social unit) but inside the township (as an economic unit). This new population formed the social fabric over which the interwar administration of the local Assiros notables ruled.

The influx of refugees to the Assiros area brought to the forefront the growing schisms in community and property relations that had developed since the late Ottoman period. The notable families of the Christian elite that had risen to prominence at the turn of the century began to transform themselves into a local ruling class during the decades that followed the Balkan Wars. Incorporation with the Greek nation-state had brought township notables new forms of power and influence over their community through new administrative institutions and positions. But the Land Redistribution Program of 1928–1929 threatened to destroy that power base.

6

ADMINISTERING THE "NEW LANDS"
OF GREEK MACEDONIA
Class Reformation and National Homogenization,
1913–1940

[We] listened to the president articulate to the council that in accordance with the decision [#122770] of Mr. Minister, General
Governor of Macedonia, all municipal and township councils
would forbid, through [administrative] decision, the speaking of
other idioms of obsolete languages within the area of their jurisdiction for the reconstitution of a universal language and our national glory. [The president] suggested that [the] speaking
of different idioms, foreign [languages] and our language
in an impure or obsolete manner in the area of the township
of Assiros would be forbidden.

Assiros Township Decision No. 134, 13 December 1936

When Raktivan, the first official Greek administrator, arrived in
Thessaloniki by steamship at the end of October 1912, he brought
with him ten consulate clerks, two judges, five customs officers, a contingent of journalists, and 168 gendarmes from Crete under the leadership
of a military officer (Raktivan 1951:12). The administration of the "New
Lands" (*Nees Hores*), as Macedonia and Thrace came to be referred to,
was entrusted to Greek officials assigned by the state government to various posts in cities and towns throughout the region. But in most rural
communities the presence of formal officers of Greek state authority had
been largely indirect. In Guvezna, the only "outsiders" to assume administrative functions were a policeman (who later became township
secretary) and new taxation supervision officers (actually stationed in
Langadhas). By and large, local-level offices and posts were filled by select
members of rural communities themselves.

After 1912, civil administration, taxation, education, conscription,
and ecclesiastical affairs were linked to a single state hierarchy, which
also empowered local elites as agents of the state bureaucracy. Moreover,
the area's growing integration with the commercial economy of Greece
wrought profound transformations in occupational differentiation, class

structure, and local political affairs. Although Balkan warfare and new developments in transportation infrastructure had led to the decline in the passing caravan trade and with it the once thriving Guvezna market, nevertheless grocery stores and other shops in the village *aghora* continued to do a bustling business, especially after the arrival of the refugees.

To many local inhabitants of Greek Macedonia during the years between the Balkan Wars and World War II, the nation of the Hellenes was largely an abstract entity that was invoked and symbolized through flags, schools, holiday celebrations, and official commemorations. The state, on the other hand, had a very concrete existence to area residents, embodied in the form of civil administrators, tax collectors, and policemen posted to the village. The local township (*kinotita*), situated between the abstract nation and the concrete state, became a key political field in the Greek nation-building enterprise. During the 1920s and 1930s, the administrative township was a veritable local mini-state, a self-financed and largely self-regulated corporate community with its own governors, elected representatives, tax collectors, teachers, and security personnel. The *tsorbadjidhes* who came to personify Greek authority in the township were also patrons and benefactors for township residents, providing them with jobs and services, as well as groceries and credit. As issues of cultural assimilation and national homogenization rose to priority on Greek government agendas during the interwar era, the words and actions of this emergent class of local elites helped to cultivate among township residents an ideology of commonness and a conscious identification with the Greek nation-state.

After the departure of the Muslims, the Greek-speaking notables of Guvezna who had risen to prominence during the late Ottoman era diversified their economic activities, building new businesses and establishing a near monopoly over both private landownership and the use and management of newly designated township properties. Challenges from above, such as state-mandated land redistribution, as well as from below, exemplified in local conflicts over land use, were key factors in the formation of new notions of what it meant to be a citizen of Greece and a resident of Greek Macedonia. In fact, the struggle for control over these former Muslim properties became a major issue in local affairs during the interwar era. Land contests reshaped the local agro-pastoral economy, leading to new relationships of patronage and dependency between the *tsorbadjidhes* and the newly endowed smallholders. This dimension of patronage, I will argue, was to have a profound influence on the spread of Greek national consciousness among area residents. In their actions and their reactions to such challenges, the *tsorbadjidhes* played an active, if not a conscious, role in creating a new local class structure re-inforced by the diffuse social ties they maintained with other villagers, co-parishioners, and fellow citizens. Clientelistic relations with the laboring village poor and cultural institutions such as ritual kinship were as impor-tant to the regulation of material life and the formation of new categories of identity as were civil administration, church management, and educa-tion in the township.

A new, common national identity among the diverse inhabitants of Greek Macedonia was not simply imposed by national elites in Greece, although the propagation of Hellenism through their agency was an im-portant part of this process. Rather, nation-building entailed a cultural revolution (Corrigan and Sayer 1985), and was a dialectical process in which both state and local interests were renegotiated and redefined through the mediating agency of local elites with a national orientation. As de Certeau (1984:xiii) put it,

> The presence and circulation of a representation (taught by preachers, edu-cators, and popularizers as the key to socioeconomic advancement) tells us nothing about what it is for its users. We must first analyze its manipulation by users who are not its makers. Only then can we gauge the difference or similarity between the production of the image and the secondary produc-tion hidden in the process of its utilization.

Greek national identity was such a "representation" employed by the *tsorbadjidhes* of Guvezna/Assiros, and the manner in which they used it, often in support of their own economic interests, played a key role in defining its meaning to other township inhabitants.

REDISTRIBUTING "NEW LANDS"
Sales and Seizures of Muslim Properties

Official Greek government documents from the Historical Archives of Macedonia/General Directorate of Macedonia (HAM/GDM) indicated that, as of March 1914, few Muslim residents of the Langadhas district had departed from the area, despite the advent of Greek rule a year ear-lier. After the violent turmoil of the Balkan Wars, all was peaceful and quiet, at least according to a report the District Director (*Eparch*) of Lan-gadhas had sent to the Prefect of Thessaloniki (*Nomarch*).[1] And yet that same year, the Ottoman General Consulate of Salonika was protesting to the Governor General of Macedonia that a number of atrocities had been committed against Muslims in the Langadhas district, just north of the city.[2] Allegations mainly concerned involuntary or even forcible removal of Muslims from their property, in some instances by local village authorities acting in the name of the Greek state. Muslim homes, barns, and shops were being taken over, it complained, by recent refugees who had fled from Bulgaria and eastern Thrace during the Balkan Wars, and growing numbers of Muslims were obliged to migrate to the relative safety of Thessaloniki. Muslim lands, businesses, and homes were being seized by rural Christians.

The legal status of (former) Muslim properties became even more ambiguous after the general exodus of Muslims under the Treaty of Lausanne in 1923. Some Muslim landowners had transferred properties to local Christians on the eve of their departure, either willfully or under coercion.[3] Large abandoned properties were quickly taken over by influential or powerful local Christian notables, who claimed them by fact or fraud as their own. The massive influx of refugees from Asia Minor and East Thrace complicated the land question and created mounting pressure for land reform. In the late 1920s, a large-scale land redistribution campaign was undertaken by the Liberal Party government of Prime Minister Eleftherios Venizelos. All abandoned Ottoman *chiftlik* estates were declared "exchangeable lands" (*andallaksimes ghees*), and marked for expropriation and redistribution by the Refugee Settlement Commission in the forthcoming reform program.

In Guvezna, the impending prospects of a Turkish exodus in the late 1910s and early 1920s led many Christian villagers to prey upon Muslim landowners. Abandoned homes and buildings in the Otmanli *mahaladhes* were stripped of timber and other materials. Granaries at the Gnoina *chiftlik* were raided by armed men from Guvezna and Drimos. The majority of Christian families, rich and poor, local and refugee alike, simply began to "squat" on abandoned fields following the Muslim evacuation. Yet most were soon obliged to surrender those plots for redistribution. Greek law provided only for the protection of former "foreign" (i.e., Turkish) properties that had been sold or legally transferred to private Greek citizens prior to the Muslim evacuation. These lands, referred to in the Assiros land registry as "foreign properties" (*ksenes idhioktisies*), were exempt from government expropriation in the coming land redistribution. In contemporary Assiros, these fields constitute 36 percent of cultivated land in the township (see map 8), and many are still in the possession of those families that obtained them earlier this century. Most of these "foreign properties" are large contiguous fields, the largest of which was 763 *stremmata*. Some wealthy Guvezna families had been in a position to purchase these properties and their legal titles.[4] Many others, how-

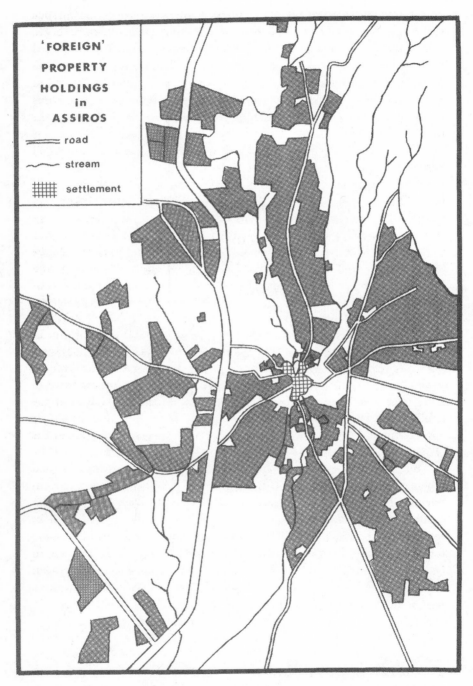

Map 8. "Foreign" property holdings in Assiros

ever, found less costly though more questionable means of acquiring such lands. A few powerful and influential families were alleged to have forged Turkish legal deeds of purchase. Others, it was said, actually purchased more modest amounts, say five to ten *stremmata,* and then added additional zeros to the numbers on the deeds to increase their claims ten or even a hundred fold. Still others simply enclosed new plots. In discussing the seizure of these "foreign properties," one Assiros man told me that the *tsorbadjidhes* had used stones or other available markers to designate the borders of their new properties. Most of them, he maintained, "never paid a drachma for those lands."

While some Christians begged or enticed Muslims to sign over their land titles, others resorted to threats, violence, and even murder to accomplish their ends. For example, it was said that one day in the 1910s, the Guvezna president, two schoolteachers, and another *tsorbadjis,* all four of whom had previously been "Macedonian Fighters" for the Greek cause, and who were all at the time members of the newly created and powerful township council (see below), had killed a local Muslim landowner called Sefik *effendi* for his properties. Some elderly Assiriotes claimed, it might be noted, that these men did not actually kill "the Turk," but merely threatened him by putting a burning iron ring (*pirosia*) around his neck. In an incident in 1923, two Guvezna *tsorbadjidhes* were said to have taken the crop-watcher and their weapons up to the Otmanli *mahaladhes* one day with the intention of forcing the Muslims there to hand over their property titles and livestock. After they arrived at the first settlement but failed to find anyone, they again mounted the slopes and continued up to the second *mahala.* There they allegedly killed the brother of a Turkish miller.[5]

But not all Christian families had the weapons to carry out such schemes, nor the political clout to do so with relative impunity. In neighboring Gnoina, local farmers watched as the lands of the former *chiftlik* estate they had been cultivating were confiscated by the RSC for the land redistribution campaign. Several told me that they regretted not having followed the advice of the Assiros *tsorbadjidhes,* who had urged them to beg the Turkish landowners for papers or other legal documents that would have given them title to the *chiftlik* estate on which they worked. As one put it, "We were not as cunning [*poniryi*] as the Assiriotes."

CREATING STATE-SPONSORED SMALLHOLDERS

The Land Redistribution Program (*Dhianomi*), having been legislated for several years, finally reached Assiros in 1928-29. The issue of land re-

form had been raised over a decade earlier, by the Liberal Party government of Venizelos in 1917. But its implementation would have never
come about, some Assiriotes claimed, if not for the influx of refugees in
the 1920s. Initially, compulsory land redistribution had been intended to
break up large agricultural estates in Thessaly and Macedonia.[6] Yet the
campaign also contributed to the homogenization of national identity
among the population of Greek Macedonia. Endowing both the "local"
poor and recent refugees alike with a share of the New Lands was
an important part of this process, for it provided material recognition of
the claims of locals and refugees to a rightful place in the Greek nation-
state.

Under the terms of the redistribution, male heads of land-poor families received allotments calculated to provide for the subsistence needs of
their nuclear families as well as a modest surplus. A basic allotment of
nine *stremmata* was allocated for each member of a family, supplemented
by additional plots totaling 25 percent of the aggregate sum of the family's basic allotments. Thus a family of three received a *kliros,* or redistributed lot, equal to thirty-six *stremmata.*[7] Recipients acquired land in four
different categories, depending on location and suitability for cultivation.[8] Property titles went to the husband of each married couple, a policy
that encouraged the partition of larger, extended-family units that contained more than one married couple by endowing each adult married
male with his own independent property base. For example, one of the
large joint families that had moved to Guvezna from Palehora in 1905
divided into several independent family units after the redistribution, as
each brother gained title to his own landed property.

Although the land reform of 1928–29 redistributed a total of
15,085.544 *stremmata* of land among 344 families in Assiros,[9] some *tsorbadjis* families continued to cultivate large estates for which they lacked
legal titles. Most were able to avoid expropriation of such lands because
of the influence they commanded or enjoyed within the new township
administration. But in 1933, some of these local elites lost their influence
over the township council, whose newly elected members voted to enact a
second land redistribution (*Dhefteri Dhianomi*) that specifically targeted
those holdings.[10] In this second redistribution, officials from Langadhas
were sent to supervise the process in conjunction with a committee of
three prominent villagers (Apostolakoudhis, Mantsos, and Palepolitis)
appointed by the new township council. Together, this team decided to
expropriate for redistribution an additional 2,000 *stremmata* of land
(ATA 1933). The amount involved was much less than that of the first
redistribution, and most of it was said to have been of poorer, more mar-

ginal agricultural quality, situated at a considerable distance from the village.

In deciding which (and whose) plots were to be appropriated for redistribution in this second *dhianomi,* the newly empowered oversight committee revealed a growing rift or rivalry between particular families of Assiros *tsorbadjidhes.* By 1934, the second redistribution had been declared complete, and the village had become a community of many small landholders governed by a powerful but factionalized local elite who continued to compete amongst themselves for economic dominance and political supremacy. Their conflicts and rivalries pointed to hidden legacies of the national contest that had so polarized identity and social relationships at the turn of the century.

RIVALRIES BETWEEN LOCAL NOTABLES

The fact that only some *tsorbadjidhes* were forced to surrender some of their large landholdings in the second redistribution is suggestive of the partisan undertones of that campaign. In some cases, families suffered expropriation despite their claims to legal titles of ownership. As a descendant of the teacher, Sapountzis, assured me, referring to his family's losses during the second redistribution:

> We all had papers for all the plots that were seized. The harvest was just completed when the clerks came. They took the land of Sapountzis, the Asteriou brothers (especially Stylianos), Tamtakos, and the Vayiatzis brothers. The families managed to save some plots because they bribed the head clerk. Whoever was loyal to the Populist [pro-Royalist] Party did not lose their land. Apostolakoudhis had 600 *stremmata,* Halepis 2,000, Artousis 3,000. They all had Turkish deeds, like us. They bought the land. But theirs was not taken away from them. Villagers at that time used to send their complaints to politicians. The case of the Assiros lands was specifically raised during a session of the Greek parliament. In 1933, the Minister of Agriculture, Mr. Theotokis, vowed to take personal responsibility for the confiscation and redistribution of the lands of Asteriou and Sapountzis. So they took our lands but left other plots in the possession of those who were their political supporters. We had no power and we lost. The only solution was to kill the redistribution clerks, as a Venizelist parliament deputy had suggested to Sapountzis.

This narrative reveals the intense and intimate manner in which local political developments in rural communities of Greek Macedonia had become linked to the national political arena of Greece during the interwar period. Greek national political parties, most notably the Liberals (i.e., Venizelists) and the Populists (i.e., pro-Royalists), became the focal point of national political identity. But they also provided a legitimate new channel for expression of ethno-national sentiments and social divisions that were legacies of the turn-of-the-century conflict over Macedonia.[11]

Mavrogordatos (1983b) has argued that throughout the 1920s the Liberal Party (*Phileleuthero Komma*) lacked a significant power base in Greek Macedonia, where supporters and followers of Venizelos were regarded by many Slavic-speakers as agents of Greek nationalism and irredentism. The pro-royalist Populist Party (*Laiko Komma*), on the other hand, had enjoyed a strong electoral base in the region, owing to the assurances of local Populist politicians that they would protect Slavic-speakers from government abuses and land expropriations. Moreover, during the 1920s, the still-active IMRO had urged its followers in Greek Macedonia to vote for Populist Party candidates in elections.[12]

This is not to suggest that local Populist politicians in Assiros were receiving orders or directives from the IMRO. But some Slavic-speaking families in the region did harbor equivocal opinions about the extension of Greek political sovereignty into Macedonia, and many resented both the presence of refugees as well as the expropriation of their lands in the first redistribution. Recall, for example, the case of Pashos, who had resigned his commission as a Greek teacher rather than work as a "Macedonian Fighter" for the Greek cause. Born of a mixed marriage between a Slavic-speaking Palehora man and the daughter of a Greek-speaking merchant settler, Pashos had been raised in the household of his stepfather, the Greek teacher Garoufalidis, whom his widowed mother had married. By the 1920s and 1930s, Pashos had become a leading Populist Party supporter in Assiros, despite his apparently ambivalent feelings towards Greek national homogenization in the region, as I will show below.

When local supporters of the Populist Party emerged as a new leading faction in township politics in 1933, they replaced the local Liberals (such as Vranas and Stylianos Asteriou) who had dominated the township council throughout the previous decade. Moreover, the newly elected Populists quickly enacted a series of administrative decrees that struck at the family economic base of Liberal *tsorbadjidhes,* confiscating fields they alleged the latter to have seized forcibly and illegally from departing Muslims. In a 1933 decision, the new township council ordered village families still holding Turkish properties to surrender those lands and to pay a fine (ATA 1933, 10.5.1933).

In their attempt to undermine the influence of their Liberal rivals, one of the first targets of the newly empowered Populist *tsorbadjidhes* was the state-appointed township secretary, a fervent Venizelist from Crete named Petrakis, who had originally come to the village under assignment as local policeman (see below). Petrakis had close ties to the family of Liberal *tsorbadjis* Stylianos Asteriou, who had been the wedding sponsor of Petrakis and had baptized his children. But in 1933, a number of villagers submitted a formal written complaint to the newly elected Populist township council, accusing Petrakis of embezzling funds and misappropriating land allocations during the 1928–1929 redistribution. They demanded his removal. Although the township council voted to defer the decision to the General Directorate of Macedonia (ATA 1933, Decision #11, 11.1.1933), Petrakis was obliged to resign a few months later. He was replaced temporarily by Apostolakoudhis, a *tsorbadjis* supporter of the Populist Party.[13] This local coup in township politics was made possible, in part, by the backing of the nationwide Populist Party organization, which had won a victory in the Greek national elections the same year. Recall from the Sapountzis narrative above, that the minister of agriculture at the time of the second redistribution was said to have personally taken responsibility for redistributing the lands of Sapountzis and Asteriou, two key local Liberal politicians.

Ascribing motives to such actions is more difficult than documenting their occurrence. Memory and local history are many-layered phenomena, and the same key figures in these political machinations of the township council had also, as younger men, been active local participants in the Macedonian Struggle. In fact, throughout Greek Macedonia, prominent (pro-Greek) activists in the turn-of-the-century national contest came to fill positions as local administrators and township officials during the decades following 1913 (Gounaris 1990). In Assiros, such leading political figures as Artousis (b.1873), Asteriou (b.1885), Pashos (b.1880), Halepis (b.1865), and Apostolakoudhis (b.1870) all had been active in the partisan conflict in one way or another, although the sentiments or loyalties of some had been equivocal. The political involvement of these men in that national conflict had been expressed in the context of local social relationships, and that history of activism had left legacies of interfamily tensions which continued to be a subtext of local elite rivalry in Assiros during the interwar period.

It is important to stress, however, that the *tsobadjidhes* had come to work within—if not to identify with—the major national political party organizations of Greece, while simultaneously expanding their own economic power in the 1920s and 1930s. As township president, Pashos made frequent trips to Athens to confer with Populist Party officials there. Vranas, it was said, with whom the Mavrorahi Pontic refugees danced when the Liberals won elections, once treated Venizelos to dinner in Thessaloniki. Yet political rivalries notwithstanding, *tsorbadjidhes* merchants, landowners, and stockbreeders in Assiros, both Liberals and Populists alike, deftly used their privileged position in the local arena to advance their own wealth and influence.

The extent to which local affairs in Assiros had come to be linked intimately with the national arena was illustrated in a political crisis that shook the country during the mid-1930s. The military seizure of power in Greece became an unequivocal expression of violent or coercive potential of the state. It was also a historical moment that demonstrated how vulnerable even the most locally prominent and powerful village notables could be to external policing by nation-state elites.

Following an attempt on the life of recently deposed former Prime Minister Venizelos in June 1933, after which the new pro-royalist government failed to make any arrests, part of the Greek armed forces under Plastiras, an anti-royalist, staged an unsuccessful coup to topple the Populist government. For a period of roughly ten to fifteen days, much of Greece was embroiled in violent clashes between opposing factions of the armed forces. Several cities came under bombardment. Elderly villagers in Assiros recalled that airplanes had been flying in the skies over the basin, soldiers had passed through the area, and cavalry troops had camped down near the river Boidana. The coup was eventually suppressed and a backlash of virulent anti-Venizelist sentiment swept many parts of the country, forcing the former prime minister into exile. A year later, General Metaxas seized power and imposed a pro-royalist military dictatorship, under which the military was purged of pro-Venizelist officers.[14]

In Assiros, all men in the village were summoned to appear before military authorities. Several were arrested and detained, mainly leading members of the local Liberal Organization (*Orghanosi Fileleftheron*), including the priest, the teachers Sapountzis and Asteriou, two refugees, and two other local men. Asteriou, who it was said had been a member of the Liberal Party's Democratic Guard (*Dhimokratikos Frouros*), was imprisoned for fifteen days in the old Hadji-Osman Turkish warehouse in the Thessaloniki port. A period of anti-Liberal fervor took hold in Assiros. An effigy was made of Venizelos and then violently beaten by villagers.

Developments such as these contributed to a reorientation of local concepts of identity, as political party affiliation, sentiments towards the monarchy, and perceptions of socioeconomic stratification came to supersede any conscious sense of cultural, ethnic, or national difference. The administrative infrastructure that the Greek state extended into the New Lands of Macedonia played a key role in effecting this shift. Acting in the capacity of local officials, both Liberal and Populist *tsorbadjidhes* brokered a restratification of local society and the development of a common national identity among local inhabitants. Their political authority was based in large part on state backing, but it was also rooted in the complex web of interfamily relationships that enabled the local elite to sustain their own economic dominance over the township community.

OFFICIATING THE TOWNSHIP LOCAL STATE

The advent of Greek rule in Macedonia introduced new formal administrative institutions, offices, and regulations among the new citizenry living in the region. Either appointed by the new governing authority of the General Directorate of Macedonia (headquartered in Thessaloniki) and its district subdirectorate in Langadhas, or popularly elected through the support of local allies and those among the local poor whom they patronized, the *tsorbadjidhes* of Assiros became executive officers of new Greek state administration at the township (*kinotita*) level. Many of them quickly assumed active participation in the flurry of new administrative activities that took place after the Second Balkan War and during the refugee settlement process. This was important to the *tsorbadjidhes,* as such profitable matters as tax collecting privileges and township pasture grazing rights were auctioned (*dhimoprasia*) by the township council to the highest bidders.

The "Christian Township of Guvezna [Assiros]," as it was referred to in official records until 1930, had been chartered under Greek legislative reforms and endowed with the right to maintain its own corporate property, fiscal autonomy, and internal security through a hierarchically structured executive administration. After 1913, the Greek state, which could not possibly finance the operations of hundreds of new *kinotites* in the New Lands of Macedonia, vested local township councils with considerable authority and discretion to determine what taxes, fees, and surcharges would be levied in the township, and at what rates.[15]

The distinguished "Macedonian Fighter" and teacher of Greek, Sapountzis, was appointed as first president of Guvezna in 1912. Elderly villagers recalled how Sapountzis had adopted a red hat as a symbol of his status, but also that the Bulgarian army had taken the cap away from

him as a gesture of defiance towards Greek authority when they came to
Guvezna later that same year. The presence of Bulgarian troops in the
village, however, proved to be brief, and after the region came firmly
under Greek control in 1913 men from local *tsorbadjidhes* families with
a Greek orientation had quickly come to dominate the newly created
township council. Their economic stature, education, and experience in
fiscal management of *wakf* corporations and commercial family enterprises made them eminently qualified to serve in new local administrative
capacities.

The township council (*kinotiko simvoulio*) was a regularly elected
governing board and decision-making authority responsible for the general oversight of the township, taxation and surcharges, and market regulation, as well as the fiscal management of township and church-owned
properties, both commercial and agro-pastoral. Councillors were originally elected every two years, but four-year terms were adopted after
World War II. The names of such powerful Guvezna families as Apostolakoudhis, Artousis, Asteriou, Halepis, Mantsos, Pashos, Sapountzis, Tamtakos, Velikas, and Vranas appeared repeatedly in rosters of township
council membership (see table 11). So too did those of a few others, such
as Galianos and Karamagiris, who had more recently risen to prominence
through successful commercial, mercantile, landowning, and stock-
breeding enterprises. The occupational livelihoods of most councillors
who served between 1919 and 1940 (i.e., schoolteachers, merchants, real-
estate owners, stockbreeders, grocers, millers, blacksmiths, or factory
owners) suggest that they had been wealthy, literate, or both.

The township president (*proedhros*) was the most influential member
of the council. Prior to World War II, councillors selected a member from
their own ranks as president. Since the war, however, presidents have
been elected directly by township residents. The president's power was
derived largely from the fact that he signed the taxation lists, attesting
that proper levies have been imposed and the revenues collected. Presidents also served as the formal representative of the community to the
outside political world, while representing that world to fellow villagers.
They were present at all village public activities, officiated at ceremonial
events from civil holidays to religious feasts, presided over public auctions
and township council meetings, signed administrative decisions, and read
or conveyed government directives to fellow villagers. Many township
presidents have come from the ranks of notable families, such as Asteriou,
Galianos, Pashos, and Vranas. The prominence of Assiros township presidents was heightened by their strong ties with major national political

parties in Greece, and many have personally known politicians in Thessaloniki and Athens, as noted above.

The position of government-appointed township secretary (*ghrammateas*) was another important innovation in civil administration following formal incorporation into Greece in 1913. Formerly appointed and paid by the township, since World War II the secretary has been nominated by the township council and confirmed by the state, which now also provides a salary. As a nonelected local official, the secretary is a full-time professional administrator, an interpreter of state directives, and a keeper of local records, such as tax rosters, family registries, male conscription rolls (established in 1933), and records of property transfers (which required validation from the secretary's office).[16] The power and influence of the position was underscored by the fact that, unlike the township presidents, who are elected politicians, township secretaries enjoyed life tenure and served until retirement, resignation, impeachment, or death.

While the teachers Asteriou and Sapountzis, as literate local notables, initially maintained township records, in 1924 the Cretan policeman Petrakis was formally appointed as first township secretary.[17] His successor was another powerful and feared man, Mouhtaris, whose family long has exercised an informal influence over village affairs that extends beyond formal administrative officeholding. As one member of the family boasted to me, "We have been governing the village all these years." During the German occupation, Secretary Mouhtaris was accused of collaborating with the occupation forces; he was murdered by communist partisans in 1944 and his body was dumped in a ditch outside the village (see chapter 7).

Mouhtaris was replaced by Yeorgios Pashos, son of the wealthy tobacco merchant, Populist Party supporter, and sometime township president, Ioannis Pashos. The younger Pashos had been widely regarded as a concerned and efficient secretary who would often open the office even in the evenings for villagers' needs. Although he himself was not engaged in husbandry or stock-breeding, his position as keeper of the township records enhanced his ability to tap into the then profitable pastoral economy, and he repeatedly won the annual auction for tax collection on slaughtered animals. Pashos remained in office until retirement in 1980, when his assistant, Yiannis Vranas, was appointed as successor. Described by some villagers as forceful patrons, both men came from prominent mercantile families. Both also had cultivated images of themselves as influential local brokers adept at mediating not only intravillage affairs but also relations between the township and society at large. Although the fathers of Pashos and Vranas had been bitter political rivals during the interwar period, the two sons were said to have cooperated in managing township duties and responsibilities.

The introduction of a Greek police (*astinomia*) presence in the village was another key aspect of state-strengthening and nation-building efforts in the area. The first to be assigned to Guvezna after 1913 had been the Cretan, Yeorghios Petrakis, who eventually became the first township secretary in the 1920s. Cretans played an important role in the turn-of-the-century Macedonian Struggle, as well as in the subsequent integration of Macedonia into Greece. Raktivan, recall, had brought with him a security force of Cretan gendarmerie when he arrived in Thessaloniki in 1912. Mavrogordatos (1983a:71) argued that Cretan policemen treated the population of Macedonia with contempt, similar to sentiments that colonizers and conquerors often show toward those they subjugate. They ridiculed the refugees settled in Macedonia as "Turkish seeds" (*Turkosporyi*) planted among a countryside filled with "Bulgarians."

Consider a brief anecdote related by an Assiros villager: "In the early years of Greek rule, a policeman from southern Greece was assigned here. His mother and father kept crying. How would he survive up there, among 'Bulgarians'? The policeman came [to Guvezna], and wrote his parents a letter telling them not to cry because everybody here was Greek." Such tales illustrate the preconceptions of many Greeks in the south in the early twentieth century that Macedonia had indeed been inhabited by "Bulgarians." They also call into question the claims of contemporary polemicists that Macedonia has always been completely Greek. But the anecdote also testifies that there had been a strong Greek presence in some rural communities of the region and in Guvezna/Assiros in particular. Always "outsiders,"[18] policemen (or *zandarmadhes,* as they were formerly called, after the French *gendarme*) embodied the coercive power and legitimizing force of the national government, while offering loyal citizens security. For many years, police in Assiros actively carried out surveillance on local residents, discouraging dissent and unrest while promoting (and sometimes enforcing) compliance with local and state authority, including enforcement of mandatory labor service requirements.

The power of local police officers was expanded greatly during the Metaxas dictatorship of the 1930s. In 1938, for example, a tense confrontation erupted between the village policeman and then township president Ioannis Pashos. The policeman, whose surname suggested Asia Minor refugee origins, went to the home of Pashos, threatened his family members and bystanders at gunpoint, beat up the president, arrested him, and led him away to the local police station where a high official of the Metaxas security forces was waiting for him. The incident reportedly centered around a book on local history, mentioned in chapter 1, which Pashos had in his possession but which government authorities sought to confiscate. The township council, dominated at the time by Pashos' Populist Party allies, immediately called for the removal of the policeman (ATA 1938, Decision #126). Pashos, it was said, eventually had to appear in court in Langadhas. But no other details concerning the incident or the case survive in township archives; members of those families involved could either not remember the incident or were disinclined to discuss it. Nevertheless, the confrontation stands as testimony to the violable status of the local township officeholding vis-à-vis the sanctioning force of external state power and authority.

FISCAL MANAGEMENT AND LOCAL STATE AUTHORITY

The management of community affairs and finances had been a key issue in local politics even under the Ottomans, when the Christian notables of Guvezna had overseen *wakf* charitable estates and competed for profitable positions as tax farmers. After 1913, the administrative township joined the church and school as the three central institutions of local community organization, each with a particular affiliation to the Greek state and to the ideological movement of Hellenism. Between 1913 and 1930, township, church, and school had been joint institutional coowners of a corporate property base in Guvezna characterized as "vakouf" (*wakf*), a term which in the Ottoman era had denoted property or land granted for a pious cause.

The revenues generated from these properties, most of which were rented out, were directed to the township administration, the local church, and the township school. The *tsorbadjidhes* served on the managerial boards of each of these three institutions, collaborating in the financing of many activities, events, and celebrations that promoted sentiments of community solidarity and common affinity with the Greek nation-state. This tripartite corporate partnership had been a vestige of the Ottoman past, when local Christian notables, the church, and school had worked closely together at the service of the idea of Hellenism. As one villager put it, "School, township, and church had been like brothers [*san adhelphia*] until they separated." The *wakf* corporation of the township, church, and school was dissolved in 1930, at the command of the General Directorate of Macedonia (ATA 1930, GDM Order #7504).[19]

Of greater significance, however, had been the tax burdens that increased following the advent of Greek rule, primarily because most new local township governments were made fiscally responsible for their own administration. They received orders and guidelines from the General Directorate of Macedonia (GDM) concerning tax increases and new tax categories, but were generally given a good deal of discretion in deciding which taxes to raise or what new surcharges to issue in order to meet state extractions and rising costs of local administration.[20] During the 1920s, 20 to 30 percent of township expenditures went to salaries of the secretary, bailiff(s), and to reimburse the expenses of the township president (see table 10), suggesting that local administrators had an active material interest in tax assessment and collection. Determining *what* would be taxed, and at what rate, became central issues in local politics.

Fixed taxes, periodic levies, and supplemental surcharges constituted a key category of township revenues, referred to in local records as "specific revenue" (*idhika esodha*).[21] Such extractions focused on three principal sources: taxes on agricultural products, fees for access to pasture lands, and taxes on purchase and sale of animals. Despite the liberation of Macedonia from Ottoman rule, the 10 percent *dhekati* tax on agricultural products (wheat, tobacco, and vineyards) continued to be imposed on farmers in the region until its abolition in 1928, following a violent confrontation between protestors and state authorities in Thessaloniki.[22] In addition, "crop-watching contributions" (*isfora aghrofilakis*) were also collected.[23] Rural residents faced a number of other taxes during the 1920s, including those on property transfers, profits from industrial and commercial enterprises, and on gross income. Taxes were also levied on land rentals and on the fees or wages of independent of freelance laborers. New surcharges were imposed on residents who applied for permission to build houses or other structures.

Tax collection continued to be farmed out through public auctions, as in the Ottoman era. Bidding was open to township residents and nonresidents alike, the only stipulation being that the winner had to secure the cosignature of two other responsible individuals, local "men of the *aghora*," who would act as guarantors (*engiites*). Township archives contained extensive documentation on the highly competitive bidding for tax contracting privileges. Whether they collected taxes from local residents in cash or in kind, local *tsorbadjis* tax contractors were often able to retain roughly 10 percent of collected revenues for themselves, providing a lucrative source of income.

In addition, the township council also claimed nonremunerated compulsory labor service from residents in order to undertake public works projects, such as drainage for roads and fields. Each able-bodied male resident between eighteen and sixty years of age had to supply the township with free labor service each year, although the number of required days tended to vary based apparently on the jobs the township council planned in each particular year (see ATA 1927–55). Those who owned animals and wagons, however, served fewer days, chiefly because they provided their animals and wagons as services. Moreover, those who could afford to do so were permitted to pay a cash fee in lieu of labor service, if they so desired. Wealthy villagers purchased exemptions but most residents were obliged to provide this service. As noted above, the police enforced the labor service requirement, and those who refused to serve faced fines.

Township fiscal records from the 1910s and 1920s indicate that local revenue became increasingly dependent on fees for pasture grazing rights and taxes on animal products, reflecting the rising prominence of animal husbandry and stock-breeding.[24] Each herder's calculated grazing fees were posted seasonally outside the churches of the township's three villages (Assiros, Examili, and Mavrorahi). Nonresidents were required to pay fees double those of resident herders. Annual lists of herdowners and herd sizes documented the development and consolidation of large-scale stock-breeding enterprises at the expense of small-scale herding activities during the interwar period. This change was closely related to the impact of land redistribution as well as the replacement of ethno-national distinctions by class-based divisions. It also had far-reaching consequences for patterns of clientelism and dependency in the local economy.

FROM ANIMAL HUSBANDRY TO STOCK-BREEDING
The Changing Character of Pastoral Economy

Shortly after 1913, grazing lands were figuratively (and in some instances literally) enclosed by the township council as community property, and rights of access and use were publicly auctioned each year. *Tsorbadjidhes* families such as Asteriou, Galianos, Halepis, Velikas, and Vranas were able to use their political influence and wealth to secure grazing rights to those township pastures. In the process, they wrestled livestock production away from small-scale herders through a series of administrative and economic measures.

With the enclosure of a large portion of the best grazing land in the township, many smallholder families found themselves increasingly mar-ginalized in the pastoral economy. Previously, animal husbandry had been a key part of diversified family economies, providing even the poor with milk and cheese for domestic consumption or for cash sale to mer-chants, as well as with wool for winter blankets.[25] After enclosure, fami-lies who endeavored to maintain a few animals but could not afford the expensive bids for private grazing rights could still place their animals under the care and custody of the collective village herd (agheli), which was tended by hired shepherds and enjoyed access rights to township grazing lands. As a result, prospects for upward mobility through small-scale husbandry became limited or even negligible after the tsorbadjidhes gained effective monopoly over use of township grazing lands.

Tensions and conflicts began to emerge between large herdowners and agricultural smallholders following the appropriation of some large areas, used primarily for grazing, by the Refugee Settlement Commission during the redistribution campaign. Sharp reductions in available pas-tures not only added market value to livestock and the by-products of husbandry, but also put new ecological pressures on the land (see Kostis 1987). Newly endowed smallholders grew concerned about crop damage by grazing animals, for in the 1930s agricultural output on small farms could barely meet the subsistence needs of families, after taxes and debts were paid. Tsorbadjidhes stockbreeders, on the other hand, had been par-ticularly anxious to keep substantial tracts of arable land out of cultiva-tion, especially the northern uplands of the township which were valued both as grazing lands and as access routes to pastures even further uphill.

Given the large amount of animals, land, and revenue involved (see tables 12 and 13), the township council spent a great deal of time deliber-ating over pastoral matters. Most controversy centered on winter grazing, when most of the agricultural fields had been sown and when the Sarakat-san and their herds were present in the area. Following the land redistri-bution of 1928–29, the township council announced prohibitions against animals grazing in cultivated fields and demarcated a "forbidden zone" (apaghorevmeni zoni) in which animals were not permitted at all (ATA 1930). Zoning regulations were in effect from November 15 (when local farmers usually began to sow winter crops) until July 20 (when the local wheat harvest was usually completed; see table 14).

It was in the context of these new regulations that the post of crop-watchers (aghrofilakes) became increasingly important to economic and political affairs in the township.[26] Appointed by the township council, the authority and responsibilities of crop-watchers gave them considerable power. Often, such men were nominated or backed by wealthy large landowning and stock-breeding *tsorbadjidhes* patrons. Animals caught grazing in forbidden zones were taken to the *toukat* (pen), from which an owner had to pay a fine in order to have his animals released.[27]

Some *tsorbadjidhes* herdowners did not heed the zoning regulations, however, and their animals continued to enter planted fields, sometimes with the connivance of bribed crop-watchers. As one *tsorbadjis* explained to me, "From the *toumba* down, all the land was forbidden [to grazing]. The sheep were dying [from overpopulation] and only those who had money could pay the crop-watchers to allow their sheep in." The clash of interests between the local *tsorbadjidhes* and other families in the township, including both local and refugee farmers as well as Sarakatsan herders, may be illustrated in a number of disputes over grazing rights.[28] These cases, moreover, also evidence the degree to which the *tsorbadjidhes* of Assiros had begun to regard themselves, and to act as, a particular class of villagers, a local economic elite who had much in common despite earlier differences expressed in family histories, national orientation, and political party loyalties.

The most heated of these confrontations involved conflicting claims to coveted winter grazing lands owned by the township in "unrestricted zones." Winter saw the return of the Sarakatsan and their herds, who had settled in the Kalivia *mahala* of Otmanli during the 1920s and had since leased the Kambili pastures from the Settlement Commission as annual winter grazing lands. The land redistributions of 1928–29 had involved as many as 15,000 *stremmata,* much of them outlying fields that, while arable, had been exploited mainly as grazing lands since late Ottoman times. Having lost those lands to the control of agricultural smallholders, the *tsorbadjidhes* stockbreeders directed their attention to the Kambili pastures near Mavrorahi.

Assiros stock-breeders had maintained that the Kambili pastures were more than sufficient for the needs of the Sarakatsan, who, they argued, should be obliged to share the winter grazing lands. In 1931, Vranas, a *tsorbadjis* stockbreeder who was then also the Liberal Party township president, testified that stock-breeding in Assiros had expanded considerably in the last five years and more grazing lands were desperately needed. It was argued that the Sarakatsan, with 22,000 (royal) *stremmata* for their 1,400 sheep, enjoyed more pastureland than they needed. Assiros herders, by contrast, had to maintain their 6,000 sheep and 500 large animals on only 12,000 (royal) *stremmata.* Citing Law 4818, Article 1033, of the General Directorate of Macedonia, Vranas and the council claimed the right to repossess some of that land for the exclusive use of Assiros herders. By the end of the year, the Kambili-Karakotzali pastures appeared in township records as Assiros lands, providing village herd-owners with their largest single pasture, covering some 5,000 *stremmata* (see table 13; ATA 1931).

During the next ten years the dispute over the Kambili lands grew increasingly bitter, developing into a protracted legal battle in which the local *tsorbadjidhes* used their ties to influential officials in the Greek state bureaucracy to pursue their collective interests. In November 1934, when Assiros herdowners took their animals up to the Otmanli pastures, the Sarakatsan chased them away with angry warnings that they would kill anyone who dared trespass on their grazing lands. The township council decided to sue the Sarakatsan in court for eviction (ATA 1934).[29] The following year, the RSC finally and officially handed over jurisdiction of the pastures to Assiros township, and the council immediately decided to charge the Sarakatsan triple the grazing fees paid by local herders (ATA 1936). Frustrated and increasingly desperate, the Sarakatsan decided to fight the case in Athenian courts (ATA 1938). Although they won the right to retain their long-term lease (*enikiostasio*) to the disputed winter pastures, they were eventually pushed out of herding by continuing high local administrative surcharges. By 1940, the Sarakatsan leader had only 115 sheep left (ATA 1940).[30]

The actions of the Assiros *tsorbadjidhes* during their protracted dispute with the Sarakatsan underscored the extent to which they had collectively come to regard their ties with state officials and national elites in Greece as critically important to their own family interests. The struggle also highlighted the extent to which the *tsorbadjidhes* were able to protect their economic interests through the institution of the township council. Empowered by the Greek government following incorporation in 1913, the township council functioned much like a local state bureaucracy itself, exercising its nationally backed authority to regulate economic matters from rents to taxes, as well as social affairs in the township. Its officials both dominated and patronized the local poor.

THE LABORING POOR
Work, Wages, and Worries

These changes in the agro-pastoral economy also affected the fortunes of the class of agricultural smallholders created through the land redistributions of the 1920s and 1930s. In contrast to the rising prosperity of the *tsorbadjidhes,* the majority of the township population (locals and refugees alike) continued to live close to the margins of subsistence. Many remained dependent upon the patronage of the wealthy local elite for wage-labor opportunities, loans, and credit, while others found themselves struggling to escape persistent debt to local *tsorbadjidhes* creditors.

During the interwar era, most family farms consisted of scattered plots of uneven quality, the fertility of which declined as land rose toward the northern hills. Some villagers recalled having to plow their fields six or seven times before planting.[31] Farming was highly labor-intensive: plowing, sowing, and harvesting were done by hand, making for difficult and strenuous work. Returns were low, but taxes as well as threshing and milling fees were high. Most smallholders produced only enough grain to feed themselves through Christmas. By January or February, many were obliged to purchase grain and groceries from local merchants on credit.[32] At harvest time, a substantial portion of their crop went towards taxes and debts with local grocers and creditors. As one villager recalled, "First came the *dhekatistis* and then came the *bakalis* [grocer]." This often compromised family subsistence supplies for the coming year and pushed many smallholders into an almost perennial cycle of debt.

Thus, temporary or seasonal work as hired laborers for local *tsorbadjidhes* was a principal means by which both refugees and local poor alike supplemented their family incomes. Relations between employers and employees were far from ideal, and hired laborers were often addressed as "servants" (*dhoulyi*).[33] As one elderly villager recalled, "Those who had animals were the big farmers as well. The rest of us either became shepherds or carried brush to Drimos."[34] Each *tsorbadjis* family regularly hired male and female laborers from among poor families in the village at harvest time, offering pay based on the number of *stremmata* harvested. Women remained actively involved in the agricultural wage-labor force, and participated in all kinds of agricultural jobs, from cultivating lentils and hoeing corn to harvesting wheat and processing tobacco. During harvest seasons, fields were crowded with hired laborers, and women recalled how they carried their babies to the fields and left them under the shade of a tree or made a small tent to protect them from the burning sun. Landowners usually delivered a snack of olives, sardines, cheese, bread, and water to their hired laborers around ten o'clock in the morning, but most workers had to bring their own lunch from home.[35] Pay was always poor. As one woman put it, "We worked many days just so we could go to the Langadhas market and buy a dress. That was it." Most families also actively sought employment for their young boys, especially as shepherds. In fact, many village men worked as shepherds during their youth, often following in the footsteps of their own father.

Shepherds were hired on a short-term basis (rarely exceeding six months). Twice each year, on St. George's Day (23 April) and St. Dimitrios's Day (26 October), herdowners and shepherd candidates would meet in the village *aghora*, where negotiations over the terms of labor contracts took place. A new pair of shoes came with the job, but if a shepherd quit in the middle of a season then he had to return the shoes to the herdowner. Shepherds were paid (usually in a quantity of wheat) at the end of their appointment. Older and more experienced shepherds enjoyed reputable status and better pay. Such individuals were often clients of large herdowners and stockbreeders, who as ritual kin patrons frequently rehired them year after year.

By contrast, many younger shepherds, especially those fresh out of primary school, lacked both experience and clientele ties. Little negotiation was involved in the terms of their contracts. Rather, they were often obliged to accept whatever terms were offered to them. Take the example of Petros, who had been born into a "servant" family. At the age of fifteen, he started tending the flocks of Sapountzis. The next year he was hired by Asteriou but claimed he had been cheated in his pay. The following year, he switched to the industrialist Galianos, receiving thirty *oka* of corn as his pay for a year of labor. When he asked Galianos for some extra sesame, he was fired. Galianos threw him out, but not before taking back the lad's shoes and sending him home barefoot. As Petros recalled,

> We were not allowed to enter the house of the *tsorbadjidhes*. We could hear them inside the house saying, "The servants have come to get paid." We had to stay outside and wait. . . . In order to receive our pay, we either had to have a gun or to kneel in front of them and kiss their hands, as in the old Turkish system.

Faced with such working conditions, many former shepherds (Petros included) emigrated to Australia in the 1950s in search of better jobs and lives.[36]

Employment as a transporter or wagoner (alternatively referred to in Assiros as *kiradjis, aghoghiatis,* or *karaghoghefs*) became an important source of cash income for the local poor during the 1910s and 1920s. By 1919, over one-fifth of Assiros men were employed as wagoners, working either for local grocers or those in rural towns as far away as Lahanas, Serres, and Nigrita.[37] Each grocer employed one or more of his own transporters. But some of these laborers eventually saved enough money to purchase their own wagons, and contracted out their services and labor to merchants in cities and towns, ferrying goods across the countryside.

Many older villagers maintained that living conditions in Assiros during the interwar period had been worse than those under Ottoman rule.

Some reflected critically that after "liberation," the exploiters and ex-ploited were now Christians alike. Winters were remembered by the el-derly as particularly difficult times. Most families had neither beds nor blankets, it was claimed, and slept on mattresses filled with rye stalks and placed atop boards, sheets of tin, or aluminum. Clothes provided their main source of warmth; only the large herdowning families were said to have had wool mattresses, along with fur blankets. The poor lacked even pillows, instead resting their heads on shoes. Or at least this had been the case for the shepherds, who slept outside or in the animal pens by the river and in the hills. Most lived on a diet of beans, bread, and freshwater fish. Meat was eaten only three times each year, on Christmas, Easter, and Prophet Elias's Day (20 July), or occasionally when a *tsor-badjis* married off one of his children and invited the entire village to a feast. Poverty was said to have been so endemic that some families could not find anyone worthy enough to help carry the coffin to the village cemetery when a family member died. Others recalled how their families had waited expectantly in election years for their *tsorbadjidhes* patrons to come around and offer money for their votes.

The establishment in 1929 of the state-run Agricultural Bank of Greece (*Aghrotiki Trapeza tis Elladhos,* or ATE) was an attempt to open new channels of credit to small-scale farmers who had always been depen-dent on local merchants, grocers, and usurers.[38] The ATE immediately began what became a common practice of purchasing crops from Assiros cultivators at standardized prices. Prior to this, most local grain had been purchased by Galianos, a *tsorbadjis* who served as township president in the mid-1930s, at prices set by the township council.[39] Yet despite the efforts and attractiveness of the ATE, most Assiros villagers continued their client dependency on local *tsorbadjidhes* benefactors, selling pro-duce to them in order to maintain their patronage in other areas of life, such as seasonal employment.

The inauguration of the village Agricultural Cooperative (*Aghrotikos Sineterismos*) several years earlier in 1924 had likewise done little to ease the dominance of the *tsorbadjis* elite. It did, however, have a much more successful impact in contributing to the emergence of a common sense of national identity among villagers. Affiliated with a broad organization of similar institutions at local, regional, and national levels, the coopera-tive promoted the integration of the local economy with that of the Greek state. Moreover, members of its management committee came to partici-pate in regional meetings and national conferences on agricultural devel-opment, as well as in pan-Hellenic or prefectural seminars on agricultural themes. In a very important way, the cooperative accentuated a feeling of common solidarity among the new class of agricultural smallholders, helping to bridge some of their cultural or ethnic differences of the past. Although it was nominally a popular organization intended to represent the interests of smallholders in particular, the cooperative itself quickly became a wealthy institution dominated by *tsorbadjis* large landowners, a development that alienated many of the local poor.[40]

Likewise, the introduction of new technological innovations such as threshing machines (*patozes*) to the village during the 1930s did little to alter popular dependency on the Assiros *tsorbadjidhes*. The Artousis brothers were the first in the village to acquire a threshing machine, followed soon afterwards by the Agricultural Cooperative, then by Asteriou and Velikas in a partnership, then Vranas, then Voukinas, and finally Asteriou bought a second one on his own. Both the *tsorbadjidhes* and the cooperative charged a 10 percent commission for threshing grain. This offered little incentive for smallholders to turn away from their *tsorbadjidhes* patrons, who unlike the cooperative (which they also dominated) could also offer their client families credit, arrange permissions to plant tobacco (a profitable cash crop),[41] or perhaps hire a shepherd boy (leaving his family with one less mouth to feed).

In this manner, the families of the *aghora* continued to dominate local community affairs long after the advent of Greek rule in 1913. They oversaw local taxation, security, and fiscal management of a tripartite property-owning corporation of local church, school, and township (even after its formal state-mandated dissolution in 1930). Yet the growing self-aggrandizement of the *tsorbadjidhes* in the face of continued material paucity among the working poor contributed to shifting boundaries of group identification and to an increasingly polarized class structure. Many of the local poor, *dopyi* and *prosfighes* alike, sought out client-like relationships with these families, symbolized in part through the idiom of ritual kinship in baptismal and wedding sponsorship, to which I will turn in the next chapter. But it was the role of the *tsorbadjidhes* as local brokers of state authority that defined political power and influence following the advent of Greek rule. They mediated relationships between the national government and the local poor, and took an active part in efforts to construct a Greek national consciousness at the local level.

Brokering Local State Action, Negotiating Local National Identity

The development of Greek national consciousness among the population of the New Lands of Macedonia had been a concern of state elites long before the "liberation" of the region in 1912, as Part I of this work has shown. Yet the years following the formal extension of Greek national sovereignty over the region witnessed more concerted efforts on this front. A number of national government directives issued to local councils during the 1920s and 1930s had a profound impact on social relations and notions of identity in Greek Macedonia. Most significant among these was that prohibiting the use of any language except Greek in public. In particular, the use of "Bulgarian" (a term, as noted earlier, frequently used in Greece to describe or categorize Slavic language[s] spoken in Macedonia) was forbidden in all public places, shops, and markets. This directive segregated community space into "public" and "private" spheres.

During the interwar period, *gendarmes* were always keeping an eye (or an ear, as it were) on the local population, issuing steep fines to any who spoke "Bulgarian" or any language other than Greek in public. The use of Slavic was effectively restricted, spoken mainly by women amongst themselves. As children entered school, where the use of any language but Greek was strictly forbidden throughout Greek Macedonia, this cultural and linguistic balance was further disrupted. Night schools were also established for older men and women (*dopyi* and refugees alike) to learn Greek. This measure was probably one of the most effective tools of cultural assimilation. By the 1940s, only a number of older women in Assiros still spoke Slavic, and by the conclusion of my fieldwork there remained only one woman whom villagers described as "Bulgarizing" the Greek language when she spoke. Yet a few words from the (former) local vernacular lexicon survive, particularly kinship terms, as evidence that Slavic had been once used there.

In Assiros, the construction of Greek linguistic hegemony apparently came about with relative ease. But in other locales, this process was more violent. According to Cowan (1990:43), the Sohoians to the east of Langadhas had been forced to drink castor oil or were even sent to prison if they spoke in any language other than Greek. In western Greek Macedonia, where Slavic consciousness among the local population was stronger and the influence of Greek language and culture had been historically weaker than in communities of central Greek Macedonia such as Assiros, the Hellenization campaign was more aggressive (and more strongly resisted). There, for example, even young schoolchildren were thrashed for speaking Slavic (see Karakasidou 1993b). Clearly, on the local level, the ideological frontiers of Hellenism did not always keep pace with the rhetorical ethnological boundaries of Hellenism championed by national elites in Greece (cf. Kyriakidis 1955).

Refugee settlement in the 1920s also had a profound impact on the spread of Greek national consciousness in Macedonia. As individual families sought to legitimize their claims to a rightful place in the New Lands, the relative Greekness of various groups became a vocal part of popular discourse. The national culture of coexistence that emerged in Greek Macedonia was no simple result of a heavy-handed acculturation campaign directed by national elites, although such pressures were exerted. Rather, it was a dialectical product of the interaction of state and local interests, in which perceptions of solidarities and differences were reshaped by conflicts, challenges, and contests in everyday life.

While many of the circumstances had changed significantly, including the symbolic and ideological clothing of their authority, the Guvezna/ Assiros *tsorbadjidhes* under the early Greek state were not unlike the Christian *dimogherondhia* during the Ottoman era, who had once had the power to determine each year what the "required" taxes were to be submitted to the Metropolite, who in turn, remitted a portion to the Patriarchate (see Vasdravellis 1941–52). During the 1920s and 1930s, the *tsorbadjidhes* consolidated themselves, despite their differences and rivalries, into a dominant local class whose interests were focused strongly on assumptions that they were part of the Greek state and the nation of the Hellenes. They moved concertedly to further their control over the ownership and management of productive resources in the township, closing off many avenues of upward mobility to the laboring poor. The enclosure of grazing lands and the competitive bidding for grazing rights devastated small herders, who had neither the funds nor the political connections to win at auctions. Some were effectively disenfranchised from pastoralism and were obliged to take up jobs as shepherd laborers for large herdowners. As one such man told me, "They [i.e. the *tsorbadjidhes*] would not even give us a couple of sheep to start our flocks. They would not even give us some wool to make blankets to cover ourselves." These actions and developments led to a restratification of local society, fostering new perceptions of difference and commonality among township residents. Social boundaries became expressed, both verbally and through action, along the lines of class rather than national orientation. Greekness continued to feature prominently in local rhetoric of difference, but the settlement of refugees had added new dimensions to the concept, its meaning, and its relevance. The interwar years were a period of concerted state-making and nation-building in Greek Macedonia, and this dual process dramatically reshaped local life in rural communities throughout the region.

It was thus within the arena of the local township that the ideology of the nation of the Hellenes and the politics of the Greek state were played out. The incorporation of the New Lands into the Greek state in 1913 gave new territorial and administrative definition to the arbitrary and imaginative boundaries of Hellenism, and created new "citizen" groups out of the local population (see Verdery 1983). Village residents were addressed as "patriots" (*patriotes*) by the township bailiff (*klitiras*) each time he was called upon to make a public pronouncement. Beating a drum and summoning their attention with a loud cry of "Patriots! Patriots!" he would announce the will of the state, the glory of the nation, and the decisions and demands of the village elite.

When the teacher of Greek, Garoufalidis, an "outsider," suggested that the name of Guvezna be changed to Assiros, he conveyed to local inhabitants a sense of place in ancient Greek history that harkened back to the Great Alexander and Greek civilization in Macedonia. In fact, townships throughout Greek Macedonia began to undergo name changes in the 1920s. This trend became especially pronounced or even proceduralized during the Metaxas dictatorship of the 1930s when concerted efforts were made to erase symbols of Ottoman, Slavic, and other non-Greek culture in the region (see Karakasidou 1993b). Even families were obliged to change their names. In Assiros, Slavic-sounding surnames listed in the old 1918 Guvezna township family registry (*dhimotologhio*) were absent from the new registry started in the 1950s. Even the given names of women, such as Velika and Dona, were transformed into Greek names. The local *tsorbadjidhes* played an active role in this process. As baptismal sponsors, it was they who named newborn children. As local benefactors, it was they who offered jobs to the laboring poor. As township administrators, they sponsored national holidays and local festivals, stood in at church-officiated rituals and ceremonies, and oversaw the education of their schoolchildren. In a very real way, the Assiros *tsorbadjidhes* sponsored the local citizenry's rite of passage to Greek nationhood in Macedonia.

7

SPONSORING PASSAGES TO NATIONHOOD

Material and Spiritual Patronage in Assiros

[E]lites dominate not only the physical means of production but
the symbolic means of production as well—and . . . this symbolic
hegemony allows them to control the very standards by which
their role is evaluated.

James Scott, *Weapons of the Weak*

On the morning of 21 June 1941, a column of German motorcycle
troops rode up the dirt road from Langadhas alongside the Ambelo-
lakos stream to occupy the village of Assiros. At least half the community
was said to have turned out in the *aghora* to greet them as friends. The
young girls of the village offered the soldiers eggs and flowers. The commanding officer of the 120-man force quartered his troops in the mansion
of the tobacco broker, Pashos. Later that same day, the leaders of the
local fascist youth organized an official welcoming ceremony.

These festivities, and the National Youth Organization (EON) that
sponsored them, grew out of the national homogenization efforts during
the Metaxas years in the late 1930s. In Greek Macedonia, the authoritar-
ian rule of military dictatorship had been accompanied by a period of
concerted pressure toward cultural or ethnic assimilation within the Hellenic nation-state. As described in the previous chapter, compulsory
Greek language classes, fines, and even corporal punishment contributed
forcefully to the promulgation of a national language. In fact, the
Metaxas years led to the development of a protocol and pageantry of
national ritual. State-issued ceremonial directives, often quite specific in
their orchestration of details, came to provide the basis for national holiday celebrations and other commemorative festivals throughout the
Greek Macedonia (Karakasidou 1995a).

I have argued that the era between the Balkan Wars and the German
occupation witnessed a dramatic restructuring of economic stratification
and notions of social identity in Assiros, as the village became increasingly polarized along lines of class differentiation. The relevance of ethnicity, national orientation, or religious affiliation—issues that had been
so prominent and divisive at the turn of the century—began to fade. In

the context of daily life, the mundane concerns of subsistence and peonage, of occupational livelihood and clientel dependency remained overwhelming concerns for most of the township's residents. Yet these developments were accompanied by conscious efforts in the realm of symbol, ritual, and education to foster the amalgamation of a Greek national identity among the region's inhabitants. During this period, many local rituals and celebrations came to adopt new symbols and meanings that encouraged or even guided national imaginings of a common Hellenic heritage and patriotic sentiments toward the Greek nation-state. It was in their capacities as local patrons that the *tsorbadjidhes* subtly cultivated images of beneficence, sponsoring employment opportunities, credit arrangements, ritual kinship, and festive community-wide celebrations and commemorations.

Material aspects of clientelism notwithstanding, the symbolic expression and legitimation of such ties of patronage and dependency played a critical role in reshaping local notions of identity and collectivity, as well as perceptions of affinity and difference. Drawing on the cultural institutions of ritual kinship and communal festivities, for example, the *tsorbadjidhes* of Assiros created an ideological foundation for their dominance that was rooted in a local cultural repertoire. This development also promoted the spread of Greek national ideology among the local poor, Slavic-speakers and Greek-speakers alike, who relied on the patronage and beneficence of the local elite. In this sense, the new state-backed authority the *tsorbadjidhes* had acquired as township officials was only one layer of ideational stratigraphy grafted on to local perceptions of power and difference—albeit an important one in that it supported the creation of a common sense of local membership in a larger, encompassing nation-state.

SOCIAL DYNAMICS OF PROPERTY, POWER, AND PRIVILEGE
Symbolizing Status and Prestige in a Changing Class Structure

Ritual kinship (*koumbario*), created through sponsorship in religious rites of passage such as baptism and marriage, was an important marker of the competitive influence of the local *tsorbadjidhes*.[1] Unlike affinal alliances, ritual kinship was often perceived as an expression of hierarchical, clientel ties between prestigious and influential families of the local elite and those of the nonelite or working poor. Each prominent *tsorbadjis* family was associated with a largely mutually exclusive ritual kindred, which it attempted to maintain or even to expand across generations.[2]

During the years 1926–40, for example, when Yeorghios Vranas served several terms as Liberal Party township president, his family sponsored no less than twenty-three baptisms (ATA, baptismal registry). Today, his descendants continue to honor the ritual kin relationships he established over half a century earlier. As descent groups proliferated, affinal ties broadened, and ritual kinship relations extended over time, networks of alliance and support were intensified. Members of *tsorbadjidhes* families who ran for office in local elections were able to draw on sizeable electoral support. As mentioned earlier, they also reportedly engaged in vote-buying practices, cultivating a clientel base of support from among the working poor, who with few exceptions enjoyed no direct representation on the powerful local township council. This material imbalance of power received further elaboration and definition through symbolic expressions in local ritual.

Consider the meanings that grew out of life-course rituals involving baptismal and wedding sponsors (*nona* [f.] or *nonos* [m.]). While parents now decide the name their child will be given during baptism, during the interwar period such decisions were the privilege of the baptismal sponsor. This practice contributed to the gradual disappearance of Slavic and other non-Greek Christian names in Assiros, as Greek-oriented *tsorbadjidhes* sponsors favored names from Hellenic traditions. Moreover, ritual kinship sponsorship was serial: a wedding sponsor often would be expected to act as baptismal sponsor for the couple's first child, and either that sponsor or another representative of that family would again serve as the child's wedding sponsor years later. Villagers themselves recognized that sponsorship was (and still is) often transmitted and reproduced across generations. Once a relationship was established, it was expected to be continued and renewed in the future, barring some unforeseen major change in the relationship between the families concerned. Furthermore, sons or daughters of sponsors were sometimes expected to succeed to that status of their parents.

While sponsorship thus was sometimes passed through generations with a remarkable degree of continuity, it was an acquired rather than an ascribed status. Not only did upwardly mobile families aspire to such status, but patterned variation in baptismal and wedding sponsorship over time may have reflected the rise and fall from prominence of particular families. The sons and daughters of Paskhalina, "the Bulgarian," for example, have come to occupy prestigious social positions in the Assiros of the 1990s, in contrast to the hostility Paskhalina endured. The rituals of sponsorship included symbolic expressions of submission to benefactors, such as the obligatory kiss of hand that all brides and grooms were expected to offer their wedding sponsor after the religious ceremony. Recall from the account of the shepherd Petros in chapter 6 that *tsorbadjidhes* employers expected their hired laborers to kiss their hands when they were paid. Also in deference to the wedding sponsor, a bride was expected to present to all her sponsor's relatives, friends, and guests handkerchiefs (*mandilia*) she had handwoven herself. In light of the prominence the *tsorbadjidhes* enjoyed as employment patrons, local representatives of the Greek state, and promoters of Greek national ideology, such practices contributed to the legitimation of the new patterns of dominance and authority following the Balkan Wars.

Sponsorship and Ritual Expressions of Group Identity

Consider the role of sponsors in the rituals involved in local marriage celebrations. During the two weeks of preparations leading up to the wedding, the words, instructions or wishes of the sponsor were (and still are) intimately respected.[3] On the Sunday of the wedding, musicians accompanied the groom's relatives as they called on the sponsor, escorting the latter—along with his or her selected guests—back to the home of the groom. There, a prewedding feast was given in their honor. Sponsors and their guests ate in a separate room, apart from the groom's family and guests. During this feast, the sponsor performed a short ceremony (*varakoma*), dipping pieces of gold paper (*chrisoharto*) into *retsina* (resin wine) and affixing them to three apples (*varakia*). The sponsor then placed these fertility symbols on ends of a cross, set atop a flagstaff. From this pole was hung the Greek national flag, to be carried by the groom's relatives or friends at the head of the wedding procession while enroute to and from the church on the coming Sunday.

It is noteworthy that expressions of national identification were voiced in wedding rituals. The symbol of the identification banner in local wedding ceremonies has a history that predates the specific form of the Greek national flag. During the late Ottoman era, patrilineally organized pastoralist groups throughout Macedonia had maintained their own descent-group banners and used them in wedding rituals. Such identification banners, known in Assiros as *hamblos* (origins unclear) or *bairaki* (*bairak*; Turkish: "flag"), were made by the women of a groom's family. They usually consisted of a red and blue cross embroidered in the middle of a white field, a pattern similar to that used by pastoralist groups throughout the southern Balkans. (Karapatakis, 1960; Loukas 1981)

In the late nineteenth century, as Bulgarian Exarchist propaganda activities intensified in Macedonia, those groups that retained a strong orientation to or ties with the Ecumenical Orthodox Patriarchate began to carry in their wedding processions the latter's banner: a red field embroidered with a twin-headed eagle, a Byzantine symbol. In this emblematic shift, the family-designed *hamblos* banners, which had once symbolized local descent groups engaged in their own livelihoods amid loose and shifting boundaries, were replaced by Byzantine Patriarchist symbols, reflecting a ritual refocus of group identity toward a common religious cum national group (i.e. Greek-oriented Patriarchate loyalists). After 1913, such Patriarchist banners were themselves replaced by the Greek national flag, at least in communities where incorporation into Greece signified liberation and not subjugation.[4] The Sarakatsan, who prided themselves on their Greek descent, were among the first pastoralist groups to replace their descent-group banners (which they called *flamboura*) with the Greek flag. The adoption of the Greek national flag represented the emergence of popular notions of a national group sharing descent from common ancestors, such as the ancient Hellenes and the Byzantines, sentiments that were reinforced in flag-devotion campaigns of the Metaxas era (see Karakasidou 1996a).

The ritual actions and behavior of those associated with the transport of the banner/flag during the wedding procession suggest an emotional symbolic link between notions of the nation and those of biological or social reproduction. The groom's male friends, or "brothers" (*bratimia*; from the Slavic *brat,* or "brother"), were the focus of these activities. On the Friday preceding the Sunday church ceremony, the groom's *bratimia* took his family's banner and went into the hills to collect shrub and firewood, to be used as cooking fuel for a feast that evening at the home of the groom. The banner was placed on the rooftop of the house, where it remained until Sunday morning, when the groom and his delegation carried it to the home of the wedding sponsor (*nonos*), to invite him formally to a midday feast in his honor.[5] There, the sponsor offered the couple his wishes or blessings for fertility and well-being in the ritual of the golden apples. Afterwards, the procession of the wedding party and guests to the church followed, led by the groom's *bratimia* with the banner. Yet such processions were often long-drawn-out. The bride and other wedding guests were obliged to wait patiently as the "brothers" celebrated their bonds of (descent group and male) solidarity to the music of the *orghana* from nearby Liti and Kolhikon. Under cross, flag, and fertility symbols of gold, the "brothers" dance, drink, and sometimes sprawl atop each other on the ground in celebration of this rite of passage.

Owing to their status, prestige, and influence, the Assiros *tsorbadjidhes* came to sponsor many weddings and baptisms.[6] The symbolic power of sponsorship was affirmed in the material living conditions for township residents in the first half of the twentieth century. Infant mortality was high, landholdings were modest, taxation was heavy, and opportunities for mobility were largely limited for many locals and refugees alike. As ritual kin patrons, wedding sponsors often served as benefactors, arranging employment or even providing food. For example, a *tsorbadjis nonos* could serve as a guarantor for a sponsoree who sought to participate in a township auction. The word of the sponsor was heard and heeded, and the actions of such benefactors were respected and emulated. Expressions of symbolic submission to the *nonos,* such as deference to the sponsor's "word" or the obligatory kissing of the hand, were also highly personalized acts that represented one's gratitude and loyalty to the patron sponsor, a relationship that mediated an individual's passage or transition between key phases of the life course.

The *tsorbadjidhes* presented a lifestyle, status, and standard of living that were matters of fact, but they were also guarded in their displays of wealth. Although their homes were usually larger than those of other local residents (owing to the need for storage facilities for their agropastoral enterprises), they were not particularly fancier or more elaborate. The most conspicuous displays of their wealth were expressed in activities surrounding ritual ceremonies, such as weddings and baptisms. Recall how several Assiros women remarked on how, as young girls from poor families, they had waited expectantly for a local *tsorbadjis* to marry one of his children. A wedding feast meant a good (and free) meal with a rare treat of meat, as all villagers were welcome to come and eat at the home of a *tsorbadjis* on such occasions.

Through such roles in life-course rituals, the Assiros local elite cultivated an image as personal and familial benefactors. At the same time, in their capacity as local administrators of township government, the *tsorbadjidhes* also sponsored public holidays and ceremonial commemorations. Some of these were local in character, such as the *kourbani,* promoting the notion of a local community. Others were linked to national celebrations designated by the Greek state, such as the commemorative ceremonies honoring the Hellenes, the descent group writ large.

CELEBRATING RITUALS OF COLLECTIVE IDENTITY

The annual *kourban* or *kourbani* feast was an important symbolic expression of local corporate beneficence in community life.[7] Jointly sponsored by the township and the church, it is still held each year on Prophet Elias's Day (20 July), the patron saint to whom the (old hilltop) church in Assiros was dedicated. In the past, the *kourbani* had been a family-based celebration, prominent among pastoralists, in which a family would open its home to relatives and friends on the day of the family's patron saint. As such, it was not unlike the *slava* celebration in rural Slavic culture, which commemorated the patron saint of a family or descent group (see Rheubotton 1976).[8] Today, however, the principal celebrations hosted by individual families are the personal name days (*onomastikes yiortes*). Like the *kourbani*, personal name days are also based on the calendar of Christian patron saint days. In contrast to the *kourbani*, however, name days focus on individuals rather than on the family as a collective unit of identity. The *kourbani* itself also underwent transformation over time. It is now a public—rather than family or descent-group—celebration, commemorating the community of the village through metaphors of family and commensality.

The *kourbani* is now held on the grounds of the Prophet Elias Church, above the village *aghora*. There, a stew of meat and potatoes is cooked in large cauldrons by a group of local men regarded as good cooks, some of them having jobs as cooks elsewhere. As the stew boils, the men drink and joke, or recount stories to the visiting ethnographer. Formerly, local *tsorbadjidhes* would bid against each other for the honor of providing the animals to be sacrificed for this ritual feast. It was a privilege that a sponsor paid for, and proceeds went into church accounts. Now, however, the township sponsors and funds the celebration. Around noon on the day of the *kourbani*, families in the village eagerly await the ringing of the church bells, which signal that the food is ready. After that, a steady stream of old women and young children may be seen making their way up the church hill, small dishes in hand, to receive a portion of the food, blessed by the priest. In the past, many would eat and dance there at the church. During my fieldwork, however, that privilege was reserved mainly for honored guests, such as district leaders of the New Democracy political party, high-ranking officers from a nearby military base, and perhaps a visiting anthropologist and her husband. Most village families now eat together at home that day, many celebrating the name day of their relatives named Elias, a common Christian name in the village.

The Assiros *tsorbadjidhes* also expanded their status as local patrons through other public celebrations over which they officiated as members of the township council. The interwar period saw a number of national holidays and public ceremonies celebrating the nation of the Hellenes and commemorating heroic figures in its collective history. The township council and the school played a key role in organizing, sponsoring, and funding these activities. Sometimes they determined the protocol and content of such programs themselves. In other instances, they followed guide-lines issued by state authorities, such as directives regarding national flag adoration (see Karakasidou 1996a). As with the *kourbani*, generous ex-penditures of public funds on festivals promoting collective identity under the Greek nation also reinforced the image of *tsorbadjidhes* township administrators as gift-giving and resource-allocating patrons. At the same time, the local elite came to express and portray themselves more con-sciously as representatives of the celebrated and ritualized Greek nation-state.

Not all of these efforts at national enculturation achieved their de-sired results. Consider the example of a small "popular library" (*laiki vivliothiki*), established by the township council in the 1920s. The library was stocked almost exclusively with books of a strong nationalist con-tent. The township council continued to add to the collection over the next two decades, acquiring a number of notable titles along the way, including: *King Constantine,*[9] purchased in 1921 (they also bought his icon in 1937, so that "he would not be forgotten"); *Communism in Greece, Ioannis Metaxas,* and *The Contribution of the Macedonians in the 1821 War of Independence,* all added in 1937; *Greece Before and After the 4th of August,*[10] bought in 1938; as well as *The Macedonians in the Fights for Independence,* 1796–1832, acquired in 1941. The library, however, proved tremendously unsuccessful. The township council noted that "families go to bed early" rather than utilize the library collection in their leisure hours (ATA 1937). Eventually the library was shut down.

In contrast, ritualized public holidays and national celebrations proved much more popular. On 22 March 1925, for example, the Assiros township council decided to sponsor a celebration of the 25 March na-tional holiday, commemorating the Greek War of Independence against the Ottomans which began in southern Greece on that day in 1821 (ATA 1925). Township councillors distributed gifts to school children and a public feast was given in honor of the holiday. The following year, 1926, a similar celebration was held in which the council purchased Greek flags and distributed them to the school children. Funds were also allocated for the erection of a memorial stele in the village green dedicated to the memory of "Greek Heroes" (*Ellines Iroes*) who had sacrificed their lives in the wars of liberation against the nation's enemies, Turkey and Bul-garia (ATA 1926). In 1929, the council voted to sponsor a commemora-tive mass on that holiday as well, and has continued the "tradition" ever since.

Through the township council, the Assiros *tsorbadjidhes* continued to promote other Greek national activities and celebrations throughout the politically tumultuous 1930s. In 1936, the council sponsored two commemorative masses in the village church, one for King Constantine and Queen Sofia and another for martyrs killed in battle for the freedom of Greece. When they learned later that year that the king would pass by Assiros while enroute to visit the town of Serres, the council decided to erect a commemorative arch over the public highway under which the king's car could pass. Township councillors also extended warm sentiments to dictator Ioannis Metaxas, then head of the Greek government. When Metaxas made a visit to Thessaloniki that year, the Assiros township president went to the city to take part in the welcoming ceremony (ATA 1936). In 1937, the General Directorate of Macedonia informed township presidents that they should send a representative to the August 4 commemoration of the Metaxas coup to be held in Athens. It also instructed them to donate funds for an ambitious campaign by Metaxas to create a Royal Air Force in Greece.

The Assiros township president at the time echoed national patriotic sentiments when he formally addressed the township council on 9 May 1937:

> [T]he president has expressed his deepest gratitude and devotion to his Royal Highness, our King, and to our national leader, Ioannis Metaxas, who has resolved once and for all the poisoned political party atmosphere of Greece through his patriotic gesture of 4th August 1936. [The president] proposes, so that our township will not do less than others, [that we] should express our patriotic enthusiasm and glory of the Greek soul . . . [and provide] funds to support the Royal Air Force and to express our love to the creators of today's Greek State, our Venerable King and the National Governor Ioannis Metaxas (ATA 1937).

It is of no small significance that the author of the statement was none other than Pashos, the former schoolteacher and tobacco merchant who had once been a vocal critic of Greek nation-building activities in Assiros. By the late 1930s, a growing sense of Greek national identity had taken root in the consciousness of local residents, even among those who a decade or two earlier had expressed ambivalence toward the extension of Greek sovereignty over Macedonia.

In present-day Assiros, three national holidays are celebrated. The most locally significant is the twenty-sixth of October (or St. Dimitrios's day, when the Ottomans surrendered Thessaloniki to Greek forces in 1912), but also observed are the twenty-fifth of March (discussed above) and the twenty-eighth of October (*Ohi* ["No"] Day, commemorating the refusal of Greece to support the Axis alliance in 1940).[11] On such days, schoolboys wear the "traditional" costumes of the Greek Independence fighters of 1821, while girls don local costumes or blue and white dresses (the colors of the national flag). All parade with the Greek flag down the streets of the village to the *aghora,* where a wreath is placed at the foot of the monument to the village's heroes. Veterans who fought against the Italians on the Albanian front in 1940 also dedicate a wreath on those days. Following the ceremony, the township offices offer soft drinks or cognac with nuts and sweets to all villagers. When I inquired why they did so, they replied that it was their "tradition." Curiously enough, Examili and Mavrorahi celebrate separate holidays, contributing to a picture of "local nationalism."

The veneration of heroes, worship of martyrs, and honor of veterans in these ceremonies were also important facets in the creation of a Greek national consciousness among the region's population, as likewise have been conscription and compulsory military service for male citizens. Since independence from the Ottomans, local township offices in Greece have maintained a special archive, the Male Registry (*Mitroo Arrenon*), in which are recorded the names and addresses of all males within an administrative jurisdiction in order that local authorities may monitor compliance with compulsory conscription.[12] Through basic training, recruits are exposed to educational programs intended to transform them not only into good soldiers but good citizens as well.[13] This basic training is a classic rite of passage in which old identities are shed during a period of liminality until inductees emerge with new status.

During this process, which is complete with its own ritual repertoire, young men from diverse backgrounds are brought together in close, stressful contact for extended periods of time. In addition to rigorous training in basic combat skills, conscripts are also conditioned to think and respond on the basis of a sense of group identity centered around national sentiments, often sharpened by the assertions of military trainers that the country, or rather the nation, is under constant threat from hostile outsiders that surround it: Slavs, Turks, Bulgarians, communists, or more recently "Skopians" from the FYROM. Upon "graduation" from their training, these young Greek soldiers are summarily dispatched to various corners of the motherland, often far from their native place, where they learn through firsthand experience what it means in other areas of the country to be Greek.

In an important sense, Greek state-strengthening innovations and nation-building efforts went hand in hand during the interwar period. Through actions such as those described above, the *tsorbadjis* local elite in Assiros contributed to a reconstruction of local notions of community, collectivity, and solidarity. They spent money on ceremonial and festive activities, established a public library and built the village school, made donations to hospitals and orphanages,[14] put out funds for legal expenses and school maintenance, and financed public works projects. These efforts had a strong national orientation and content, repeatedly promoting a sense of Greek identity that over the years helped to amalgamate the various ethnic groups living in the area under a single national culture that was officially depicted (and popularly perceived) as homogeneous. One might even argue that if not for the success of Greek nation-building efforts in the region, which helped to legitimize new state dominance, Greece might still have lost Macedonia when it was confronted by new Bulgarian aggression during the German occupation of the 1940s.

TEMPERING NATIONAL IDENTITY THROUGH OCCUPATION AND RESISTANCE

It is in the context of such growing popular national sentiments that one might revisit the welcome extended by the Assiriotes to the German occupational force in the summer of 1941. By their own accounts, many villagers had come to harbor strong resentment towards the British and French during the 1930s, to whom they attributed Greece's defeat by Turkey in the Asia Minor War of 1921–23. In the early years of World War II, these feelings found reexpression in sympathy and support for the Germans, and many Assiriotes listened to the "Robin" radio broadcasts of the Third Reich in Greece. Moreover, by the end of the Metaxas era in 1940, most young people in Assiros had been organized into a local chapter of the National Youth Organization (*Ethniki Orghanosi Neon* or EON). Some had joined out of family conviction, others out of political necessity.

The National Youth Organization actively promoted strong nationalist and community sentiment throughout the country. The Assiros EON was largely successful in its solidarity-building efforts, in part because many of its activities were festive outings for village youths who otherwise had few opportunities to socialize outside the village. The local branch was under the direction of the township secretary, Mouhtaris. A local merchant rented space to the township for use as an EON office. In 1938, the branch requested and received funds from the township to purchase uniforms (ATA 1938), which by their very character tend to facilitate group identity and solidarity.

Among the activities sponsored by the EON were the 4 August holiday celebrations of 1938 and 1939, which were underwritten with EON funds and carried out with a great air of festivity. The township council purchased beverages, sweets, firecrackers, candles, and a commemorative wreath for the occasion. In 1939, the local EON branch sent a telegram of Christmas greetings to the king and one to the president, General Metaxas, providing a special thrill for the youthful members. Under the EON, prominent Assiros men also cooperated with regional government authorities. For example, when the Governor General of Macedonia informed the township in 1939 that vehicles were needed to transport several EON companies for an outing, three local men volunteered to drive the Assiros bus and received remuneration from the township. Only a few days before the Germans arrived, the township was elated when several local EON members went to Lahanas to participate in a commemoration of the victorious 1913 battle against the Bulgarians (ATA 1938, 1939, 1940).

When villagers were asked about the German occupation, many insisted that the Germans harmed no one and never had any intentions of that sort. They recalled the soldiers as humane and polite, and claimed they displayed a great deal of respect for local women and young girls. Troops at the public fountain surrendered their place to women returning from the fields or fetching water for their households. Villagers maintained that the township president at the time, a local merchant *tsorbadjis* named Athanasios Karamagiris, went to great lengths to ensure the village kept out of trouble. He was remembered as a diplomat rather than as a collaborator. No reprisals occurred in Assiros during the German occupation.

Yet it was not long before villagers came to realize that the German forces had come as occupiers, not as friends. Many poor villagers were left without draft animals and suffered terrible hunger as the Germans requisitioned all their horses. Some wealthier families or those with oxen suffered marginally less. Assiriotes recounted how they even ate turtles during those years. Hungry people came from as far away as Thessaloniki to beg for wheat or food, but most Assiriotes had nothing to spare. Their common subjugation to a foreign occupation army and the decline of their own means of subsistence forced the Assiriotes through a collective rite of passage. As Bulgarian nationalist forces and later a militant communist movement challenged Greek national hegemony in Macedonia during the 1940s, the *tsorbadjidhes* rose to new prominence in defense of the nation, leading the local population to new levels of national consciousness yet again through baptisms of fire.

Assiros was situated on the perimeter of the thirty-kilometer occupation zone that the German command maintained around major cities, such as Thessaloniki. With its administrative border at the twenty-seventh kilometer mark on the public highway, Assiros was the northernmost village of the Langadhas basin under German occupation. Beyond that point, the Bulgarian allies of the Nazis had been given responsibility for the occupation of the Macedonian hinterland.

Aligning themselves with Germany, Bulgarian leaders had harbored visions of restoring the short-lived Greater Bulgaria of the 1878 San Stefano Treaty (see map 7), although their efforts to control the region as far south as Mount Olympus were checked by the Germans. Bulgarian activity had been particularly forceful in eastern Greek Macedonia (the area east of the Strimon River) and in Thrace. Bulgarian occupation in those areas, according to local inhabitants themselves, was particularly harsh. Strong efforts were made once again to "Bulgarize" the local Slavic-speaking population. Propaganda and torture accompanied the teachers and priests that the troops brought with them from Bulgaria. As had been the case during the Macedonian Struggle, many rural residents of the region fled Bulgarian occupational forces to seek protection in more secure Greek strongholds, such as Assiros.[15]

On 2 July 1941, less than two weeks after the arrival of the German occupation force in Assiros, a three-man governing committee consisting of Asteriou, Galianos, and Karamagiris (as president), all men of the *aghora,* was set up in the village. The township council was suspended, as were elections (ATA 1941). The committee cultivated amicable relations with the Germans in an effort to keep out the Bulgarians and their propaganda efforts. Consider the following account:

> One day during the German occupation the villagers awoke to find themselves surrounded by Bulgarian troops. The soldiers ordered the president to gather all the men of the village in the *aghora.* The bailiff, who knew no Bulgarian, called the president, Athanasios Karamagiris. Then a German patrol arrived and approached the crowd. "The Bulgarians are not our friends," the president told the German officer. "Our friends are the Germans." The officer telephoned to German headquarters in Langadhas and the issue was resolved.

Not all local villagers, however, shared the attitudes of the president towards the Bulgarians. One Assiriotissa woman was said to have warmly greeted the Bulgarian troops as they marched past a doorway where she stood sweeping. She spoke with them at length, presumably in "Bulgarian," telling them that the Assiriotes were of the same "race" (*ratsa*) as they. It is unclear whether she did so out of emotional conviction, or from a lack of Greek national consciousness, or simply as an expedient survival strategy. But such an incident does indicate that a degree of non-Greek Otherness was still registered in the minds or memories of some Assiros villagers.

For the majority of local villagers, however, "the Bulgarians" by the 1940s had become objectivized as an alien, hostile, national other. Recall how during the turn-of-the-century national conflict, the Greek-speaking local Christian notables had cooperated in impeding the infiltration of Bulgarian national propagandizing in Guvezna. In the decades that followed the advent of Greek rule, they further mediated the cultivation of a strong sense of Greek national consciousness among local Slavic-speakers, creating a belief in Hellenism among local residents.

One popular story of the occupation era reaffirmed the importance of the local *tsorbadjis* elite in safeguarding Hellenism in Assiros:

> During one night later in the German occupation a knock came at the door of the president's house. "Open up," someone said, "I am a friend," Karamagiris took out olives, onions, and ouzo and treated the stranger. The latter in turn confided his secret. "The Bulgarians are offering money to those who will register as Bulgarians." After a pause he continued. "President, I will go to the Middle East and join the resistance there, but be careful and promise me that nothing like this will happen in your village."

The rather cryptic aura surrounding this account, of a stranger knocking on the village president's door in the middle of the night, may be attributable in part to the reputation Assiros enjoyed throughout the century as a stronghold of Greek patriotic national sentiment. Karamagiris reportedly kept his promise to the midnight visitor. No one from Assiros registered as a Bulgarian. Villagers recalled that in the distance they could hear the Bulgarians call out periodic announcements: "Whoever registers with us will not go hungry!" But once again, Bulgarians and Bulgarian nationalism remained outside the physical and social space of Assiros.[16]

Despite, and in part because of, the foreign occupation, the Assiriotes emerged from the Second World War with a stronger sense of collective national identity vis-à-vis neighboring states. But new markers of difference were beginning to take form among the local population, distinctions that were based on occupation, livelihood, power, and influence rather than on ethnic or national orientations. The social tensions generated by developments of the interwar era eventually erupted in the trauma of yet another violent conflict: the Greek Civil War (1947–49), in which the Macedonian countryside was fiercely contested. In Assiros, this new conflict was expressed largely in terms of a struggle between social groups divided along lines of local political alliances and class identities, rather than in terms of ethnicity or nationality. By contrast, in other parts of Greek Macedonia, especially in the west, the conflict had strong national-istic undertones, as many Slavic-speakers joined or supported communist partisans in the hopes of creating an autonomous Macedonia.

THE RETURN OF PARTISAN TERROR

Organized resistance to the German occupation began in September 1941 with the formation of the National Liberation Front (*Ethniko Apeleftherotiko Metopo* or EAM; Jelavich 1983:278). Early members of this initial resistance organization were later stigmatized for its communist ties, but at this stage in the resistance many volunteers had been fighting for na-tional liberation rather than communism. While Assiriotes joined the ranks of the EAM, a rival right-wing National Guard resistance organiza-tion, the Panhellenic Liberation Organization (*Panellinia Apeleftherotiki Orghanosi* or PAO) was set up shortly after the establishment of the EAM. It was to this organization and its PAO brigades that many Assiros men flocked, leading to a progressive deterioration of the peaceful (if ten-uous) coexistence that had initially held between local villagers and the Germans. Partisan terror, rather than German reprisals, was responsible for most casualties in Assiros during the 1940s.

The national resistance movement against the German occupation soon became embroiled in partisan factionalism between Left and Right that rapidly divided the Greek Macedonian countryside. Many Assiriotes claimed they had been more afraid of the PAO brigades than of the Ger-mans or even the Bulgarians. Local right-wing villagers would loot the houses of the few leftist EAM members, while the latter looted the houses of the Assiros *tsorbadjidhes* whenever they had the opportunity. Consider that five houses reportedly were burnt down by leftist partisans in 1944. All belonged to wealthy and politically prominent village families men-tioned earlier: Galianos (a member of the governing committee under the German occupation), the two Velikas brothers, Vranas, and Mouhtaris (the township secretary, who was assassinated by leftist partisans a year later). In the course of the war, a total of eleven village houses and one barn were destroyed, while seven Assiros men were murdered. Of these, only one was killed by the Germans; the rest were victims of local civil strife.

Following the German retreat from Assiros in September 1944, Left-ist EAM partisans occupied the village and placed it under "Popular Government" (*Laokratia*), as they did in other rural Greek communities that came under their control. It was said that those placed in charge of the *Laokratia* even set up courts, so as to put on trial the Assiriotes who had fought with PAO brigades and had terrorized the surrounding countryside. I have scant details on events of the *Laokratia* period in Assiros; few villagers were willing to discuss it.

In the spring of 1945, EAM partisans left Assiros, surrendering their weapons and withdrawing to positions at least thirty kilometers from all major towns, in accordance with the provisions of the Treaty of Varkiza (see Clogg 1979:156). Assiros reverted to the control of Greek national forces and, of course, the local *tsorbadjidhes*. The latter now possessed stronger, reinforced ties to the conservative anticommunist national government. Reprisals against left-wing partisans came quickly. In November 1944, four villagers were labeled as "war criminals" and accused of having "committed many murders in Assiros and elsewhere" (ATA 1944). In June 1945, the office of the Thessaloniki Prefecture demanded the names of anyone who had taken part in the partisan movement's formation (ATA 1945). Authorities particularly wanted to know whether any public servants or township clerks had been involved with the EAM.

The ensuing national campaign of government harassment and leftist suppression eventually culminated in the Greek Civil War of 1947–49. During that civil conflict, which lasted almost three years, Assiros was again a Greek national government stronghold. Only three Assiriotes joined the communist partisans in the hills. Many respondents attributed such a low number to the forceful role played by the township president at the time, Voukas, who reportedly threatened leftist sympathizers in the village with reprisals should any mishaps befall any inhabitants of Assiros. Incidents did occur, however, and many respondents recalled scenes in which leftist partisans in positions on the church hill shot at Greek national guardsmen stationed at the schoolhouse.

The violence and terror of the era were openly manifest. What distinguished conditions in 1940s Assiros from those of early 1900s Guvezna was that the ethno-national conflict of the past had been rendered largely irrelevant. As mentioned earlier, the Civil War conflict in Assiros lacked the nationalistic undertones expressed in western Greek Macedonia. Moreover, Assiros was not seriously contested by leftist forces. The few local residents who did join the communist partisans were not recruited by or assigned to the Slavo-Macedonian SNOF brigades (see Karakasidou 1993a). The early twentieth-century rhetoric of anti-Bulgarianism had been replaced by that of anticommunism, and socioeconomic grievances rather than ethnic or national injustices were a rallying cry in many areas where the Cold War grew hot. Developments of the Civil War period had an important influence on the processes of class restratification and national homogenization discussed earlier. The dominance of local *tsorbadjidhes* families was augmented through new policing authority, including the command of new local militia units.

Shortly after the start of the Civil War, the government sponsored the organization and arming of local paramilitary troops to "protect" villages from communists. Originally, these forces were known as "Rural Security Units" (*Monadhes Asfalias Ipethrou,* or MAY) and their members were referred to as *maidhes.* The strength of each local unit was proportionate to the size of the local population. During the Civil War years in Assiros, some thirty to fifty armed *maidhes* guarded the village inhabitants, the water supply, and the nearby telegraph poles from those whom some of them described as "bloodthirsty" communists. In 1948, the Assiros MAY had thirty members, including members of the Artousis, Asteriou, Galianos, Velikas, Halepis, and Tamtakos families.[17] Each of these men carried a gun (some weapons were provided by the Greek army; others were privately owned) and were outfitted with bedding, coats, shoes, boots, and ammunition. Villagers suspected of subversive activities were taken by local *maidhes* to Langadhas for interrogation.

These paramilitary forces remained active even after the communist threat had diminished. They were renamed, however, as "National Security Units" (*Monadhes Ethnikis Asfalias,* or MEA) and were charged with broader responsibilities to safeguard the nation (*ethnos*) rather than merely the countryside (*ipethros*). After the Civil War, these paramilitary groups were again renamed as "National Security Battalions" (*Taghmata Ethnikis Asfalias,* or TEA). In addition to protecting villagers working in the fields, the *maidhes* (as they continued to be called, colloquially) were to ensure that no one left the village after sunset and were authorized by police to shoot anyone who tried to do so. Throughout the 1950s, 1960s, and early 1970s, the TEA continued to enforce a curfew in the village. Coffee shops had to close by 10 P.M., when all houses also had to extinguish lights. If a villager needed to venture outside, to call on a doctor for instance, permission was first required from the armed guards on duty. Although the curfew was lifted and the activities of the TEA were formally suspended following the fall of Greece's military *junta* in 1974, local *maidhes* retained their weapons and continued to "guard" the village with patriotic fervor until the election of the PASOK socialist government of Andreas Papandreou in 1981.

By the end of the 1940s, Assiros had developed a reputation in the region as a conservative national stronghold, in which most villagers were supporters of the crown and conservative political parties. Even at the height of the Civil War, the township council made a point of sending their warm regards to King Paul II on his name day, receiving in return a telegram of thanks from the Royal Palace in Athens (ATA 1948). Having served as a Greek nationalist center during the turn-of-the-century Macedonian Struggle, Assiros once again played a similar role during the Civil War era. As an armed bastion of conservative and nationalist sentiment, Assiros offered sanctuary to several outsiders who sought refuge from the reprisals of leftist partisans.[18] By then, however, local constructs of identity had been radically transformed. Cultural differences and ethnic boundaries had been rendered irrelevant. In contrast to former leftist partisans with whom I have spoken in northwestern Greece, no one in Assiros ever mentioned having supported or fought for an autonomous Macedonia.[19] In Assiros, the conflicts of the Civil War era were predominantly class-based. It was of no little significance that by the late 1940s the *tsorbadjidhes* of Assiros, regardless of their own family histories, had been united in their struggle against communism. Using their influence, they mobilized much of their clientele in this effort, creating a reputation for the village as a conservative national stronghold.

STRUCTURING TERRORISM AND CLIENTELISM IN POSTWAR ASSIROS

As noted above, the years leading up to the Civil War saw the adoption of several police measures aimed at eradicating leftist influence in the Greek countryside. Following the leftist defeat, government directives again ordered the township council to compile lists of leftists and leftist sympathizers. The Assiros elite were given broad, virtually unchecked, discretionary powers in this process. Later, as postwar reconstruction and development aid arrived in Assiros, not only did families with good relations with council members receive preferential treatment, but others were literally black-listed, stigmatized, and excluded from these benefits for years to come. The disestablished were disenfranchised.

As early as 1945, for example, the prefectural office in Thessaloniki demanded the names of villagers who had left for Bulgaria with the retreating Bulgarian forces, as well as those of newly arrived refugees who had settled in the area. That same year the District Director (*Eparch*) of Langadhas sent a memorandum to all township presidents, requesting townships to list all "antinational" activities perpetrated in their communities by "Bulgarian" speakers (*Voulgharofoni*), Romanizers (*Roumanizondes*),[20] Armenians, Serbs, Circassians, and members of other "foreign minorities" (ATA 1945). The memorandum demanded not only names and identification card (*taftotita*) numbers, but details of espionage, betrayals, extortions, murders of loyal Greeks, and the like. It promised that all information would be kept confidential but stressed the need to scrutinize carefully the actions of certain individuals. The following year, the sub-directorate of the gendarmerie ordered township presidents to compile lists of villagers who had been drafted into the army, and to indicate beside each name the individual's political ideology (*fronima*; ATA 1946). Later, in 1948, the office of the prefecture of Thessaloniki again required lists of suspected leftist collaborators and names of local children "abducted" by communist partisans and taken to Bulgaria and other Eastern European countries.[21]

Clearly, these state initiatives assisted Assiros *tsorbadjidhes* in consolidating a more diverse power base reinforced by unequivocal state backing and legal sanctions. Individuals and families who had dared to challenge this emergent local ruling class were harassed and persecuted for years to come. Nine alleged "murderers" from the village were either sent into exile or imprisoned (ATA 1954). Both during their years of imprisonment and following their release, these men were obliged to write "letters of confession" denouncing their former political ideology and their alleged affiliations with the Communist Party of Greece (*Kommounistiko Komma Elladhos* or KKE). These "confessions," essentially public letters of contrition which testified that foreign communists had tricked and deluded their authors into subversive activities, were read aloud to the Assiros congregation during the Sunday mass.[22] Even with the restitution of democracy in 1974, communist supporters have remained, not surprisingly, a small minority in village politics. In 1990, some Assiriotes proudly claimed to me that theirs was a "clean" (*kathari*) township with no more than 120 communists (mostly from refugee families) out of a total population of approximately 2,000 residents.

It is no exaggeration to say that the powerful and sometimes feared leaders of the local TEA brigade literally determined the flow of people in and out of the village for many years. When migration to Australia became a popular alternative for poor villagers in the 1950s and 1960s, those wishing to emigrate were required to obtain a letter from the township certifying that they were of good patriotic standing in village political life. Prospective migrants sometimes had to resort to bribery, and women were alleged to have been obliged to sleep with certain local authorities, in order to obtain such papers. Certification also required the signature of a local guarantor, preferably a *tsorbadjis* patron or sponsor.

The 1940s were therefore chaotic years marred by much violence on both the Right and the Left. But the pattern of local social life which emerged in the following decade was clear-cut and decisive. The ruling elite of Assiros used force liberally to accomplish their ends and to extend their influence and patronage. One prominent village TEA leader illustrated this practice in a story he related to me. It concerned, I believe, not a real incident but rather was an allegory through which he intended to demonstrate that threat or use of force was an effective political tool in village society.

> A man from Thessaloniki wanted to marry a girl from Mavrorahi. He had politely asked for the girl's hand, but her parents refused. Rebuffed and dejected, he returned to Thessaloniki, where one of his friends asked him why he seemed so troubled. Upon hearing the story, this friend told the man to leave the matter in his hands, for he knew how to resolve the problem. This friend then got dressed, took up his weapons, slung bullet belts around his neck and shoulders and went up to Mavrorahi. The girl's parents quickly assented to the marriage.

Reflecting on his story, this powerful conservative village leader and former *mais* assured me that "people are illiterate and stupid. They only understand force, nothing else."

As *maidhes,* the conservative local elite and their allies on the political right carried their weapons prominently and impressively for many years, exercising undisputed rule over the community. The manifest willingness of the Assiros *tsorbadjidhes* to employ violence, terror, or extortion in pursuit of their goals and defense of their interest was an important aspect of their dominance, both political and economic. It certainly left them well positioned to further enhance their local economic power through the management and distribution of postwar international development aid.

CONSOLIDATION AND CHALLENGE
Postwar Uneven Development

In the years following World War II, a substantial amount of financial and material aid flowed into Assiros, much of it in the form of seeds, animals, fertilizers, plows, and other farming equipment. Although this aid had originated in developmental assistance programs run by national and international agencies and governments, its local distribution was administered by the township council and the *tsorbadjis* elite. Decisions concerning the eligibility of recipients, for example, were left to the discretion of the township officials. Families whose members were suspected of collaborating with or supporting leftist partisans were disqualified. On the other hand, developmental assistance became a concrete symbol of reward to those who had been active supporters of their local patrons and loyal citizens of the Greek state.

In 1945, immediately following the German withdrawal, the Greek government began distributing production materials such as tools, grain, and seed to villages in the Langadhas area. International relief efforts reached Assiros that same year when the British delivered canned goods. Villagers began, as some put it, to "fill our stomachs" (*ghemise to stomahi mas*), ending the long suffering brought on by the occupation. Additional assistance was provided to Assiros by the state-run Agricultural Bank and the Treasury of Agricultural Insurance (*Tamio Aghrotikis Asfalias*). Yet Some of the most significant forms of material assistance were introduced through the postwar reconstruction programs of the United Nations Refugee Relief Agency (UNRRA) and the U.S. government's Marshall Plan.[23] These programs delivered plows, tractors, harvesters, and chemical fertilizers to the township, new resources that again transformed the local agrarian economy, contributing to the development of large-scale mechanized farming. The organizational networks through which such aid was locally distributed offered opportunities for self-aggrandizement on the part of the *tsorbadjidhes* as local administrators and community managers.

In 1945, the Assiros township council formed a Committee for Agricultural Provisioning, authorized to determine which villagers were eligible to receive relief supplies and in what specific form and quantity. The committee drew up lists of farmers they considered most in need of assistance.[24] Funds and resources, however, were not distributed solely on the basis of need. Rather, they overwhelmingly found their way into the hands of the large, powerful, and wealthier families in the village and to their clients; disproportionately little assistance reached the smallholders who were arguably most in need of it.[25] "Dollars," several villagers maintained, "were coming in and farm vehicles were driven down to the village *aghora*, though the money reached only some pockets." Consider some concrete examples of how aid tended to go to those families who "already had enough."

Under the Marshall Plan, any villager in possession of more than 40 hectares (300 *stremmata*) was classified as a "landowner" (*idhioktitis*), and was eligible to receive a tractor at a low subsidized price.[26] The Assiros Committee of Agricultural Provisioning compiled a list of such families in 1946. The Velikas family was the first to receive a foreign (British) tractor from UNRRA on credit. Tamtakos, the former teacher Asteriou, Halepis, the Artousis brothers, and the Assiros Agricultural Cooperative all received foreign tractors as well, along with drills and harvesters (ATA 1946).[27] By 1952 a wide variety of farm machinery and "modern equipment" (*moderna mihanimata*) were being used in Assiros, including wagons, plows, and harrows, as well as threshing, harvesting, and grinding machines. The first modern threshing machines were purchased in 1958, by the same entrepreneurs who obtained the first combine harvesters: the Artousis brothers, the son of Stylianos Asteriou, the Velikas brothers, a partnership between Vranas and Voukinas, and the village Agricultural Cooperative. Many of these families had sold their herds of livestock in order to finance these new purchases, thus precipitating the decline of the large-scale stock-breeding that had come to dominate the Assiros economy during the interwar era.

Equipped with their new threshing machines, some of these wealthy and prominent Assiriotes went as far afield as Halkidhiki to thresh the crops of other villages. The Velikas brothers, for example, who sold their large herds to buy a new threshing machine, took their equipment to Lahanas, Vertiskos, Arakli, Krithia, Dorkas, the Kilkis District, and Halkidhiki, charging a 13 percent commission for their services. To other Assiriotes, the Velikas brothers symbolized quintessential successful farmers; they were praised for having effectively used their resources and equipment to make new profits that were then reinvested.

Agricultural mechanization in the 1950s also led to the monocultivation of wheat and to the further consolidation of large landholdings. It allowed for the opening of new arable lands for cultivation, at least by those who possessed the machinery necessary to make such investment profitable. As late as 1940, fully 40 percent of Assiros lands still remained uncultivated, while both crop yields and investment returns were low. However, following the introduction of mechanization and chemical fertilizers,[28] virtually all arable land was brought under cultivation. Wheat production, which required no irrigation, quickly became the dominant new source of wealth.[29] Assiros farmers today claim they cannot grow anything other than wheat in the area because of crop destruction from the "Vardar Wind" (*Vardharis*), which blows cold and hard each winter from out of the Vardar (Axios) river valley. Monocultivation of wheat, however, was actively encouraged by the government's efforts to attain self-sufficiency in grain production, although subsequent subsidies also attracted wheat producers to the European export market.[30] On the eve of

World War II, Greece had imported 45 percent of its wheat from abroad (Jelavich 1983:277); by the 1970s the country was generating a surplus, and 122,287 tons of its 1,946,000-ton wheat harvest were exported abroad (Apergis 1978:172).[31]

FULL-TIME FARMERS AND PART-TIME CULTIVATORS

Developmental aid had a significant impact on local social stratification in Assiros, especially for the new generation of land-poor villagers in the postwar era.[32] As the *tsorbadjidhes* sold off their herds of livestock in order to finance mechanization, employment opportunities for shepherds disappeared. As large landowners purchased combine harvesters, women found it increasingly difficult to find jobs hoeing or harvesting. Unable to keep pace with rising production costs involved in mechanized agriculture and industrial fertilizers, many smallholders in Assiros began to rent out their plots, often to the large-scale mechanized farmers of the village.[33] While some smallholders continued to cultivate their land, most families owning twenty *stremmata* or less began to turn to new wage-labor opportunities in rapidly expanding industrial and commercial centers, both in Greece and abroad. Not surprisingly, farming has become a secondary occupation in Assiros, save for a few *tsorbadjidhes* families who have been able to expand their production base in the years following World War II. Today, only ten men in the village are involved exclusively in agriculture, most of whom inherited large landed estates and farm machinery from their fathers.[34] They rent additional fields in other villages, including plots in the hills which, although they offer lower returns, help extend their growing season with crops that mature later than those cultivated on the plain. After harvests, fields are burned and plowed under at least three times to aerate and mix the soil. Smallholders claimed they cannot afford such extensive soil preparation. Efficient and profitable farming has become the domain of the mechanized.

Many Assiriotes in the 1950s and 1960s migrated either to Thessaloniki or to Australia, often as families.[35] Some financed the move through property sales, usually to siblings, but in other instances large landowners purchased such plots. Others stayed in the village and found whatever employment they could in the area. At harvest time, villagers went as far afield as the Axios River valley in search of work. Shepherds worked in other villages, such as Krithia and Examili; some even went to the Kilkis District, where they tended sheep flocks of Pontic Greek refugees. Thus, prior to rural industrial development in the Langadhas basin during the 1960s, few of the laboring poor enjoyed job security and steady, reliable incomes. Often, personal and familial ties with local *tsorbadjidhes* patrons remained the only means through which laborers could gain access to the limited employment opportunities in Assiros village itself. Many maintained that, in order to secure such jobs, they had to demonstrate to their prospective *tsorbadjidhes* employers which political party they had voted for in the previous elections. Many villagers insisted that even until the late 1970s, it had been common practice for wealthy villagers to buy votes when local elections came around. Poor villagers, particularly women, were said to have sold their votes, like their labor, hoping that they would find some kind of employment from these wealthy patrons or at least temporary employment at harvest time.

These patterns, however, were radically altered by the proliferation of medium-scale rural industries in the late 1970s and early 1980s, fostered by government tax breaks and subsidies. Industrialists were encouraged to set up or relocate their plants in designated development zones which lined provincial and national highways, such as the Thessaloniki-Serres road which passed by Assiros. Village men now find work in nearby factories and receive medical benefits (which cover the whole family) and retirement pensions. In the past two decades Assiros women have also risen to prominent roles in the modern labor force.[36] Cottage industry in the village is thriving. By the 1990s there were no less than fifteen small-scale textile factories (*viotehnies*) in Assiros, most of them family-owned and employing local girls and young married women.[37] Few women receive any kind of benefits with these jobs, but most said they did not mind; it was the cash they sought. By remaining in the village at benefit-less jobs, such women appear on government rolls as farmers and thus qualify for agricultural subsidies.

By the postwar era, many smallholders in Assiros found the modest property base they had acquired during the land redistributions of the 1920s and 1930s threatened by the long-term impact of demographic growth and estate partition through inheritance. The *tsorbadjidhes* also faced such pressures, and their practical responses to this predicament provided further evidence of their ability as a local elite class to adapt to new challenges. In their strategies of property management, the *tsorbadjidhes* employed a common repertoire of cultural conventions surrounding inheritance and succession, title transfer, dowry, affinal and ritual kin alliance, and the timing and calculus of family division in order to protect their bases of power and positions of dominance.

THE PURSUIT OF PROPERTY MANAGEMENT

The era of developmental assistance in the 1950s and 1960s was also a period marked by the relative lack of major political rivalry among the *tsorbadjidhes*. When a new land redistribution program was announced by the national government in the 1950s, the *tsorbadjidhes* managed to avoid expropriation of their large landholdings.[38] They had come to form a united front. This they accomplished through their strong, well-developed ties with district, prefectural, and other regional government offices and bureaucratic staff, as well as by manipulating legal loopholes and local practices regarding property management and transfer. For example, although relatively uncommon in Assiros until the 1970s, the institution of landed dowry began to come into use in the 1950s and 1960s in the face of mounting pressures for new land expropriations.[39] Some local *tsorbadjidhes* were able to avoid the 500 *stremmata* ceiling on landholdings by transferring property titles to their daughters. But unlike dominant dowry practices in other parts of Greece, these transfers were temporary rather than permanent. When the restrictive landholding statute was later repealed, fathers retrieved the lands in question from their daughters.

These practices were facilitated by intensified affinal alliances among large landowning families during the postwar era. During this period, for example, several marriages were arranged between unusually close relatives, such as first cousins in the case of the Halepis family (see Genealogy E). These endogamous unions provided a means of closure through which *tsorbadjidhes* families could evade new restrictions on the size of landholdings by temporarily shifting documentation of ownership between each other in a mutually agreeable manner. Some negotiated direct reciprocal exchanges or land transfers with their affines, such as with the family of a daughter's husband. These innovative strategies of temporary title transfer were critical to the *tsorbadjidhes* in their efforts to maintain the large continuous estates that made mechanized farming profitable. When the crisis precipitated by government investigation into local landholdings had passed, allied families re-exchanged the properties they had transferred to one another.

New strategies of inheritance and family division were also adopted by the *tsorbadjidhes* in an effort to safeguard their properties. Greek inheritance laws now provide for equal partible inheritance, although many agriculturalists recognize that such practices rapidly lead to land fragmentation.[40] Most Assiros families consequently employed a modified form of ultimogeniture: the youngest son inherited the bulk of the family estate, while older brothers would receive a relatively smaller share of the family's estate at the time of or shortly after their marriage.[41] Elderly villagers claimed such practices had been prevalent in the region before Macedonia was incorporated into the Greek state, and many Assiriotes claimed that ultimogeniture was and still is the only fair form of inheritance as it is the youngest son who bears the heavy responsibility of caring for the aging parents.

Tsorbadjidhes strategies of property management and estate succession, however, were markedly different from this approach. While most brothers in present-day Assiros, for example, undertake to cultivate family lands individually, most *tsorbadjidhes* sons (and even some cousins) form partnerships that continue after the death of a father, as in the cases of the Artousis and Velikas families, for example. Property division among brothers was not commonly practiced by the *tsorbadjidhes*, and several villagers recounted a story of one man who committed suicide because of his father's refusal to give him his own share of the family's estate when he got married. The shareholding corporate character of *tsorbadjidhes* family economies allowed for the maximization of family resources.[42] Joint ownership of the Artousis family lands provides an example of how Assiros *tsorbadjidhes* prevented division and fragmentation of their land holdings. Even in the 1990s, the Artousis family claimed title to 1,000 *stremmata* of undivided land, currently exploited jointly by two first cousins. At the time of my field research the cousins were both on the eve of their retirement, and their children, themselves second cousins, planned to continue exploiting the estate jointly.

NEW UNIFICATION, NEW DEMOCRACY

The decades between the Balkan Wars and World War II were a period of intense competition over property rights and the structuring of occupational relations. Issues of cultural difference, ethnic identity, and national consciousness progressively receded from political relevance. The land conflicts that have been discussed here were but one indication of the growing consolidation of class hegemony in Assiros and the tensions created by this process. Land redistribution and the subsequent transformations in the local agrarian economy precipitated fundamental changes in the way local villagers conceived of themselves and each other. The material aggrandizement of the Assiros *tsorbadjidhes* in the postwar era was by no means a new development in the history of the community. But the dominant tenor of the newly emerging class relationships had a homogenizing effect on ethnic or national distinctions that had been expressed in the past but had faded as issues of property ownership, occupation, income, and access to influence networks rose in importance.

The economic context and political climate in postwar Greece provided the *tsorbadjidhes* with new resources with which to pursue their entrepreneurial activities. They acquired new forms of power, yet became increasingly dependent on the source of this material and political support: the district, prefectural, and national governments. At the same time, the local elite also drew their smallholding neighbors and ritual kin into relations of patronage and dependency, at least until migration and industrialization began to offer new modes of exit for the local poor. Sponsors of life-course rituals and employment opportunities, the *tsorbadjidhes* were also brokers of the local population's passage to nationhood. The Greeks of Assiros established new traditions to celebrate their collective identity and their affinity with the Hellenes.

But the local distribution of developmental assistance in the Cold War era reflected the emerging new class structure of Assiros following World War II and the Greek Civil War. Measured in terms of such neoclassical economic indicators of growth as average per capita income, Assiros was clearly making rapid strides in economic development. But this increased wealth and prosperity also contributed to a growing polarization between village families. Growing class differentiation came to dominate popular consciousness. Through no small effort of the *tsorbadjidhes*, Assiros became and remained a stronghold of conservative Greek national sentiment throughout the course of the twentieth century. One *tsorbadjis* showed me a photograph of King Constantine, deposed in 1973. "We will bring him back," he told me with a determined smile.

Militancy was a vocal theme in the nation-building process as it developed in Assiros. It had been evidenced in the actions of partisan fighters during the Macedonian Struggle, and again in the Civil War. Many villagers, rich and poor alike, remarked to me that Assiros had enjoyed its most intimate relations with the Greek state during the Papadopoulos years (1967–74), when Greece was governed by military junta. In the 1990s, only a few Assiros men, mostly former TEA members, possessed carbines, which they kept for hunting small game. On one occasion, on a cool evening in late summer near the start of the hunting season, I had been talking with some Assiriotes over ouzo in a *kafenion* when two men walked by sporting rifles pointed towards the sky. They were greeted with cheers from friends, who urged them (almost successfully) to fire rounds into the air. My companions explained that the men were hunters. Having once hunted communists, they now hunted animals.

Industrialization and the proliferation of mass media have reshaped the lives and livelihoods of the Greeks of Assiros. There are new occupations, new channels of exchange, and new avenues of mobility. With these have come new ways of conceiving of oneself and one's relationships with others. Images of Greece and imagined notions of what it means to be Greek pervade the lives and minds of those who now live amid the fields of wheat in Greek Macedonia. Whether commuting daily to factory jobs in Thessaloniki, preparing for university entrance exams, vacationing in the Greek islands, or relaxing at home with the dozens of new television stations now broadcasting in Greece, the Assiriotes are intimately immersed in the culture and economy of the Greek nation-state. They live off regular wages and salaries, retirement pensions, European Union subsidies, and rents from farmlands they have since quit and leased to the few remaining farmers in the village.

The *aghora,* once the focus of community life in late Ottoman Guvezna, continues to be a field of action for the new relationships that now pervade village life. Young adults gather in cafeterias and café-bars. Young children occupy themselves in an electronic video game shop. A discotheque pumps music in the air, sometimes softly, sometimes in great blasts. The streets have been paved, but the streambeds hold no water. The women no longer sing or bake. Even signs of gentrification have reached the village *aghora,* as a once favorite *kafenion* of the elderly has become a fancy *ouzeri.*

Across the *aghora,* the new Byzantine-style Church of Constantine and Eleni is being raised, a symbol of the past, present, and future of the nation of the Hellenes and the centrality of the Church in maintaining that identity across centuries. Today, the village priest (who is of Pontic refugee descent) has new forces with which to contend, as he seeks to keep his flock in the Christian way of life represented by Greek Orthodoxy. The new church, of much larger proportions than those of the old Prophet Elias Church, is built not on a hilltop so as to identify the community from afar. Rather, it is sited on the township's public green, at the center of the *aghora,* where it faces off against the café-bar-discos of Greek youth culture in an attempt to preach morality to modernity.

In many ways, the past has become very much a foreign country, to the Assiriotes. Its remaining physical symbols have taken on new meanings, as villagers debate not their Greekness but their Europeanness. It is to the imaginative civilization of modernity that they now aspire. Many of the identities of the past have become strangely alien, buried beneath the stratigraphy of memory and history among the fields of wheat and hills of blood in a land called Macedonia.

CONCLUSION

Reconstructing the Passages to Nationhood

The contest for Macedonia between Greece and Bulgaria at the turn of the century was a national political and economic contest, a contest largely over a sizeable region of fertile lands not only ideally suited for grain and pastoral production but sitting astride major trade routes. The significance of this fact cannot be underplayed: the caravan routes which crossed Macedonia directly linked the economies of at least two world systems (and indirectly many more). The economies of East and West, or southeast and northwest Eurasia, were linked in the nineteenth century directly and vibrantly by the overland trade of grain, cotton, and other goods which passed through Macedonia and Salonika on their way to Istanbul and points east, or to European cities to the north. This was the lifeline of trade which, despite the numerous wars that occupy such a dominant position in conventional history, kept alive and connected the economies of Europe (that complex "tapestry") and the Ottoman Empire (that vast expansive "bloc" of economy and society that has been frequently portrayed in Orientalist scholarship as exotic, somehow backwards, and vaguely threatening).

This overland trade was conducted by camel and pack-animal caravans, pushing on slowly from town to town, market to market, crossing the Balkan land bridge between three continents. Too often we are tempted to envision these extensive and far-reaching trade routes as single, quick lines between two points, East and West. In reality, this commerce was dependent upon local societies and communities through which it passed, which fed it, watered it, gave it resting places, provided

218

it with forums for small or large-scale exchanges. In the patchwork of cultures, linguistic groups, ethnic groups, subregional communities which characterized much of the southern Balkans, this trade and commerce-oriented exchange was facilitated and sustained through the medium of the Greek language. As Tsoukalas (1977:39) put it, "the Greek language, which was for centuries the official language of the Orthodox Church, was used from approximately 1750 as the *lingua franca* of the upwardly mobile petty bourgeois merchants." Many of these merchants, regardless of their cultural or ethnic identity, lacked a national consciousness of their own. But they were eventually Hellenized through religion, occupation, and education. The use of the Greek language slowly facilitated the gradually growing hegemony of Greek national identity. Greek had been the language of the Eastern Orthodox Church for longer than the Ottoman Empire existed. Indeed, even back to the days of Byzantium it had been the *lingua franca* of administration, commerce, religion, education, and higher learning.

The establishment of the independent Bulgarian Exarchate in 1870, however, brought all this into jeopardy. Up until that point, it had been the Orthodox Patriarchate, rather than the tiny, largely weak and irrelevant new Greek kingdom down on the extreme tip of the Balkan peninsula, that had enjoyed this hegemony and reaped its benefits. But the Exarchate embodied not only a conceptual realm of jurisdiction but a territorial area of administration. As the Bulgarian Church bureaucracy sought to extend its influence (and thus its administrative control and tax revenue base) over a larger area of what was, or later became, Macedonia, it threatened to deprive the Christian Orthodox "subempire," that state within a state so to speak, of its very heartland. A glance at any map of the region for the late nineteenth century graphically illustrates the extent to which the ambitious Bulgarian Exarchate sought to tap into that great wealth of commerce which constituted the region. And the Patriarchate, far from being a territory-less vestibule which simply preserved secular Greek society and culture over the centuries since the fall of Byzantium, rose to defend its hegemony and took an active role in nurturing the growth and expansion of the nation of the Hellenes.

The region of Macedonia had been no backward, isolated *terra incognito* of subsistence or peasant agriculture. Rather, it had been characterized, even defined, largely by the vibrant exchange that gave it life. In the preceding chapters I have attempted to trace a pattern of cultural creation, the processes which have transformed the cultures and identities of the inhabitants of central Macedonia, as well as some of the events which have marked those processes. Macedonia, and indeed the Balkans in general, has long been not one culture area but a *cultures* area, inhabited by a plethora of various ethnic groups tied together in a complex web of interaction.

For the past several hundred years the central Macedonian countryside was dotted with innumerable settlements, linked together in slightly insular (but not isolated) pocket-like communities, continually interacting through exchanging goods, services, and betrothals. For most of the inhabitants of these exchange- or market-communities, this was "the world." The boundaries of these communities, however abstract to the minds of contemporary analysts, often were quite real to the minds of local villagers. They represented the area in which inhabitants made a living from the land, exchanged the goods they produced or came to possess, and the area within which they looked to marry and reproduce. These boundaries were demarcated by natural geography (rivers, mountains, etc) and human agency (administrative divisions, markets and exchange networks, and trade routes). Yet they were only ephemeral products of historical processes and contemporary circumstances, continuously subject to change.

This is not to say these "pocket-like" communities were in any way isolated from a larger social fabric. Quite the contrary, they were all linked together by larger trade networks and caravan routes which crisscrossed the region, not to mention the administrative structures and institutions of the Ottoman state and the Orthodox Church. Community inhabitants certainly knew of the "outside world," since enough commerce and goods were passing through their communities continually to remind them. But for most of the rural population, the agriculturalist serfs and peasant sharecroppers alike, those exchange-communities represented the immediate world in which they lived.

According to local legends, more than one hundred years ago migrants from the area of Trikala in Thessaly crossed the mountain of Olympus and made their way northward along the trade caravan route which led to the market town of Serres to the east and the Bulgarian frontier to the north. Coming down from the Derveni pass and through the village of Aivati, these migrants continued across the Langadhas basin plain until they reached the caravan stop of Guvezna. There, some decided to stay, settling in the community, setting up shops or mercantile enterprises which fed the passing caravan trade. Those who did so eventually married local women, either from the village of Guvezna itself or from the communities of Christian agriculturalists which lay around it.

When these settlers arrived in the Guvezna area, they had little choice but to map on to those preexisting patterns of exchange and interaction which were in place at the time of arrival. I believe it would be mistaken to consider this marriage pattern, or for that matter the establishment of commercial ties of dependency over the Slavic-speaking villages of the area, as a conscious or conspiratorial plan of these migrants to Hellenize local Slavic-speaking inhabitants. There was, in fact, little else these arriving Greek migrants could do. They married in the directions and along the lines that their local neighbors did. Within the structures and organizations of everyday life, these Greeks soon came to manage the affairs of the Orthodox community of Guvezna. They collected taxes, built a church, set up a school, and developed the village *aghora* into a thriving marketplace.

On deciding to settle in Guvezna, these Greek-speakers established themselves as merchants, controlling and mediating the exchange which took place there between sedentary agriculturalists, Muslim herders in the mountains, and the passing trade caravans. This position provided them with a considerable degree of control over the organization of social life in the community, and the local Slavic-speaking inhabitants who had cause to interact with them had little choice but to do so on terms set by those who became community leaders. Over time, Slavic-speakers also established themselves in mercantile and commercial enterprises, learned the Greek language, intermarried with Greek mercantile notables and adopted many of their social customs.

As their gold pieces accumulated, many of these merchants began to diversify into livestock breeding and later purchased (or enclosed or were granted) land from Ottoman Muslims. Thus these Greek-speakers cum Greeks came to dominate the local agro-pastoral commercial economy. For the most part, the bulk of the local Slavic-speaking population continued to be herders and agriculturalists, tending the flocks or working the lands of either the Ottoman estates or the few "free-holding" settlements in the area. With a mode of subsistence very different from their new mercantile neighbors, these agriculturalists had their own language, customs, beliefs, origin myths, kinship terms, and worldviews. Yet as Greek influence grew in the area, so did its Hellenizing effect. Alongside the forum of the Guvezna market, another principal agent in this process was the Orthodox Church, which held a monopoly on the iconicity and symbolism in the countryside. Prior to the area's incorporation into the expanding Greek nation-state, the Church was the principal conveyor of cultural and ideological change in the region. The priests not only mediated marriages and baptisms but regulated the production of history, identity, and belief through their control over language, both spoken and written. Under their influence the wedding ceremonies of this ritual community underwent change, as the descent-group banners of patrilineal descent groups were replaced, first by a red Patriarchist flag with the double-headed Byzantine eagle, and later by the Greek national flag. New idioms of identity were introduced through which people reconceptualized their relationship both to each other and to the larger cosmos.

But Macedonia was by this time already caught between two confrontational national forces: the southward-looking Bulgarians to the north, and the northward-looking Greeks to the south. A moving frontier of political, economic, and national struggle was racing towards the region. In the early years of the twentieth century, the Langadhas basin, like many other areas of what was to become Greek Macedonia, were scarred and set aflame by the terror and bloodshed of nationalism commonly referred to as the Macedonian Struggle.

It is within this historical contextual framework that we must approach the Macedonian question. Failure to do so simply ignores the material realities and influences of the region's history. Now, in the 1990s, the arena of contest threatens to move beyond scholarly forums of argument and debate. The voices which rise above the din are often those of combatants themselves, the modern-day Macedonian Fighters, nationalist historians and regional specialists whose scholarship is dedicated to their national cause. The poles of the contest are currently being realigned from their nineteenth- and early twentieth-century south-northeast (Greek-Bulgarian) confrontation to a new south-northwest (Greek-FYROM) conflict. The claims advanced by scholarly advocates of nationalist causes on all sides echo each other hollowly. Nikolaos Martis (1984) and others of his persuasion have been concerned to demonstrate the eternal Greekness of Macedonia. Their FYROM counterparts, in entirely comparable claims, are to an equal degree reductionist. It is no accident that both sides have been equally committed to the rhetoric of truth and falsehood; neither can encompass the contingent view of national identity that emerges from an ethnographically informed analysis of the region's history.

To the victors, the adage maintains, belong the spoils. Or as Marx once put it, to the victors belong the rights to write history. But the losers, or those who simply have become subsumed within the group of the victorious, also construct their own histories. Their voices may not be carried free of static over the airways, and they may even be deprived of soap-box platforms from which to address the multitudes. Yet they too tell a part of history, and in our efforts to seek truth from facts, we must at least give a critical ear to all the voices which claim to recount it: oral or written, scholarly or popular, secular or ecclesiastic, past and present. These texts are themselves social facts. They may or may not proclaim The Truth, but as historical constructs they certainly embody a part of it.

The reconstruction and analysis of the processes which affected Macedonian history, and thus influenced the histories of not only regional nation-states but interlinked world economic systems, necessitates a critical perspective on prevalent or dominant (Gramsci would have said hegemonic) strains of scholarly and popular interpretation of Macedonian history. Prevailing wisdom of historical scholarship clamors, sometimes angrily, sometimes without elegance, that it alone proclaims the gospellike incontrovertible truth of historical fact and reconstruction. Greek Macedonia did not magically appear out of the ashes and ruins of a crumbling Turkish, Muslim, "Oriental," Ottoman Empire. It was not a new land of promise and salvation miraculously created intact by the good graces of surrounding nations. It was, simply, a largely administrative assumption and restructuring of a pattern of relations which were in place before the advent of Greek rule, an economy in which a predominant role was being played and expanded, particularly by commercial merchants, landlords, and large stockbreeders.

These *tsorbadjidhes* were Greeks, regardless of whatever they had been before. As they were drawn to the expanding economy of the young Greek nation-state, they assumed new roles and identities as they oriented their activities, their trade, their broader network of resources, to the area of Thessaloniki and points south, as well as to Sofia, Istanbul, and points north and east, and to Kilkis, Monastiri (Bitola), and other points northwest. These were other Greek places; that is, they were settlements, villages, towns, and cities in which there was a Greek-speaking, and an Orthodox-practicing, community with a network of organized, semiorganized, or unorganized allies, countryless countrymen, and acquaintances. These particular contacts or networks were, in each instance, both personal or open-ended, but never or rarely formally or officially recognized as being so. These were the Greeks who came into the inheritance of a nation, a tradition or idea of a supranational (or supraethnic) economy and its society, after the collapse of the Ottomans.

Make no mistake; this was not an uncontested, easy, or inevitable process. At least three major wars were fought in this part of the Balkans in the decades of the twentieth century before World War II. The Macedonian Struggle, two Balkan Wars, World War I, World War II, and the Greek Civil War brought bloody terror on Slavs, Greeks, and other "Others." But the passage to Greek nationhood was forged through this process, and through the organizational context of the Church and the vast commercial mercantile network that expanded beyond the limits of the territorial state created in the south in 1829.

The liberation of Macedonia from Ottoman rule in 1912 and the incorporation of the region into the formal political economy of the Greek nation-state in 1913 radically altered the dynamics of local life and concepts of identity. Now fully under the nation-state's hegemony, the reconstruction of personal and social identity, or the particular construction of national Greek identity, began in almost uncontested earnest. This was accompanied by, and perhaps inseparable from, the long-term process of agrarian development in the region. The case histories recounted in this work offer ethnographic detail through which we can uncover and better understand the opaque clues to this puzzle. The aid and assistance projects of the national government and its supernational patrons and allies provided the material catalysts which transformed culture, ethnicity, and identity in Greek Macedonia. Undoubtedly there was protest and opposition at the local level, and the preceding pages have documented how such objections were raised and dealt with in the township of Assiros.

The Greek nation-state offered a different set of pressures or influences over production activity at each locale. In the region of Macedonia, those which had been more closely aligned with the Greek economy to the south were least adversely affected. Those families and communities which suffered most, whose members were killed or pressured to flee, were those that had held on, for whatever reason, to non-Greek or pre-Greek identities. These identities were shaped not only out of their participation or interaction with a different set of social ties and networks (i.e., Slavo-Macedonian, Bulgarian, etc.) but also by their nonparticipation in those Greek (and Greek-dominated) networks of interaction and exchange.

Exchange binds society together, gives it definition and meaning. But exchange is often unbalanced, and is symbolized and creatively reproduced through the generalized network or structure of stratification that characterizes and defines all aspects of society: from kinship and affinal relations, to ties between neighbors and coparishioners, tenants and owners, tax collectors and tax payers, merchants and patrons, husbands and wives, parents and children. Through an understanding of how these patterns of exchange were arranged, acted through, and endured through time, or how they have changed or ultimately balanced out materially, one begins to get a sense of the processes of ethno-national creation. It was not a process of ethnogenesis, for it did not create something out of nothing; it reshaped creatively preexisting relations and nonrelations.

Trying to heal the wounds of a decade and a half of fascism and armed conflict, Greece crossed the threshold of the 1960s with trepidation but also with a rejuvenating hope for the future. The nation, now accepted as a natural social collectivity, bore the ugly scars of civil war.

But the inhabitants of central Greek Macedonia carried those crosses, so to speak, as Greeks, as full-fledged citizens of the nation-state. The partisan resistance and the Civil War had brought a unique opportunity for those who sought to assimilate if only given a chance. On the postwar southern NATO flank of Europe, the only people deprived of the rights of citizenship and new democratic equality were those unrepentant (as well as some rather repentant) communists.

The new character of the international order in the region peripheralized, suppressed, or censored ethnic and national divisions within the nation-state. Many former Slavic-speakers, Pontics, East Thracians, and Asia Minor Greeks could finally find a welcome refuge in Assiros as long as they were anticommunist and submitted quietly to the domination of the local ruling class. By the 1960s the Assiros *tsorbadjidhes* had transformed themselves from a local elite to a hegemonic class. The basis of their power, interests, and identity lay in the distinctive privileged access they enjoyed to the means of productive activity and its management in the township. These included large tracts of land, both arable and pasture; large herds; advanced industrial technology in the form of plows, tractors, harvesters, threshing machines, and combines; and, above all, their influence in the political administration of the township.

Postwar development aid and reconstruction assistance, as well as Greek government and EEC/EU subsidies, accomplished what they intended to achieve. "Development" it was, but not of the kind that many expected. These monies and benefits had been intended to aid and assist in the reconstruction of post–World War II and post–Civil War Greece. Instead, they were appropriated and applied in ways that restructured and re-formed (as opposed to reformed) established patterns of class dominance in agrarian Greek Macedonia.

The *tsorbadjidhes* both sustained and reproduced their material power base and thus themselves as *tsorbadjidhes* over subsequent generations. Under changing circumstances they diversified their holdings and activities and developed subtle yet efficient means of protecting the resources they had already come to command. By the 1960s, most of Assiros' notable families were concerned with not only making their fortunes but protecting them as well. Equally dramatic as the ways they developed to protect their property was the relentless effort of the township's laboring class to defy dependency. They struggled to secure and retain that little piece of land, or machine, or job which would enable them to make ends meet, to feed hungry mouths, and maybe to pull oneself or one's children up a rung or two on the ladder of social mobility, even if it meant leaving the community, temporarily or permanently, to do so.

Class differences grew increasingly pronounced and articulated in the postwar era, but the differences had themselves grown out of the former ethnic distinctions which once separated township inhabitants into different social groups. Those ethnic markers, boundaries, or identities had now faded under the banner of patriotic Greek nationalism. Decades of ideological education and propaganda under first the Patriarchate, then the Crown, the Venizelos Liberals, the Populist Royalists, the Metaxas dictatorship, the military junta of 1967–74, and more recently the Pan-Hellenic socialists and the New Democracy conservatives, have taught inhabitants to love their country, their homeland, *Elladha.*

The Assiriotes were drawn into an even larger expanding economy, that of the Euro-American western empire, which gained hegemony through the blockade and eventual defeat of its continental communist contestors. Like its neighbors in NATO and the EEC, Greece arose from the rubble and ashes of World War II through the help of the Marshall Plan and international efforts which restructured, refocused, and reoriented exchange networks. This restructuring was no sudden accomplishment but a protracted and painful transformation of a way of life. The poor, the less influential, the ill-connected, the laborers, were pushed off the land, often by far from subtle means, to become the wage-earning rural proletariat of an industrializing economy. Transformed were ways of life, ways of looking at the world, ways of making a living out of or in the world. Occupations became more regulated and standardized, and the rapid developments in occupational and residential mobility fostered a more comprehensive form of collective identity under the state political economy of modern Greece.

After nearly a century of Greek nation-building in central Greek Macedonia, however, important social distinctions continue to divide the population. In the second part of this study, we have followed how inhabitants of the Assiros township were drawn into a new mode of production. Yet families were drawn into this brave new world in different ways, under different circumstances. The important discriminations between social groups in township life are embodied in stereotypes. While differences are now more frequently expressed in the rhetoric of class relations, residual concepts of ethnic distinctions remain: *endopyi, Voulghari, Pontyi, Thrakiotes,* and the like.

But interaction and social exchange between and among rural inhabitants of central Greek Macedonia continue to be articulated through one's position in the local political economy. The current structure of the regional division of labor and the social segregation of status differences between individuals employed in different occupations are to a limited extent still expressed in an ethnic idiom, but the grammar of class relations has gained considerable sway in the political dialogue which narrates social life in township society. The protracted processes of agrarian development have introduced powerful new factors which have restructured the give-and-take of daily life. EEC (now EU) subsidies, government directives concerning grain production, and other pressures have influenced the patterns of economic interaction. These forces do not represent a radical break with an ill-defined past; they are part of the on-going processes of social change.

The twentieth century has provided us with an overwhelming display of what people can do with the power of culture. It has also given us some not too subtle warnings of what will befall humanity as time goes by. As the century draws to a close in Macedonia, the disturbing rumblings of war roll over the hills of the Balkans again today, much as they did when this century opened. Regardless of political dispositions, national inclinations, economic position, or personal temperament, the one common theme most observers of the world today share is anxiety. And, perhaps, anger.

The Greek nation or the Hellenic national body, as Tsoukalas termed it, "was formed by a sum of minorities" (Tsoukalas 1977:50). The chapters of this study have documented the Hellenization of a township in central Greek Macedonia. They were written with a degree of local detail in the hope of making plain the concrete impact which this tumultuous course had on lives, families, and communities. Yet these developments were not uniform throughout Greece; in other parts of Greek Macedonia, resistance to Hellenization is still audible. In this part of the Langadhas basin, however, Hellenization was a protracted process stretching the length of the twentieth century. For some, it was gentle, even profitable. For others, life in turn-of-the-century Guvezna was like the Hobbesian state of nature: nasty, brutish, and short. When waxing hegemonic nation-states collide, those of us who pick through the historical fragments must not fail to see the trees for the forest. The so-called liberation of Macedonia in 1913 was the symbol marking the beginning of uncontested hegemony in culture-nation production. Whatever people of central Greek Macedonia had been, it was clear that henceforth they were to be Greeks. And so they became.

Culture and history weave an inextricably complex pattern across the face of the land. Deciphering the jumble of produce man and land create here, as anywhere, has brought us back from a journey across time. Settlements vanish and people die, and history is recreated a thousand times in a day in the things people say, or do, or write.

AFTERWORD

> Nationalism is, essentially, the general imposition of a high culture
> on society, where previously low cultures had taken up the lives of
> the majority . . . of the population. It means the generalized diffu-
> sion of a school-mediated academy-supervised idiom. . . . It is the
> establishment of an anonymous, impersonal society, with mutually
> substitutable atomized individuals, held together above all by a
> shared culture of this kind, in place of a previous complex struc-
> ture of local groups, sustained by folk cultures.
>
> Ernest Gellner, *Nations and Nationalism*

Eight years have passed since I first began work on this project in 1988.
In the early 1990s, after my field research in Assiros township had
been completed, the Macedonian controversy rose to national and international attention once again with the independence of the Former Yugoslav Republic of Macedonia and the heightened nation-building activities
there. These developments led me to new research in western Greek Macedonia, across the territorial border with the FYROM, where transcripts
of resistance, some hidden, some open, are still discernible.

The recent Macedonian controversy has drawn on and inflamed passionate patriotic sentiments among the general public. Authorities in
Greece have been concerned that political turmoil in the southern Balkans
following the breakup of Yugoslavia and the fall of communist governments in Albania and Bulgaria may yet spill over into Greece. These concerns had been heightened in September 1991 when the southernmost of
the former Yugoslav republics dropped the word "Socialist" from its title
and through public referendum declared itself the independent "Republic
of Macedonia." This had been followed there by a series of developments
that were interpreted (some of them correctly so) by many in Greece as
of hostile intent: the adoption of a name that many Greeks have been
taught is a part of their own national heritage, dating back to the time
of Alexander the Great; of a new national flag (eventually changed) emblazoned with a sunburst or star uncovered by Greek archaeologists at a
tomb in northern Greece believed to have been that of Alexander's father,
Philip II of Macedon; and of "novelty currency" bearing the image of an
architectural landmark in Thessaloniki, the White Tower of the city's
waterfront.

Greek authorities and lay citizens alike responded to what they perceived emanating from the FYROM with a public campaign that included an unilateral economic embargo against the FYROM and punitive sanctions against some pro-FYROM elements in Greece. Yet behind the rhetorical devices and the visual images lay a heated debate over the relative Greekness or non-Greekness of the region of Macedonia. Authorities in the FYROM claimed to have "unliberated brethren" living in northern Greece, referring to Slavic-speakers and their descendants, whom they assert are not Greek. In Greece, reaction to such claims has been vehement and sometimes extreme: the population of Macedonia has been nothing but pure Greek since antiquity, it is claimed; the Slavs who migrated into the area during the sixth and seventh centuries had been assimilated into Greek culture, although some Greeks in Macedonia picked up a Slavic "idiom" of speech.

Greek national ideology on the Macedonia issue has been manifest in various aspects of popular material culture, including T-shirts and cigarette lighters, taxi cabs and bumper stickers, Pavlos Melas telephone cards and international media advertisements. It has generated a number of new television stations that employ names or symbols relating to Macedonia. New houses are being constructed with facade designs adapted from ancient Macedonian tombs. The Thessaloniki airport has been renamed as the Macedonia Airport; the Aegean port of Kavala has been renamed as the Port of Philip II. Gold-colored 100 drachma coins have been minted with a profile of the Great Alexander on the face and the Star of Vergina on the reverse. Each midnight, the Metropolite's radio station in Thessaloniki broadcasts a succession of three songs: a popular nationalistic song, a Byzantine piece, and the Greek national anthem.

Given such a context, the reaction to my work in Greece, as well as among Greek diaspora abroad, has been often sharp and hostile. In particular, one Athenian journalist, a columnist for a weekly magazine, took it upon himself to champion the defense of Greece. In the first of what became a series of articles, he accused me of "cannibalism" (*kannivalismos*) in attempting to dismember the Greek nation (Kargakos 1993a). The polemic was picked up and circulated widely within the Greek media, including Greek American newspapers and magazines in New York City. One local newspaper in the Langadhas area likened me to Efialtis, who had betrayed Greece to the Persians in ancient times (*Vardaris* 1993). Then after learning that I had written a doctoral dissertation on ethnicity and nation-building in a central Greek Macedonian township (Karakasidou 1992), he challenged the people of Assiros to declare publicly their position on what he alleged were my assertions concerning the non-Greek character of their community (Kargakos 1993b).

Community leaders in Assiros became deeply alarmed over the possible consequences of such characterizations, particularly in light of the highly charged political atmosphere of the time. Their concerns were heightened when they received a request from the Ministry of Macedonia and Thrace (formerly the Ministry of Northern Greece) for a statement of clarification following the publication of the journalist's allegations. To make matters worse, they began to receive telephone calls from former township residents now living in Thessaloniki, from individuals serving on township councils in neighboring communities, from police and security officials, and from private citizens with no personal knowledge of or familiarity with Assiros but who on the basis of the journalist's allegations nevertheless accused the Assiriotes of being "Skopians," a reference to authorities, citizens, and agents of the FYROM.

Local notables in Assiros responded in a collective letter sent not only to the national magazine that had printed the journalist's allegations (see Kargakos 1993c), but also to the Ministry of Macedonia and Thrace and to the Director of Internal Affairs at the prefectural office of Thessaloniki. In it, they defended themselves by maintaining they had supported my research on local history, thinking it had been a "national deed" (*ethniko ergho*). They declared that if I had indeed claimed that they were not Greek, they considered such assertions to be an "insult" (*ivris*). They went on to assert in their letter that Assiros had never been a bilingual community and that they were all "pure Greek, twenty-four karat, in both language and national consciousness." As for my personal character, they claimed to have known me well, adding that I was a Greek of Asia Minor descent, married (without religious ceremony, they stressed) to a Yugoslav (an assertion, I might add, that came as a startling surprise to both me and my husband—who is not a Yugoslav). They concluded their letter by stating that they were waiting for their "traumatized Greek sentiment to be satisfied" before they took any actions against me. The letter was signed in numbered sequence by (1) the township president, (2) the Assiros village priest, (3–4) the superintendents of the high school and primary school, (5) the president of the Assiros Agricultural Cooperative, (6) the township secretary, and (7–8) the presidents of the high school and primary school Parent-Teacher Associations. All of the signatories had, in fact, been personal acquaintances of mine, but none had direct knowledge of my published or unpublished material on Assiros.

My relations with Assiros were abruptly terminated after this incident. I do not know if local villagers gathered informally in their *kafenia* to discuss and debate the allegations, as they often had done during my fieldwork when issues of local history, politics, and popular concerns were raised. I have learned from a friend in the community that local leaders had attempted to keep news of the journalist's allegations secret from village residents in general, hoping to prevent a larger scandal from emerging. I was told that they had also tried to determine who had told me what.

Part of the problem lay, no doubt, in the different language that anthropologists often use to present their findings. Such deviations may take on added force when the anthropologist is a native of the country or culture about which he or she writes. In Greece, where heightened international tension has made the study of Macedonia (in the words of one Assiros young man following the incident with the Athenian journalist) a "national issue" (*ethniko thema*), much added significance is ascribed to writings that appear to go against the grain of popular nationalism. The anthropological reconstruction of local history presented in this work differs from the ways in which local respondents conceptualized their own historical past. Beginning as early as primary school, all Greeks, myself included, have been taught an official narrative of Greek national history which maintains that Macedonia has been Greek since antiquity. When the Athenian journalist remarked, "Greece does not only have a history, it has a qualitative history" (Kargakos 1993a), he was alluding to a so-called High Culture: a history of glorious achievement; of history as national destiny. National history has a magical quality, collapsing time and capturing past, present, and future in its comprehensive breadth and promoting the survival of the nation in both space and in ideology (see Karakasidou 1994b). As an ideology, national history conveys both a sense of a collective past as well as a collective destiny. The past is no longer a foreign country but a familiar place easily recognizable to those enculturated by the myths of nationalism.

Analytically, one may discern at least three distinct strains of historical narratives expressed by local villagers. The first was made up of the generic national history they had learned in school. When Assiriotes spoke about history, per se, they invoked narratives of the nation that had been taught to them from a young age in school and in church. These verbal texts followed the same canonized and homogenized traditions as periodized national history, referring to oppression under the Turks, Bulgarian efforts to seize Greek lands, struggles against communist subversives, and the like.

The second form of historical narrative linked local events, landmarks, and artifacts to the grand heritage and destiny invoked, preserved, and defended by national history. Both these first and second genres of narrative were considered by local villagers to be part of the historical record. For example, imaginative local legends dated the community to antiquity, claiming the settlement had been established by Alexander the Great or one of his generals following their return from the Trojan War. These nonlinear uses of time linked historical figures from the fourth century B.C.E. to developments or events of the Bronze Age. Similarly, local legends that linked present-day Assiros with a nearby Byzantine site of considerable size and wealth may be interpreted as complementary rather than antithetical to origin accounts set in antiquity, because they echoed the Paparrigopoulos paradigm of the continuity of Hellenism from ancient to modern times through Byzantium. Even popular local accounts of the more recent past, such as the tale of a Greek military hero of the Balkan Wars whose successful campaign to drive Bulgarian forces from the area began in Assiros, supported the ideology of national history by conveying a veritable morality that conformed to prescribed patterns of thought, action, and emotion.

The third type of local narratives, however, those of mundane personal and family histories, were not considered by villagers to be "history" as they had been taught to understand it. Rather, such accounts were regarded as mere recollections of personal experiences that were largely irrelevant to the historical record, as defined by established (and hegemonic) national canon. "History," for the Assiriotes, carried an aura of sacredness and grandeur; memories were mundane and profane. This duality of the past provided an elasticity through which certain elements in local oral accounts, apparently anomalous to the paradigmatic national history, were either rationalized or dismissed with little or no conscious reflection. Villagers in Assiros related to me accounts of the Slavic-speaking ancestor who had migrated down from Montenegro in the 1860s to settle on a nearby *chiftlik;* of Slavic-speaking mothers or grandmothers (*Voulghares*) who were prevented by their Greek-speaking husbands at the turn of the century from using their natal language at home; of the Greek teacher-cum-national activist who was released from prison and escaped death during the Macedonian Struggle through the intercession of a relative in the Bulgarian army; of the local woman who struck up conversations with Bulgarian soldiers during World War II, telling them that villagers were "of the same race" as the Bulgarians. Yet none expressed any sense that such mundane occurrences were in any way anomalous to the standardized national history they had been taught in school. It was only when confronted with externally imposed labels, such as "Skopians," that any suggestion of anomaly took form.

Such views, however, have had a direct and immediate significance for contemporary constructions of identity, both in the past and the present. Local notions of identity in turn-of-the-century Macedonia had been derived primarily from one's place of origin, from one's occupational livelihood, or from one's vernacular language. The national categories employed by politicians, propagandists, and polemicists on all sides at the time, such as those used in census surveys, were largely anachronistic to most of the region's present-day inhabitants, save for activists who had been drawn into the growing national contest for Macedonia. Villagers in Assiros did not consider it in the least significant to have had Slavic-speaking parents or grandparents; it was simply a fact of life. During my field-work in the late 1980s, conducted before the recent resurgence of a renewed Macedonian controversy, local residents did not use terms such as ethnicity, nationality, or national consciousness in their discourse with me and with each other. In the mid-1990s, however, such terms have become an integral part of Greek national historical narrative. This development has come about largely through heavy media exposure. Print capitalism was critical to the development and transmission of nationalism and national ideology (Anderson 1983); today, celluloid and television capitalism have added a new channel or dimension for the proselytization and proliferation of national consciousness and sentiment.

To most Greeks, terms such as nationality and national consciousness have a specific content and meaning, derived from the contemporary rhetorical posturing of national movements in the Balkans. When anthropologists working in Greece today employ similar terms as heuristic devices in their analysis of local culture, society, and history, they cut against the grain of established conventions: the newly invented traditions of identity that are endowed with national ideology's magical force of timelessness. Nationalists today with an almost arrogant disregard for the subtle and complex nuances of local history, blindly categorize Slavic-speakers and bilinguals of the past as contemporary national anomalies: as "Skopians" who threaten the integrity of the Greek nation.

THE MORALITY OF THE NATION AND THE IDEOLOGY OF "PEOPLEHOOD"

National ideology, as Greenfeld (1992) has argued, is diffused through local relationships. In Assiros, this process of dissemination was brokered by Greek-speaking local elites who assisted state authorities in establishing effective economic and political administration over the area. The morals of the nation were (and still are) so hegemonic that local villagers showed little or no consciousness of their active participation in this process, or of the ways in which national morality continues to shape their conceptions of themselves and their families' pasts. The ideology of the nation "locates the sense of individual identity within a 'people,' which is seen as the bearer of sovereignty, the central object of loyalty, and the basis of collective solidarity" (Greenfeld 1992:3). Nationalist ideologies, as Fox (1990:3) has put it, refer to the "production of conceptions of peoplehood."

Greekness is celebrated and legitimized continuously through national holidays, which as ritual celebrations capture the imaginations of the public, particularly impressionable school children. Moreover, as shown in Part II, national holidays replaced the significance of those festivals in the past that had once marked changes in agricultural or pastoral cycles. A cult of national ancestors, commemorating heroic figures who contributed to the establishment of the modern Greek nation-state, to the "liberation" (*apeleftherosi*) of Macedonia, and to its "incorporation" (*ensomatosi*) within Greece, has overtaken local villagers' appreciation and commemoration of their own personal ancestors. Celebrations and legitimations of Greekness are mediated by the mass media, teachers, and civil administrators. Villagers are full participants in the Greek body politic. They vote in national elections; they read the national press; they follow programs on nationwide television; they vacation in Greek islands to the south. In short, they are full-fledged (but often unconscious) participants in the state apparatus and its means of legitimation.

In this sense, Assiros township authorities were not disingenuous in their letter of response; they were not attempting to conceal a hidden history. Rather, personal experiences have become subsumed under national history, and genealogies have been used (subconsciously) to emphasize to the rest of the nation the "pure Greekness" of the local population. The founder of one of the largest surname groups in Assiros today is remembered not as a Slavic-speaking migrant from Montenegro who settled on a nearby *chiftlik*, gradually accumulated sizeable wealth and property, and eventually established his family among the ranks of the village's Greek-speaking mercantile and landowning elite. Rather, he is remembered as a Greek patriot who sent his son to Greek school to become a teacher of Greek and a partisan fighter for the Greek cause in the Macedonian Struggle. Today, there are new Macedonian Fighters to defend the community, both local and national, from "propaganda agents of Skopia."

NATIONAL (FALSE) CONSCIOUSNESS AND THE SUPERSCRIPTION OF MEMORIES

The historical consciousness of the Greek nation has been overwritten upon localized memories of personal experience. Written and oral histories, in this sense, have as much to do with so-called High Culture–Low Culture dichotomies and "qualitative history" as they do with Anderson's theories of print capitalism and nation-building. When discrepancies appear between the established canons of generic, homogenizing national history and the personal memories, family experiences, and even archival documents from a specific locale, the latter are assumed to be anomalous and therefore often dismissed or ignored altogether.

Recall the tragic story of Paskhalina, "the Bulgarian." She had always told the Greek-speaking residents of Assiros that her natal Slavic-speaking village had been destroyed, and her siblings abducted, by the Bulgarian army as it retreated from the region. Initially, she had likewise given me the same account. It was only through the benefit of extended, intensive local fieldwork that she confided, on my fourth visit with her in three years, that the story was a fabrication. In truth, her siblings had voluntarily left the area for Bulgaria. She and her parents had moved to Assiros because they had relatives living there. Paskhalina, however, never confided with her neighbors that it had been the Greek army that had burned their village. On the contrary, she fought them in the Greek courts during the 1960s to stop them from taunting her with the label "Bulgarian." Her legal victory never had any real effect, however, and she carried the stigma until the day she died. Nevertheless, I am certain that at the time of her death she felt nothing other than Greek. Years of schooling and a lifetime of intimate contact with local Assiriotes (having married in the village, as well) had superscribed a Greek national identity upon her own memories and interpretations of local history.

History, in its nation-proper sense, unfolds in a periodized account, imagined or real, of events and illustrious personages that contributed to the shaping of national destiny. National history's nonlinear use of time enables it to ignore or label as anomalous those local memories that would otherwise challenge both the logic of its construction and, ultimately, its power. Bilingualism had been an important element in the community's nineteenth-century past. It had helped make Guvezna a thriving marketplace, dominated by a Greek-speaking merchant class that had profitably mediated social exchange across occupational, linguistic, ethnic, and religious boundaries. Yet this very bilingualism is today condemned, by outside guardians of the nation, as somehow subversive, somehow "Skopian." And such rhetorical aggression has led local villagers to deny their own pasts for fear of recrimination. There are no longer any so-called "Bulgarians" or bilinguals in Assiros, and through the hegemonic censorship of nationalist activists there never were. Greekness is now measured through the metaphor of gold: twenty-four karat, the most precious, the most pure. National history creates ellipses in the local historical record, and some scholars and national advocates in Greece are not averse to publishing only those materials from historical archives that conform with established canons of national history. When the anthropologist explained to local residents that she was researching the history of their community, they interpreted her objective through their own frames of reference as a "national deed." Yet they regarded the inclusion of their multicultural, multilingual past in such a history as an "insult" that "traumatized [their] Greek sentiment."

Such constructed national (false) consciousness invokes the ancestors not as everyday people but as those heroes who fought boldly and bravely against the enemies of the nation earlier in this century. And yet there were others, whose descendants still live in Assiros, that played a dual role in the Macedonian Struggle, aiding or supporting both Greek and Bulgarian agents and forces. It would be improper to pass judgment upon them, for they acted without the benefit of hindsight, without the vision of latter-day constructs of national history and national destiny, struggling to survive the terror of those years without knowing which side would emerge victorious. The Bulgarian army reportedly camped outside Assiros in 1912 during its unsuccessful attempt to capture Thessaloniki from the Turks before the Greek forces could do the same. Its commanding officer, described by some villagers as a "Bulgarian prince," was hosted in a village home with warm hospitality. And yet, after the Balkan Wars, when Slavic-speaking affines from neighboring villages sought refuge in Assiros, they were refused shelter and asked repeatedly to leave. Those who did remain were able to do so only by attaching themselves as servants to the households of Greek-speaking merchants and stockbreeders, as in the case of Paskhalina's family. With the liberation of Assiros and its embodiment within the Greek polity, loyalty to the new state came to supersede other identities and loyalties.

The mundane aspects of nation-building and state formation in Greek Macedonia brought in a new administrative structure, new tax directives, new conscription obligations, and new family laws. These, in turn, generated new social and economic hierarchies, especially after the resettlement of Greek national refugees from Asia Minor and the massive land redistributions of the 1920s. But the spiritual aspects of this process touched on what Chatterjee (1993:6) called an "inner" domain that bears the "essential" marks of cultural identity. The mundane national imagination, with its borders and boundaries, its state sovereignty and foreign enemies, pales in comparison to the spiritual national imagination, which provides for the uniform, homogeneous, and continuous history of the nation. Thus, as Greenfeld (1992:7) concluded, "Every member of the 'people' thus interpreted partakes in its superior, elite quality, and it is in consequence that a stratified national population is perceived as essentially homogeneous, and the lines of status and class as superficial."

Local ethnographic history writes against the grain of nationalism when it challenges the manner in which national ideology imposes its constructs of the present onto the developments of the past. When oral accounts of mundane experiences are rewoven into the fabric of national history, they reveal texture in an otherwise even surface. They may also threaten to disrobe the emperor of his new clothes, so to speak, and thus attract scornful attention and retribution. Yet when nationalist authoritarianism threatens to disrupt violently the peaceful coexistence of peoples, it is time we participant-observers in this charade of modern chauvinism make an effort at dismantling boundaries rather than raising them.

At very least, I sincerely hope that readers, regardless of their reaction to this work, will have the decency to leave the Assiriotes to themselves and to their memories.

APPENDIX: GENEALOGIES

Genealogy A: The Tamtakos patriline

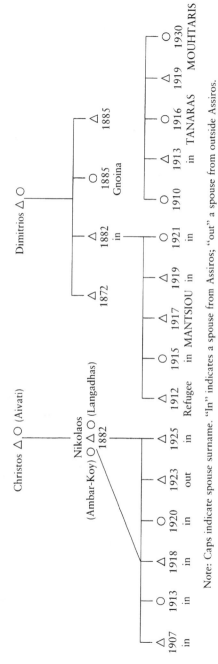

Note: Caps indicate spouse surname. "In" indicates a spouse from Assiros; "out" a spouse from outside Assiros.

Genealogy B: The Asteriou patriline

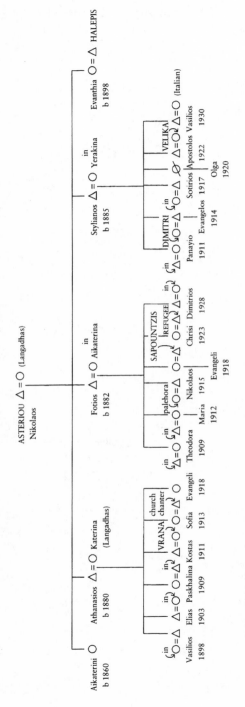

Genealogy C: The Velikas patriline

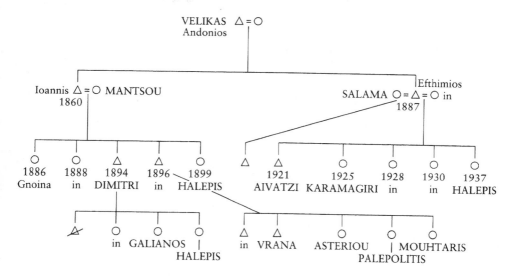

Genealogy D: The Halepis patriline

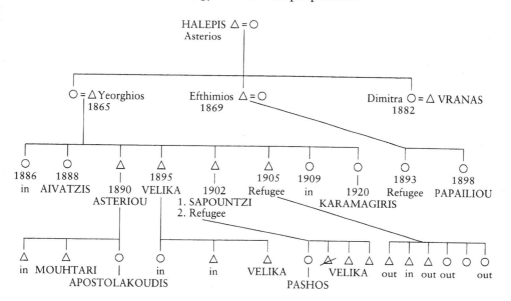

Genealogy E: The Artousis patriline

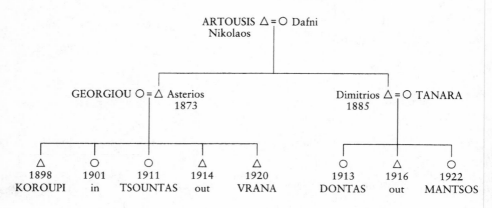

Genealogy F: The Vranas patriline

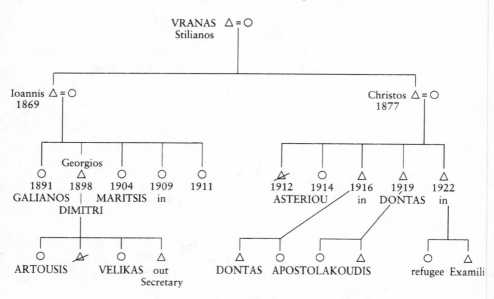

Genealogy G: The Sapountzis patriline

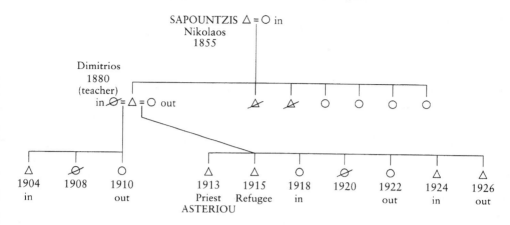

TABLES

Table 1. Langadhas Basin Population Statistics, 1920–81

Township	1920	1928	1940	1951	1961	1971	1981
Aghios Vasilios	582	767	1,059	1,251	1,247	1,051	1,026
Assiros	1,383	1,685	2,051	2,301	2,256	1,938	2,010
Assiros	1,206	1,412	1,635	1,775	1,776	1,654	1,767
Examili	99	158	306	340	282	192	190
Mavrorahi	78	115	110	186	198	92	53
Chrisavgi	458	525	596	644	701	641	707
Drimos	2,133	2,295	2,396	2,139	1,972	1,794	n/a
Iraklio	200	631	822	875	866	788	747
Kavallari	493	762	1,008	1,125	1,241	1,210	1,375
Kolhikon	770	1,192	1,569	1,932	1,977	1,666	1,558
Krithia	333	1,258	1,473	1,518	1,417	1,198	1,278
Laghina	944	1,247	1,403	1,291	1,380	1,465	n/a
Langadhas	26,198	38,976	47,335	50,285	52,277	42,961	40,234
Liti	1,495	1,579	3,688	3,213	1,852	1,722	n/a
Melissohori	1,689	2,456	1,548	1,403	1,192	941	n/a
Perivolaki	652	645	895	1,010	903	705	754

SOURCE: Chouliarakis (1988)

Table 2. "Ethnic" Composition of Basin Villages

Village	"Ethnic" Composition
Aghios Vasilios	Former Slavic-speakers
Assiros	Former Slavic-speakers, Greek-speaking settlers, East Thracian refugees
Chrisavgi	East Thracians, Asia Minor refugees, Pontics
Drimos	Greek-speakers (some former Slavic-speakers?)
Examili	East Thracians
Iraklion	East Thracians
Kavalari	Former Slavic-speakers, Asia Minor refugees
Kolhikon	Former Slavic-speakers, Pontics, East Thracians
Krithia	East Thracians
Laina	Former Slavic-speakers, Greek-speakers, some Vlah, some Sarakatsan, and some Pontics
Lahanas	Pontics
Langadhas	Former Slavic-speakers, refugees
Liti	Former Slavic-speakers
Melissochori	Former Slavic-speakers, Greek-speakers
Mavrorahi	Pontics
(Nea) Dorkas	East Thracians, Sarakatsan
Pente Vrises	Pontics, some Vlahs
Perivolaki	East Thracians
Polidhedri	Pontics, Sarakatsan
Ossa	Former Slavic-speakers, refugees
Vertiskos	Former Slavic-speakers, Greek-speakers
Xiliopolis	Former Slavic-speakers

Table 3. Assiros Township Population Statistics, 1920–81

Village	1920	1928	1940	1945	1951	1961	1971	1981
Assiros	1,206	1,412	1,635	1,780	1,775	1,776	1,654	1,767
Gnoina	99	n/a	*	*	*	*	*	*
Palehora	53	0	0	0	0	0	0	0
Examili	—	158	306	**	340	282	192	190
Krithia	—	1,090	*	*	*	*	*	*
Mavrorahi	—	115	110	**	186	198	92	53

SOURCE: Assiros Township Archives

* Withdrew from Assiros Township in 1930
** Inhabitants evacuated to Assiros during the Greek Civil War

Table 4. Population of Macedonia, 1914

National Group	Bulgarian Claims	Greek Claims	Serbian Claims
Bulgarians	1,181,336	332,162	57,600
Greeks	228,702	652,795	201,140
Serbs	700	0	2,048,320

SOURCE: Christoff 1919:31

Table 5. Ottoman-Era Agricultural Estates in the Guvezna Area

15th Century	Gaina timar Muslims		Cedid Yuruk garrison
16th Century	Guveyna wakf chiftlik Christians	Guveyna-Yeni wakf chiftlik Christians	
Late 18th Century	Guveyna chiftlik Christians	Guveyna chiftlik Muslims	Yeni-Koy hanekesan
Mid-19th Century	Guneyna wakf chiftlik Christians	Guvezna "village" Muslims, Christians	Yeni-Koy chiftlik Christians
Present-day	Palehora (abandoned)	Assiros	Gnoina

SOURCE: Dimitriadis 1980

Table 6. Occupations of Assiros Males (Percentages), 1911–39

Year	Shopowner	Herder	Artisan	Clerk	Transporter	Laborer	Merchant	Farmer	Orphans
1911	10.0	n/a	17.0	5.6	18.6	7.1	2.8	29.0	10.0
1912	5.8	n/a	22.1	3.4	14.0	23.1	13.0	10.4	7.0
1913	n/a	n/a	n/a	n/a	n/a	n/a	n/a	n/a	n/a
1914	5.0	n/a	23.9	2.5	15.7	19.0	6.6	19.0	8.3
1915	4.6	n/a	24.8	3.7	12.8	12.0	6.4	24.8	10.0
1916	4.4	0.9	14.9	4.4	22.8	20.2	7.0	25.4	n/a
1917	7.2	0.7	16.7	5.8	17.4	18.1	5.1	29.0	n/a
1918	10.5	1.3	18.3	7.8	21.6	5.9	7.2	20.2	7.2
1919	7.9	0.7	14.3	5.7	18.6	15.7	7.1	30.0	n/a
1920	5.7	0.6	15.5	3.4	10.3	13.8	4.6	37.4	8.7
1921	5.8	n/a	18.1	2.9	10.1	14.5	7.2	31.9	9.5
1922	6.6	n/a	13.2	1.1	6.6	8.8	3.3	50.5	9.9
1923	6.9	n/a	12.6	1.3	6.9	11.9	4.4	45.9	10.1
1924	5.1	n/a	13.1	2.9	2.3	3.6	2.9	55.5	14.6
1925	3.4	0.7	14.4	2.7	n/a	8.9	4.1	50.7	15.1

1926	5.1	n/a	10.8	0.6	0.5	14.6	4.4	47.5	16.5
1927	5.7	2.7	10.2	0.7	—	11.6	1.4	51.0	17.0
1928	3.9	1.9	9.0	1.3	—	12.3	1.3	52.9	17.4
1929	2.6	0.6	9.8	1.3	—	4.5	4.5	62.3	14.4
1930	3.3	0.6	10.4	11.0	—	7.7	3.3	53.3	11.0
1931	4.5	0.6	10.1	2.8	—	11.2	2.2	54.5	14.7
1932	4.1	0.6	9.9	1.7	—	14.5	1.2	56.4	12.2
1933	5.2	0.6	8.5	2.3	—	21.6	0.7	51.1	10.9
1934	3.8	0.8	12.4	3.2	—	13.5	1.7	53.5	11.9
1935	3.9	0.6	11.3	3.9	—	8.4	2.2	60.1	10.2
1936	5.0	0.6	9.4	2.8	—	19.4	1.1	52.2	10.1
1937	7.0	0.6	10.2	4.8	—	14.4	0.5	52.4	10.7
1938	4.5	0.5	10.4	5.0	—	16.3	2.5	52.0	8.8
1939	4.5	—	10.1	4.5	—	20.2	1.7	52.2	6.8

SOURCE: Assiros School Archives; not all rows tally to 100% owing to illegible print, incomplete entries, or rounding. Male heads of families with more than one child enrolled in school were only counted once; table does not include families without school children.

Table 7.   Slavic Kinship Terminology in Greek Macedonia

English	Standard Greek	Kilkis Area	Serres Area	Florina Area
father	pateras	tatko	tatko	tatko
mother	mitera	male	male	maika*
son	yios			sin
daughter	kori			herka
brother	adhelfos	brat	brat	
sister	adhelfi	sesra	sesra	
cousin (f.)	eksadhelfi	bratotsetka	bratotsetka	bratsela
cousin (m.)	eksadhelfos	bratotset		bratset
uncle	thios	tsiko		striko*
mother's brother	thios	vouiko		vouiko
aunt	thia	teto**		strina
mother's brother's wife	thia	vouitsino		vouina
co-daughter-in-law	sinifadha	yiatoura		
husband's sister	kouniadha	baldouza		
husband's brother	kouniadhos			zolva
husband's elder brother	kouniadhos	afendi		
nephew	anepsios	fnouk		unoutsi
niece	anepsia	fnouka		unouka
grandson	engonos	fnouk		unoutsi
granddaughter	engoni	fnouka		unouka
grandfather	papous	dedo		dedo
grandmother	yiayia	babo		babo
grandmother's sister	thia	teto		

* Still used by some elderly in Assiros
** Commonly used in Assiros

Table 8. Place of Birth, Household Heads, Assiros Township
(Percentages as of 1986)

Birthplace	Assiros		Examili		Mavrorahi	
	Male	Female	Male	Female	Male	Female
Pontos	—	—	—	—	25.2	18.2
East Thrace	1.9	2.1	35.3	28.7	—	—
Asia Minor	0.6	0.8	0.5	2.4	0.9	0.6
Mavrorahi	—	0.2	—	—	52.2	34.0
Examili	—	0.3	48.1	18.2	—	—
Assiros	85.5	63.1	—	—	—	—
Flamouri*	—	—	—	—	6.1	5.0
Other Villages	11.7	32.5	13.9	47.8	11.3	39.6
Outside Greece	0.3	1.0	—	2.4	4.3	—
Unknown	—	—	2.1	0.5	—	2.5
Total	1,158	1,196	187	209	115	159
Total Village Population	2,354		396		274	

SOURCE: Assiros Township Registry

* Several families from Flamouri, a mountain village near Lahanas, were evacuated to Assiros during the Greek Civil War.

Table 9A. Marriages of Daughters, Assiros Township
(Born 1915–40)

	Assiros	Assiros Refugee	Examili	Mavrorahi
Total Counted	159	36	103	33
% marrying in	72.3	31.0	19.4	51.5
% marrying out	27.7	69.0	80.6	48.5
% Married Out to:				
Thessaloniki Prefecture	62.9	40.0	41.7	66.7
Kilkis Prefecture	20.0	30.0	20.8	16.7
Halkidhiki Prefecture	2.9	—	12.5	—
Serres Prefecture	5.7	10.0	4.2	8.3
Western Greek Macedonia	—	—	6.9	8.3
Eastern Greek Macedonia	2.9	—	2.8	—
Thrace	2.9	—	—	—
Elsewhere in Greece	2.9	5.0	2.8	—
Outside Greece	—	—	—	—
Unknown	—	15.0	8.3	—

Table 9B. Marriages of Sons, Assiros Township (Born 1915–40)

	Assiros	Assiros Refugee	Examili	Mavrorahi
Total Counted	217	56	90	43
% marrying in	67.3	55.6	18.9	23.3
% marrying out	32.7	44.4	81.1	76.7
% Married Out to:				
Thessaloniki Prefecture	44.4	44.0	26.7	51.4
Kilkis Prefecture	11.1	20.0	30.7	28.6
Halkidhiki Prefecture	5.6	—	1.3	2.9
Serres Prefecture	9.3	12.0	4.0	—
Western Greek Macedonia	9.3	8.0	6.7	11.4
Eastern Greek Macedonia	—	—	2.7	2.9
Thrace	1.9	—	2.7	—
Elsewhere in Greece	11.1	12.0	9.3	2.9
Outside Greece	7.4	—	4.0	—
Unknown	4.0	4.0	—	—

Table 10. Assiros Township Budgetary Expenses, 1921–31 (Percentages)

Item	1921	1922	1923	1924	1925	1926	1927	1928	1929	1930	1931
President	n/a	12.0	12.8	10.2	10.5	10.7	8.7	n/a	n/a	n/a	n/a
Secretary & bailiff	n/a	6.0	9.6	13.3	19.2	26.7	23.3	n/a	n/a	n/a	n/a
Salaries	29.9	n/a	n/a	n/a	n/a	n/a	n/a	13.8	17.1	16.4	13.7
Office supplies	5.3	n/a	n/a	n/a	n/a	n/a	n/a	1.6	1.9	1.0	1.4
Office expenses	n/a	9.7	6.9	7.2	6.7	6.9	17.2	9.3	9.4	8.9	7.4
Public works	53.3	65.6	64.4	41.4	45.0	43.2	36.4	46.5	61.6	61.5	68.3
Public services	4.9	n/a	n/a	n/a	n/a	n/a	n/a	1.5	2.0	4.2	4.4
School	n/a	2.5	2.1	22.1	11.9	6.7	8.5	23.3	3.2	1.5	1.6
Donations	6.6	2.0	1.2	0.8	0.0	2.2	1.2	0.9	1.6	3.4	1.6
Officials' fees	n/a	2.2	3.0	5.0	6.7	3.6	4.8	n/a	n/a	n/a	n/a
Court expenses	n/a	n/a	n/a	n/a	n/a	n/a	n/a	3.1	3.2	3.1	1.6

Table 11. Assiros Township Presidents and Councilmen, 1919–35

Year	Position	Occupation
1919		
Tamtakos, Nikolaos	president	farmer/grocer/merchant
Asteriou, Stylianos	councilman	teacher/stockbreeder/farmer
Mantsos, Athanasios	councilman	merchant/tax farmer
Apostolakoudis, Elias	councilman	merchant
Danelis, Anastasios	councilman	merchant
1921		
Pashos, Ioannis	president	merchant
Halepis, Yeorghios	councilman	real estate/stock-breeder
Karavidas, Ioannis	councilman	crop-watcher
Vayiatzis, Konstantinos	councilman	grocer
1923		
Tamtakos, Nikolas	president	
Sapountzis, Dimitrios	secretary	teacher
Karavidas, Nikolaos	bailiff	cripple
Asteriou, Stylianos	councilman	
Artousis, Asterios	councilman	grocer/merchant/real estate
Vaniotis, Efthimios	councilman	miller
1925		
Asteriou, Stylianos	president	
Artousis, Asterios	vice president	
Velikas, Ioannis	councilman	real estate/stock-breeder
Vranas, Yeorghios	councilman	grocer/merchant/stock-breeder
Pashos, Ioannis	councilman	
Andreadis, Panayiotis	councilman	refugee (in Assiros village)
1926		
Kalamis, Yeorgios	president	horse-shoer
Galianos, Anastasios	vice president	merchant/industrialist
Velikas, Dimitrios	councilman	stock-breeder
Karamagiris, Athanasios	councilman	grocer/merchant
Vayiatzis, Fotios	councilman	cheese merchant
Pashos, Ioannis	councilman	
1929		
Vranas, Yeorghios	president	
Vasiliou, Alexander	councilman	merchant/refugee (Assiros village)
Asteriou, Stylianos	councilman	
Tamtakos, Nikolaos	councilman	
Pashos, Ioannis	councilman	
Apostolakoudhis, Elias	councilman	
Artousis, Asterios	councilman	
two refugees from Examili	councilman	
1931		
Vranas, Yeorghios	president	
Asteriou, Stylianos	vice president	
1934		
Galianos, Anastasios	president	
Asteriou, Stylianos	vice president	
1935		
Voukas, Dimitrios	president	farmer
Karamagiris, Athanasios	vice president	

SOURCE: Assiros Township Archives

Table 12. Assiros Township Tax Revenues, Available Years, 1935–54 (Percentages)

Source	1935–36	1946–47	1947–48	1948–49	1950–51	1951–52	1953–54
Stock-Breeding	35.2	58.6	67.2	73.7	80.2	23.7	32.7
Agriculture	56.6	41.4	32.8	24.7	16.9	74.6	67.3
Corvee labor	—	—	—	—	—	1.4	—
Property Taxes	6.6	—	—	1.4	—	—	—
Rents	1.6	—	—	—	—	—	—
Other	—	—	—	0.2	2.9	0.3	—

Table 13. Assiros Township Grazing Lands, 1920–40

Pasture	Area in Stremmata	Pasture Capacity	
		Small Animals	Large Animals
Assiros	9,500	500–1,000	village herd
Debella	1,000	500–1,000	n/a
Sporadikes	1,500	500–1,000	n/a
Outs-Agats[1]	2,000	1,000	300 (village herd)
Kambili,[2] Pournar	5,000	2,000–3,000	300 (village herd)
Mavrorahi Otmanli[3]	4,000	500	100–150 (village herd)
Examili Skotomeni-Isar	3,000	1,000	150–250 (village herd)

SOURCE: Assiros Township Archives

1. Came under Assiros jurisdiction in 1931.
2. Incorporated into Assiros township in 1937; formerly state property (*dhimosio*) rented out regularly to Sarakatsani since 1922.
3. Incorporated into Assiros township in 1943.

Table 14. Grazing Cycle and Forbidden Grazing Zones

Time Period	Forbidden Zones
15 November–15 March	Cultivated and fallow fields (*niama*); vineyards; melon patches; village circular plain located in the *koula* region and devoted to pear-tree cultivation; animal pens permitted only alongside cattle routes and inside village (*aghelatharia*); animals brought back to village for milking
15 March–10 July	Same as above; pens and animals permitted in summer pastures
20 July–15 November	Only vineyards, melon patches, and village pear-tree plots forbidden

Table 15. Baptismal Sponsors, 1880–1985 (Settlement Groups by Percentage)

	1880–1950				
Sponsor	Mavrorahi	Examili	Assiros Refugee	Kalivia Sarakatsani	Assiros Local
Mavrorahi	54.5	—	—	4.2	0.1
Examili	—	70.8	1.2	—	0.2
Assiros Refugee	—	1.0	40.2	—	1.8
Sarakatsan	5.5	—	—	58.2	—
Assiros	1.8	4.9	34.6	4.2	8.8
Outsider	20.0	11.4	16.8	16.7	8.8
Unknown	18.2	11.9	7.2	16.7	7.8
	1951–85				
Sponsor	Mavrorahi	Examili	Assiros Refugee	Kalivia Sarakatsani	Assiros Local
Mavrorahi	60.0	—	—	—	—
Examili	—	41.0	—	—	1.2
Assiros Refugee	—	4.5	7.1	—	3.7
Sarakatsan	—	—	—	44.4	1.9
Assiros	4.0	4.5	42.9	11.2	65.9
Outsider	32.0	45.5	42.9	44.4	26.7
Unknown	4.0	4.5	7.1	—	0.6
	Total 1880–1985				
Sponsor	Mavrorahi	Examili	Assiros Refugee	Kalivia Sarakatsani	Assiros Local
Mavrorahi	56.2	—	—	3.0	0.1
Examili	—	67.9	1.0	—	0.3
Assiros Refugee	—	1.3	35.7	—	2.0
Sarakatsan	3.7	—	—	54.5[1]	0.2
Assiros	2.5	4.9	35.7	6.1	79.6
Outsider	23.8	14.7	20.4	24.2	10.8
Unknown	13.8	11.2	7.2	12.2	7.0

SOURCE: Assiros Baptismal Registry

1. Three percent from the Assiros Sarakatsan group, the remaining 51.5 percent from the Assiros "local" population.

Table 16. Farmers Involved in Grain Production, 1990

	Assiros			Examili			Mavrorahi			Total	
Crop	no.	%	Stremmata	no.	%	Stremmata	no.	%	Stremmata	Farmers	Stremmata
Soft wheat	287	93.1	19,558	33	80.5	1,590	7	100	271	327	21,418
Hard wheat	118	38.3	6,745	29	70.3	1,582	1	14.3	148	148	8,353
Barley	19	6.2	333	7	17.1	119	0	0	0	26	452
Total	308		26,636	41		3,290	7		296	401	30,223

SOURCE: Assiros Township Archives

NOTES

INTRODUCTION

1. Salonika (Thessaloniki) was one of the chief market ports of the sixteenth-century Aegean grain trade, servicing mainly Macedonia (Braudel 1966:579). For more on the role of Thessaloniki as a commercial center since the eighteenth century, see Moskoff (1964).

2. Many elderly residents of the Langadhas basin recalled the camel caravans that passed through the area during their youth. Bactrian camels were regarded as superior transport animals for Balkan commerce, for unlike the desert-adapted dromedary, the Bactrian camel was able to withstand low temperatures and to climb high mountains (Braudel 1966:96).

3. The Langadhas plain is regarded as a "basin" by Greek archaeologists working in the area, as its waters have no outlet to the sea. The basin's boundaries are defined by Lake Aghios Vasilios and the Derveni foothills to the south, the Kamila mountain (Deve Karan) to the west, and by Vertiskos mountain and its extensions to the north and east (Kotsakis 1986).

4. Encompassing an area of approximately 192 square kilometers, the basin consists of several zones, distinguishable by either geomorphology or socio-ecology and patterns of land utilization. The lowlands surrounding Lake Aghios Vasilios, whose marshes were drained through government water-control projects of the 1930s, have a high water table and consist mainly of irrigated corn and clover fields. The rolling plains of the western basin are devoted largely to dry wheat cultivation. In the hills and mountain peripheries of the basin, animal husbandry is the principal economic livelihood, and here one may find remnants of nineteenth-century herding hamlets (see map 2a).

5. The last published census, in 1971, put the population of Langadhas town at just over 6,700, fully half of whom were refugees from East Thrace, Asia Minor, the Black Sea, Russia, and Bulgaria who settled in the area after 1922 (for population statistics of pertinent Langadhas basin communities, see table 1). Administratively and financially, the basin belongs to the Prefecture of Thessaloniki, which comprises the districts of Thessaloniki and Langadhas. Encompassing eighteen townships (*kinotites*) in 1945, the district today has grown to include a total

of fifty. Communities in this area, as elsewhere in Greece, experienced substantial emigration in the 1960s and the 1970s, with more than a fifth of district residents departing for the urban centers of Thessaloniki, Athens, Australia, and Western Europe.

6. In addition, there are groups of migrating Gypsies who periodically set up their tents in some areas of the basin, particularly outside the town of Langadhas. Muslim seasonal agricultural and industrial workers also come to the area from western (i.e. Greek) Thrace. While Gypsies and so-called "Greek Muslims" participate in the region's economy, they do not form marriage alliances with the basin's sedentary population. In 1990, migrant laborers from Albania also began to cross into Greece in search of employment. Unprotected by law, many suffer harsh treatment at the hands of local residents and officials.

7. *Toumba* refers to the prehistoric mounds of the Macedonian countryside.

8. The *stremma* (pl. *stremmata*) is the unit of land measure used in Greece. One *stremma* is roughly equivalent to one-quarter acre (or four *stremmata* to the acre). According to the National Statistic Bureau (1962), 43 percent of the land in Assiros township is agricultural. Another 43.5 percent of township land is designated as "common lands" (*kinotikes*) devoted to herding.

9. Inhabitants of such clustered neighborhoods in Balkan villages were often close agnatic relatives, sometimes comprising localized descent groups (see Hammel 1968:19; Halpern and Kerewsky Halpern 1986 [1972]:22).

10. Situated at the foot of the Chrisopetra hills, the area around Examili is considered prime grazing land, and Assiros township collects considerable revenue through head taxes on livestock, pasture access fees, and taxes on agricultural products. Fully half of Examili's 11,500 *stremmata* are grazing lands, although the best herding land in the area lies still further north, in the hills around the village of Mavrorahi.

11. The *kafenion* opens only occasionally for the evening, especially when friends from Thessaloniki or a visiting ethnographer come to call. In this tiny settlement, the *kafenion* fills a dual function as a small-item shop. Here villagers can buy candy, chocolates, cigarettes, napkins, toilet paper, rubbing alcohol, canned food, and other such goods, or use the village's only telephone, installed in 1958 and affectionately referred to by the villagers as "gargle." A small yellow mailbox adorns the exterior wall of the *kafenion* beside a plaque bearing the date 1958, the year it was constructed with funds from the Marshall Plan. Even in this small community, the *kafenion* remains the center of social life, a place for meeting, socializing, arguing, drinking, playing music on homemade instruments, and singing.

12. Most of Mavrorahi's 18,500 *stremmata* are devoted to herding, though there are a few patches of cash-bringing tobacco cultivation. The eight cows still kept in the village are free-ranging, quite a rare phenomenon in modern-day Greece. Under new government incentives, a few villagers have attempted to clear a plot or two for cultivation of "hard" macaroni wheat or rye, while others have planted almond trees. Yet the water crisis has utterly destroyed any thoughts of irrigation, leaving all plots totally dependent on the sparse rainfall.

13. Around the ninth century, Armenians in Macedonia began to play important roles in the political, military, and administrative sectors of the Byzantine Empire (Charanis 1963). They were reportedly settled in the area of Thessaloniki

in A.D. 988, and a number were established by the Byzantine emperor Basil II in Aivatovo or Aivatzik, the present-day village of Liti in the Langadhas area. Nakratzas (1988:47) maintained that Aivatzik is an Armenian name, but that by the nineteenth century its population had been Slavicized and spoke a Slavic dialect. During the Ottoman period, however, Armenian and Greek Orthodox priests were virtually indistinguishable to outsiders (Curtis 1911:4).

14. These Gypsies were probably descendants of Rom or Indic speakers who migrated to the Balkans early in the second millennium (A.D.)

15. Rheubottom (1976:21) noted that in Yugoslav Macedonia there were widespread popular beliefs that prior to Christianity the Slavs had been a "'wild people' who lived without customs or morality. But this state of nature came to an end when they converted to Christianity. The saints taught them religion, morality, and the arts of civilization. . . . The saints wrought a state of culture out of a state of nature."

16. See Borza (1990) for a concise review of the literature on, and a discussion of, the relative Greekness of the ancient Macedonians. In contrast to many contemporary Greek writers, Borza (1990:277) contended that "As far as the ancient Greeks were concerned, the Macedonians were not Greeks," despite the fact that they spread some aspects of Greek civilization to Western Asia.

17. Mavrogordatos (1983a) was among the few Greek scholars to recognize the existence of a "Slavo-Macedonian" ethnic group within the borders of Greek Macedonia, noting that, when Epiros and Macedonia were "liberated," the Greek population constituted a numerical minority in those regions, where "Slavo-Macedonians" controlled agricultural production. He claimed that Jews, Turks, and Slavo-Macedonians constituted the majority of the electorate in the national Greek elections of 1915 and 1929, and that their votes played a key role in those results (Mavrogordatos 1983a:71). Tsoukalas (1977:36) maintained that "Slavs were dominant in Macedonia. Greeks were only an important minority which became smaller and smaller as one moved north."

18. Such reasoning was part of the Greek government's unsuccessful effort within the European Union and the United Nations to block international diplomatic recognition of the Former Yugoslav Republic of Macedonia (FYROM), which declared its independence from the former Yugoslavia in September 1991. The European Union finally accorded recognition to the new country late in 1993, just prior to Greece's assumption of the union's chairmanship. The U.S. had stationed several hundred American troops there as peacekeeping forces.

19. Instrumental in the construction of a "tradition" (*pace* Hobsbawm and Ranger 1983) of the Greek nation which harkens back to the golden age of Byzantium and even to the prehistoric Mycenean and Minoan civilizations has been the work of Greek national historians such as Konstantinos Paparrigopoulos (see chapter 3). Regarded in Greece as the father of modern Greek history, Papparigopoulos sought to establish a direct continuity between ancient and modern Greece through the Byzantines, and his work has been highly influential among Greek politicians and writers concerned with national issues (Karakasidou 1994b).

20. Here, too, critics have sharply attacked such positions. Georgevitch (1918: 191) maintained that Macedonian language includes considerable regional variation, divisible into several dialects. More recently, Friedman (1986) identified

Macedonian as a Balkan language containing many dialects transitional between Serbian and Bulgarian.

21. Serbian national activists reportedly became involved in Macedonia later than those from Greece and Bulgaria, dispatching teachers and propagandists to the region beginning in 1889 (*Pro-Macedonia* 1923:3–4). But the extent of Serbian involvement in the region has been debated. Haskell (1918a:14) claimed that Serbia became involved in Macedonia only because it lost Bosnia to the Austro-Hungarian Empire and was seeking to recoup territorial losses by expanding southward. Christoff (1919:24) maintained that prior to 1878, when the borders of the autonomous Bulgarian principality were negotiated by international diplomats, "Servian national leaders, with the exception of a few ethnic chauvinists, did not claim any portion of Macedonia to be Servian." The conflict between Bulgaria and Serbia over Macedonia heated up dramatically after the partition of the region in 1913 (see Tosheff 1932). During 1896–97, a total of only seventy-seven Serbian schools were reportedly operating in Macedonia, a number that paled in comparison to the 843 Bulgarian schools (Christoff 1919:27).

22. Elsewhere, I have addressed competitive Greek and former Yugoslav Macedonian nation-building activities in the Florina prefecture of northwestern Greece, near the contemporary border with Albania and the FYROM (see Karakasidou 1993, 1994a). For a recent study of Macedonian nationalism among the former Yugoslav Macedonian diaspora, see Danforth (1995).

23. For a review of national-genesis historiography from the FYROM, see Kofos (1992).

24. In 1996, many Greeks still refused to use the word "Macedonia" in reference to the nation-state on their northern border. Instead, the terms "Skopia" and "Skopians," derived from the name of that country's capital and principal city, Skopje, have been employed in a demeaning and derogatory manner to refer to the FYROM, its government, and its population.

25. This rhetoric was blended with socialist rhetoric or what Kolisevski (1959) called a "Marxist approach to national history" (p. 43) in which the working-class poor play an important role since "socialist and national development are but two aspects of the same process" (p. 32).

26. For more on how concepts of ethnicity and nationality are collapsed together in contemporary Greece, see Karakasidou (1993b).

27. A number of scholars have indeed dealt explicitly with the issue of ethnicity as a nonstatic and ever-changing product of global developments. Some have maintained that ethnicity must be examined on both the "micro" and the "macro" levels (e.g., Clammer 1986, Salamone 1986). As Epstein (1978:109) put it, "ethnic identity . . . is the product of the interplay of internal and external factors. . . . [It] becomes intimately interwoven with questions of hierarchy, stratification and the pursuit of political interests . . . [thus] the [ethnic] categories become 'social facts.' " Ethnicity as collective identity is "generated, transmitted and perpetuated," and no study of ethnicity can ignore those formulative and reproductive processes within the context of specific historical circumstances (Epstein 1978).

28. Consider a man of Arvanitis (i.e., Orthodox Christian Albanian) descent whom I met in a village in western Greek Macedonia. His grandfather had migrated to the area from Albania at around the turn of the century and subse-

quently learned to speak Slavic (and later Greek). When he sang his laments, he began in Arvanitika, then continued in Slavic, and finished in Greek. Although he was a Slavic-speaker living in Macedonia, it would be unjustified to describe him as a Macedonian Slav.

ONE

1. Keesing's (1986) comparative evaluation of oral Kwaio versions and written English accounts of an attack on an English slave-ship in the nineteenth century is enlightening in this regard, for he found that local oral accounts were more internally consistent and historically accurate than written versions of the incident authored by English participants. Herzfeld (1991a) also discussed in detail the issue of "multiple pasts, multiple presents" in his treatment of monumental history in the old town of Rethemnos, Crete.

2. Similarly, Anastenaria fire walkers in contemporary Greece often link their origins to St. Constantine and the fall of Constantinople (see Danforth 1989).

3. Reports on the archaeological excavations of the Assiros *toumba* may be found in Wardle (1989).

4. For example, the letter claimed that Herodotus (Z 122) had mentioned a city called "Assa," while in Aristotle's *History of the Animals* (G 112) there was mention of an ancient settlement called "Assiritis" in Halkidhiki through which the Cold River (*Psihros potamos*) flowed. The letter also maintained that Claudius Ptolemeus (A.D. 108–60) mentioned a settlement called "Assoros" or "Assiros" (in Book G 13,56), while Pliny and Ptolemy (III, 12,33) referred to a settlement called "Assiros," and Stefanos of Byzantium spoke of an "Assira."

5. The vast majority of villages and towns throughout the Greek province of Macedonia were given new Greek names, replacing former Slavic and Turkish ones, after the region was incorporated into Greece in 1913.

6. Current archaeological evidence indicates that Aghia Anna was a sizeable estate possessing scattered farmsteads. Habitation of the site in general dated to Neolithic times, and occupation apparently continued throughout the Byzantine and Ottoman eras. During the Ottoman period, inhabitants were concentrated south of the Neolithic site in a relatively small area of scattered houses. Archaeologists working in the area have concluded that it was probably a single operating farm (Kotsakis, personal communication, 1991). Following the abandonment of Aghia Anna, the area reverted to agricultural and grazing land. Sarakatsan residents of Assiros currently maintain their herd pens near the site of Aghia Anna. While some of the nearby farmland was redistributed to landless Assiros villagers during 1928 (see chapter 6), some thirty *stremmata* has still remained the *wakf* property of the Assiros church, which rents it out to wheat cultivators.

7. An Ottoman tax document of the late nineteenth century, for example, referred to a small hamlet (*mahala*) in the area, called "Ayna Hanli" (Turkish: "Mirror Inn"), consisting of four houses (Dimitriadis 1980). The name bears some resemblance to "Ayana," although it may have been a different settlement. One of the oldest families in Assiros bears a surname that suggests they may have come from Ayna Hanli.

8. Laiou-Thomadakis (1977) noted that during the late Byzantine era, Macedonia had been divided into two principal regions or *themes,* Thessaloniki and

Strymon, and that many villages and lands had actually been owned by monasteries on Mount Athos.

9. I have encountered this term in other parts of Macedonia, always describing a small town. Apparently, it had been a term used widely by the Ottomans.

10. Assiros men secretly dug in the area of Aghia Anna for many years in a vain quest to uncover buried golden treasure.

11. I heard similar stories of descent from migrants originating in the forests of Central Europe from inhabitants of other former Slavic-speaking villages in the Langadhas basin.

12. As I will explain in detail below, Palehora was formerly known as "Guneyna," and Gnoina as "Yeni-Koy." The conceptual merging of the two settlements, both said by Assiriotes to have been formerly Slavic-speaking villages, was probably facilitated by the similarity of the names "Guneyna" and "Gnoina." Lefort (1986:154) noted that in 1862 the names "Gknoina" [sic] and "Palaiochora" [sic] were alternatively used in reference to a settlement also called "Guneyna."

13. Aivati (Liti) was the village from which musicians (*orghana*) who played at all festivities in the Langadhas basin came.

14. Structuralist approaches to social theory by scholars as diverse as Douglas (1975), Freud (1960), and Radcliffe-Brown (1952) have addressed the manner in which jokes and joking relations may reveal certain fundamental social cleavages and unresolved structural tensions.

15. Ambar-Koy ("Grain Cellar Village"), west of Guvezna, had been an important grain market and "mixed village" of Muslims and Slavic-speaking Christians situated on the Salonika-Kukush-Monastir-Serbia trade route. In the 1860s, it was inhabited by twenty-one Muslim and twenty-seven Christian families, but by 1920 it had a population of 524 (Dimitriadis 1980). Ambar-Koy inhabitants regularly shopped in Guvezna; a prominent Guvezna grain merchant (Apostolakoudhis) did much of his business in Ambar-Koy. Balaftsa, southeast of Guvezna, had been a *chiftlik* and charcoal-producing village of three Muslim families and sixty-six (Slavic-speaking) Christian families in the 1860s (population 770 in 1920; ibid.). Langaza, south of Guvezna, recall, had been an Ottoman *kaza* seat with a large Slavic-speaking population. Zarova, northeast of Guvezna, had been a charcoal-producing *chiftlik* inhabited by ninety-eight households of Slavic-speaking Christians in the 1860s, all of whom left for Bulgaria after the Second Balkan War (ibid.).

16. A colleague has suggested that the stories of local respondents concerning their descent from settlers from Trikala may be an "invented" construction that attempts to lay claim to "real" Greek descent. I remain skeptical of such interpretations, however. Even assuming, for the moment, that some settlers did seek to "fabricate" claims to Greek descent, this rather conspiratorial hypothesis is of no analytical value in explaining *why* Trikala and Thessaly were selected as ancestral lands when other locations could have served equally well.

17. The only written source I have found that mentions such a migration from Thessaly is the work of X. S. Strukova (1971), a study based on Russian diplomatic records. Strukova dated the population movement to the 1860s.

18. Vucinich (1965:44), for example, traced the origins of feudalization under the Ottomans to Persian, Seljuk, and Byzantine institutions. During the last two

centuries of Byzantine rule, agricultural estates had been gradually parceled out to a succession of landlords. Laiou-Thomadakis (1977) argued that peasants (*paroikoi*) lost freedom of movement and were obliged to pay both taxes and rents, collected in kind. The largest institutional landowner under the Byzantines, however, had been the Orthodox Church, whose properties had been endowed by the emperors. By the Ottoman conquest, agricultural productivity in Byzantium had fallen precipitously and much of the countryside had been depopulated, plagued by repeated civil unrest.

19. *Sipahi* were permitted to retain certain revenues from *timar* lands in return for providing soldiers for the empire's army. But they could not sell such lands nor transfer them to descendants. *Timar* land was worked by *rayah* (i.e., subjects), Muslim and Christian farmers who paid fixed taxes and provided labor service to their *sipahi* landlords (Vucinich 1965:46; see also Moutaftsieva 1990, and Asdrahas 1978).

20. To shelter themselves from taxes, many wealthy Christians donated their land to Church-owned *wakf* trusts while still retaining the right to exploit it productively and to extract from it a profitable surplus (McGrew 1985:25–27).

21. The early Ottomans have been depicted as a community of *ghazis*, or frontier warriors of the Islamic faith, during their period of formation and expansion (Vucinich 1965:9; Stavrianos 1959:35–36). Inalcik (1985) described the Ghazi as leaders of mounted warrior bands that raided the lands of non-Muslims. Their origins, some contend, may be traced to Turkoman pastoral nomads who had been dislodged from their more easterly lands and had migrated into western Anatolia following Mongol invasions in the thirteenth century. On the frontiers of the Byzantine empire, Turkoman tribal loyalties and rivalries were gradually overcome by emergent *ghazis*, under whose flags mounted troops raided Byzantine areas and clashed with Byzantine frontier guards (*akrites*). Ghazi Osman is considered the founder of the Ottoman Empire.

22. I believe that Guveyna-yeni (or 'New Guveyna') was the precursor of the settlement that eventually became Guvezna/Assiros, while Guveyna later became known as Guneyna/Palehora ("Old Village").

23. Inalcik (1985:113) argued that the development of *chiftlik* properties represented an evolutionary step beyond the "Asiatic" mode of production that had characterized Ottoman society, as it led to new social and economic formations dependent upon European capitalism. Vergopoulos (1975:64–81) outlined six major factors leading up to the institutionalization of this new form of landholding: (1) the end to Ottoman conquests of new lands; (2) the development of capitalist commercial activity; (3) inflation and increased tax burdens; (4) depopulation of the countryside; (5) the development of agrarian social movements; and (6) looting. For extensive discussion of the formation, function, and division of labor on *chiftliks* in Macedonia, see Karavidas (1931:111–200).

24. McGrew (1985), however, argued that the *chiftlik* economy operated only during the last two centuries of Ottoman rule in the Balkans, and that in southern Greece the term *chiftlik* implied something quite different: the "right to collect a specified portion of the agricultural produce of a particular village" (McGrew 1985:31). Collectors were either Muslim or Christian, and such villages were defined or referred to as the *chiftliks* of that individual. In popular historical dis-

course throughout Greece, however, the term *chiftlik* is often applied rather loosely to any large landholding under the Ottomans.

25. By the first few decades of the twentieth century, preoccupation with grain supplies in Mediterranean markets had led to a new shift in agriculture, and 70 to 80 percent of Macedonian lands came to be devoted to wheat cultivation (Vergopoulos 1975:134). In fact, throughout the eighteenth and nineteenth centuries, as much as 400,000–480,000 kilograms of Macedonian wheat were exported to Europe annually (Zdraveva 1981:180). As Braudel (1966:573) noted succinctly, "Grain was a preoccupation simply because it was always scarce: Mediterranean harvests usually verged on the inadequate. . . . Richer kinds of farming, vines, and livestock were in constant competition with cereal growing. . . . Wheat in the Mediterranean took up a great deal of room . . . particularly since the same land could not be sown every year. . . . The practice of dry-farming required plowing the same land at different times. . . . And all government measures— taxes on grain, the regulation of sales—were so many blows on the back of a peasantry. . . . And then there were the recurrent tragedies of winter floods and summer droughts. . . . The final result was extreme instability of price levels which fluctuated with the slightest news."

26. As Vincent (1982) noted in her study of Uganda, the American Civil War had a dramatic effect on global cotton production and trade around the world.

27. During the years 1876–1908, this market was so well integrated that fluctuations of grain prices in Istanbul closely reflected those in London (Quataert 1983).

28. This Christian *chiftlik* of "Guneyna" most likely referred to the now abandoned settlement known locally as Palehora, previously recorded in Ottoman tax records as the Christian *chiftlik* of Guveyna.

29. Situated just west of Guneyna (i.e. Palehora), nineteenth-century Yeni-Koy (i.e., present-day Gnoina) had been a *wakf chiftlik* made up of a few low, single-storied, mudbrick houses clustered tightly together. Lefort (1986:131) also recorded descriptions of seven houses there in 1862 and twenty-five houses in 1889. Referred to by the Serbian Gopcevic in 1889 as "Bogorodica" (a Slavic name), and by the Bulgarian K'ncov as "Eni Kjoj," Yeni-Koy reportedly had as many as 250 inhabitants in the late nineteenth century (ibid.).

30. The "free Christians" of *kefalohoria,* such as those in nearby Dirmil (Drimos) and Baltza (Melissohori), acquired land of their own either through a *cift-hane* small family farm, a *wakf* trust, or rights over a *chiftlik* estate (McGrew 1985:25–29). Unlike in other villages in which the entire settlement was held collectively responsible for meeting taxes and fees, families living in a *kefalohori* paid their taxes individually and independently of each other through an officially designated collection agent. Ownership of a *cift-hane* was inherited jointly by the sons of a father after his death (Inalcik 1985:105). Such "free-held" farms were frequently found in mountainous areas where productivity was low and Ottoman authority was relatively weaker (McGrew 1985:32–33); they were also known as *mulks,* under the control of a *malik* (Gibb and Bowen 1950:236; Moutaftsieva 1990:112). Landless laborers who had residence in *kefalohoria* often worked either as sharecroppers on a nearby *chiftlik* or as hired hands on non-*chiftlik* lands (Inalcik 1985:123). Vergopoulos (1975:135) maintained that by 1913 there was

nearly a 3:2 ratio in the number of *kefalohoria* (610) and *chiftliks* (421) in Macedonia. Guvezna had never been a *kefalohori*.

31. Although present-day Assiriotes claimed that the first village church was built in 1810, it is unlikely that Cousinery would have failed to note the existence of a church in the then largely Muslim Guvezna. Other local accounts maintained that there had been a small church dedicated to St. George (a popular saint among pastoralists) in the dell near the village *aghora* by as early as 1835, which would have been several years after Cousinery passed through Guvezna. Evidence suggests that the larger, more prominent hilltop church of the Prophet Elias, said to have been built with funds donated by local Greek merchants, was not constructed until the fourth quarter of the nineteenth century (see chapter 4).

32. In fact, as early as 1857, the British Foreign Office was actively involved in the free distribution of seeds, as well as new technologies, to agricultural estates in Macedonia (Vakalopoulos 1987:217–18). Cotton, mainly from the Serres area and other parts of central Macedonia, became the second most important crop (after grain) collected and exchanged in the warehouses of Salonika, from where it was packed and shipped to Marseilles and other European ports (Vakalopoulos 1987:224).

33. Asserting the importance of their local market, some local villagers claimed that the Guvezna market predated that of Langadhas, that there had once even been a bank in the village, and that laborers opening a road through the village had found Austrian coins there. By one account, the postal service (*posta*) between Greece and Russia formerly passed through Guvezna. Heavily laden mules, it was said, came through the village and their drivers, guarded by gendarmes, were sometimes carrying large amounts of cash (much of it gold pieces) from the transactions they brokered between markets, cities, and states. It was claimed that mule drivers did not like to carry money through the area, apparently for fear of bandits, and would often hide it near Guvezna, burying it under a tree in a field in Yianik-Koy (present-day Dorkas).

34. One local myth concerning the origins of the (Turkish) name Guvezna focused on this passing trade. It maintained that the old village cemetery had been situated near to the caravan road and that passing travelers frequently saw women crying at the tombs of their deceased family members, wailing "Gou! Gou!" For this reason, it was said, strangers began to refer to the village as "Guvezna."

35. Koliopoulos (1980:422–30) maintained that bandits in nineteenth-century Thessaly, for example, were not heroic peasant revolutionaries of the sort described by Hobsbawm (1959, 1981), but rather had been shepherds or seminomadic pastoralists who took to the mountains and expressed the antagonisms between their groups and landed villagers through their raids and looting.

36. Vergopoulos (1975:95) noted that Ottoman regulations required owners of such *chiftlik* colonies (usually absentee landlords who employed estate managers while they themselves resided in urban comfort, as with the principal Ottoman *chiftlik* owners in Guvezna) to meet certain stipulations before they received authorization to cultivate their lands. Most significant had been the provisioning of local cultivators with draft animals, seeds, and implements, as well as a requirement to bring settlers with "foreign" status (i.e., not citizens of the Ottoman Empire).

37. The mosquitoes have since discovered the location of the village, as anyone who has ever spent a summer night in Assiros may attest.

38. At the same time, some families left Guvezna for other settlements in the basin. There are, for example, still families in Langadhas who bear the surname Guveznyi ("From Guvezna"). It was common practice at that time to register new settlers or migrants to a community by giving them family names depicting their place of origin. Pertinent examples may be offered from Assiros, but I have opted for the use of pseudonyms in order to protect the identity, privacy, and sensitivity of local residents.

39. Present-day Assiriotes claimed that the population of Guvezna had grown to some thirty Turkish and ninety Christian families by the end of the nineteenth century, making a total population of 120 families. But Greek demographer Chalkiopoulos (1910:13) recorded a population of 870 Greeks and 101 Turks (i.e., Muslims) living in "Givezna." Official Greek government documents dating from 1914 reported that, within a year following the incorporation of the region into Greece, only twenty-two Muslim Turks remained in Guvezna, alongside a Greek population of over 1,000 (Historical Archive of Macedonia/General Directorate of Macedonia [HAM/GDM], File No. 51 ["Educational Statistics of the Langadhas District"], letter from Vakalopoulos, District Director [*Eparhos*], to the Prefect [*Nomarhis*] of Thessaloniki, 3 February 1914, Protocol No. 20).

40. In some cases, Ottoman authorities would move in and retake possession of villages that defaulted on their tax obligations, often selling the land under *chiftlik* status to newcomers able to pay for land titles and all outstanding taxes.

41. Vucinich (1962) noted that the word *tsorbadjis* (Turkish: *corbaci*) initially meant an officer in charge of an *orta*, or a company of Janissaries, but eventually came to mean "well-to-do-person" (Vucinich 1962:605). Karpat (1982:147) mentioned that *corbaci* referred to a town head. Apparently the word stands for an affluent individual who can hold an office or has a position of power. Professor Joseph Rothschild (personal communication) brought to my attention the fact that in Ottoman Bulgaria, the word *tsorbadji* meant "those who eat thick soup" and was usually a term applied to relatively affluent artisans and merchants.

Two

1. Some of these oral accounts came from elderly villagers who themselves had been young children during the last years of Ottoman rule. Others were offered by those who had heard stories and tales of local life and family history from their parents, grandparents, kin, and friends.

2. Since all land in the Ottoman Empire was ultimately regarded as the property of the sultan, it is perhaps more correct in legal terms to speak of local estate management or stewardship rather than ownership. A property manager, often referred to by sharecroppers as *chiftlik sahibi* or *bey* (Vucinich 1965:49), had lived in Guvezna and looked after the local *chiftlik* estates. Yet in practice managerial stewards often acted, and were popularly regarded, as de facto owners of such properties. In order to convey how jural categories played out in actual social relations of production at the local level, I shall refer to these former Ottoman managers as (de facto) "owners."

3. The grandson of Toptop *bey* returned to Assiros once, sometime in the

1970s, and asked Turkish-speaking village elders to guide him to the site of his grandfather's former mansion and barn. While many Assiriotes had been sure the *bey*'s grandson had come back to recover hidden family treasure, the man returned to Turkey empty-handed.

4. Village legends alternatively maintained that Shei *effendi* had been a general, a governor, or a judge.

5. Legal documents pertaining to landownership and transfer in Guvezna, contained in Assiros township archives or in the possession of individual families, also indicated the presence of small, private landowners in the village by the turn of the twentieth century (see chapter 6).

6. Villagers claimed that Muslim women who had been "secret Christians" or friends of Christians had donated land to the church as well.

7. Christians in Thessaly also purchased the lands of departing Muslims in 1881, when that region became part of Greece. Vergopoulos (1975:116–162) maintained that Turkish landowners in Thessaly had gone to Constantinople to seek buyers from among wealthy Greek Phanariotes, and that within three years nearly all land titles had been transferred to Christian owners. Gounaris (1989: 141) argued that the legal transfer of farms from Muslim to Christian hands began after new "legislative regulations and bankruptcies" in the 1850s. Yet most Christian landowners in Macedonia were smallholders who collectively possessed only two-fifths of all cultivated lands in the region.

8. The *"Koinaroi* Turks," as they were referred to in Assiros, were a group of Muslim herders and laborers who migrated throughout the region with their families and animals. In late Ottoman Guvezna, they had lived in tents out on the open plain. Some claimed that the *Koinaroi* moved into Central Macedonia from Konya, in Asia Minor, perhaps around the close of the fourteenth century. Wilkinson (1951) maintained that the *Konariote* were a collection of former nomadic pastoralists from Konia, in western Macedonia.

9. Herzfeld (1991b) has argued that the public "silence and submission" of women, frequently noted in the ethnographic literature on Greece, is a product of male hegemony in Greek society. Such notions fundamentally ignore and thus distort the many subtle ways through which women, constrained by such circumstances, influence family life and public interaction.

10. In addition, Vlah pastoralists were said to have rented winter grazing lands in both Guvezna and Guneyna/Palehora.

11. There were conflicting reports regarding the "foreign ownership" of Guneyna (Palehora), suggesting that the *chiftlik* may have changed hands more than once. Some claimed that its landlord had been from France, others maintained the owner had been from (southwest) Asia, Germany, or even from Greece. These conflicting versions may all be true, as properties changed hands frequently at the turn of the century.

12. Such joint family organization is reminiscent of the *zadruga* units found in many Slavic communities throughout the Balkans (for a discussion of Slavic *zadruga* in western Greek Macedonia, see Karavidas 1931; Karakasidou 1996). I do not term these grand family units as *zadruga,* despite strong parallels, primarily because no one in Assiros referred to them as such. Hammel (1968:13) maintained that although in the past Yugoslav peasants did not use the term *zadruga* to describe an extended or joint family unit, the term nevertheless entered "the

folk lexicon from ethnographic, historical, and folkloristic writings used in the elementary schools." For details on Slavic *zadruga* organization, see Halpern and Kerewsky-Halpern (1986), Hammel (1972), Segalen (1986), and St. Elrich (1966). St. Elrich (1966:34) also noted that Yugoslavian *zadruga* often "rapidly decayed" when brides married in with dowries, especially in the form of capital resources such as land or livestock.

13. While they maintained a single domestic economy under a common budget, this single extended family occupied between nine and fourteen houses. Lefort (1986) described Guneyna (i.e., Palehora) as having twenty-four houses in 1862. Its buildings were all single-storied structures made of stone gathered from nearby Deve-Karan mountain. Short and squat, these houses were attached to *ahouria,* barns or small rooms in which animals were kept. Villagers used two-wheeled horse-drawn wagons to carry water up to the houses from the small fountain at the foot of the southern knoll. The settlement itself occupied an area of approximately fifty *stremmata* and was divided by a small dirt road into two separate neighborhoods (*mahaladhes*), apparently populated by different extended family units.

14. The assertion that these families have no legal titles to their land implies that they had arbitrarily seized them from former Muslim owners after the fall of the Ottoman Empire (see chapter 6).

15. Other Assiriotes maintained that during the late Ottoman era Christian men could avoid conscription into the Turkish army by marrying women who were either from outside their community of residence or had been widows.

16. A variety of goods and services were available in Guvezna through grocery stores, merchandise shops, commercial storehouses for agricultural products, inns for caravan travelers, and even moneylenders. This suggests that the village ranked relatively high in the regional marketing hierarchy of the Langadhas basin. The importance of these trade networks is illustrated by the fact that even after the Guvezna market began to decline following the paving of the Thessaloniki-Serres road and the discontinuation of the camel caravans in 1923, the village continued to thrive as an important commercial center. Its shops were crucial to the well-being of the refugee communities established in the surrounding hills after 1922 (see chapter 5).

17. Collectively, these hamlets belonged to the *kaza* of Avret-Isar (roughly the present-day Kilkis prefecture). According to Lefort (1986:223), who cited Gopcevic (1889) and others who observed these hamlets, the Otmanli *mahaladhes* consisted of a group of four or five small settlements. The first *mahala* was Kara Kotsane, the location of which remains unclear. The second hamlet, Karatzale *mahala,* was located four kilometers northeast of Guvezna, where its ruins still stand today. This site was chosen by the Sarakatsan transhumant pastoralists who settled in the area in the 1920s (see chapter 6). Kran *mahala* (now called Rematakia) sat 5.5 kilometers northeast of Guvezna. The fourth *mahala,* Tzami (present-day Mavrorahi), was situated seven kilometers northeast of Guvezna; named after the mosque there, Tzami was the social and religious center for Muslims in the Otmanli hamlets. K'ncov, a Bulgarian visitor, mentioned a fifth settlement, Gjuvezne Basja *mahala;* while Lefort could not place it, this hamlet may have been the Kara Kotsane *mahala.* Official Greek government documents pertaining to the 20,951 Turks living in ninety-five Turkish communities of the Lan-

gadhas District list a total of 688 Turks living in the four Otmanli *Mahaladhes* during February–April, 1914: Kara-Kotzali, 114 people; Kara-Tzali, 108; Kran, 185; and Tzami *Mahala*, 281 inhabitants (HAM/GDM, File No. 51 ["Educational Statistics of the Langadhas District"]).

18. One *oka* equals approximately 1,250 grams.

19. Present-day Artousis family landholdings include not only extensive fields around Assiros but also residential and commercial property in downtown Thessaloniki.

20. It was said that Kondos had been classified as a British citizen, presumably because of his employment by this British company.

21. Whether or not Pashos himself spoke Slavic remains uncertain, but his wife certainly did. Assiros villagers claimed that she had learned it from Bulgarian soldiers when they occupied Guvezna during the Balkan Wars.

22. Of these terms, the Turkish word *kiradjidhes* was used most widely in Assiros. The second, *aghoyiates*, comes from Greek and was also used by Slavic-speakers in Sohos, another caravan stop in the Vertiskos highlands studied by Cowan (1990). The third, *karaghoghis*, was not used verbally at all but only appeared as an occupational category in the old (1919) village registry (*Dhimotologhio*).

23. In the past, when the *dhekati* renters could not meet their payments to the Taxation Office, they faced bankruptcy and disaster. It was only in 1932 that amendments to the *dhekati* bankruptcy laws were passed, exempting *dhekati* renters of tax obligations in years of poor harvest. Villagers claimed that in the late 1920s, local notables such as Tamtakos, Pashos, and others had complained to a lawyer in Langadhas about the difficulties of their positions, and had petitioned for a legal reform.

24. Guneyna (Palehora)-born Papailiou had been another miller in the area. Brother of the Guvezna priest, papa-Yiorghos, Papailiou had served as a gendarme and became a powerful man in Guvezna during the first decade of this century, patrolling the area on his Cretan horse accompanied by his young Turkish servant (he also had many female servants at home). After being discharged from his post as gendarme, Papailiou bought a Turkish mill situated close to present-day Examili. He also acquired 250 *stremmata* of land in that area, all of which was inherited by his daughter.

25. The *dhimoyerondia* were committees of three to twelve men who were endowed with administrative, judicial, and taxation powers. Christian affairs in nearby Baltza (present-day Melissohori), for example, had been managed by a twelve-man committee of distinguished Christian elders known as the *dhimoyerondia*, many of whom also served on the school and church boards of the village (Kabasakalis 1974:28). Yet unlike Guvezna, Baltza had been a village of "free cultivators" (*kefalohori*), and most of its inhabitants were free farmers who paid taxes on their agricultural products. Baltza also had slaves who worked the local *chiftliks* without pay as well as peasant sharecroppers. The local priest collected taxes for the Patriarchate as well as funds to maintain himself and to run the local church.

26. *Dhekati* revenues were split 8:2 between Ottoman authorities and the local collection agent. Vergopoulos (1975) noted that the *dhekati* tax survived in the Greek kingdom for sixty years after its independence in 1829, amounting to as

much as 12 percent of state revenues. He also argued that the abolition of the *dhekati* in 1881 on the eve of Thessaly's incorporation into the expanding Greek state was a gift or goodwill gesture by then Greek prime minister Trikoupis to the large Greek *chiftlik* owners of Thessaly (Vergopoulos 1975:146). It was replaced by a 3.4 percent tax on draft animals, which was subsequently restricted in 1910 to *chiftlik* owners only, exempting free cultivators and sharecroppers (Vergopoulos 1975:171). The *dhekati* tax remained in place in Greek Macedonia until 1928 (see chapter 6).

27. In Macedonia, a plethora of taxes were in place during the late nineteenth and early twentieth centuries, including those on land, sheep (herdowners with special legal status were exempted) and hogs, in addition to a tax for the military, other "occasional" taxes, and surcharges for the Christian bishop as well as fees collected for rural guards, local priests, and local teachers (Gounaris 1989).

28. The Old Township Registry, compiled by the Guvezna priest in 1918, which provided Greek authorities with an inventory of their new citizens, listed twenty-three women with Slavic names married to Guvezna men. Seven were from the Kilkis area, and the rest apparently from either Guvezna or elsewhere in the Langadhas basin.

29. The 1918 township registry listed some fifteen families made up of extended domestic units.

30. The partitioning of such family units was often delayed until the death of the family patriarch, and when it did occur took the form of equal partible inheritance among brothers. Over time and given supportive economic circumstances, the individual conjugal units that split off from such domestic units might also develop themselves into similar joint families, as sons matured and married but remained with their parents. Not all families, of course, were able to achieve a joint organizational form during their developmental cycle. The implementation of land reform legislation by the national Greek government in the late 1920s heavily influenced the decline of such family forms in Greek Macedonia (see chapter 6).

31. See Hammel (1972) for a critique of such approaches and an alternative perspective on *zadruga* corporate family organization.

32. See, for example, the account of the Palepolitis family in chapter 4.

33. These exchanges usually occurred in three discrete installments: one at the time of betrothal, one during the intervening period between betrothal and wedding, and one on the occasion of the wedding itself. Some observers reported that a bride's father would sometimes return a token portion of the aggregate sum to the family of the groom (Natsis 1990:60). Goody (1973) has referred to such exchanges as "indirect dowry," with the initial payments of the groom's family being used by the bride's family to defer the costs of preparing her dowry. Bridewealth payments could be quite substantial, in some cases totaling even twenty gold pieces (Karavidas 1931:214).

34. Skouteri-Didaskalou (1991:220) noted that the practice of bridewealth was widespread among agriculturalists and pastoralists throughout "traditional" Epirus, Macedonia, and Thrace and was referred to alternatively as "the right of the father" (*dhikeoma tou patera*), "the milk of the mother" (*ghala tis miteras*), "purchase" (*aghora*), or "bargaining" (*pazarema*).

35. The terms *tsino* and *teto* are now used interchangeably in Assiros in reference to aunts.

36. For an excellent discussion of ethnic divisions of labor in Ottoman Macedonia, see Vermeulen (1984).

THREE

1. Consider, for example, the manner in which Yugoslavs and Bulgarians were depicted in a pamphlet entitled *A Sketch of Southern Slav History,* published in 1928. The Yugoslavs were described as a homogeneous nation "full of youth and vitality," who went through empire construction, conquest, resistance, and liberation. But the Bulgarians were regarded as far from heroic, as they had fallen to the Ottomans in a single moment, unlike (it was argued) the Yugoslavs, who had resisted until their last drop of blood was offered up for the nation. The Yugoslavs, and not the Bulgarians, it maintained, saved Europe from Ottoman conquest. "Our nation," the authors of this pamphlet declared, "served Europe as a rampart and bulwark in her need; we sacrificed ourselves for her, and gloriously fulfilled the duty imposed upon us by the moment." This kind of rhetoric continues to survive today, perpetuating divisions among the inhabitants of the region.

2. In Greece, the role of European commercial interests and the romanticism of many European Philhellene intellectuals played an important role in the creation of a modern Greek nation-state (originally headed by a Bavarian king) independent of Ottoman domination.

3. Serbian involvement, as noted earlier, had been centered mainly on the areas of Macedonia close to Serbia and was not as fierce as Greek and Bulgarian activities in central Macedonia. Romania was also involved in a national consciousness-building campaign in Macedonia, having established a Macedon-Romanian committee in 1862. Romanians based their interests in the area on the pretext of protecting the nomadic Vlahs, with whom they claimed cultural and linguistic affinities. Although the ethnic origins of the Vlahs has been widely disputed, some scholars claim their language is derived from Roman Latin roots. For more on the Vlahs, see Balamaci (1991) and Winnifrith (1987).

4. Wilkinson also argues that the publication of A. Boue's (French) map of Macedonia in 1847 triggered "the attention of the European powers towards the idea of a possible Slav hegemony in the Balkans." At the same time, it also stimulated Bulgarian nationalist activity towards the establishment of an independent Church (Wilkinson 1951:37–39).

5. In 1876, representatives of leading European powers met at an international conference in Istanbul where they decided that Macedonia should become an autonomous province of the Ottoman Empire with the name of Western Bulgaria (Pro-Macedonia 1927:6). Within two years, however, gains in a Russian sphere of influence following the Russo-Turkish War prompted other European states to demand a renegotiation of the San Stefano Treaty that nominally returned Macedonia to the Ottomans, primarily as a buffer zone between neighboring empires.

6. As Cvijic (1907:12) argued, the Slavic-speakers of Macedonia might have become Bulgarians just as easily as they might have become Serbians.

7. Baron (1947:13) argued that "Catholic clerics, being the main intelligentsia in medieval society, were also the main promoters of national literature and recorders of national history." Fletcher (1982:316) made similar claims regarding

the role of religion in England, where the Protestant cause was an important factor in the growth and development of a national identity among the gentry during the sixteenth and seventeenth centuries.

8. In the years prior to the establishment of the Bulgarian Exarchate in 1870, living conditions for rural inhabitants of Ottoman Macedonia were reportedly so poor that a delegation of Bulgarians even made a trip to Rome in an attempt to negotiate a union between the Bulgarian Church and the Catholic Church. Several towns and villages in the Avret Hizar *kaza,* such as Kukush (Kilkis) and Todorak (Theodoraki), reportedly became Roman Catholic (Christoff 1919:12).

9. For more on the work of American missionaries in Bulgaria, see Tsanoff (1919), Haskell (1919), and the Carnegie *Report* (1914).

10. The close ties between the Patriarchate and the Ottoman Porte were reflected in the reaction of the former to the 1821 Greek War of Independence. At that time the Peloponnese was a semiautonomous region where landed notables (known as *kodzabasidhes*) and high Church officials had opposed the revolution against the Ottomans. When the rebellion broke out, both the notables and the high clergy fled to Tripoli, where they found sanctuary under the protection of the Turkish army (Todorov and Trajkov 1971:15).

11. Brailsford (1906) described how bishops administered the laws of marriage, divorce, and inheritance, controlled schools and hospitals, amassed considerable wealth, and lived in great houses. Their avarice and corruption displayed little concern for the spiritual and material welfare of the population. Brailsford also found that, unlike the bishops, most local priests in the Macedonian countryside were a relatively uneducated group, living a lifestyle not unlike that of the peasants around them. Their ties to the ecclesiastical hierarchy, however, made these priests village leaders or local notables. He also stressed the religious convictions of the Macedonian population but argued that local belief in God and the "glorious legion of saints, sometimes visible and always active, [was] not very clearly distinguished from the traditional Slavonic fairies. . . . [The] prehistoric ritual which survives in the heart of the Balkan peasants, [was] a paganism more native, more congenial, more deeply-rooted than the Orthodox Church itself" (Brailsford 1906:71–75). Even in 1990, the village priest in my fieldsite once complained to me about the residual elements of pagan religion to which some villagers, he maintained, stubbornly clung.

12. Papaioannou researched and wrote his study in 1987, while working for the Greek Ministry of Education as a member of a council for the study of ecclesiastical affairs. He reportedly faced considerable difficulty in securing a publisher, for many influential Greeks were said to have found his interpretations and characterizations of the Patriarchate to be objectionable. The impasse was resolved in 1991 when the publisher of the Athenian liberal daily newspaper *Eleftherotypia* ("Free Press") agreed to print Papaioannou's work.

13. Sigalas (1940:289–90) offered additional insight on the strength of the Ecumenical Patriarchate within the Ottoman state: "While the Sultan had to [approve] the appointment of an archbishop and Metropolite, the clergy were clearly the civic leaders of the Christian community under Ottoman rule. They [sent] their representatives to collect the public taxes, both in cash and kind. The Metropolite, the churches and the monasteries could own vineyards, gardens, *metohia, wakf,* pastures, mills, holy springs, feasts, and monasteries as well as

houses, shops, land, furniture, money and animals. No one interfered with the Church's management of this property."

14. Stewart (1994) argues that, in the context of the late nineteenth century, the Greek term *filetismos* might better be glossed as "chauvinism" or "ethno-nationalism" rather than "racism."

15. For years following its excommunication by the Patriarchate, the Exarchate still enjoyed the patronage of the Ottoman sultan and was permitted to maintain its administrative seat in Istanbul (Raikin 1984).

16. This famous Article X stipulated that "if the whole orthodox population, or at least two-thirds thereof, desire to establish an exarchy for the control of their spiritual affairs in localities other than those indicated above, and this desire be clearly established, they may be permitted to do as they wish. Such permission, however, may only be accorded with the consent or upon the request of the whole population, or at least two-thirds thereof" (Carnegie Endowment, 1914:5).

17. K. Vakalopoulos (1970), for example, traced the development of Greek national consciousness to the period following the first crusades in 1204 A.D., when the Byzantines took on the struggle against the Westerners. He claimed that people came to understand that being a Byzantine citizen was in itself rather meaningless, and that people therefore sought to establish a sense of belonging and to share a common identity focused on a Greek heritage. The constant presence of Greeks in high intellectual and administrative positions was greatly attractive to the people of Byzantium, he argued, who sought to Hellenize themselves.

18. This sort of "nationless" national consciousness seems akin to what Diamandouros (1983:54) termed "traditional" consciousness (where identification takes place on many levels, including the village, the community, etc.), and which contrasts with so-called "modern" national consciousness that exists within a nation-state.

19. The inhabitants of Macedonia, in fact, did not constitute a single ethnic group but were rather composed of several distinct populations. For example, Wilkinson identified eight "Macedo-Slav" groups that existed in 1903: persons speaking the Macedo-Slav dialect; Slavs without any specific national inclination; Slavized Vlahs; Greek Macedo-Slavs; Bulgarian Macedo-Slavs (the so-called "Bulgarians"); Serb Macedo-Slavs (the so-called "Serbs"); Albanized Macedo-Slavs; and Moslem Macedo-Slavs (Wilkinson 1951: fig. 84).

20. The presence of southern Greek settlers was not a phenomenon unique to Guvezna. Cowan (1990) noted that as early as 1700 Greeks from Epirus and Halkidhiki reportedly came to Sohos, a market town situated in the hills east of Guvezna, between Langadhas and Serres. They arrived as "traveling merchants and caravaners (*kiradzidhes*), transporting merchandise on pack animals,—mules, horses, oxen, even camels" (Cowan 1990:31). But within a century or so, roughly four generations, these Greeks had emerged as an "indigenous" merchant class in that market town. In the nineteenth century, this commercial Sohoian elite actively cultivated a strong Greek identity and began to send their sons to Thessaloniki and Constantinople to be educated. On the other end of the social stratification continuum in Sohos there existed a class of peasant-laborers, composed of "Macedonian-speaking Christians and the 'Turks'" (Cowan 1990:41). Cowan likewise noted that the contestation of Macedonia by several "powers" led to the destruction of its cultural diversity.

21. For a Greek account of Dragoumis's contribution to the Macedonian Struggle, see Evrygenis (1961).

22. Dragoumis's younger brother, Philipos, many years his junior, later served as a parliamentary deputy from Florina, the district of Greece just across the border from Monastiri/Bitola. Ion Dragoumis himself was killed (either assassinated or executed, depending on who is telling the story) in 1915.

23. Pavlos Melas (1870–1904) had been a wealthy Athenian who led one of the earliest groups of Greek partisans into Macedonia to fight against pro-Bulgarians. He was killed, allegedly by Ottoman troops, in Statista (Kastoria District) in 1904, just shortly after his arrival in Macedonia. Pavlos Melas quickly became enshrined as an iconic symbol of national martyrdom in Greece. His name and face have been hung on school walls throughout this century, and are easily recognizable to most Greeks today. During the period of national ferment over the Macedonia issue in the early 1990s, his portrait was printed on new public telephone calling cards issued throughout Greece.

24. The contribution made by Hellenized Vlahs to modern Greek nation-state building in Macedonia is beyond the scope of this monograph, but see Balamaci (1991).

25. Dragoumis's descriptions of turn-of-the-century Bitola (Monastiri) were also noteworthy in their evocation of a Byzantine past. In a passage marked by a montage of past and present, "Alexis" reflected on the many narrow alleyways running off a main street that led to a railway station: "Monastiri appears to me as a Byzantine city," he contended (1992:13). Dragoumis also depicted the Virgin Mary (*Panaghia*) as an important iconic image of Hellenism in Macedonia. He likened Macedonia to a virgin woman, and to the Virgin Mary in particular. "The Barbarians," he cried in the closing paragraph of chapter 4, "look without shame at your virginity, step on you, and pollute you" (1992:58).

26. The *Phanariotes* were Greek merchants, financiers, and clergymen who lived in the district of Phanari in Istanbul, where the Ecumenical Orthodox Patriarchate had been headquartered since 1601. This elite had prospered through the prominence they came to enjoy in Ottoman imperial affairs and bureaucracy, especially after the eighteenth century. "They became imperial tax farmers, they rented the salt monopoly, undertook contract works, became purveyors to the court, and gained control of the Black Sea wheat trade" (Stavrianos 1959:270). From 1711, the *Phanariotes* served the Ottomans as governors of Wallachia and Moldavia. The Ecumenical Patriarchate had extensive connections with the *Phanariotes*, and in the nineteenth century the Church had been instrumental in transferring commerce from the foreigners throughout the Ottoman Empire to the control of Greeks and even determined the value of foreign currencies. Like the Patriarchate, the *Phanariotes* had also initially opposed the establishment of an independent kingdom of Greece.

27. Among those that eventually became most noteworthy in their activities surrounding the Macedonian issue were the Athens-based Association for the Propagation of Greek Letters (established 1874), Committee for the Reinforcement of the Greek Church and Education (1886), Epicurus Council of the Macedonians (1903), and Melas Infantile Chamber (1904). Similar organizations also of significance but based in Istanbul included the Greek Philological Association (1861), Macedonian Phil-Educational Brotherhood (1871), Hellenic Literary As-

sociation (1874), and Educational and Philanthropic Brotherhood or Love Each Other (1880). There were numerous similar associations at local district levels, such as in Langadhas (see below).

28. Irredentism, of course, was not a phenomenon unique to the Greek state. It has been a long-standing phenomenon in the Near and Middle East, defined as "an ideological or organizational expression of passionate interest in the welfare of an ethnic minority living outside the boundaries of the State peopled by [members of] the same group" (Landau 1981:1). Landau maintained that Pan-Turkism was one form of irredentism among the Turkic groups throughout Russia and Central Asia, although it has been particularly strong in Turkey proper where it led to the formation of a new type of nationalism.

29. By 1905, the Ottoman *vilayet* of Salonika had 521 Greek schools and 319 Bulgarian schools, as well as 21 schools run by Serbs and 10 by Romanians; the *kaza* of Langaza (Langadhas) had 28 Greek schools, with 36 teachers and 1,736 students (The Population of Macedonia 1905:20).

30. Dragoumis (1992) also had been critical of the fact that pupils were learning only ancient Greek mythology in their history lessons, rather than the general history of Greece.

31. For more details on the functioning of such "secret" schools, see Zisis (1990).

32. Surviving school documents indicate that during the 1912–13 school year, the first two grades followed lessons in "sacred subjects" (*Iera* or, plainly speaking, religion), language, arithmetic, knowledge of the nation (*Patridhoghnosia*, or mainly geography and history lessons on the Greek nation), music, and embroidering. The four higher grades took courses on "sacred subjects," language, geography, music, calligraphy, arithmetic, and history. This curriculum changed little in 1914, when new directives arrived from the recently established national government authorities in Greek Macedonia.

33. After the introduction of compulsory attendance requirements, school enrollments in Guvezna rose from 77 (8 female) students, aged eight to fifteen, in 1911, to over 300 students in 1937 (ASA). While some of the increase may be attributable to growing village population, demographics alone cannot account for such a steep rise, which is rather a reflection of a new national educational policy on the part of the Greek state.

34. In much the same vein as their Greek counterparts, scholars from the FYROM have argued that the Macedonian national movement had even earlier roots. Pandevski (1978:13–20), for example, claimed that Macedonians formed a distinct group, possessing its own "national" consciousness, that had staged repeated struggles for independence from the Ottomans in 1876, 1878, and 1879. Tashkovski (1976) adopted a similar position, maintaining that even the Bogomil religious movement was an expression of Macedonian desires for independence from Bulgaria, which had attempted to establish a feudal system in Macedonia in the thirteenth and fourteenth centuries. Such claims, however, are often tinged by the imposition of present-day national labels on categories of identity in the past. In such a manner, historical events are interpreted through teleological assumptions concerning their role in the predestined emergence and consolidation of contemporary nation-states of the late twentieth century.

35. For details on IMRO history, politics, and intrigue, see Perry (1988) and Fischer-Galati (1972–73).

36. Bulgarian *comitadjidhes* were members of "committees," formed in Sofia, that proselytized the Bulgarian cause to Slavic-speakers in Macedonia. Moore (1906:9) noted that most *comitadjidhes* in Macedonia had been organized by a local leader (*voivoda*) from a village, who also served as representative to the Central Committee in Sofia. These partisan groups were usually trained in Bulgaria, regardless of where their recruits came from, and were then dispatched across the border into Macedonia. The *comitadjidhes,* as well as rural bandits, grew beards to conceal distinguishing characteristics of their physiognomy, but they were often readily identifiable since the rest of the rural population (with the exception of the priests) were clean-shaven.

37. See, for example, A. Vakalopoulos (1987:17) and Svolopoulos (1987).

38. See A. Vakalopoulos (1987) for an overview of local Greek-oriented uprisings in Macedonia as well as participation by Macedonian inhabitants in the 1821 War of Independence in Greece.

39. The incident has come to be referred to as the "Ilinden" Uprising (or the St. Elias Uprising) because it began on July 20, Prophet Elias Day in the Orthodox calendar.

40. Some historians from Yugoslav Macedonia have claimed that the uprising was initially so successful that "at dawn the next day, women and children began to leave their villages for the mountains, carrying with them food for the rebels. The peasants set up bakeries in the forests, workshops for repairing arms and first aid centers" (Pribichevich 1982:127).

41. IMRO had initiated the uprising in hopes that the "Great Powers" of Europe would intervene in support of the rebels (Sowards 1989). But European governments did not act, perceiving their interests better served through internal reform of the Ottoman Empire rather than through violent national conflict. At the turn of the century, Austria, Germany, and Russia all had been opposed to the breakup of Ottoman Macedonia, proposing instead a series of reforms that included the recruitment of a new police force from both Christian and Muslim populations, expanded public works projects, and a reform of the education system (Sowards 1989:1–27), issues to which I will return later.

42. Dragoumis (1992) described a scene in which his (autobiographical) character observed a group of "Bulgarians" celebrating the anniversary of the Ilinden Uprising in a Thessaloniki cafe with drink, song, and pro-Bulgarian talk. "It is too bad that I am not a Bulgarian at this moment," he wrote. "Macedonia belongs to whoever takes her."

43. For further details, see Kazazis (1904) and Anagnostopoulos-Paleologos (1987).

44. Previously, Greek activists established the National Society (*Ethniki Eteria*), which had supported both Greek schools and armed fighters in Macedonia (Bitoski 1981:226; Perry 1988:16), although its influence had not been as strong as that of this new Macedonian Committee.

45. Serbian partisans also began to appear in Macedonia in 1904, especially in the northern part of the region where the indigenous population was said to have supported Serbian national efforts in Macedonia (Kofos 1987:230). See

Karathanasis (1990) for a broader overview of different national partisan activities in various parts of Macedonia.

46. A study of these Greek "Macedonian fighters" based on their family and individual life histories, education, and occupations would prove very interesting. Given the bourgeois character of national revolutions, it is perhaps not surprising that many were merchants, millers, commercial entrepreneurs. A *somata* captain in the Langadhas area named Ramnalis, for example, was described as a "peaceful" miller, who was "murdered in cold blood by outlaw bands" (*Makedoniki Zoi* [1988] 264:22–23).

47. The metaphor of the school is striking, as church-operated (and frequently church-housed) schools throughout Macedonia were critical vehicles for the transmission of basic literacy, arithmetic, and theology.

48. Georgevitch (1918:256–81) claimed that during 1903–4 alone, 466 Macedonians, mostly peasants, were murdered.

49. A history of modern Macedonian nationalism is beyond the scope of this present study. Suffice it to say that there had been conscious, organized efforts at least as early as the turn of the century to build a movement for national autonomy, independence, or liberation for Slavic-speakers in Macedonia. Part of the confusion over this issue stems from the poorly coordinated leadership of such efforts, their limited resources, and the active efforts of pro-Bulgarian activists to coopt such movements. In fact, many early twentieth-century contemporaries now praised in the FYROM as heroes and martyrs of the national campaign for independence were themselves unclear as to what an independent Macedonia would mean or entail. For example, Gotse Delcev, a schoolmaster from Kukush (present-day Kilkis) who because of his leading role in organizing the Ilinden Uprising of 1903 is often called the "father" of the modern Macedonian nation, had supported the slogan "Macedonia for Macedonians." But he and others who attempted to popularize slogans, such as those among Macedonian diaspora communities in the United States who in the 1920s publicized their case to the international community through books and pamphlets, often left the links between an independent Macedonia and the neighboring state of Bulgaria ill-defined. For a detailed account of the formation of the Macedonian nation, see Danforth (1995).

50. The distinction between the terms "ethnicity" and "nationality" is a recent one in Greek discourse on Macedonia, whether scholarly, journalistic, or popular. "Nationality" (*ethnikotita*) continues to be used far more frequently, and often uncritically, particularly in reference to issues of descent and collective consciousness. For an overview of the epistemological and political consequences of such conceptualizations, see Karakasidou (1993b).

FOUR

1. The village cemetery had been moved to a new site adjacent to this church sometime later, as evidenced by a marble plaque discovered in the cemetery that read: "The cemetery of the Orthodox Community of Guvezna [*Orthodhoksi Kinotita Guveznas*], established in 1899."

2. The prefix *Hadzi-* ("pilgrimage") was often added to the names of individuals and their descendants who had made a pious pilgrimage to the Holy Land.

3. There was no mention of papa-Souliotis in the 1918 village registry; perhaps he had left Guvezna by that time, having completed his "mission."

4. The term *Tsetes* refers to a category of irregular armed forces who frequently lacked a well-coordinated hierarchical chain of command and who sometimes had no superiors from whom to receive orders. As such, they have been popularly described at times as "bandits."

5. I believe that this document, although undated and unsigned, was most likely written by Karamanis, a local teacher and native of Assiros, around 1952.

6. Serbian activists also made efforts to establish their own schools in Macedonia, but with limited success. At times, there were reportedly more teachers than pupils in Serbian-sponsored schools (Tosheff 1932:69–70).

7. This source (Chatzikiriakou 1962) had been originally written as a report to the Greek general consul of Thessaloniki, Lambros Koromilas, who had orchestrated and overseen Greek activities in the region during the Macedonian Struggle. Koromilas was removed from his post in 1908, at the demand of the Ottoman Porte. Ottoman censors had also removed the word "Macedonia" from the original title of this report, but it was secretly published in Thessaloniki in 1906. Ottoman authorities subsequently confiscated copies of the book and Koromilas was asked to leave Ottoman Macedonia and to return to Greece. Incidentally, the report's author, Chatzikiriakou, subsequently became Greek minister of education and signed the directive establishing the University of Thessaloniki in 1926 (Plastiras 1987:256–57).

8. At the time, one man (Koroupis, a Guveznan) and two women (both outsiders) served as teachers for the 82 male and 28 female students (HAM/GDM, File No. 51).

9. This information comes, in part, from a copy of that list retained by the village school for its own records (ASA).

10. Yeorgios had a son, Alexandros, of whom it was said that he also served the "Greek cause." Born in Guvezna in 1889, and like his father educated at the Ottoman Gymnasium and later the School of Education (*Dhidhaskalion*) in Serres, Alexandros was upon his graduation appointed schoolteacher in various places throughout Macedonia during the 1910s, including Guvezna. He retired seven years after his father, in 1931.

11. Among Garoufalidis' students had been Yeorghios Vranas, Ioannis Pashos, and Dimitrios Artousis, all of whom became prominent village leaders during the interwar period (see Part II).

12. Sapountzis also became a major landowner in the village, acquiring much of his property (including the former mansion of the Tortop *bey*) from departing Muslims in the 1920s. He owned large animal herds and employed local boys as shepherds, whom he fed with sardines, bread, and vinegar.

13. When Garoufalidis suggested the new name "Assiros" to be given to Guvezna, Sapountzis did not object.

14. Asteriou's eldest son became a herder, caring for the family's large flocks, while his second son eventually took over management of the family's agricultural activities. Stylianos, the youngest, was sent to become a teacher.

15. Later, a small structure at the Guneyna/Palehora *chiftlik* was designated as a schoolroom and one of the teachers from Guvezna would walk to Palehora to conduct lessons.

16. The villager who used this term was referring to the Ilinden Uprising in Krusovo of 1903.

17. This heavy capital sentence, notable for its redundancy, suggests that Stylianos was deeply involved in illegal political activities such as national propagandizing.

18. "Martso" is a Slavic form of "Maria."

19. See especially Delta (1937, first edition).

20. The building compound that once housed the Ottoman-era Greek consulate of Salonika is now the Museum of the Macedonian Struggle in Thessaloniki.

21. Another version of this story maintained that the *bey*'s own son had been in love with his young stepmother and had hired Apostolakoudhis to murder the *bey*. Yet all accounts I heard of this young man had a common theme: he had been a murderer and a thief who had terrorized the population of the basin.

22. It was said that as a poor boy thirteen years of age, Salamas returned home from school one day, found nothing to eat, and threw away his school bag. He left Guvezna for Salonika, where he worked beside his father's brother making salami for the city's European residents. He later established his own factory, employing young men and boys from Guvezna.

23. After its eventual abandonment, Guneyna became known locally as Palehora ("Old Village").

24. "Kapetan Thanasis" was remembered in Assiros both as a hero and as a man who took money from the poor and gave it to the rich. Villagers related to me many legends of his exploits, which ended with his assassination in the *Ilisia* coffeeshop of Thessaloniki, and songs are still sung of him.

25. Two other separate family units, apparently Stoinos cousins of Yeorghios "Palepolitis," also came to Guvezna, while another family chose to relocate from Palehora to Drimos.

26. Some accounts maintained that Palepolitis had been betrayed by his shepherds, while others insisted that it had been Halepis. Recall that Halepis, also a stockbreeder with large herds, had been known to offer secret assistance to partisan groups.

27. In 1952, for example, Assiros township received a letter from the prefecture of Thessaloniki and the Committee of National Rights (*Epitropi Ethnikon Dhikeon*) informing it that the Holy Metropolite of Thessaloniki was directing all priests in the region to help organize a "Pan-Macedonian" fund-raising campaign. Donations were to be used in the construction of busts of the famous Macedonian Fighters which would decorate parks, squares, public spaces in villages and towns throughout Greek Macedonia. Along similar lines, in 1974 the Assiros township council asked the school principal to organize a committee for an October 13 celebration commemorating the death of famed Macedonian Fighter and national martyr, Pavlos Melas. For more on the effect of such festive commemorations on the formation of a Greek national consciousness and ideology among the Assiriotes, see chapter 7 (see also Karakasidou 1995a).

28. *Evzonakia* is a diminutive of *evzonas* (pl. *evzones*), referring to Greek soldiers wearing white *foustanella* skirts, similar to those worn today by the guards of the Tomb of the Unknown Soldier in Athens.

29. In his memoirs of the First Balkan War, Zoroyiannidis (1992), general of the Greek army, made specific reference to Guvezna, noting that on November

13, 1912, he and his men arrived in the village at the same time as a Bulgarian army battalion. Both units left a small number of armed men in Guvezna before moving on, the Greek army towards the north and the Bulgarian forces southward. For detailed descriptions of events of the First Balkan War in the Langadhas basin, see also Mazarakis-Ainian (1989:183–228).

30. Tsountas, recall, also gave part of his house for use as village classroom space while the Greek army reportedly occupied the Guvezna school building during 1912–15.

31. Kukush (Kilkis), recall, had been an area heavily populated with Slavic-speakers before 1913. In the Battle of Kilkis during the Second Balkan War, Greek forces burned villages throughout the area and set fire to the fields of the entire valley, driving thousands from their homes.

32. Curiously, the account also offers a version of the liberation of Thessaloniki that differs from that portrayed in most Greek historical accounts, maintaining that the Bulgarian army had entered Thessaloniki first, rather than the Greek army.

33. As one villager in Assiros counseled me, "Don't write about these things or they will put you in prison."

34. Perhaps women in general, or Slavic-speaking women in particular (especially in-marrying affines), were not considered by Greek-speakers to have been members of the local Guvezna community. On the other hand, perhaps such reasoning was applied to all Slavic-speakers in general, effectively denying their historical existence in the contemporary, purely Greek village of Assiros.

35. Apparently, the standardized Bulgarian that Paskhalina was exposed to in Sofia was so different from the local or regional spoken vernacular she had used that she likened the difference to that between *katharevousa* (atticized Greek) and the *dhimotiki* spoken vernacular.

36. The spring grazing cycle ran from St. George's Day (April 23) to St. Dimitrios's Day (October 26).

37. Limitations of space preclude a full treatment of how World War I influenced local developments in Guvezna. Suffice it to say that not long after the conclusion of the Balkan Wars, Greece entered World War I on the side of the Allies. Britain and France had constructed a small railroad running from Thessaloniki up the Axios valley to the Kilkis District, where it turned east through the village of Volvot (present-day Nea Sanda). The railway line terminated near the 25th kilometer mark on the present-day Thessaloniki-Serres public highway, where Allied forces maintained a garrison and small supply depot. The British hired many villagers from the surrounding countryside to break stones and do other work on railroad construction. Even Guvezna children found employment, carrying water for the thirsty workers. When Allied forces departed, they left the structures intact, reportedly for Guvezna villagers to use as they deemed fit. A train would bring supplies, and village transporters (*kiradjidhes*) would ferry merchandise by wagons to the Guvezna market. The British would sometimes come to Guvezna in the evening and enjoyed dancing with the local women, though they reportedly never held their hands. One village woman recalled that the dancing partners would always hold a handkerchief between them.

38. Tounda-Fergadi (1986) argued that some 15,000 "Bulgarians" had already left Greece by the time the Bulgarian army retreated at the end of the Second

Balkan War in 1913. Tosheff (1932:97) maintained that some 300,000 "Bulgarians" from Macedonia, Serbia, and Dobrudja (which had become part of Roumania) were received in Bulgaria during the years following the Balkan Wars and World War I. On the other hand, Kyriakidis (1941–52) accused Bulgarian sources of "counterfeiting history" with their claims that a total of 152,144 "Bulgarians" had migrated to Bulgaria from Macedonia and Thrace by 1922. He maintained that League of Nations statistics indicated only 33,620 "Bulgarians" left Greece for Bulgaria.

39. One of the most prominent folklorists in Greek Macedonia, Kyriakidis (1941–52:333) claimed that these numbers, when compared with those of "Bulgarian" emigrants from Greece, suggested that Bulgaria was more "Greek" than Macedonia and Thrace were "Bulgarian."

40. For more on the protocol and the diplomatic maneuvers leading up to its signing, see Touna-Fergadi (1986).

41. Subsequent developments and nationalization campaigns among ethnic or national minorities in Bulgaria and Serbia are beyond the scope of this study (but see, e.g., Poulton 1991). After gaining control of the northwestern region of Macedonia, Serbia issued a "public security" decree (October 4, 1913) which the Carnegie *Report* (1914:160–62) likened to the establishment of a military dictatorship. Slavo-Macedonians in Serbia who allegedly had been involved with the IMRO and its activities were expelled, many eventually settling in Bucharest, where they attempted (unsuccessfully) to reopen negotiations with representatives of the Serbian government (Tosheff 1932:6). Macedonian diaspora groups also stepped up efforts to present their versions of the Macedonian reality to the international community. The Central Committee of the Union of the Macedonian Political Organizations of the United States and Canada, for example, undertook the publication of a series of pamphlets, called "Pro-Macedonia," in which they sought to document how Greek and Serbian authorities had continued to deny the existence of a "Bulgarian" element in their respective countries. For this organization, the presence of Bulgarian churches, chapels, monasteries, and bishoprics, as well as schools, teachers, pupils, newspapers, and magazines attested to the "Bulgarian" character of Slavo-Macedonians (see Pro-Macedonia 1927).

42. Wilkinson (1951:315–23) listed ten criteria that have been used by such national academic propagandists to delineate the ethnic affiliations of the people of Macedonia: language, religion, economy, historical associations, common customs, long-established political allegiances, similar material customs, place of birth, political nationality, and pseudo-racial studies. He cited ignorance, patriotism, lack of data, methodological flaws, and conflicting, overlapping, or undefined criteria as the reasons behind the great diversity of works on the ethnic composition of Macedonia.

43. Another productive strain of scholarship on ethnic identity comes from the work of A. Cohen (1981), who argued that, while ethnicity has many aspects, its political character is most relevant to understanding the social context within which ethnicity is expressed. For example, Roosen's (1989) work among Huron Indians of Quebec, maintained that a conceptual construct of ethnicity was imposed on the indigenous population through European political dominance: "Political leaders can create stereotypes that give almost religious exaltedness to eth-

nic identity and, via stereotypes, lead to economic and cultural wars with other groups and even to genocide" (Roosen 1989:18).

Five

1. For details, see the report of the Inter-Allied Commission on Eastern Macedonia (1919).

2. There is a large literature concerning negotiations leading to the post–World War I treaties and Bulgaria's unsuccessful attempts to justify its claims to Macedonia and Thrace despite its defeat. A prominent American missionary working in Bulgaria urged negotiators to consider the ethnic makeup of the disputed areas, arguing that if the victorious allies were to penalize Bulgaria for having sided with Germany then no harmony would be attained in what he called this "plague spot of Europe." "If the Peace Congress ignores the personality of the Macedonians . . . and hands them over like cattle to masters whom they detest, in order to penalize Bulgaria, we may expect such results as followed the Berlin and Bucharest Treaties" (Haskell 1918b:8).

3. Western Thrace (comprising the present-day prefectures of Xanthi, Rodhopi, and Evros), once predominantly populated by Muslims, became part of Bulgaria under the terms of the Treaty of Bucharest (August 1913) following the Second Balkan War (Jelavich 1983:99). Bulgarian occupation and administration continued through World War I, after which the Treaty of Neuilly gave western Thrace and its Aegean coastline to Greece (Jelavich 1983:125). However, for a brief interim period (1919–20), the region was placed under a joint Allied administration, led by the French and supported with detachments of British, Italian, and Greek troops. Greek administration finally took hold after the signing of the Treaty of Sèvres (August 1920), which established guarantees for the protection of national minorities in the region (Mavrogordatos 1983:239).

4. Mavrogordatos (1983:246) argued that this 1919 convention "allowed a sizeable and compact Slavo-Macedonian population to stay in Greece, largely upon instructions from the IMRO, whereas Greeks left Bulgaria practically to the man." Recall from chapter 4 that 46,000 Greeks came from Bulgaria and 96,000 Slavic-speakers departed from Greek Macedonia (Pearson 1983:104).

5. Mavrorahi residents referred to their amalgamation with Assiros (the new name of Guvezna) by saying "we went with Assiros" (*pighame me tin Assiro*) or "Assiros took us" (*mas pire I Assiros*), suggesting their passive, if not reluctant, role in this process. It is likely that little choice was involved in their integration with the township, as they lacked the authority to determine for themselves to which township they would be affiliated (see below).

6. Jelavich (1983) claimed the victorious World War I Allies were divided over Greece's expansionist plans and actions. Initially encouraged by early British diplomatic posturing, Greece had been opposed in its designs by both Italy and France. At a critical moment in Greece's Asia Minor campaign, Great Britain reportedly rejected appeals for assistance. Petroleum interests were said to have figured prominently in the maneuvering. In the early twentieth century, Asia Minor had become an important focus of European attention and petroleum pros-

pecting. Some popular claims in Greece have attributed British "betrayal" of the Greek nationalist campaign in Asia Minor to the Foreign Office's desire to secure an oil concession from the Turkish government.

7. Thrace refers to the geographic region between the Nestos River and the city of Istanbul. West Thrace is that area of the region between the Nestos and Evros Rivers, while East Thrace consists of the zone from the Evros River (the present-day international border between Greece and Turkey) to Istanbul. At Lausanne, Italy had objected to the incorporation of West Thrace into Greece because only a minority of the region's inhabitants had been Greek-speakers at the time. More than two-thirds (67 percent) of the population had been Muslims (owning 84 percent of the land), while less than a fifth (18 percent) had been Greeks (mostly traders whose landholdings amounted to only 5 percent of the region's total; Whitman 1990:1–2). The remainder of the population comprised Slavic-speakers, Jews, or Armenians. As in Macedonia, the percentage of Greeks in the region increased sharply following the settlement of Asia Minor refugees after 1923.

8. The Treaty of Lausanne included provisions that exempted two specific cohorts of "religious minorities" from this compulsory exchange of populations between Greece and Turkey (Kettani 1980:153–54; Jelavich 1983,2:122–29). Roughly 110,000 Greek Christians (including the Orthodox Patriarchate, at the insistence of the Allies) were permitted to remain in Istanbul (Whitman 1992:1), and some 124,000 Muslims were left in West Thrace (Bahcheli 1987:11–12). Both groups were to be guaranteed religious protection and equal rights under the laws of each country, although compliance by authorities in both Greece and Turkey has not always been satisfactory (see Whitman 1992; Karakasidou 1995).

9. Kassimatis (1988:135), however, maintained that the number of Orthodox Christian refugees coming into Greece was as high as 1,800,000. Mavrogordatos (1983b), on the other hand, put the figure at 1,222,000. As for Turkish refugees, Pelagidis (1994) claimed that in 1923 alone some 310,000 had been resettled from Greece to Asia Minor, while the rest eventually moved into evacuated Greek villages in East Thrace. For more detailed figures, see Clogg (1979:121).

10. Some surviving family members found such expedient measures alienating, if not barbaric, as they did not entail a proper Christian burial or funeral ritual. Mass burials conveyed a symbolism significantly different from the practice of secondary burial, now nearly universal in contemporary Greece, in which after a period of at least three years the bones of the dead are exhumed from individual graves, cleaned, and placed together in a communal resting place. Pontic refugees apparently had not engaged in such cultural practices in Turkey, and still do not do so in Mavrorahi today.

11. These Pontics had not been interested in the plains for a number of reasons. Their initial inquiries in Langadhas basin villages had encountered profound resistance from local residents, who guarded their property zealously. The remaining uninhabited areas on the plains had been mostly mosquitoe-infested marshes where malaria was said to have been rampant. On the other hand, the site of the Otmanli *mahaladhes* was located in an eco-niche resembling that which these Pontics had been accustomed to exploiting in their native area near the Black Sea. These Pontic refugees found three of the five Otmanli hamlets still occupied by Turkish herding families as well as a group of Turkish-speaking Orthodox

Christian refugees from the area around Ankara, whom the Pontics referred to as "Ankares." All but two of these Ankares families eventually moved to a new settlement in the Kavala District in eastern Greek Macedonia. Those that remained at Otmanli developed quite harmonious relations with the Pontic refugees.

12. For example, in the Florina Prefecture of western Greek Macedonia, where the number of Greek-speakers among the pre-refugee population has been relatively small, Greek administrators, educators, policemen, and military personnel repeatedly suggested in reports to their superiors that the government should actively encourage the settlement of Greek-speaking (especially East Thracian) refugees in the region (see Karakasidou 1994a).

13. Many Assiros locals also downplayed the capabilities of East Thracian refugees, claiming that, when the latter had first arrived, those "fishermen" had to be shown how to harvest and thresh, as they had known nothing about it. Refugee families in Examili strongly resented such depictions and objected that they had been very capable farmers in Thrace.

14. Far from a homogeneous group, upon their arrival in Greece refugee families had many different idioms of identity: local, regional, national, and religious. Thus, an East Thracian refugee considered herself/himself a "Greek" (national) from "Eksemil" (local) in "East Thrace" (regional) and a Christian Orthodox (religious). One might even argue that *Thrakiotes* was a category of *ethnic* identity, as it signified cultural traits that were markedly different from those of the *Pontyi* or *Mikrasiates*. Idioms of identity were sometimes expressed as mutually exclusive or competitive, but they actually coexisted and overlapped. The Treaty of Lausanne had made Orthodox religion a principal defining characteristic of their national identity, but even religion had local variations. Examili villagers, for example, related what they considered a humorous story of how their local customs had led to problems with the regional Orthodox Metropolite when they had lived in East Thrace. In old Eksemil, they said, betrothed couples often lived together during an engagement period of several years prior to their formal religious wedding. At one point, the Metropolite learned of the practice and became very upset, threatening them with excommunication if they did not stop the practice and marry immediately. One Sunday, some twenty marriages were reportedly performed. Only one couple had missed out, as the young man, a herder, had been away tending his flocks at the time and knew nothing about the Metropolite's order.

15. In contrast, many wealthy Muslim landowners had left Macedonia earlier, some as early as 1912 with the outbreak of the First Balkan War. A large number of urban Muslims from Thessaloniki departed in 1917, and the rest in 1922–23. Most Muslim herders and sharecroppers of the Guvezna area remained there until 1922.

16. Ernest Hemingway, for example, had been a correspondent in Thrace at the time and wrote several communiqués about local conditions and abuses by the Greek army against the departing Turks. See, for example, a piece Hemingway published in the *Toronto Daily Star* on 14 November 1922.

17. The Commission had main offices in major cities and towns such as Thessaloniki (Hirschon 1989:39–40). Its regional wings (*Ghrafion Epikismou*), such as that based in the district seat of Langadhas, were responsible for house and

farm plot allocations. For a general discussion of refugee settlement, see Cassi-matis (1988:135–49), Hirschon (1989:36–45), League of Nations (1926), and Pentzopoulos (1962).

18. This was the case, for example, in Ayia Eleni in the Serres District of east-ern Greek Macedonia (Danforth, personal communication). In fact, in many "mixed villages" of Slavic-speaking locals and resettled refugees throughout Greek Macedonia, the latter tended to dominate political affairs and administra-tion.

19. These families from Asia Minor eventually settled in the Thessaloniki sub-urb of *Saranda Ekklisies* ("Forty Churches").

20. The name of the neighborhood, recall, was derived from the fact that it had been originally established by Muslim refugees settled there as sharecroppers by Ottoman authorities. *Matziria* had been abandoned after the departure of the local Muslims in 1922. Houses in the neighborhood were of a distinct architec-tural style, built in two parallel rows, and lacked the tall walls that surrounded most other Guvezna homes. Only two East Thracian families were said to have received houses in the old part of the village proper. Local villagers in Assiros alleged that these two refugee families had been involved with the local RSC office and had used those connections to arrange allocation of two of the best aban-doned Turkish properties for themselves. Both houses came with large plots of land, as well as facilities for produce storage and animal keeping.

21. Until the 1950s, there was no road linking the neighborhood with the village proper. The hilltop road running between the neighborhood and the vil-lage school on Thessaloniki Street was constructed only in 1954–55; the road connecting *Matziria* with the national public highway was put in a year later.

22. Subsequently, some of these East Thracian families decided that conditions in Guvezna/Assiros were unacceptable and they departed for western Greek Mac-edonia. Only fifteen families from among this group of East Thracians eventually remained in the village. Table 8 shows that approximately only 2 percent of both the Assiros men and women were born in East Thrace.

23. Some of these refugees maintained that their town's name originated from *krithari* (barley), while others claimed it came from the word *krifia,* signifying a hiding place. The Kallipoli coastal town of Krithia was said to have produced a large surplus of barley; it was also said that the town had been a favored refuge for pirates, who sought shelter in its scattered, quiet, tiny bays. Its population (approximately 5,000) was said to have been evacuated in 1922 after the town was bombarded by Turkish artillery.

24. Guvezna paid 62.9 percent of the agricultural tax, while Palehora paid 12.5 percent, Examili 5 percent, and Mavrorahi 0.5 percent.

25. Inhabitants of Gnoina remained marginal in social and political affairs in Krithia township, despite a growing trend of intermarriage between the two settlements in later years. As of the early 1990s, on only one occasion had a Gnoinan been elected to a seat on the Krithia township council. During the first years following the settlement of Krithia, relations between the East Thracian refugees and local Gnoinans had been strained and limited, as the former fre-quently accused the latter of being "Bulgarians." Mavrogordatos (1983b) noted that the relative Greekness of "locals" and "refugees" was often disputed by the

other (see also Drettas 1985). The refugees, he maintained, spoke their own dialects and remained segregated in separate neighborhoods, two factors that accentuated the cultural differences between the groups (Mavrogordatos 1983b:75).

26. For several years after Krithia's secession, the Greek state continued to hold Assiros responsible for providing funds and material support to help sustain Krithia until the refugees there could firmly establish themselves as a fully functional, self-supporting township. These allocations or donations were referred to in Assiros township records as *prika* (dowry). Yet township archives also indicated that the *tsorbadjidhes* of Assiros often objected to such instructions and sometimes refused to comply.

27. This group of refugees had comprised families from two separate villages in East Thrace, Plaghiari and Eksemil. Upon their arrival in Greek Macedonia, refugees from Plaghiari had dispersed into three separate groups, the smallest of which came to the Langadhas basin. They had settled first in the village of Stefania (situated in nearby Karterai township in the hills to the north), but had stayed there only a year. Most of the former Muslim inhabitants of Stefania had been herders, but the Plaghiari refugees had boasted of their capable agricultural skills and had no intention of converting themselves to husbandry or pastoralism. Instead, they moved down to settle on the basin plain, just northwest of Guvezna. They were joined shortly thereafter by a second group of East Thracian refugees, from Eksemil. In 1926, another group of *Thrakiotes* from Eksemil moved to the new Examili from an initial resettlement site near Edessa (Vodena) in western Greek Macedonia.

28. Since the 1940s, the principal political divisions in Examili have been along the lines of conservatives versus leftists, with the former aligning themselves with the Assiros elite.

29. More recently, Examili socialists attempted to bridge the divide within the village by establishing a Cultural Association. Their effort failed to unite the people, however, as did the village soccer team (the "Lions") which was said to have fared rather well in local matches.

30. The prominent Guvezna *tsorbadjis* miller and industrialist, Galianos, owner of a sesame processing plant, won the publicly auctioned contract to transport the necessary building materials from Thessaloniki to Krithia. He later did very good business with the Krithia farmers, who were excellent sesame producers.

31. In 1928, the RSC filed suit in Langadhas court on behalf of the Pontic refugees against Assiros township, disputing the boundaries between Otmanli and the Outs Agats *mahala* and seeking to allow the refugees to use those grazing lands. The township won the case. Otmanli (Turkish: "lots of grass") and the surrounding hills northeast of Guvezna/Assiros were an essential resource in the development of large-scale commercial stock-breeding by the local *tsorbadjidhes* during the 1920s and 1930s, as well as a key factor in the reconfiguration of class stratification in the township.

32. Dorkas (Yianik-Koy) had once been populated by Slavic-speakers who left for Bulgaria after the Second Balkan War. Karterai village (the township seat), as well as Stefania, had been inhabited by Muslim herders who left after 1922.

33. It was only in 1992 that Mavrorahi succeeded in seceding from Assiros and

joining the Karterai township. This much-wanted "victory" was accompanied by the paving of the dirt road in the spring of 1996 for the sole purpose of creating a dump for the Thessaloniki garbage near the village.

34. Vlahs are generally regarded as (former) transhumant pastoralists who once had spoken a Latin-based language similar to those used in Romania or Wallachia (hence, Vlah). As noted in Part I, Romanian nationalists had attempted to propagandize among Balkan Vlahs. Some, in fact, had left Greece for Romania, but most remained and became staunchly aggressive proponents of Hellenism.

35. Several theories have been suggested to account for the origins of the Sarakatsan (see Campbell 1964:1–6), although many such theories are based on modern-day national categories projected onto the past. They have been labeled as Aromoun Vlahs, descendants of Illyrian and Thracian tribes; as Balkan inhabitants fleeing the Romans; or as just plain Greeks who went up to the mountains and became stockbreeders at the time of the Ottoman conquest. The Greek identity of the Sarakatsan is widely assumed in Greek historiography, in which they are generally depicted as descendants of Greek-speakers who had fled the plains for the mountains in order to escape Slavic invasions more than 1,200 years ago. Another theory depicted the Sarakatsan as Turkish-speaking descendants of nomads from the Russian steppes who came to the Balkans during the eleventh through thirteenth centuries and were Christianized (Guboglo 1970:112), a thesis based largely on claims that the Sarakatsan had been once extensively involved in horse-breeding, which declined after their sedentarization. One Sarakatsanos in Assiros claimed that all Sarakatsan were descended from the inhabitants of the village of Sirako, in Epirus, who had fled after an attack by the notorious Ali-Pasha of Ioannina during the 1820s.

36. The name "Vlahika" originated from the fact that Sarakatsan are often referred to in Greek Macedonia by the generic name "Vlah." The name "Kalivia" ("Huts") was said to have been derived from the fact that the Sarakatsan had put simple thatched roofs atop the old Turkish houses of the hamlet.

37. This first Sarakatsan family to settle in Kalivia was soon joined by a brother and a widowed sister-in-law of the patriarch, and not long afterwards by his wife's brother and sister. The last additions to the group arrived in 1936, when distant cousins of the original settler were taken on as agricultural laborers, a status that later served them as an advantage when they received relatively more land in the redistribution campaigns than their relatives who had arrived earlier. The Sarakatsanos shepherd who had established his family herding group (*tselingato*) in Kalivia was referred to as the leader (*kehayias*), a position he retained until the group broke up in 1949 and its members dispersed to Assiros and Dorkas.

38. The practice of combining herds into cooperative summer companies (Campbell 1964:88–94) was common among other Greek pastoralists as well. These herding companies began operating after St. George's Day (April 23), and ran through June 29 (the Day of the Apostles), after which time sheep milk production reportedly dropped off (Petropoulos 1943–44:60). Each *kehayias* handled negotiations for both winter grazing lands and summer pastures, and decided which members of his *tselingato* would join his summer company and who would summer with other *kehayias* elsewhere. It was during the summer months of dispersal that marriage and other alliances tended to be formed. Summer pastures

for the Sarakatsan became limited after southern Macedonia was incorporated into the Greek nation-state and its borders with Bulgaria and Serbia were redrawn and closed. A number of Sarakatsan were reportedly "caught" in Bulgaria when the partition of Macedonia took place and have remained there ever since. Currently, there is a movement in Greece to help these "unliberated brethren" to return.

39. I was told that the most notable of all had been Captain Garefas, who fought against the Bulgarians and provided weapons and provisions for Greek partisans.

40. The families of two Sarakatsan brothers had settled in the village of Examili in the 1920s, establishing a winter camp at the edge of the village made of small huts they constructed themselves. Conflicts and hostility, including violent assault and arson, plagued relationships between these Sarakatsan and the *Thrakiotes* of Examili, who were also engaged in animal husbandry. In 1938, for example, the Examili villagers accused the Sarakatsan of unauthorized cultivation of thirty-five *stremmata* of pastureland and burnt down their huts in an attempt to force them out of the village (ATA 1938).

41. "Caucasian," as used here, referred to individuals who lived in the Caucasus mountain region of Southwest Asia, and to Pontic Greeks in particular. Popular stereotypes in Greece portray such people as being "backward" or somehow possessing lower intelligence.

42. Over 80 percent of Assiros men born between 1890 and 1915 took brides from Assiros itself, suggesting a period of closure in the 1920s and 1930s. In the subsequent generation, those villagers born between 1915 and 1940, the trend towards closure weakened in Assiros (72 percent of the women and only 67 percent of the men marrying within the village; see tables 9A and 9B).

43. In a similar vein, Hirschon noted that refugees can be equally pointed in their retaliatory remarks against locals: "They [the locals] know nothing"; "They don't know how to behave"; "They don't know how to speak"; "They have no manners"; "It was we who taught them everything"; "What can you expect? They're from the mountains" (Hirschon 1989:30–31).

SIX

1. HAM/GDM, File No. 16 ("Districts of Langadhas, Sohos, Zagliveri, Lingovani, September 1913–January/March 1914"), letter from the Langadhas District Director to the Prefect of Thessaloniki, 13 January 1914.

2. HAM/GDM, File No. 76 ("Muslim Migration, February–December 1914"), letter from the Consulat Général Ottoman, Salonique to Monsieur le Gouverneur Général, 10 August 1914, Protocol No. 403.

3. A similar process had occurred in Thessaly immediately preceding its incorporation into the Greek kingdom in 1881. Ottoman landowners there sold their large estates to wealthy and influential Greeks in Athens and Constantinople. Such properties were appropriated and redistributed in the 1920s to landless cultivators in that region (Vergopoulos 1977–78:462). In southern Greece, Ottomans had departed hastily in the years leading up to the kingdom's independence in 1829. All Muslim-owned lands there had been taken over by the Greek state and labeled "national lands" (*ethnikes ghees*), which were then rented out to cultiva-

tors until a redistribution was undertaken in the 1870s. See also Mouzelis (1978–79).

4. The Sapountzis family, for example, held a number of legal deeds (copies of which I have in my possession) to properties they claimed to have purchased from Turkish landowners. One such document, dated 28 September 1922, stated that the then village schoolteacher, Sapountzis, purchased from Seremet, son of Turkish landowner Toptop Zathe Sioukri, some thirty-one plots of land totaling 317.5 *stremmata*, along with a storage facility (*apothiki*), a barn, a half "share" in a second barn, and a two-fifths "share" in still a third barn, all for the sum of 5,000 *drachmas*. A few days later, on 1 October 1922, Sapountzis made three more transactions with the same Turkish landowner, purchasing more land and two additional houses. His total purchase amounted to some 714.5 *stremmata* in seventy-two plots, the largest of which was only twenty-two *stremmata*.

5. Another version of the same incident, recounted by Pontic refugees in Mavrorahi, maintained that in 1923 three Assiros men had come up into the hills one night with their rifles and shot to death a Turkish miller and his son near the old watermill on the Boidana River. The following morning, the few remaining Turks in the Kran hamlet were said to have fled in terror, taking their cattle, goats, and sheep with them to East (i.e., Turkish) Thrace, where they resettled in villages abandoned by *Thrakiotes*. After the Turks' departure from Kran, the Guveznans came up to the hamlet and dismantled the Turkish homes, taking away windows, doors, and all the salvageable lumber they could find.

6. Redistribution had been needed most urgently in Thessaly and Macedonia where large landed estates accounted for more than half Greece's total *chiftliks* in the 1910s (Vergopoulos 1977–78:173–75; Augustinos 1981:241). Even during the 1920s, more than half of the lands of Greek Macedonia had been former *chiftlik* estates.

7. By the same method of calculation, a family of four received one and a quarter *kliros,* or forty-five *stremmata,* while a family of five received one and three-quarters *kliros,* or fifty-four *stremmata.* In actuality, the size of a *kliros* in a particular village varied, based on the quality of land. Mountain villages such as Mavrorahi and Dorkas received extra *stremmata* to compensate for rocky soil or low fertility.

8. One principal type of redistributed lands were the "in-fields" (*avlotopos*), plots of approximately 2.5 *stremmata* per family. These plots were situated within the borders of the residential area of the village and were planted primarily with crops intended for the daily consumption needs of village families (such as okra, lentils, chick peas, fava beans), with clover or barley for animal feed, or with cash crops such as tobacco and cotton.

9. These figures come from thē Directorate of Agriculture, Thessaloniki. Land is currently measured by the standard "French *stremma,*" which equals 1,000 square meters, with four *stremmata* making roughly one acre. During the Ottoman period land was measured by the "Turkish *stremma*" (1:1,600 square meters), and to complicate matters even more, township archives indicate that during the 1920s and 1930s the "Royal *stremma*" (1:3,600) was employed as the standard unit of measure.

10. Land redistribution in Mavrorahi did not even begin until 1938, some years after the process had been completed in Assiros and Examili. Influential

landowners in Assiros, Mavrorahiotes maintained, effectively delayed land redistribution in the hamlet for nearly a decade, hoping to oblige the refugees to abandon the site with its prime grazing lands. Land in that hill area was rocky, sandy, dry, and of low fertility; families there attempted to cultivate any plots they found available, but crops and vines repeatedly withered and died. Most refugee families in Mavrorahi soon gave up attempts at agriculture, although a few continued to cultivate tobacco. By the late 1920s, most village residents were making their living through animal husbandry, some with herds as large as 200 goats or 50 to 80 sheep.

11. During research elsewhere in Greek Macedonia, I have heard allegations that in some villages Slavic-speakers were denied land or received little of it in the 1920s redistribution, obliging some to migrate out of the region. It remains unclear the extent to which natal language, a family's history of national orientation, or degree of national consciousness were relevant factors in the Assiros *tsorbadjis* rivalries during the 1920s and 1930s. But it was said that some Slavic-speaking families, such as that of Palepolitis who had been forced by Greek partisans to abandon Palehora, had been excluded from the land reform process as administered by Liberal Party township councillors. They did, however, receive land in the second *dhianomi* initiated by Populist or pro-royalist *tsorbadjidhes* who came to power in 1933.

12. Mavrogordatos (1983b:250) offered five reasons why Slavic-speakers in Greece supported the Populists over the Venizelists after 1912. First, local Populist politicians (mostly from local notable families) had promised to protect them from harassment by Greek authorities; second, the Populists exploited the sensitive land question; third, the Populists had promised to reverse some of Venizelos' policies and to remove the refugees from Macedonia; fourth, Slavic-speakers were conservative peasants and supporters of Bulgarian irredentism; fifth, the IMRO had directed Slavic-speakers in Greece to vote for the Populists. Yet, as I have shown in Part I, not all Slavic-speakers in Macedonia supported Bulgarian irredentism. Rather, such political allegiance was largely conditional upon the activities and leanings of powerful and influential local elites in each rural community.

13. Apostolakoudhis was removed from the post of secretary a few months later, reportedly because of mental problems. He was replaced by Mouhtaris (ATA, 1933, Decision #19, 28.5.1933), another pro-royalist. That same month, former secretary Petrakis was given some funds (apparently as a sort of severance pay) and left his post (ATA 1933, Decision #21, 11.5.1933). It might be noted that he remained politically active in the area, becoming a fierce anticommunist partisan during the Civil War years (see chapter 7).

14. After leading a coup d'etat on 4 August 1936, Metaxas ruled as dictator until his death in 1941. The Metaxas dictatorship actively sought to purify the Greek nation (*ethnos*), imposing many cultural prohibitions and language restrictions and imprisoning leftists and Slavic-speakers alike (see Karakasidou 1993b).

15. The township council enjoyed considerable latitude in determining how revenues were to be collected and allocated. Archival records indicated that roughly half of all township revenues has been consistently allocated to public works projects, particularly the construction and maintenance of the village's water system and cisterns as well as bridges and roads. Other major expenditures included school operations, salaries of nonelected township personnel, and fees

to the state government; very few funds, however, were redistributed as relief directly to needy families (see table 10).

16. In the 1990s, the township secretary maintained the Township Registry, the Male Registry for conscription, the Marriage Registry, and the Baptism Registry. He and his assistant were also responsible for documentation required of farmers applying for subsidies from either the Greek government or the European Union (formerly the EEC). The secretary also functions as the local representative to the Organization for Agricultural Development (*Orghanismos Gheorghikis Anaptikseos*), which provides pensions and medical insurance to farmers.

17. During his tenure as secretary, Petrakis also served as head of the Refugee Resettlement Commission's township branch office. Recall that he had been accused of mismanaging funds and plot reallocations in the first land redistribution, and while such allegations were never proven, Petrakis resigned or was dismissed in 1933. He and his family remained in Assiros until the 1937–38 school year, when apparently he was transferred to a new posting in Karterai township. Petrakis became a firm supporter of the dictatorship of General Ioannis Metaxas in the 1930s. During the 1940s, Petrakis became a feared anticommunist who, under the nom de guerre "Kapetan Psiloritis" (the name of a well-known mountain in Crete), directed the Panhellenic Liberation Organization (PAO) brigades of the Langadhas district in a number of aggressive campaigns during the German Occupation (see chapter 7). It was said that at one point during the Civil War communist partisans had almost assassinated him, but that his life was spared through direct intervention by British forces in the area.

18. Policemen in Greece are assigned rotational posts throughout the country but never in their native region. Some officers have remained in the community in which they once served, resigning their commissions or taking early retirement. In Assiros, several former policemen married local women, left the force, and took up agricultural livelihoods. Assiros, formerly a one-man post, now has three policemen assigned to it.

19. At that point, the state assumed direct control over the financing of the local public-school system. Under the terms of the partition, the local school was given a *kliros* of farmland and an additional plot set aside during the land redistributions of the 1920s on which to construct a new facility. The township and local church, on the other hand, retained only the properties they had acquired as *wakf* holdings under the Ottomans. Yet even after the formal dissolution of the partnership, the three institutions of township, church, and school continued to accommodate each other. For example, the township offices were formerly located on a plot owned by the school; the new village church is situated on a township plot. The township continued to support the school for years, providing money as extra pay for teachers, for the construction of a new school facility, for firewood during the winter months, and the like. Even as late as 1951, the township was providing the salary for one of the schoolteachers.

20. A GDM decree (#10.16.1926) issued in 1926, for example, gave township authorities the right to issue, raise, or lower taxes as they pleased, depending on village needs (ATA 1926). It was only after the 1950s that the national government began to tax villagers directly. Although farmers paid no formal income tax (those with large incomes excepted), their liabilities were increased indirectly as merchants were required to pay a 3 percent tax on the purchase prices of ag-

ricultural products. Vergopoulos (1975:266) has argued that, through this taxation system, Greek farmers in fact pay even heavier taxes than urbanites. He calculated that although, on average, farmers made seven times less income than urban Greeks, they paid 2.4 times more taxes (Vergopoulos 1975:196–99).

21. In addition to "specific revenues" derived from taxation, township records included another category of local finances, referred to as "general revenue" (*ghenika esodha*). This was derived primarily from the leasing to private contractors of township-owned properties, which included a drinking house (*kapilio*), demolished in 1936; a storage room (*apothiki*), known as "The *Dhekati* Collector's Shop" (*To Maghazi tis Dkekatis*), in which the 10 percent tax in kind on agricultural products was stored; a kiosk (*periptero*) in the village *aghora* which sold cigarettes, candies, and other small items (contracts for kiosk operation were restricted to war cripples and their families); an inn (*khan*), equipped with an oven, that once stood on the site of the current *kinotita* offices; and a number of plots in the *aghora* along the riverbank.

22. In 1928, the president of the Union of Cooperatives in Langadhas organized a massive demonstration in Thessaloniki to demand the abolition of the *dhekati* tax. Many farmers from Assiros and other villages of Greek Macedonia gathered with their horses in the *Sindrivani* (Fountain) area of the city, near the site of the present-day International Trade Fair grounds. From there, demonstrators moved westward along Egnatia Avenue to the Governor General's Palace (*Dhiikitirion*), stopping streetcars along the way. The cavalry was called out, and charged the crowd with drawn swords. One elderly Assiriotis who participated in the demonstration remembered how terrified the farmers had been, and how they defended themselves by throwing stones. The Governor General of Macedonia eventually appeared on the balcony of the mansion to announce that all the demands would be met. Farmers were also granted the right to make their own *ouzo*, as permission had been formally required to convert grapes into alcohol and until then relatively few villagers enjoyed such privileges. Eventually, after 1928, the *dhekati* tax was replaced by a 2 to 3 percent "tax on products of the earth" (*foros engion proiondon*), which was also contracted through a public auction. Each year, the Langadhas district tax office sent to rural townships lists of agricultural products subject to such kind of taxation.

23. Crop-watching fees were usually paid in kind, and were collected from individual farmers based on the number of *stremmata* planted and the number of draft animals owned (ATA 1924). In 1924, for example, if a man had one horse, he paid two *koutli* of wheat (one *koutlos* equaled 100 *oke*), while a man with two horses and a plough paid three *koutli*. For each ox owned, a farmer had to pay one *koutlos* of wheat as well (ATA 1924). Sometimes, as in 1935, the fees were set by the Supervision of Agricultural Security Office of the Prefecture of Thessaloniki. By 1937 fees were determined solely on the basis of the amount of *stremmata* cultivated. Even in 1938, however, Assiros farmers paid significantly less crop-watching fees than their counterparts in Examili and Mavrorahi (3.5 drachmas per *stremma* compared to five and seven drachmas, respectively; ATA 1938).

24. There was, for example, a tax on slaughtered animals (*foros sfaghiasthendon zoon*), which later became a tax on sold and purchased animals (*foros aghorapoloumenon zoon*). There was also a tax on the number of animals reared

(*foros dietomenon zoon*), as well as a local fee for grazing rights (*dhikeoma voskis*), and a number of taxes on dairy products (*foros ghalaktokomikon proiondon*) including cheese, butter, cream, and milk (payable in drachmas per *oke* of product). Not until 1951 did the percentage of township income derived from animal products and pasture fees begin to decline markedly, from over 80 percent of town revenues in the fiscal year 1950–51 to just under a third in 1953–54 (see table 12). This drop was matched by a correspondingly sharp rise in the proportion of local revenues derived from agricultural taxes, which rose from just shy of 17 percent to over two-thirds of township revenues. This change can be attributed largely to the impact of agricultural mechanization in the 1950s and to the decline of the pastoral sector of the local economy (see chapter 7).

25. In contrast to smallholders, whose involvement in animal husbandry centered mainly around subsistence needs, the *tsorbadjidhes* saw animals as *zoiko kefaleo* or "live capital" (Halstead 1990:152). Not only did they provide manure for the fields, but in the event of poor harvest or crop failure, livestock could be sold to meet expenses, wages, and debts. Livestock, slowly built up over time, were later sold to support these families' agricultural mechanization in the 1950s. These changes in the pastoral sector of the local economy had a significant impact on social stratification in the township, as well as on perceptions of identity, difference, and solidarity.

26. The township council usually hired three permanent and two seasonal crop-watchers. The latter were employed from July to October, after which time zoning regulations were suspended and animals were free to graze in recently harvested wheat fields. Seasonal crop-watchers were mainly responsible for protecting the vineyards and other crops still in the ground. They would build two-story wooden structures (*dhraghasies*) upon which they would sit overlooking the vineyards all day long.

27. In 1926, fines were set by legislative decree at 0.50 drachmas per small animal and five drachmas per large beast. If more than 100 animals belonging to one owner were seized, the maximum penalty imposed was limited to 100 drachmas (ATA 1926). In addition, fees were levied for feeding and guarding animals during detention. Unclaimed animals were eventually auctioned by the Agronomy Service in Langadhas (ATA 1955).

28. In 1931 the animals of Artousis and Halepis were reported to have entered a number of fields, causing considerable damage to growing crops. The township council, however, dismissed complaints filed by angry smallholders, and the animals were even permitted to graze in sown fields, despite zoning prohibitions (ATA 1931).

29. The first court hearing took place in Thessaloniki a month later. The Assiriotes hired a Langadhas lawyer to press their claims, while the Sarakatsan sent their own *kehayias* to represent the group. After the hearing ended inconclusively, the township president made a trip to Athens to visit the Ministry of Agriculture, where he pressed the township's case over the Kambili-Karakotzali pastures. The ministry soon sent the Sarakatsan a telegram demanding that they vacate the disputed grazing lands immediately (ATA 1935). They refused, and subsequently received a summons from the Thessaloniki district attorney to appear in court.

30. Faced with mounting pressure from the township government, the Sarakatsan families decided to move down to Assiros in 1955–56 in hopes of acquir-

ing residency, legitimate status, and better treatment. Within a short time, they had become tobacco cultivators, an occupation most of them still undertake as a principal form of livelihood.

31. Both large landowners and smallholders in Assiros generally practiced a two-season system of fallow and crop rotation. Kostis (1987:82–83) noted that in 1929 only 28.1 percent of cultivated lands in Greece were actually sown with crop each year, while another 11.4 percent went fallow. Noncultivated lands were made up of 20 percent pasture, 40 percent forest and 1 percent marshlands. For example, a farmer owning 100 *stremmata* would plough all his fields in October but sow only half the area with wheat. Another forty *stremmata* would be *niama,* left fallow until the planting of sesame, the principal spring crop, in May. On the remaining ten *stremmata* he might have planted oats (as horse fodder), barley (for ox fodder), corn (for pigs), or *rov* (vetch, a draft-animal fodder). Only a small number of fields were devoted to *aghranapafsis,* left fallow for a whole year. This regime, it was said, produced maximum returns, and was followed until the introduction of mechanized farming and government directives encouraging the monocultivation of wheat in the 1950s. Halstead (1990) has dealt extensively with agricultural risk-buffering mechanisms in Greece and in Assiros in particular.

32. This phenomenon was, of course, not unique to Assiros. Vergopoulos (1978) argued that despite land redistribution as many as 83 percent of Greek farmers remained in debt in 1933. The Metaxas dictatorship in 1937 attempted to help farmers by canceling interest payments on outstanding loans. Some farmers were even granted amnesty from repaying the principal on their loans, if their debt burden exceeded 60 percent of their total property (Vergopoulos 1978:185).

33. In contradistinction to common Western European perceptions of "servants" as the elite of the laboring class (see Kussmaul 1981), in Assiros *dhoulos* was largely a derogatory term and such "servants" were considered to have the lowest status in the village social hierarchy.

34. Firewood collection was also an important supplementary income-generating activity opened to virtually anyone who had a wagon or a donkey. Firewood, as well as dung, had long been a principal energy source for most inhabitants of the area, and township-owned lands (even leased grazing pastures), were open to firewood scavengers. Villagers recalled that sometimes as many as 100 to 150 donkeys, led by men, women, or children, would go up into the hills and mountains northwest of Assiros looking for such fuel. Firewood was usually sold or bartered either in the village of Drimos (which had depleted its own supply) or at the Langadhas market, where one horseload of firewood would fetch one kilo of corn bread. Some would also gather cow dung from the grazing pastures to sell or use as fuel in the big boilers (*kazania*) in which *ouzo* was made.

35. Most hired laborers carried with them a small package of *tarator,* a favorite field food made of bread and garlic. Others brought small bundles of *lipares,* cheap lake fish dressed with vinegar and garlic, and *kritsmas* made from flour and water which they often washed down freely with *retsina.* For those fortunate enough to work for generous patrons, a second snack of beans would arrive sometime later in the day from the landowner's house.

36. It was also in the 1950s that an unofficial union was established among young shepherds, and a designated representative negotiated better contract terms

with the large stockbreeders in the village. The union's organizer and negotiator has since emigrated to Australia, and was unavailable for interview. His departure from Assiros was rumored to have been linked to resentment among the local elite for his unionizing activities.

37. The *kiradjidhes* slowly disappeared after 1927, following the introduction of motor vehicles to the region. In Assiros, the first truck was purchased by Salamas, the cheese and salami maker, who started transporting the milk from the surrounding herding hamlets, such as Mavrorahi. Until then, he reportedly hired boys who were recommended to him by other local authorities or the boys who asked for the lowest wages.

38. Although a branch of the National Bank of Greece had opened in Langadhas in 1922, that bank's high rates of interest and numerous bureaucratic fees had greatly deterred most agriculturalists. By contrast, the establishment of the ATE was praised (years later) by the Langadhas-based Union of Agricultural Cooperatives as a victory of immense importance in the struggles of the "agricultural class."

39. Galianos also owned a flour mill. Villagers recalled that it operated around the clock and was the only processing plant in the area for sesame, another important but labor-intensive cash crop in the local economy during the interwar period. Prior to World War II, nearly 15 percent of Assiros fields were devoted to sesame, although by the 1960s sesame production had given way to the monoculativation of wheat, encouraged through the advent of mechanized farming. The Galianos family also maintained large herds of some 300 sheep and 100 cows, which they fed on "waste" produced through the sesame-pressing process.

40. These wealthy and powerful families became estranged from the cooperative following the introduction of mechanized agriculture in the 1950s and 1960s (see chapter 7).

41. *Tsorbadjis* patronage was particularly critical for those smallholders seeking permits to cultivate tobacco, which was regulated by the state through township authorities. Licenses, usually granted only for small plots, were coveted and difficult to obtain. Eligibility requirements were codified by the state Tobacco Board (*Eforia Kapnou*) in 1957. Thereafter, licenses were issued to farmers who had planted tobacco the previous year; had permission to plant the previous year but did not do so because of illness, death, or military service; were the son of a tobacco farmer; or had been involved in a joint cultivation partnership (as certified by the township president) in preceding years. Two other stipulations were attached to these regulations: that the "right to cultivate" tobacco followed a farmer wherever he was pleased to go; and that such rights were inherited by one of the family's sons upon the death of the father. Through the patronage of a *tsorbadjis* benefactor, a family might secure written authorization from the township president to cultivate tobacco, and if the prices offered by tobacco merchants (such as Pashos) were satisfactory, returns could be attractive.

SEVEN

1. For a detailed discussion of southern Slav godparenthood and ritual kinship, see Hammel (1968).

2. Herzfeld (1982b:295), for example, found patterns of "endocommunal spir-

itual kinship," often reproduced over several generations, as was common in Assiros, among Greek baptismal sponsorship in Rhodes. In contrast, Sarakatsan in
Epirus and the herders in Crete preferred sponsors who were either outsiders or
powerful local herdsmen. In each context, families looked for baptismal sponsors
in particular directions, based on their specific needs.

3. I recall encountering a neighbor of mine in Assiros who was rushing to
prepare for a Sunday wedding at which she was to be the sponsor (*nona*). When
I inquired as to whether or not I might attend the various ceremonies of the ritual,
she replied without hesitation, "Of course you can. I am the *nona*." Wedding
sponsors had the privilege of inviting whatever guests they pleased.

4. By contrast, in some villages of the Florina District of western Greek Macedonia, where Slavo-Macedonian ethnic identity has become more publicly expressed in recent years, local residents claimed that their forefathers had refused
to raise the Greek flag in such a ritual context. There were no such sentiments
of dissent expressed in Assiros, reflecting the degree of success of Greek nation-
building efforts in the area.

5. Regardless of whether or not they were the *nonos*, the local *tsorbadjidhes*
formerly also sponsored horse races on the Sunday morning of a church wedding
ceremony. Some ten or so horses and their riders would start off down near the
Boidana River and race to a finish line in the Assiros *aghora*. Great festivity surrounded these races, particularly for the *bratimia* and other friends of the groom
who participated.

6. Baptismal sponsorship in the township reflected a tendency towards group
closure during the period 1880–1950 (see table 15). Even after 1950, with the
advent of mechanized farming and rural industrial development, when one might
expect most villagers to expand their ritual kin networks by seeking sponsors
from outside their own group in the township, Assiros locals remained largely
inward-looking in the choice of baptismal sponsors. The degree of closure among
such groups is symbolic of both their degree of self-identification and group cohesiveness, as well as their separateness from other local residents.

7. An extensive study of the *kourban(i)* celebration in Greek Macedonia is
currently being conducted by Zeta Papageorgopoulou. Apparently, the *kourbani*
was celebrated widely throughout Macedonia. Danforth (1989) noted that the
firewalking of the Anastenaria in eastern Greek Macedonia also centered around
a *kourbani* festival.

8. Halpern (1986:110), who also described the *slava* celebration in rural Serbia, argued that its origins may be traced to pre-Christian pagan religions of the
region.

9. King Constantine succeeded to the Greek throne (1913–17) after his father
was assassinated in Thessaloniki in 1913. At the time of his coronation, he represented the realization of what Clogg (1979:104) termed "the widely believed
prophecy that the Greeks would re-capture Constantinople when a Constantine
once again sat upon the throne of Hellas." The new village church is to be dedicated to Saints Constantine and Eleni.

10. August 4, 1936, was the day General Ioannis Metaxas seized power and
established a military government which lasted until 1940.

11. St. Dimitrios Day (October 26) is a municipal-sponsored national holiday
in Thessaloniki. It is not widely observed in other parts of northern Greece, let

alone in the south. The fact that it is regarded as the most important national holiday in Assiros may be related to the historical role contemporary villagers believe Guvezna played in the liberation of the city (recall the account from chapter 4). The 28th of October, in contrast to the 26th, is a major holiday celebrated throughout Greece. It exalts the negative response Ioannis Metaxas is credited with giving to Mussolini's ultimatum (see Karakasidou 1995a).

12. My own field research in other areas of Greek Macedonia, where Slavic-speakers had expressed a much stronger sense of ethnic distinctiveness, revealed that conscription was actively resisted during the first two decades following the establishment of Greek national sovereignty. In contrast, I learned of no such instances in Assiros.

13. Military service (stratiotiko) is usually referred to as "serving the motherland" (ipireto tin patridha, where ipireto is Greek for "doing service").

14. Before 1928, when villagers fell seriously ill they were sent to the Public Hospital of Thessaloniki, where they were treated free of charge because the township was always sending donations to the hospital. After 1928, the township hired a doctor to make periodic visits to the villages. A physician finally settled permanently in the village in 1934, and although the township provided a room for him, villagers always had to pay him out of their own pockets. Most illnesses, however, were treated by local women herbalists.

15. Many villagers from the Strimon valley passed through Assiros in 1941 as refugees fleeing Bulgarian occupation forces. The Assiros township council allocated funds from their budget to provide them with food. The council stated that it was their duty to help their fellow Greeks, although they did so at considerable expense to their own coffers (ATA 1941).

16. The Bulgarian forces were widely regarded as a greater threat than Nazi troops. On 30 January 1943, for example, a large demonstration organized by members of the resistance and attended by a few Assiriotes was held in Langadhas to protest the German occupation. Some present-day elderly villagers who had been present at the rally claimed that they had gone expecting to attend a German food distribution rally. They were surprised to find, instead, a large crowd gathering in protest at the Aghia Paraskevi square opposite the cathedral. Before the crowd stood one German and two Bulgarian soldiers. As the crowd swelled, one man stood up on a chair and denounced the occupation, telling the crowd that although everyone was hungry, soon the Germans would be defeated and liberation would come. A Gestapo officer arrived, it is said, and pulled the man down, but a woman grabbed the officer's gun. The Bulgarian soldiers prepared to fire on the crowd, but they were ordered by the Germans to fire in the air instead. The demonstration was dispersed without bloodshed. Several Assiriotes men were arrested during the incident and imprisoned in the Pavlos Melas military installation in western Thessaloniki. Yet the story was recounted as an example of how the Bulgarians were more aggressive towards Greek citizens than were the Germans.

17. General Directorate of Western Macedonia (Gheniki Dhiikisi Dhitikis Makedhonias), File 19B/14.

18. Among those who came seeking shelter and sanctuary were several Sarakatsan families, twelve refugee families from Examili, and five from Mavrorahi.

Even inhabitants from villages as far away as Kilkis and the mountainous regions of the northern Langadhas District, areas occupied by leftist forces, found refuge in Assiros.

19. In western Greek Macedonia, where support for leftist partisans among Slavic-speakers had been much greater, autonomist aspirations had been stronger and more prevalent. There, many local Slavic-speakers who had openly aided or fought within the ranks of Greek communist forces fled north with them to Yugoslavia following their defeat in 1949 (see Kofos 1964; Karakasidou 1993a).

20. This category referred mainly to Vlahs in Macedonia who had followed Romanian propaganda.

21. When Greek communist partisans retreated into Yugoslavia following their defeat in 1949, many children were taken with them, either sent voluntarily (if reluctantly) by parents who feared reprisals, or forcibly abducted. Villagers in Assiros maintained that only one abduction had taken place in the 1940s: a young shepherd boy tending a flock in the hills was allegedly seized by Bulgarian troops as they withdrew from the area during World War II. I have been unable to verify the account; the individual involved has since died and his son, who now lives in Assiros, claimed to have no knowledge of the incident. Nevertheless, Paskhalina's accounts of her own siblings' "abduction" by the retreating Bulgarian army suggests that such allegations should be treated with care. In this case, the parents of the individual alleged to have been abducted had moved to Assiros from Xiloupolis, once a predominantly Slavic-speaking village, most of whose inhabitants had departed for Bulgaria after the Second Balkan War. The family was said to have moved to Guvezna during the Macedonian Struggle, but they were not listed in the 1919 township registry.

22. Many such letters written by former partisans are held in the archives of the General Directorate of Western Macedonia.

23. In addition to monetary and material assistance offered through the Marshall Plan and the UNRRA, there were also a number of international organizations directly involved in reconstruction work in the northern part of the country, including the UNESCO village Educational Rehabilitation Committee for Northern Greece (whose chairman came from the University of Thessaloniki), the Queen's Fund Institution, the Congregational Christian Service Committee, the Quaker Domestic School, and the Ecumenical Work Camp. For details concerning postwar U.S. reconstruction aid to Greece in general, see McNeil (1957).

24. Based on such lists, disproportionally large amounts of aid went to Assiros village, while relatively little was allocated for Examili and Mavrorahi. Some eighty Assiros farmers were deemed needy, compared with only four in Examili and three in Mavrorahi, despite the fact that residents of Examili and Mavrorahi had suffered burdens of comparable magnitude during the occupation.

25. Jelavich (1983:308) argued that in Greece, "Although supplies were sent in by the UNRRA, a considerable percentage ended up on the black market. The obvious corruption and the prevalence of profiteering caused great social bitterness." A number of Assiriotes also claimed that even of the clothing items delivered to the village by the UNRRA the largest quantity and those of the best quality were kept by the tsorbadjidhes, who had been responsible for their distribution to needy families.

26. Tractors were also available to farmers classified as "nonowners," but

such families were required to purchase them at going market rates. Few families in Assiros could afford to do so.

27. Tractors were rapidly introduced into Greek agriculture during the 1950s, and by 1964 as much as 86 percent of Greek Macedonian lands were cultivated with machinery. Although by 1964 the regions of Macedonia, Thrace, and Central Greece (*Sterea Hellas*) contained 54.4 percent of cultivated lands in Greece, farmers in those areas possessed just over 80 percent of all tractors in the country (Kamarinou 1977:79–80).

28. Kamarinou (1977:81–83) noted that use of chemical fertilizers increased at double-digit rates during 1955–64, with most concentrated in grain production.

29. While some Assiros farmers are involved in the cultivation of semolina, also known as macaroni wheat or "hard wheat" (*skliro stari*), the majority concentrate production on more profitable "soft wheat" (*malako stari;* see table 16). Baltas (1986) maintained that soft wheat is preferred (3:1 over hard wheat) in Greece because of soil considerations. In Assiros, however, even taking account of subsidies, soft wheat is nearly twice as profitable as hard wheat.

30. European Union subsidies for semolina production, introduced under the E.E.C. in the late 1970s, were oriented to the demands of the Western European market.

31. Most wheat is produced in Thessaly, Macedonia, and Thrace. In 1970, 40 percent of all cultivated lands were devoted to grain production, more than half of which were producing wheat (Baltas 1986:21).

32. Postwar developmental assistance and the paving of the old Thessaloniki-Serres public highway in 1948 (with aid from the U.S. government) also contributed to incipient social stratification in more economically peripheral villages in the Langadhas basin, such as Mavrorahi. Some Mavrorahi families were rewarded for their patriotism and anticommunist activities with livestock and draft animals. Following the Civil War, Anatolia College (an elite private American high school located in the exclusive suburb of Panorama overlooking Thessaloniki) formed a committee that applied for a Point Four Technical Assistance grant to help in the reconstruction of eight villages within a five-mile radius of Assiros, including Mavrorahi. An American of the Congregational Christian Service Committee was appointed to oversee the implementation of the program, which worked through "Friends of the Village" (FOV), an organization established by the Greek royal family to "adopt" small villages and guide them through a model development and reconstruction program.

33. Moisidis (1986) claimed that over 30 percent of all cultivated lands in Greek Macedonia are now rented out, more than twice the rate for Greece in general (Tsoumas and Tasioulas 1986:44). Vergopoulos (1975:216) attributed this in part to the preference of emigrant laborers to lease out rather than to sell family properties.

34. Government subsidy lists in 1990 revealed that only four (1.3 percent) of Assiros' 308 farmers cultivate more than 300 *stremmata* of land. Another ten (3.2 percent) farm between 200 and 300 *stremmata*, while nearly half (47.4 percent) possess plots ranging from only 1 to 50 *stremmata*.

35. While 57 percent of the Greek population had been farmers in 1928, the ratio had fallen to 35 percent by 1971 (Kamarinou 1977:92). During the period

1955–71 alone, some 1.5 million rural people, nearly a third of the country's population, left the Greek countryside for work in urban areas, most from villages predominantly involved in cash-crop production (Vergopoulos 1975). In 1951, less than a quarter (23.4 percent) of Greek farming families had members employed in nonagricultural occupations, but by 1981 that figure had risen to over 40 percent (Moisidis 1986:226–31). The flow of rural labor out of Greece in search of overseas factory jobs in the 1960s was remarkably well-organized, with regional associations established to help arrange visas, passage, housing, and sometimes even employment in the immigrant community abroad.

36. In 1967, the first small-scale "putting out" or contracting work started in Assiros for a textile firm in Thessaloniki. Pieces of embroidery were brought in for local women to work on, and they were paid on a piecework basis. For seven years this provided an important source of cash for Assiros families, until the firm's profits fell and it discontinued the practice.

37. Many women are still not permitted by their fathers or husbands to work outside the village, although approval is often given for employment within Assiros.

38. In 1951, the Greek government of Plastiras announced a new land-reform campaign. It intended to confiscate (appallotriosi) and to redistribute all lands in excess of 500 stremmata per family. The Assiros tsorbadjidhes embarked on a concerted letter-writing campaign to high government officials in the late 1950s, including the then prime minister, Konstantinos Karamanlis (himself a native of the Serres area). Many in Assiros claimed that local elite families in the village had asked Karamanlis to order a stop to the measuring of village plots intended for redistribution, and that Karamanlis agreed.

39. For details on dowry, upward mobility, and land fragmentation in Greece, see Friedl (1962). In the 1980s, PASOK-sponsored legislation abolished the institution of dowry. Today, when women inherit or receive property from their fathers at the time of marriage, they remain the sole owners of that property and can dispose of it as they please. This is in contrast to former legal rights over the ownership and disposal of dowry, the transfer or sale of which required the agreement and signature of the husband. For more on changes in gender relations in Greece under the PASOK era, see Pollis (1992).

40. Herzfeld (1985) argued that Greek legislation governing partible inheritance was not motivated by concern over land fragmentation but rather that such laws were derived from European notions of Hellenic "individuals" set against the "communism" of the Slavs and the oriental passivity of the "Asiatics." Partible inheritance, he concluded, reflected "the progressive domination by an ideologically 'European' and neo-classical elite over the rural peasantry" (Herzfeld 1985:180).

41. Property divisions included not only family land but also the rooms of a family's house. In some cases, additions were built onto existing homes and new, separate entrances were constructed for each new nuclear family unit emerging from the division process. If more resources were available, siblings sometimes built new houses on plots allocated to them in the occasional redistributions administered by the township. If less land were available but funds were sufficient, brothers might also build their new homes in the family's yard or an adjacent area. Parents in contemporary Assiros begin to transfer property to their children

as soon as they become old-age pensioners. Some now prepare legal wills in which they stipulate particular details for the division of their estate, outlining specific ratios, amounts, and even physical plots that each heir will receive, or other forms of property a child will inherit in lieu of land. Children with more formal education frequently receive less inheritance than other siblings. In most instances when there is no will specifying how the estate is to be divided, a man's surviving descendants (or in practice usually his sons) get together to agree on a division scheme. Daughters usually get a small share, referred to as a *miraz*, but this depended largely on the willingness of her brothers. Land disputes, mainly between brothers or between brothers and sister(s), are discussed freely by most respondents and are a popular topic in virtually all social circles and gatherings. Sometimes, in order to ensure an equitable division settlement, mediators have been brought in to arbitrate disputes. This was the case following the death of Stylianos Asteriou in 1956. Two years after his death, his sons decided to divide the family estate. The youngest brother (who had received an education in Italy, had married an Italian woman, and suspected he was going to receive less) and the only sister brought a mediator to the negotiation sessions which the siblings were conducting. When the agreement the Asteriou brothers reached between themselves proved inequitable to their sister, she sued them in court and obtained an equal share in the family estate through legal redress. Her brothers had protested her claims, citing the fact that she had received a large *rouha* (trousseau) when she married in 1931. She successfully contended that what she received as a *miraz* or *rouha* was insufficient in light of the size of the family estate.

42. Consider the case of the Velikas brothers, who had kept their large holdings together for many years. In the summer of 1992 it was rumored that they were finally preparing to divide their property. Village gossip maintained that the division was to be conducted "in true *tsorbadjis* fashion." Most villagers followed a common practice of equal partible inheritance, dividing plots between themselves and parceling out the fragmented remains to ensure equitable distribution of quality land. The two Velikas brothers, in contrast, were said to be working out an arrangement which would prevent fragmentation of the family's estate.

BIBLIOGRAPHY

Abbot, G. F. 1969. [1903] *Macedonian Folklore*. Thessaloniki: Institute for Balkan Studies, No. 110.

Anagnostopoulos-Paleologos, Thanos. 1987. "Neoklis Kazazis and the French Philhellenes during the Macedonian Struggle." In *O Makedonikos Agonas: Symposio*. Thessaloniki: Institute for Balkan Studies, No. 211, Museum of the Macedonian Struggle, pp. 259–71. [in Greek]

Anderson, Benedict 1983. *Imagined Communities: Reflections on the origin and spread of nationalism*. London: Verso.

Angelopoulos, Athanasios. 1973. *The Foreign Propagandas in the Polyani District in the Period 1870–1912*. Thessaloniki: Institute for Balkan Studies, No. 137. [in Greek]

Apergis, Stavros. 1978. *Re-formation of Agricultural Production*. Athens: Agricultural Bank of Greece, Studies on Agrarian Economy, No. 5. [in Greek]

Apostolski, Mihajlo, et al., eds. 1969. *From the Past of the Macedonian People*. Skopje: Skopje Radio and Television.

Appadurai, Arjun. 1981. "The Past as a Scarce Resource." *Man* 16(2):209–19.

Asdrahas, Spiros. 1978. *Mechanisms of Agrarian Economy in the Ottoman Period (15th-16th centuries)*. Athens: Themelio. [in Greek]

Augustinos, Jerry. 1981. "The Peasant Question and the Greek Intellectuals." *Bulletin of the Greek Historical and Ethnological Society* 24:229–43. [in Greek]

———. 1977. *Consciousness and History: Nationalist critics of Greek society, 1897–1914*. Boulder, Colo: East European Quarterly (distributed by Columbia University Press).

Bahcheli, Tozun. 1987. "The Muslim Turkish Community in Greece: Problems and prospects." *Journal: Institute of Muslim Minority Affairs* 8(1):109–20.

Bailey, F. G. 1957. *Caste and the Economic Frontier*. Manchester: Manchester University Press.

Balamaci, Nicholas S. 1991. "Can the Vlachs Write Their Own History?" *Journal of the Hellenic Diaspora* 17:9–36.

Baltas, Nikos K. 1986. *Analyzing the Demand for Agricultural Products: The case of grains.* Athens: Agricultural Bank of Greece, Studies on Agrarian Economy. [in Greek]

Baron, Salo W. 1947. *Modern Nationalism and Religion.* New York: Meridian Books.

Barth, F., ed. 1969. *Ethnic Groups and Boundaries: The social organization of culture difference.* Oslo and London: Allen and Unwin.

Belia, Eleni D. 1987. "The Educational Policy of the Greek State Towards Macedonia and the Macedonian Struggle." In *O Makedonikos Agonas: Symposio.* Thessaloniki: Institute for Balkan Studies, No. 211, Museum of the Macedonian Struggle, pp. 29–40. [in Greek]

Belić, Aleksander. 1919. *La Macédoine; études ethnographiques et politiques.* Paris: Blond et Gay. [in French]

Bhabha, Homi K. 1994. *The Location of Culture.* London and New York: Routledge.

Bitoski, Krste. 1981. "The Attitude of the Kingdom of Greece Toward Macedonia and the Macedonian Revolutionary Organization (1893–1903)." In *Macédoine: Articles d'Histoire Nationale.* Skopje: Institut d'Histoire Nationale, pp. 223–41.

Blu, Karen I. 1980. *The Lumbee Problem: The making of an American Indian people.* New York: Cambridge University Press.

Borza, Eugene N. 1990. *In the Shadow of Olympus: The emergence of Macedon.* Princeton: Princeton University Press.

Brailsford, H. N. 1906. *Macedonia: Its races and their future.* New York: Arno Press and the *New York Times.*

Braudel, Fernand. 1966. *The Mediterranean and the Mediterranean World in the Age of Philip II.* Vol. I. London: Harper Collins.

Campbell, John. 1964. *Honour, Family and Patronage.* Oxford: Clarendon Press.

Carnegie Endowment for International Peace. 1914. *Report of the International Commission to Inquire into the Causes and Conduct of the Balkan Wars.* Sofia: The "Balkan Question" Library, Book No. 1, Al Paskaleff and Company.

Cassimatis, Louis. 1988. *American Influence in Greece: 1917–1929.* Kent, Ohio: Kent State University Press.

Chakaloff, George, and Stanislav J. Shoomkoff. 1904. *The Macedonian Problem and Its Proper Solution.* Philadelphia: John C. Winston.

Chalkiopoulos, Athanasios. 1910. *Macedonia: Ethnological statistics of the Thessaloniki and Monastir Vilayets.* Athens. [in Greek]

Charanis, Peter. 1963. "How Greek Was the Byzantine Empire?" *Bucknell Review* 11(3):101–16.

Chatterjee, Partha. 1993. *The Nation and Its Fragments: Colonial and postcolonial histories.* Princeton: Princeton University Press.

Chatzikiriakou, Georgios. 1962. *Thoughts and Impressions from a Tour in Macedonia (1905–1906)*. Thessaloniki: Institute for Balkan Studies, No. 58. [in Greek]

Christoff, A. T. 1919. *The Truth about Bulgaria*. Kansas City.

Christowe, Stoyan. 1935. *Heroes and Assassins*. New York: Robert M. McBride.

Clammer, John. 1986. "Ethnicity and the Classification of Social Differences in Plural Societies: A perspective from Singapore." In *Ethnic Identities and Prejudices: Perspectives from the third world*, Anand Paranjpe, ed. Leiden: Brill, pp. 9–23.

Clogg, Richard. 1979. *A Short History of Modern Greece*. Cambridge: Cambridge University Press.

Cohen, Abner. 1981. "Variable in Ethnicity." In *Ethnic Change*, Charles Keyes, ed. Seattle: University of Washington Press, pp. 306–31.

Comaroff, John, and Jean Comaroff. 1992. *Ethnography and the Historical Imagination*. Boulder, Colo: Westview Press.

Corrigan, Paul, and Derek Sayer. 1985. *The Great Arch: English state formation as cultural revolution*. Oxford and New York: Basil Blackwell.

Cowan, Jane K. 1990. *Dance and the Body Politic in Northern Greece*. Princeton: Princeton University Press.

Curtis, William E. 1911. *Around the Black Sea*. New York: Hodder and Stoughton.

Cvijić, J. 1918. *La Péninsule Balkanique Géographie Humaine*. Paris. [in French]

Danforth, Loring. 1995. *The Macedonian Conflict: Ethnic nationalism in a transnational world*. Princeton: Princeton University Press.

———. 1989. *Firewalking and Religious Healing: The Anastenaria of northern Greece and the American firewalking movement*. Princeton: Princeton University Press.

de Certeau, Michel. 1984. *The Practice of Everyday Life*. Trans. Steven Rendall. Berkeley: University of California Press.

Delta, Pinelopi. 1988 [1937]. *In the Swamp's Secrets*. Athens: Estia Bookstore. [in Greek]

Diamandouros, P. Nikiforos. 1983. "Hellenism and Greekness." In *Hellenism-Greekness: Ideological and vital axes of modern Greek society*, D. Tsaousis, ed. Athens: Estia, pp. 51–58. [in Greek]

Dimitriadis, Vasilis. 1980. "Taxation Categories of the Thessaloniki Villages During the Ottoman Period." *Makedonika* 20:375–459. [in Greek]

Dimitsas, Margaritis. 1879. *History of Macedonia from Ancient Times until The Ottoman Conquest*. Athens: Palamidis Printing. [in Greek]

Dirks, Nicholas B. 1993. *The Hollow Crown: Ethnohistory of an Indian Kingdom*. 2d ed. Ann Arbor: University of Michigan Press.

Dirks, Nicholas, Geoff Eley, and Sherry Ortner, eds. 1994. *Culture, Power, History: A reader in contemporary social theory*. Princeton: Princeton University Press.

Douglas, Mary. 1975. *Implicit Meanings*. London: Routledge and Kegan Paul.

Dragoumis, Ion. 1992. *Martyrs' and Heroes' Blood*. Athens: Nea Thesis.

Drettas, George. 1985. "Questions de Vampirisme." *Etudes Rurales* 97/98:201–18. [in French]

Drukheim, Emile. 1965 [1915]. *The Elementary Forms of the Religious Life*. New York: The Free Press.

Epstein, Arnold, L. 1978. *Ethnos and Identity: Three studies in ethnicity*. London: Tavistock.

Evrygenis, Dimitrios I. 1961. *Ion Dragoumis and the Macedonian Struggle*. Thessaloniki: Institute for Balkan Studies, No. 41. [in Greek]

Fallers, Lloyd A. 1974. *The Social Anthropology of the Nation-State*. Chicago: Aldine.

Faubion, James D. 1993. *Modern Greek Lessons: A primer in historical constructivism*. Princeton: Princeton University Press.

Fischer-Galati, Stephen. 1972–73. "The Internal Macedonian Revolutionary Organization: Its significance in 'Wars of National Liberation.' " *East European Quarterly* 1(4):454–72.

Fox, Richard. 1990. "Introduction." In *National Ideologies and the Production of National Cultures*, Richard Fox, ed. Washington, D.C.: American Ethnological Society Monograph Series, No. 2.

Frazee, Charles A. 1969. *The Orthodox Church and Independent Greece, 1821–1852*. London: Cambridge University Press.

Freud, Sigmund. 1960 [1905]. *Jokes and Their Relation to the Unconscious*. London: W. W. Norton.

Fried, Morton. 1975. *The Notion of the Tribe*. Menlo Park: Cummings.

Friedl, Ernestine. 1962. *Vasilika: A village in modern Greece*. New York: Holt, Rinehart and Winston.

Friedman, Victor A. 1986. "Linguistics, Nationalism and Literary Languages: A Balkan Perspective." In *The Real World Linguist: Linguistic applications in the 1980's*, U. Raskin and P. Bjarkman, eds. Norwood, N.J.: Ablex, pp. 287–305.

Geertz, Clifford. 1973. *The Interpretation of Cultures*. New York: Basic Books.

Gellner, Ernest. 1983. *Nations and Nationalism*. Ithaca: Cornell University Press.

Georgevitch, T. R. 1918. *Macedonia*. New York: Macmillan.

Gibb, H. A. R., and H. Bowen. 1950. *Islamic Society and the West: A study of the impact of Western civilization on Moslem culture in the Near East*. 2 Vols. London: Oxford University Press.

Glazer, Nathan, and Daniel P. Moynihan. 1970. *Beyond the Melting Pot: The Negroes, Puerto Ricans, Jews, Italians, and Irish of New York City*. Cambridge: Massachusetts Institute of Technology Press.

Goody, Jack. 1958. *The Developmental Cycle in Domestic Groups*. Cambridge: Cambridge University Press.

Goody Jack, and S. J. Tambiah. 1973. *Bride wealth and Dowry*. Cambridge: Cambridge University Press, Cambridge Papers in Social Anthropology, No. 7.

Gounaris, Basil C. 1990. "Parliamentary Deputies and Kapetanareyi: Clientelistic relations in postwar Macedonia." *Ellinika* 41:313–35, 1990.

———. 1989. "Railway Construction and Labour Availability in Macedonia in the Late Nineteenth Century." *Byzantine and Modern Greek Studies* 13:139–58.

———. 1987. "The Macedonian Struggle Towards Its End: Attempts for re-organization and new directions." In *O Makedonikos Agonas: Symposio*. Thessaloniki: Institute for Balkan Studies, No. 211, Museum of the Macedonian Struggle, pp. 113–24. [in Greek]

Greenfeld, Liah. 1992. *Nationalism: Five Roads to Modernity*. Cambridge: Harvard University Press.

Guboglo, M. 1970. "On the Subject of the Origin of the Sarakatsani." *Bulletin of Slavic Bibliography* 7(27):103–14. [in Greek]

Haarland, Gunnar. 1969. "Economic Determinants in Ethnic Processes." In *Ethnic Groups and Boundaries,* F. Barth, ed. Boston: Little, Brown.

Halpern, Joel, and Barbara Kerewsky-Halpern. 1986 [1972]. *A Serbian Village in Historical Perspective*. Prospect Heights, Il.: Waveland Press.

Halstead, Paul. 1990. "Waste Not, Want Not: Traditional responses to crop failure in Greece." *Rural History* 1(2):147–64.

Hammel, Eugene A. 1972. "Zadruga as Process." In *Household and Family in Past Times,* P. Laslett and R. Wall, eds., pp. 335–73. Cambridge: Cambridge University Press.

———. 1968. *Alternative Social Structures and Ritual Relations in the Balkans*. Englewood Cliffs: Prentice-Hall.

Haskell, Edward B. 1919. *American Influence in Bulgaria*. New York: The Missionary Review of the World.

———. 1918a. "The Truth about Bulgaria." *Alumni Magazine,* Oberlin College, November.

———. 1918b. "Bulgaria and Macedonia: A study of the vexed problems of nationality in Macedonia and the Dobrudja by a missionary who knows the Balkan peoples well." *Springfield Republican,* 8 November 1918, Oberlin, Ohio.

Hechter, Michael. 1975. *Internal Colonialism: The Celtic fringe in British national development, 1536–1966*. Berkeley: University of California Press.

Herzfeld, Michael. 1991a. *A Place in History: Social and monumental time in a Cretan town*. Princeton: Princeton University Press.

———. 1991b. "Silence, Submission, and Subversion: Toward a poetics of womanhood." In *Contested Identities: Gender and kinship in modern Greece,* Peter Loizos and Evthymios Papataxiarchis, eds. Princeton: Princeton University Press, pp. 79–97.

———. 1985. " 'Law' and 'Custom': Ethnography *of* and *in* Greek national identity." *Journal of Modern Greek Studies* 3(2):167–85.

———. 1982a. *Ours Once More: Folklore, ideology and the making of modern Greece.* Austin: University of Texas Press.

———. 1982b. "When Exceptions Define the Rules: Greek baptismal names and the negotiation of identity." *Journal of Anthropological Research* 38:288–302.

Hirschon, Renée. 1989. *Heirs of the Greek Catastrophe: The social life of Asia Minor refugees in Piraeus.* Oxford: Clarendon.

Hobsbawm, Eric J. 1990. *Nations and Nationalism Since 1780: Programme, myth, reality.* Cambridge: Cambridge University Press.

———. 1981. *Bandits.* New York: Pantheon Books.

———. 1959. *Primitive Rebels: Studies in archaic forms of social movement in the 19th and 20th centuries.* New York: W. W. Norton.

Hobsbawm, Eric J., and Terence Ranger, eds. 1983. *The Invention of Tradition.* Cambridge: Cambridge University Press.

Inalcik, Halil. 1985. *Studies in Ottoman Social and Economic History.* London: Variorum Reprints.

Inter-Allied Commission in Eastern Macedonia. 1919. *An Account of Bulgarian Occupation: Report of the Inter-Allied Commission on Eastern Macedonia.* London: George S. Vellonis.

Jelavich, Barbara. 1983. *History of the Balkans: Twentieth century.* Cambridge: Cambridge University Press.

Just, Roger. 1989. "Triumph of the Ethnos." In *History and Ethnicity,* Elizabeth Tonkin, Malcolm Chapman, and Maryon McDonald, eds. Association of Social Anthropologists Monographs, No. 27. London: Routledge and Kegan Paul, pp. 71–78.

Kabasakalis, Dimitrios. 1974. *The History of Baltza (Melissohori-Thessaloniki).* Thessaloniki. [in Greek]

Kamarinou, Lili. 1977. *The Accumulation of Agricultural Surplus in Greece.* Athens: Nea Sinora. [in Greek]

Karakasidou, Anastasia. 1996. "Women of the Family, Women of the Nation: National enculturation among Slavic speakers in northwestern Greece." *Women's Studies International Forum* 19(1–2, January–April):99–110.

———. 1995a. "Protocol and Pageantry: National celebrations in northern Greece." Paper presented at the 94th Annual Meetings of the American Anthropological Association (AAA), Washington, D.C., 15–19 November.

———. 1995b. "Vestiges of the Ottoman Past: Muslims under Siege in Greek Thrace." *Cultural Survival Quarterly* 19(2):71–75.

———. 1994a. "Cultural Illegitimacy in Modern Greece: The Slavo-Macedonian 'non-minority.'" Paper presented at the workshop "Minorities in Greece," St. Anthony's College, Oxford University, 5–8 January 1994; to appear in *Ethnic and Religious Minorities in Greece,* Richard Clogg, ed. (forthcoming).

———. 1994b. "Sacred Scholars, Profane Advocates: Intellectuals molding national consciousness in Greece." *Identities: Global Studies in Culture and Power* 1(1):35–61.

————. 1993a. "Fellow Travelers, Separate Roads: The Greek communist party and the Macedonian question." *East European Quarterly* (Winter) 27(4): 453–77.

————. 1993b. "Politicizing Culture: Negating Macedonian ethnicity in northern Greece." *Journal of Modern Greek Studies* 11(1):1–28.

————. 1992. "Fields of Wheat, Hills of Shrub: Agrarian development and nation-building in northern Greece," Ph.D dissertation, Department of Anthropology, Columbia University.

Karapatakis, Kostas. 1960. *Weddings in Old Times (Folklore of the Grevena region)*. Anthens. [in Greek]

Karathanasis, Athanasios. 1990. *Essays About Macedonia: Studies and articles about the intellectual activities and life in Macedonia*. Thessaloniki: Kyriakidis Brothers. [in Greek]

Karavidas, K. D. 1931. *Agrotika: A comparative study*. Athens: Papazisis. [in Greek]

Kargakos, Sarandos. 1993a. "Hellenism and Cannibalism." *Ikonomikos Tahidromos*, 1 July 1993, pp. 44–45. [in Greek]

————. 1993b. "What Does the Defense of Karakasidou Mean?" *Ikonomikos Tahidromos*, 30 September 1993, pp. 33–34. [in Greek]

————. 1993c. "Unprecedented International (and not only) Mobilization for the Defense of the Anthropologist Mrs. Anastasia Karakasidou." *Ikonomikos Tahidromos*, 16 December 1993, pp. 35–38. [in Greek]

Karpat, Kemal. 1982. "*Millets* and Nationality: The roots of the incongruity of nation and state in the post-Ottoman era." In *Christians and Jews in the Ottoman Empire*, vol. 1, *The central lands*, B. Braude and B. Lewis eds. New York and London: Holmes and Meier, pp. 141–69.

Kazasis, Neocles. 1904. *L'Hellenisme et la Macédoine*. Paris: Imprimerie de la Renaissance Latine. [in French]

Keesing, Roger. 1986. "The Young Dick Attack: Oral and documentary history on the colonial frontier." *Ethnohistory* 33:268–92.

Kepetzis. 1908. "On the Recent Developments in Macedonian Matters." *Macedonian Almanac* 31–40. [in Greek]

Keramidziev, Mih. 1951. *The Aegean Macedonia Under Greek Sovereignty*. Skopje: Institute of National History. [in Macedonian]

Kettani, M. Ali. 1980. "Muslims in Southern Europe." *Journal: Institute of Muslim Minority Affairs* 2(1):145–57.

Keyes, Charles, F., ed. 1981. *Ethnic Change*. Seattle: University of Washington Press.

Kiril, Patriarkh Balgarski. 1969. *The Bulgarian Exarchate in the Region of Adrianople and Macedonia after the War of Liberation. 1877–1878*. Sofia. [in Bulgarian]

Kitromilidis, Paschalis. 1989. " 'Imagined Communities' and the Origins of the National Question in the Balkans." *European History Quarterly* 19(2):149–92.

Kofos, Evangelos. 1992. "Ideological Origins of Slavo-Macedonianism: Their impact on the current phase of the Macedonian Question." *Mnimosini* 11:426–40. [in Greek]

———. 1991. "National Heritage and National Identity in Nineteenth Century and Twentieth Century Macedonia." Hellenic Foundation for Defense and Foreign Policy (Athens), Occasional Paper.

———. 1987. "The Macedonian Struggle in Yugoslavian Historiography." In *O Makedonikos Agonas: Symposio.* Thessaloniki: Institute for Balkan Studies, No. 211, Museum of the Macedonian Struggle, pp. 279–317. [in Greek]

———. 1975. *Greece and the Eastern Crisis, 1875–1878.* Thessaloniki: Institute for Balakan Studies, No. 148.

———. 1964. *Nationalism and Communism in Macedonia.* Thessaloniki: Institute for Balkan Studies.

Koliopoulos, Ioannis. 1987. "The Macedonia of Ion Dragoumis: Thoughts from his personal diary." In *O Makedonikos Agonas: Symposio.* Thessaloniki: Institute for Balkan Studies, No. 211, Museum of the Macedonian Struggle, pp. 153–60. [in Greek]

———. 1980. "About Social and Other Bandits in Modern Greece." *Bulletin of the Greek Historical and Ethnological Society* 23:422–36. [in Greek]

Koliševski, Lazar. 1959. *Macedonian National Question.* Beograd: Edition Jugoslavija.

Kontoyiannis, P. K. 1911. "Aivati." *Macedonian Almanac* 4:241–54. [in Greek]

Kostis, Kostas. 1987. *Agrarian Economy and the Agricultural Bank: Facets of the Greek economy in the interwar period (1919–1928).* Athens: Educational Foundation of the National Bank of Greece. [in Greek]

Kotsakis, Kostas. 1986. "The Langadhas Basin Intensive Survey, First Preliminary Report of the 1986 Season." Manuscript.

Krader, Lawrence. 1963. *Social Organization of the Mongol-Turkish Pastoralist Nomads.* The Hague: Mouton.

Kussmaul, Ann. 1981. *Servants in Husbandry in Early Modern England.* Cambridge: Cambridge University Press.

Kyriakidis, Stilpon. 1955. *The Northern Ethnological Boundaries of Hellenism.* Thessaloniki: Institute for Balkan Studies, No. 5. [in Greek]

———. 1941–52. "Byzantine Studies VII: Momtsilos and his state." *Madedonika* 2:332–45. [in Greek]

Ladas, S. P. 1932. *The Exchanges of Minorities: Bulgaria, Greece and Turkey.* New York: Macmillan.

Laiou-Thomadakis, Angeliki E. 1977. *Peasant Society in the Late Byzantine Empire: A social and demographic study.* Princeton: Princeton University Press.

Landau, Jacob M. 1981. *Pan-Turkism in Turkey: A study in irredentism.* Hamden: Archon.

League of Nations. 1926. *Greeks Refugee Settlement.* Geneva.

Lefort, Jacques. 1986. *Paysages de Macédoine: Leurs caractères, leur évolution à travers les documents et les récits des voyageurs.* Paris: Travaux et mémoires du centre de recherches d'histoire et civilisation de Byzance. Collège de France: Monographies 3. [in French]

Loukas, Asterios. 1981, *Macedonia: Wedding customs and songs in Liti.* Thessaloniki. [in Greek]

Lowenthal, David. 1985. *The Past Is a Foreign Country.* Cambridge: Cambridge University Press.

Makedoniki Zoi. 1988. 264:22–23. [in Greek]

McGowan, Bruce. 1981. *Economic Life in Ottoman Europe: Taxation, trade and the struggle for land, 1600–1800.* Cambridge: Cambridge University Press.

McGrew, William W. 1985. *Land and Revolution in Modern Greece, 1800–1881: The transition in the tenure and exploitation of land from Ottoman rule to independence.* Kent, Ohio: Kent State University Press.

McNeill, William H. 1957. *Greece: American Aid in Action, 1947–1956.* New York: The Twentieth Century Fund.

Martis, Nikolaos. 1984. *The Falsification of Macedonian History.* Athens: Distributed by Evroekdotiki.

Marx, Karl. 1977 [1898]. *The Eighteenth Brumaire of Louis Bonaparte.* Moscow: Progress Publishers.

Mavrogordators, George. 1983a. "The *Dihasmos* as a Crisis of Greek Integration." In *Hellinismos-Hellinikotita,* D. Tasousis, ed. Athens: Estia, pp. 69–78. [in Greek]

———. 1983b. *Stillborn Republic: Social coalitions and party strategies in Greece, 1922–1936.* Berkeley: University of California Press.

Mazarakis-Ainian, I. K. 1989. "The Volunteer Scout Brigades During the Balkan Wars, 1912–1913." *Bulletin of the Historical and Ethnological Society of Greece* 32:183–228. [in Greek]

Moisidis, Andonis. 1986. *Agricultural Society in Modern Greece: Production and social structure in greek agricultural (1950–1980).* Athens: Institute of Mediterranean Studies. [in Greek]

Moore, Frederick. 1906. *The Balkan Trail.* New York: Macmillan.

Moskoff, Kostis. 1964. *Thessaloniki 1700–1912: The cutting edge of the mercantile city.* Athens. [in Greek]

Moutaftsieva, Vera. 1990 [1962]. *Agrarian Relations in the Ottoman Empire in the Fifteenth and Sixteenth Centuries.* Athens: Poreia. [in Greek]

Mouzelis, Nikos. 1978–79. "Peasant Agriculture, Productivity and the Laws of Capitalist Development: A reply to Vergopoulos." *The Journal of Peasant Studies* 6:351–57.

Nakratzas, Georgios. 1988. *The Close Ethnological Relationship of Modern Day Greeks, Bulgarians and Turks: Macedonia-Thrace.* Thessaloniki. [in Greek]

National Statistics Bureau. 1962. *Distribution of the Country's Lands on the Basis of Their Use.* Athens. [in Greek]

Natsas, Ch. 1953. *The San Stefano Treaty and Hellenism.* Thessaloniki: Society of Macedonian Studies. [in Greek]

Natsis, Konstantinos I. 1990. *Folklore Elements and Traditional Dances in the Florina Prefecture.* Florina: Aristotelis Cultural Association. [in Greek]

Nikov, Petar. 1929. *Renaissance of the Bulgarian People: Ecclesiastico-national struggles and achievement.* Sofia. [in Bulgarian]

Pamuk, Sevket. 1987. *The Ottoman Empire and European Capitalism, 1820–1913: Trade, investment, and production.* New York: Cambridge University Press.

Pandevski, Manol D. 1978. *Macedonia and the Macedonians in the Eastern Crisis.* Skopje: Macedonian Review.

Papadopoulos, Stefanos I. 1987. "Education in Macedonia and Her Contribution in the Development of the Preconditions for the Success of the Macedonian Struggle." In *O Makedonikos Agonas: Symposio.* Thessaloniki: Institute for Balkan Studies, no. 211, Museum of the Macedonian Struggle, pp. 21–27. [in Greek]

Papaioannou, Dimitris K. 1991. *The Politics of Bishops During the Ottoman Period.* Athens. [in Greek]

Paparrigopoulos, Konstantinos. 1983 [1860–72]. *History of the Greek Nation: Ten illustrated volumes.* Athens: Faros Publishers. [in Greek]

———. 1843. *About the Settlement of Some Slavic Tribes in the Peloponnese.* Athens: Library of Historical Studies, No. 209. [in Greek]

Papastathis, Charalambos. 1987. "The Church and the Macedonian Struggle." In *O Makedonikos Agonas: Symposio.* Thessaloniki: Institute for Balkan Studies, No. 211, Museum of the Macedonian Struggle, pp. 63–70. [in Greek]

Papathanasi-Mousiopoulou, Kalliopi. 1982–83. "Song-Verses of a Cretan Partisan of the Macedonian Struggle." *Laographia* 33:461–64. [in Greek]

Pearson, R. 1983. *National Minorities in Eastern Europe, 1848–1945.* London: Macmillan.

Pelagidis, Efstathios. 1994. *The Settlement of Refugees in Western Macedonia (1923–1930).* Thessaloniki: Kyriakidis Brothers. [in Greek]

Pentzopoulos, D. 1962. *The Balkan Exchange of Minorities and Its Impact Upon Greece.* Paris and the Hague: Mouton.

Perry, Duncan M. 1988. *The Politics of Terror: The Macedonian liberation movements, 1893–1903.* Durham: Duke University Press.

Petropoulos, D. A. 1943–44. "Traditions of Cooperation and Mutual Help." *Annual of the Folklore Archives* 5:59–85. [in Greek]

Plastiras, Kostas N. 1987. "Literature in Thessaloniki During the Years of the Macedonian Struggle." In *O Makedonikos Agonas: Symposio.* Thessaloniki: Institute for Balkan Studies, No. 211, Museum of the Macedonian Struggle, pp. 243–58. [in Greek]

Pollis, Adamantia. 1992. "Gender and Social Change in Greece: The role of women." In *The Greek Socialist Experiment: Papandreou's Greece, 1981–1989.* Th. Kariotis, ed. New York: Pella.

The Population of Macedonia. 1905 Evidence of the Christian Schools. London: Ede, Allom and Townsend.

Poulton, Hugh. 1991. *The Balkans: Minorities and States in Conflict.* London: Minority Rights Group.

Pribichevich, Stoyan. 1982. *Macedonia, Its People and History.* University Park: Pennsylvania State University Press.

Pro-Macedonia. 1927. *The Macedonian Slavs: Their national character and struggles.* Indianapolis: Central Committee of the Union of the Macedonian Political Organization of the United States of America and Canada.

Psomiadis, Harry. 1968. *The Eastern Question: The last phase; A study in Greek-Turkish diplomacy.* Chicago, Distributed by Argonaut Inc., Publishers.

Quataert, Donald. 1983. *Social Disintegration and Popular Resistance in the Ottoman Empire, 1881–1908.* New York: New York University Press.

Radcliffe-Brown, A. R. 1952. *Structure and Function in Primitive Society.* New York: The Free Press.

Radeff, Simeon. 1918. *La Macédoine et la Renaissance Bulgare au XIXe Siècle.* Sofia: Edition de l'Union des Savants, gens des Lettres et Artistes Bulgares. Imprimerie de la cour Royale. [in French]

Raikin, Spas. 1984. "Nationalism and the Bulgarian Orthodox Church." In *Religion and Nationalism in Soviet and East European Politics,* Pedro Ramet, ed. Durham: Duke University Press, pp. 187–206.

Raktivan, Konstantinos. 1951. *Documents and Notes of the First Greek Government of Macedonia (1912–1913).* Thessaloniki: Publications of the Society for Macedonian Studies, No. 12. [in Greek]

Rheubottom, David B. 1976. "The Saint's Feast and Skopska Crna Goran Social Structure." *Man* 11(1):18–34.

Roosen, Eugeen. 1989. *Creating Ethnicity: The process of ethnogenesis.* Newbury Park: Sage.

Rothbard. 1992. *Sunday Avgi,* March 1992. [in Greek]

Sahlins, Peter. 1989. *Boundaries: The making of France and Spain in the Pyrenees.* Berkeley: University of California Press.

Salamone, Frank A. 1986. "Colonialism and the Emergence of Fulani Identity." In *Ethnic Identities and Prejudices,* Anand Paranje, ed. Leiden: Brill, pp. 61–70.

Sarandis, Theodoros. 1987. *The Conspiracy Against Macedonia.* Athens. [in Greek]

Scott, James C. 1985. *Weapons of the Weak: Everyday forces of peasant resistance.* New Haven: Yale University Press.

Segalen, Martine. 1986. *Historical Anthropology of the Family.* Cambridge: Cambridge University Press.

Sigalas, A. 1940. "Patriarchal Deeds, Firmans, and Other Documents." *Makedonika* 1:277–323. [in Greek]

Singleton, Fred. 1976. *Twentieth Century Yugoslavia.* New York: Columbia University Press.

Skouteri-Didaskalou, Nora. 1991. *Anthropology and the Women's Issue.* Athens: Politis. [in Greek]

Smith, Anthony D. 1987. *The Ethnic Origins of Nations*. Oxford: Basil Black-well.

Smith, Arthur D. Howden. 1908. *Fighting the Turk in the Balkans: An American's adventures with the Macedonian revolutionists*. New York and London: The Knickerbocker Press and G. P. Putnam's Sons.

Souliotis-Nikolaidis, Athanasios. 1993 [1959] *The Macedonian Struggle: The "Organization Thessaloniki." 1906–1908, memoires*. Thessaloniki: Institute for Balkan Studies, No. 28. [in Greek]

Sowards, Steven W. 1989. *Austria's Policy of Macedonian Reform*. Boulder, Colo.: East European Monographs (distributed by Columbia University Press).

St. Elrich, Vera. 1966. *Family in Transition: A Study of 300 Yugoslav villages*. Princeton: Princeton University Press.

Stavrianos, L. S. 1959. *The Balkans Since 1453*. New York: Rinehart and Company.

Stewart, Charles. 1991. "Syncretism as a Dimension of Nationalist Discourse in Modern Greece." In *Syncretism/Anti-Syncretism: The politics of religious synthesis*, Charles Stewart and Rosalind Shaw, eds. London and New York: Routledge.

Stoianovich, Trajan. 1960. "The Conquering Balkan Orthodox Merchant." *Journal of Economic History* Vol. 20, pp. 269–73.

Strukova, Xenia. 1971. "Concerning the Case of the Socio-Economic Condition of the Thessaloniki Sanjak During the Seventh Decade of the 19th Century." In *Bulletin of Yugoslavian Bibliography* 8(1):75–85. [in Greek]

Svolopoulos, Konstantinos. 1987. "The Decision for Organizing the Armed Struggle." In *O Makedonikos Agonas: Symposio*. Thessaloniki: Institute for Balkan Studies, No. 211, Museum of the Macedonian Struggle, pp. 51–61. [in Greek]

Tashkovski, Dragan. 1976. *The Macedonian Nation*. Skopje: Nasha Kniga.

Theodoritos, Nevrokopiou. 1941–52. "Some Historical Information Regarding the Local Orthodox Greek Community since the Appearance of the Bulgarian Issue." *Makedonika* 2:414–60. [in Greek]

Todorov, N., and V. Trajkov. 1971. "The Greek Revolution of 1821–1829 and the Bulgarians." *Etudes Balkaniques* 1:3–26. [in Bulgarian]

Tosheff, Andrew. 1932. *The Bulgarian-Serbian Debate*. Sofia: The Royal Printing Office.

Tounda-Fergadi, Areti. 1986. *Greek-Bulgarian Minorities: Protocol of Politis-Kalvov (1924–1925)*. Thessaloniki: Institute for Balkan Studies, No. 201. [in Greek]

Tozis, Yiannis A. 1941–52. "Siatistina." *Makedonika* 2:311–31. [in Greek]

Trajanovski, Alexandar. 1981. "The Educational and Political Activity of the Exarchate in Macedonia in the First Few Years Before and After the Formation of the Secret Macedonian-Odrin Revolutionary Organization." In *Macédoine: Articles d'Histoire*. Skopje: Institut d'Histoire National, pp. 187–98.

Tsanoff, Vladimir A., ed. 1919. *Reports and Letters of American Missionaries: Referring to the distribution of nationalities in the former provinces of European Turkey, 1858–1918.* Sofia.

Tsoukalas, Konstantinos. 1977. *Dependence and Reproduction: The social role of the educational mechanisms in Greece (1830–1922).* Athens: Themelio. [in Greek]

Tsoumas, Th., and D. Tasioulas. 1986. *Land Tenure and Land Use of Agricultural Lands in Greece.* Athens: Agricultural Bank of Greece. [in Greek]

Vakalopoulos, Apostolos. 1987. "The Macedonian Struggle (1904–1908) as the Best Phase of the Struggles of the Greeks for Macedonia." In *O Makedonikos Agonas: Symposio.* Thessaloniki: Institute for Balkan Studies, No. 211, Museum of the Macedonian Struggle, pp. 1–19. [in Greek]

———. 1970. *Origins of the Greek Nation: The Byzantine period, 1204–1461.* New Brunswick: Rutgers University Press.

Vakalopoulos, Konstantinos. 1988a. *Modern History of Macedonia, 1830–1912: From the birth of the Greek state until the liberation.* Thessaloniki: Barbounakis.

———. 1988b. "Ethnological Map of Macedonia." *Kathimerini,* July 17. [in Greek]

———. 1987. *Macedonia and Turkey, 1830–1878.* Thessaloniki: Vanias. [in Greek]

———. 1983. "Forms of Bandit Activities in Macedonia After the 1878 Revolution." *Valkanika Simmikta* 2:125–38. [in Greek]

Vardaris. (Anonymous) 1993. "Modern Efialtes Hit Macedonia!! The Treachery Deepens, While the Number of Greeks Decreases." *Vardaris* 106, 10 November 1993, pp. 3–5. [in Greek]

Vasdravellis, Ioannis K. 1941–52. "Historical Archives of the Holy Court of Thessaloniki." *Makedonika* 2:89–128. [in Greek]

Vayiakakos, Dikeos B. 1987. "The Influence of Macedonian Struggle in Mani." In *O Makedonikos Agonas: Symposio.* Thessaloniki: Institute for Balkan Studies, No. 211, Museum of the Macedonian Struggle, pp. 209–30. [in Greek]

Verdery, Katherine. 1991. *National Ideology Under Socialism: Identity and cultural politics in Ceausescu's Romania.* Berkeley: University of California Press.

———. 1983. *Transylvanian Villagers: Three centuries of political, economic, and ethnic change.* Berkeley: University of California Press.

Vergopoulos, Kostas. 1978. *Nationalism and Economic Development: Greece in the interwar period.* Athens: Exantas. [in Greek]

———. 1977–78. "Capitalism and Peasant Productivity." *Journal of Peasant Studies* 5:446–65.

———. 1975. *The Agrarian Problem in Greece: The issue of the social incorporation of agriculture.* Athens: Exantas. [in Greek]

Vermeulen, Hans. 1984. "Greek Cultural Dominance among the Orthodox Population of Macedonia during the Last Period of Ottoman Rule." In *Cul-*

tural Dominance in the Mediterranean Area, A. Blok and H. Driessen, eds. Nijmegen: Katholieke Universiteit.

Vincent, Joan. 1993. "Ethnicity and the State in Northern Ireland." In *Ethnicity and the State,* Judith Toland, ed. New Brunswick: Transaction Publishers.

——. 1982. *Teso in Transformation.* Berkeley: University of California Press.

——. 1974. "The Structuring of Ethnicity." *Human Organization* 33(4):375–79.

Von Mach, Richard. 1907. *The Bulgarian Exarchate: Its history and the extent of its authority in Turkey.* London: T. Fisher Unwin; Neuchatel: Attinger Freres.

Vouri, Sofia. 1992. *Education and Nationalism in the Balkans: The case study of northwestern Macedonia, 1870–1904.* Athens: Paraskinio. [in Greek]

Vucinich, Wayne S. 1965. *The Ottoman Empire, Its Record and Legacy.* Princeton, N.J.: Van Nostrand.

——. 1962. "The Nature of Balkan Society Under Ottoman Rule." *Slavic Review* 21(4):597–616.

Wardle, Ken. 1989. "Excavations at Assiros, 1988: A preliminary report." *British School of Archaeology* 84:447–63.

Weber, Eugen. 1976. *Peasants into Frenchmen: The modernization of rural France, 1870–1914.* Stanford: Stanford University Press.

Weber, Max. 1968 [1925]. *Economy and Society.* Tubingen: J. C. B. Mohr.

Whitman, Lois. 1992. *Destroying Ethnic Identity: The Turks of Greece.* New York: Helsinki Watch Report (Division of Human Rights Watch).

Wilkinson, H. R. 1951. *Maps and Politics: A review of the ethnographic cartography of Macedonia:* Liverpool: At the University.

Winnifrith, Tom J. 1987. *The Vlachs: The history of a Balkan people.* New York: St. Martin's.

Zdraveva, Milka. 1981. "Territorial Changes in the Balkan Penninsula After the Berlin Congress and Their Effect on the Economic Life of Macedonia." In *Macédoine: Articles d'Histoire.* Skopje: Institut d'Histoire Nationale, pp. 177–86.

Zisis, Kostas I. 1990. *Education During the Ottoman Occupation in the Region of Agrafa.* Athens: Historical Publications, Vasilopoulos. [in Greek]

Zoroyiannidis, Konstantinos. 1992 [orig. 1975]. *Diary of Marches and War Incidents, 1912–1913.* Thessaloniki: Institute for Balkan Studies, No. 154. [in Greek]

INDEX

Kambili pasturelands, 181, 182
Kapetan Thanasis, 101, 121
karaghoghis, 64
Karakasidou, 22, 187, 189, 190,
194, 197, 205, 229, 231
Karamagiris, 201, 202, 203
Karamalidhes, 148
Karapatakis, 193
Karavidas, 46
Kargakos, 229–31
Karterai, 123, 156
Kastoria, 127
Katharevousa, 96, 97, 128
Kato Seli, 114
Kavala, 229
kazas (districts), 43
Kazazis, Neokles, 102
kefalohoria ("head" or "free" vil-
lages), 47
kehayiadhes, 59
Kemal Attaturk, 144
Kepetzis, 102
Keramidziev, 17
Kerim *effendi*, 55
Keyes, 20
khans (inns), 49, 55, 75
Kilkis, 12, 59, 115, 116, 118, 124,
127, 130, 211, 212, 223
Kilkis, Battle of, 127
King Paul II, 207
Kioutsouk Stanbul, 33, 35
kiradjidhes, 64
Kiril, 15
Kitromilidis, 79, 84, 85
Kofos, 15, 93, 96, 101
Kolhikon (Balaftsa) 40, 51, 65, 119,
121, 194
Koliopoulos, 90
Koliševski, 16, 17
Kondos, 61, 62, 63, 69, 72, 73, 120
Kontoyiannis, 53
Koromilas, Lambros, 103
Koroupis, Fotios, 114, 117
Kostis, 180
kourban, kourbani, 195, 196, 197
Koutsovlach semipastoralists, 5
Krader, 24
Kresna, 124

Krithia, 143, 153, 154, 157, 158,
159, 211, 212
Krusovo, 101
Kukush (Kilkis), 12, 40, 58, 116,
118, 120, 126, 131
Kyriakidis, 15, 133, 187

Ladas, 142
Ladino-speaking, 10
Lahanas, 124, 184, 201, 211
Lahanas, Battle of, 124
Lake Aghios Vasilios (Besik-Giol),
33, 80, 112
land redistribution, 168, 178, 169,
171, 180, 181, 182, 237
Land Redistribution Program, 161,
167
Langadhas, 5, 12, 40, 42, 49, 57,
58, 65, 70, 74, 93, 110, 112,
115, 116, 121, 128, 131, 132,
151, 154, 162, 168, 173, 177,
183, 187, 190, 202, 206, 210,
229
Langadhas basin, 1, 9, 23, 44, 47,
50, 53, 58, 70, 80, 93, 101, 103,
105, 106, 119, 135, 141, 146,
152, 202, 213, 220, 222, 227
Langadhas district, 114, 164
Langadhas, District Director
(*Eparch*) of, 112, 164, 207
Langadhas plain, 5, 8, 123, 147
Langaza, 4, 12, 40, 43, 59
League of Nations, 133, 145, 152
Lefort, 36, 48, 49, 51, 53
leftist partisans, 204, 207, 210
left-wing partisans, 205
Liberal Organization, 172
Liberal Party, 145, 170, 181, 192
Liberal Party government, 165, 168
Liberals (Venizelists), 170, 172,
226
Lingovan (Xiloupolis), 55, 123
literary associations, 93, 96
Liti (Aivati), 37, 39, 63, 119, 130,
194
Local, locals (*endopyi, dopyi*), 5, 39,
116, 146, 147, 151, 153, 157,
158, 160, 161, 181, 182, 195

Metaxas era, 194, 200
Metaxas security forces, 177
Metaxas years, 190
Methodius, 14
Metropolite (Florina), Augustinos
    Kandiotis, 141
Metropolite (Thessaloniki), 13, 111,
    113, 115, 118, 188, 229
Middle East, 203
millet system, 78, 108
millets, 43, 79
mills, 65
Ministry of Macedonia and Thrace,
    230
minority, Bulgarian, in Greece, 133
minority, Greek, in Bulgaria, 133
Minority Treaty, 132
misaridhes (yarandjidhes), 59
Mitrousis, Kapetanios, 113
monarchy, 173
Monastiri (Bitola), 90, 102, 113,
    223
Montenegro (Mavrovouni), 42, 58,
    59, 95, 105, 114, 115, 116, 232,
    234
Moore, 32
Morning Star (Zornitsa), 83
mosque (*tzami*), 10, 55, 109
Mouhtaris, 175, 200, 204
Mount Athos, 35
Moynihan, 19
municipalities (*nahiyes*), 43
Muslim herders, 10, 221
Muslim women, 152
Muslims, 12, 41–43, 45, 47, 49, 51,
    52, 54, 55, 60, 62–64, 66, 143,
    145, 147, 151, 154, 163, 164,
    165, 167, 170, 221

nahiyes (municipalities), 43
National Guard, *see* Panhellenic Lib-
    eration Organization
National Liberation Front (EAM),
    204, 205
national propagandists, 13
national resistance movement, 204
National Security Battalions (TEA),
    206, 208, 209, 216

National Security Units (MEA), 206
national symbols, 27
National Youth Organization
    (EON), 190, 200, 201
nationalism, 25, 26, 85, 89, 94, 144,
    228
NATO, 225, 226
Natsas, 80
Nazis, 202
Neapolis (New City), Assiros, 7
Nevrokopi, 81
New Democracy, 6, 196, 226
New Guveyna, *see* Guveyna-Yeni
New Lands, 162, 164, 168, 173,
    186, 188, 189
Nietzsche, Friedrich, 90
Nigrita, 49, 184
Nikopolis (Zarova), 40
Nikov, 15

October 28, 198
Olympus, 202, 220
Orghanosi Thessaloniki, 96, 118
Orthodox Christians, 94, 148
Orthodox Christianity, 94
Orthodox Church, 88, 219–21
Ortner, 27
Otmanli, 10, 12, 55, 62, 63, 146,
    149, 156, 157, 165, 167, 181,
    182
Ottoman authorities, 52, 56, 60, 61,
    67, 93, 98, 117
Ottoman Constitution, New, 104
Ottoman Empire, 25, 43, 45, 49, 55,
    77, 79, 80, 84, 92, 104, 113,
    136, 144, 148, 218, 219, 223
Ottoman era, 10, 12, 14, 15, 24, 31,
    34, 35, 37, 43, 45, 54, 76, 79,
    87, 101, 105, 143, 149, 151,
    152, 161, 163, 177, 178, 181,
    184, 188, 193, 220, 223
Ottoman era population, 133
Ottoman forces, 14, 24, 43
Ottoman Gymnasium, Serres, 113
Ottoman occupations, 15, 34
Ottoman period, 143, 161
Ottoman Porte, 45, 47, 50, 79, 84,
    86, 101

Transylvania, 134
Trapezous (Trebizond), 147
Treasury of Agricultural Insurance, 210
Treaty of Adrianople, 78
Treaty of Berlin, 80
Treaty of Bucharest, 24, 132
Treaty of Lausanne, 142, 145
Treaty of Neuilly, 132, 141
Treaty of San Stefano, 80, 202
Treaty of Varkiza, 205
Triandafillos, 113
Trikala, 12, 41, 48, 50, 62, 63, 65, 69, 73, 220
Trojan War, 36, 232
trousseau, 69
Tsanoff, 83, 132
Tsei *effendi,* 55
tselingato, see herding group
Tsernovo, 114
Tsetes, 110
Tsopanakis, 14
tsorbadjis, tsorbadjidhes, 52, 61, 66, 67, 69, 71, 72, 74, 81, 109, 118, 120, 124, 128, 136, 143, 144, 153, 156–58, 160, 163, 164, 167–74, 177–86, 188, 189, 191–97, 199, 201, 203–10, 212–16, 223, 225
Tsoukalas, 50, 83, 219, 227
Tsountas, 111, 123, 124
Turkey, 5, 109, 123, 142, 144, 145, 146, 148, 149, 151, 157, 197, 200
Turkish (language), 12, 37, 51, 56, 57, 116, 148, 150
Turkish authorities, 119
Turkish-speakers, 10, 12, 33, 42, 148
Turks, 1, 41, 42, 50, 55, 56, 57, 60, 62, 80, 89, 97, 106, 115, 123, 124, 142, 147, 150, 151, 167, 199, 231, 236
Turks, Koinaroi, 57
Tzami, 143, 156

ultimogeniture, 214, 215
Uniate Church, 82

United Nations Refugee Relief Agency (UNRRA) 210, 211

Vakalopoulos, A., 48, 90, 103, 108
Vakalopoulos, K., 15, 102, 132
Vardar Wind, 211
Vardaris, 229
Vasdravellis, 188
Vasilios II, Byzantine emperor (Voulgharoktonos), 9, 92
Vayazit I, Sultan, 44
Vayiakakos, 103
Vayiatzis, 169
Velika, 189
Velikas, 59, 66, 153, 174, 179, 186, 204, 206, 211, 215
Velissarios, 123, 124
Venizelos, Eleftherios, 141, 144, 157, 165, 168, 170, 172, 225
Verdery, 21, 82, 134, 189
Vergina, Star of, 229
Vergopoulos, 46, 47, 51, 59, 61, 67
Vermeulen, Hans, 54, 72
Veroia, 130
Vertiskos, 211
Vertiskos foothills, 33
Vertiskos hills, 115
Vertiskos mountains, 6, 9, 12
vilayets (provinces), 43
village herd, 180
village priest, 217, 230
Vincent, Joan, 20, 82
Vissoka (Ossa), 70, 119
Vlah (language), 96
Vlahika, 156
Vlahs, 50, 51, 54, 91, 142, 156
Vlah-speaking, 12
Volvot (Nea Sanda), 130
Von Mach, Richard, 77, 86
Voukas, 66, 205
Voukinas, 28, 186, 211
Voulgharoktonos, *see* Vasilios II
Vouninoudis, 111
Vouri, 50
Vranas, 64, 66, 120, 170, 172, 174, 175, 176, 179, 181, 186, 192, 204, 211
Vucinich, 46, 47, 50, 79